Word Meaning and Syntax

OXFORD SURVEYS IN SYNTAX AND MORPHOLOGY

GENERAL EDITOR: Robert D. Van Valin, Jr, *Heinrich-Heine University and the University at Buffalo, State University of New York*

ADVISORY EDITORS: Guglielmo Cinque, *University of Venice*; Daniel Everett, *Illinois State University*; Adele Goldberg, *Princeton University*; Kees Hengeveld, *University of Amsterdam*; Caroline Heycock, *University of Edinburgh*; David Pesetsky, *MIT*; Ian Roberts, *University of Cambridge*; Masayoshi Shibatani, *Rice University*; Andrew Spencer, *University of Essex*; Tom Wasow, *Stanford University*

PUBLISHED

IN PREPARATION

Word Meaning and Syntax

Approaches to the Interface

STEPHEN WECHSLER

OXFORD
UNIVERSITY PRESS

OXFORD
UNIVERSITY PRESS

Great Clarendon Street, Oxford, OX2 6DP
United Kingdom

Oxford University Press is a department of the University of Oxford.
It furthers the University's objective of excellence in research, scholarship,
and education by publishing worldwide. Oxford is a registered trade mark of
Oxford University Press in the UK and in certain other countries

First Edition published in 2015

Impression: 4

Published in the United States of America by Oxford University Press
198 Madison Avenue, New York, NY 10016, United States of America

British Library Cataloguing in Publication Data
Data available

Library of Congress Control Number: 2014945279

ISBN 978-0-19-927988-3 (hbk.)
ISBN 978-0-19-927989-0 (pbk.)

Printed and bound by
CPI Group (UK) Ltd, Croydon CRO 4YY

Contents

General preface

Oxford Surveys in Syntax and Morphology provides overviews of the major approaches to subjects and questions at the center of linguistic research in morphology and syntax. The volumes are accessible, critical, and up-to-date. Individually and collectively they aim to reveal the field's intellectual history and theoretical diversity. Each book published in the series will characteristically contain: (1) a brief historical overview of relevant research in the subject; (2) a critical presentation of approaches from relevant (but usually seen as competing) theoretical perspectives to the phenomena and issues at hand, including an objective evaluation of the strengths and weaknesses of each approach to the central problems and issues; (3) a balanced account of the current issues, problems, and opportunities relating to the topic, showing the degree of consensus or otherwise in each case. The volumes will thus provide researchers and graduate students concerned with syntax, morphology, and related aspects of semantics with a vital source of information and reference.

Word Meaning and Syntax: Approaches to the Interface addresses some of the most important issues concerning the syntax–semantics interface in contemporary linguistic theory, namely those concerning predicate argument structure. It provides an excellent critical overview of many approaches to these topics, starting with a discussion of the nature of word meaning itself and presenting a pre-theoretical survey of the major phenomena in this domain before delving into the different theoretical analyses.

Robert D. Van Valin, Jr
General Editor

University at Buffalo,
The State University of New York

Heinrich Heine University,
Düsseldorf

Preface and acknowledgments

This book examines approaches to the interface between word meaning and syntax, focusing on the issue of how the arguments of verbs and other predicators are expressed in the syntax, an area generally known as 'argument structure' or 'argument realization.' The word 'approaches' in the book's subtitle refers to the various theoretical frameworks for modeling and understanding that interface. But it also refers to the two fundamental sides from which one must approach the interface: from the word meaning side and from the syntax side. Or one might prefer to say: from the meaning side and the form side. Addressing the approach from the meaning side requires us to face an ancient question: what is the meaning of a word? The main aspects of that problem, including polysemy, vagueness, normativity, and pragmatic context, cannot be ignored when we turn to the syntax interface. So those issues are reviewed first, before we look at argument alternations, and then finally delve into specific proposals for the lexicon-syntax interface.

This book project started during a period that I spent as a visiting scholar at Stanford University in 2005, with the help of funding from a Faculty Research Assignment grant from the University of Texas. I am grateful to both institutions, and to the many people who helped out with the book, and people with whom I had conversations that helped shape my thinking. Beth Levin was especially important in the early stages of writing, providing guidance and commenting on some early chapter drafts. There are very few people with as much expertise and experience in this area as Beth has, and I am grateful to her for her help. I am fortunate to have as the series editor Robert Van Valin, who has written extensively on this area and was able to give very detailed and perceptive comments on many aspects of the book. Two anonymous reviewers gave valuable comments on the prospectus. Katrin Erk's detailed feedback on Chapter 2 improved it greatly. John Beavers commented on the section on mereologies and affectedness, and we also discussed other aspects of the book. Stefan Müller is a co-author of Chapter 6, 'The lexical–constructional debate,' which is based on a paper we wrote that appeared as a target article in *Theoretical Linguistics* (the chapter appears here with the kind permission of the journal). Stefan also generously read and reviewed other chapters of the book, and thereby saved me from making several errors. The people acknowledged in the *Theoretical Linguistics* article were also helping me with this book, perhaps without knowing it. These include Colin Bannard, Judith Meinschäfer, Frank Richter, and Dieter Wunderlich, who commented on a draft.

I am particularly grateful to my teacher, mentor, friend, and colleague Ivan Sag, who has been a major influence on my thinking in this area throughout my career. Ivan died in 2012, before this book was quite completed, and the field of linguistics is much the poorer for the loss. Ivan never stopped asking the important questions, and his answers shaped our understanding of syntax and its relation to semantics. In fact, the collaboration with Stefan Müller grew out of an online discussion initiated by Ivan. In addition to Ivan, Stefan, and myself, that discussion included Bill Croft, Charles Fillmore, Adele Goldberg, Paul Kay, and Jean-Pierre Koenig.

Students in my Fall 2010 seminar on Word Meaning (namely Telma Can Pixabaj, Luis Chacartegui, Zach Childers, Ashwini Ganeshan, Maggie Gemmell, Juwon Lee, Sandra Markarian, Charles Mignot, Michael Speriosu, I Nyoman Udayana, and Ahmed Zaheed) were subjected to drafts of Chapters 1 and 2. I have discussed various issues in this book with a number of other scholars, including Heidi Harley and Richard Larson.

The world's leading expert on the complex interactions between the writing of this book and my overall mood is my wife, Marie Carmel. I am grateful to Marie for her support, without which I might have given up a long time ago.

List of abbreviations

ABS	absolutive case
ACC	accusative case
ACT	Actor (in RRG)
AGT	agent
ANTIP	antipassive
APPL	applicative
ARG-ST	argument structure (in HPSG)
ASC	argument structure construction
ASP	aspect
AUX	auxiliary
AV	Actor voice (in Austronesian languages)
AVM	attribute-value matrix
C	complementizer
CAT	category
CAUS	causative
CG	Categorial Grammar
COMPL	completive aspect
COMPS	complement list (HPSG feature)
DAT	dative case
DEC	declarative
DEF	definite
DIR	directional
DN	derived nominal
DO	double object
DS	different subject
DTRS	daughters (HPSG feature)
ECM	exceptional case marking
ERG	ergative case
EXPL	expletive
F	feminine

FOC	focus
FUT	future
FV	final vowel
GEN	genitive case
GN	gerundive nominal
GPSG	Generalized Phrase Structure Grammar
HPSG	Head-Driven Phrase Structure Grammar
I.C.	Intrinsic Classification (in LMT)
iff	if and only if
IND	indicative
INF	infinitive
INGR	ingressive
INS	instrumental role or case
INTR	intransitive
IPFV	imperfective
LDG	Lexical Decomposition Grammar
LFG	Lexical-Functional Grammar
LMT	Lexical Mapping Theory
LOC	locative case
M	masculine
MaxEndpt	Maximal endpoint closed-scale adjective
MID	middle voice
MinEndpt	Minimal endpoint closed-scale adjective
MSE	Mapping to subevents
MSO	Mapping to subobjects
NFUT	non-future
NOM	nominative case
NPAST	non-past
OBJ	object
OBJ2	secondary object
OBL	oblique
OM	object marker
OV	Objective voice (in Austronesian languages)
PASS	passive
PAT	patient role

PFV	perfective aspect
PHON	phonology
PL	plural
PO	prepositional object
POSS	possessor
PRED	predicate (LFG feature)
PRS	present
PST	past
PTCP	participle
REFL	reflexive
RN	relational noun
RRG	Role and Reference Grammar
SBCG	Sign-Based Construction Grammar
SC	small clause
SEML	semelfactive
SG	singular
SM	subject marker
SOA	State of affairs
SPR	specifier
SUBCAT	subcategorization list (HPSG feature)
SUBJ	subject
TAG	Tree-Adjoining Grammar
TOP	topic
TR	transitive
UND	Undergoer (in RRG)

1

The role of word meaning in syntax

1.1 The syntax–lexicon interface

Syntax, the system of rules for combining words into sentences, is greatly influenced by the meanings of those words. But the exact nature of this interface between word meaning and syntax remains one of the most controversial and elusive issues in contemporary linguistics. To understand the relationship between word meaning and syntax we first devise appropriate ways of modeling each of these two relata, and then proceed to explore the relation between those two models. Each side of the interface, word meaning and syntax, presents its own challenges. Syntax is probably more amenable to definitive statements of empirical fact. It is easy to show, based on an examination of written or spoken corpora, that in English a verb precedes its object while in Japanese a verb follows its object. Although there are various alternative ways to model syntax, there is little disagreement that these are important facts about the syntax of the respective languages. But unlike syntax, where we can consult the acoustic signal or the order of written words on a page, word meaning has no physical manifestation and is accessible mainly through the introspective judgments of speakers. When it comes to word meaning, there is often disagreement about the facts. Even before bringing syntax into the picture, word meaning is already a complex relation between language and the world it represents.

Syntax may be defined as the grammatical system for combining words into utterances, so syntax in this broad sense includes phrase structure, morphosyntax, and compositional semantics. While the study of word meaning has always been an important part of linguistics, it is the combinatorial system of syntax that began to receive a new level of attention and analysis with the advent of generative grammar. Chomsky's (1957) monograph *Syntactic Structures* demonstrated that mathematical models could be applied to the study of this combinatorial system, allowing the formulation of precise, testable hypotheses. The central idea, dubbed "the autonomy of syntax," was that words belong to categories corresponding to traditional parts of speech such as Noun, Verb, Adjective, and Preposition, and that a language can be formally defined as a set of well-formedness conditions on structured combinations of such category symbols, thereby abstracting away from the meanings of the particular words themselves. A single word has rich, complex shades of meaning that interface with the extralinguistic world, while syntax, or at least an important aspect of it, is a hermetic, closed system that can be studied in isolation from the messy world outside. It was natural that the new science of linguistics would have placed its primary emphasis on combinatorics rather than words themselves. Similarly, an important part of the study of formal semantics allows for word meanings to be effectively reduced to constants like **drink'** for the word *drink,* that retain only a logical type, such as type $\langle e, \langle e,t \rangle \rangle$ for a transitive verb.

While the difficulty of modeling word meaning and the complexity of its relation to syntax pose a challenge, a look at cross-linguistic patterns reveals clear tendencies governing its relation to syntax. We know that in language after language, agentive sorts of semantic roles, such as the drinker role of the verb *drink,* are realized as subjects rather than objects—even if we cannot always say exactly what counts as an "agentive sort of semantic role." We can see that something is at work, even if we cannot say with certainty what that something is.

1.2 Predicate argument structure and its discontents

Speakers of English can be fairly confident that the object of the active verb *eat* represents the food or other thing that gets eaten, while the subject of *eat* represents the eater. This type of regularity, which is important for efficient communication, is immediately explained by the hypothesis that the lexical representation of the verb includes a "predicate argument structure": a lexical representation specifying the allowable associations between participant roles and dependent phrases for a verb or other predicator. Call this the "lexical hypothesis." The predicate argument structure for the verb *eat* indicates that its subject fills the eater role (the *agent*) and its object the role of the thing eaten (the *patient*):

(1)   *eat* ⟨ agent   patient ⟩

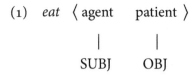

SUBJ   OBJ

This lexical representation is then handed to the system of English syntax, which specifies how subjects and objects are encoded, roughly speaking as NPs respectively preceding and following the verb. Most but not all theories assume that grammar includes lexical predicate argument structures in some form, varying however in the details.

But is this mapping between semantic roles and the phrases express-ing them really built into the lexical representation of the verb? Or does it come about some other way? The evidence seems to cut in two directions. On the one hand there are strong generalizations obtaining across the lexicon. Many verbs with similar meaning have a parallel subject–object mapping: *consume, drink, devour*, and so on. More generally, as mentioned in the previous section, agents of active sen-tences tend to be expressed by subjects rather than objects. This suggests (to some researchers) that the mapping is dictated not by the lexical item *per se* but rather by constraints holding directly between the syntax and semantic interpretation. On that extra-lexical hypothesis, the fact that the "eater" role of *eat* is the verb's subject does not follow from the grammatical representation of the verb. Instead, the rules governing the relation between subjecthood and the denotations of clauses would require that in descriptions of eating type situations, the eater must be the subject. Such rules deal in notions like 'agent' and 'subject' (or 'external argument'), but bypass any direct mention of the verb *eat*.

On the other hand, there is also considerable lexical idiosyncracy in the expression of arguments, as in these contrasts:

(2)   a. She ate it. / *She ate on it. / She ate.
      b. *She dined it. / She dined on it. / She dined.
      c. She nibbled it. / She nibbled on it. / She nibbled.
      d. She devoured it. / *She devoured on it. / *She devoured.

(3)   a. Susan trusts Mary. / *Susan trusts on Mary.
      b. *Susan relies Mary. / Susan relies on Mary.

Indeed, it has been obvious from the start of the generative program that part-of-speech categories like Noun and Verb are insufficient to determine the distribution of words, since words vary in their transitivity and, more generally, in their complement selection properties. Beyond the specification of major category, words belong to subcategories according to the morphosyntactic features of the complements they select. The pattern in (3) can be captured with the subcategorization frames posited below for the verbs *trust* and *rely*:

(4)   a. *trust*, V. [___ NP]
      b. *rely*, V. [___ PP$_{on}$]

The mapping to semantic arguments is made explicit here:

(5)   a. *trust* ⟨ agent   patient ⟩

                    | |

              SUBJ   OBJ

      b. *rely* ⟨ agent   patient ⟩

                    | |

              SUBJ   OBL$_{on}$

Here OBL$_{on}$ stands for a prepositional phrase headed by the word *on*. So subcategorization can be rather idiosyncratic, varying from word to word. In some languages this idiosyncracy is observed in subcategorization for subjects as well as complements, as in Icelandic lexically determined ('quirky') subject case (Zaenen et al. 1985).

These lexical entries represent the predicate argument structure as if it were an idiosyncratic property of each word, but this is only a useful first approximation. As noted, there are rather strong correlations, some cross-linguistic (e.g. agents tend not to be objects) and some language-specific (e.g. a particular English preposition such as *on* marks a certain range of semantic role types). This tension between idiosyncracy (in this case, lexical idiosyncracy) and rule-governed behavior leaves us on very familiar ground, as it is observed in nearly all areas of grammar, including phonology, morphology, syntax, semantics, and pragmatics. This property of the lexicon has been captured with formal devices such as default inheritance hierarchies and lexical rules with exception features.

Such lexical idiosyncracy suggests that the predicate argument structure is associated with a *word* after all. On that view, the argument–complement mapping specified in lexical structures could itself be governed by principles and language-specific rules, which would explain the cross-lexical generalizations. Those principles and rules crucially involve *the meaning of the word* (here, the word *eat*), as opposed to the denotation of a particular utterance. (Recall that by contrast the *extralexical* hypothesis above bypassed any mention of the word.) The lexical and extralexical hypotheses imply different answers to the question of what sort of thing the meaning of a word is (see Chapter 2). Ultimately it is likely that both lexical and extralexical factors are at play in the grammars of natural language, and that many problems of language can be understood in terms of an interaction between the two.

1.3 Organization of the book

This book approaches the interface between word meaning and syntax from both sides of this relation. Chapter 2 comes at the problem from the lexicosemantic side, looking at word meaning in all its richness. Chapter 3 introduces the syntactic side, surveying verb classes according to patterns of complementation and especially complement alternations, and then reviewing findings on how these aspects of syntax relate to meaning. Chapter 4 reviews models of word meaning involving sublexical structure that is visible to the rules of syntax. Chapter 5 discuss various approaches to modeling the mapping between word meaning and syntax. The controversy between lexicalism and constructional approaches is discussed in Chapter 6, followed by some specific empirical domains for testing and comparing different theoretical approaches in Chapter 7.

2

Word meaning

2.1 Introduction

To address the relationship between word meanings and argument realization, we must know what word meanings are, and how those word meanings figure into the theory of argument realization. This chapter primarily focuses on the problem of word meaning and some of the approaches to that problem. In later chapters we consider more directly the role played by word meaning in the theory of argument realization.

Word forms are typically polysemous, carrying a range of related senses. Decisions about where to draw the borders between senses can have crucial consequences for the study of the lexicon–syntax interface. Consider an analysis of the mapping between complement patterns and word meaning. When we associate a complement pattern with an aspect of the verb's meaning, must that aspect be observed in all uses of the verb? Or do we restrict attention just to certain 'prototypical' senses? Or just the sense relevant to the immediate context? (See Section 4.6 for examples.) Vagueness also poses an important problem. Rules for mapping from a word meaning to syntax must take account of the fact that speakers are typically uncertain about the boundaries of the word's denotation.

This chapter reviews various approaches to the problems of polysemy (Sections 2.2 and 2.3) and vagueness (Section 2.4). Then we consider theories of word meaning that place a heavy emphasis on the role of world knowledge (Section 2.5), before concluding (Section 2.6).

2.2 Words and senses

2.2.1 Homonymy, polysemy, and generality

Cruse (1986: 50ff.) observed: 'One of the basic problems of lexical semantics is the multiplicity of semantic uses of a single word form (without grammatical difference).' Words are said to be 'polysemous': each word form has a range of meanings that are related, whether closely or distantly. With the proviso 'without grammatical difference', Cruse is limiting his attention to variation exhibited by a single part-of-speech category, putting aside cognates such as the noun *chair* versus the verb *to chair*, as in *to chair a committee*. Polysemy is ubiquitous, 'the rule rather than the exception' (Cruse 1986: 50).

Traditionally a distinction is drawn between 'homonymy' and 'polysemy'.[1] Two words are homonyms if they accidentally take the same phonological shape but are unrelated in meaning, such as *light* in weight versus *light* in color, or *bank* 'financial institution' versus *bank* 'side of a river'. However, the line between homonymy and polysemy is not always easy to draw. For example, while the latter example of *bank* has become a standard example of clear homonymy, we will see below that even for this example the situation is not entirely clear-cut.

In contrast to homonymy, polysemy involves meaning variation, such as *bank* as 'financial institution' (1a) versus *bank* as 'physical building housing a financial institution' (1b) (Pustejovsky 1995):

(1) a. The bank raised its interest rates.
     b. John walked into the bank.

This example of polysemy differs from homonymy in two respects. First, the financial institution and the building housing it are clearly related, while in contrast there is no apparent relation between financial institutions and riversides (but see Section 2.2.1). Second, the polysemy relation connecting the two uses of *bank* in (1) is systematic. A parallel polysemy can be found across virtually all English words and phrases refering to buildings that house institutions, including even proper names such as *Austin City Hall, The University of Texas, The Performing Arts Center*, and so on:

(2) a. The University of Texas raised its tuition rates.
     b. The University of Texas is located several blocks north of the state capitol building.

---

[1] Regarding 'homophony' versus 'homonymy': Homophones have the same sound (*break* ~ *brake*); homographs have the same spelling (*bow* of a ship ~ *bow* and arrow); and homonyms have the same sound and spelling (the dogs *bark* ~ the *bark* of the tree). As long as we are concerned with spoken language, the terms homophony and homonymy are interchangeable. But some reading studies are described below.

This alternation (*institution X ~ building that houses X*) is an instance of 'systematic polysemy', since the relation is regular within the language (see Section 2.3.1).

Not all polysemy is similarly regular or systematic. Individual words are often extended to new uses that bear some semantic relation to the old ones. If these extensions catch on for a single word but fail to generalize to semantically related words of the language, they remain as isolated instances of 'idiosyncratic polysemy'. For example, Cruse (1986: 49–50) contrasts the different uses of the adjective *topless* in *a topless dress*, *a topless dancer*, and *a topless bar*. But writing in 1986 Cruse did not foresee the March 2008 coinage of *topless meeting* to refer to a business meeting where laptops, palmtops, and other portable electronic devices are forbidden.[2] The 2008 coinage is a play on *laptop* and presumably a deliberate *double entendre* based on the sort of uses Cruse referred to. For speakers using that coinage this is an example of lexically idiosyncratic polysemy. Such idiosyncratic polysemy is extremely common.

With idiosyncratic polysemy, one of the two criteria distinguishing polysemy from homonymy has been lost: idiosyncratic polysemy is not regular. The connection between senses may still be 'motivated', in that one can explain it after the fact (as in the case of *topless meetings*), while not being 'predictable', in the sense that a general rule applies (on this distinction see Lakoff 1987). This leaves only the criterion of semantic similarity. But if the connection between uses becomes opaque over time, due either to semantic drift or to changes in the extralinguistic world, then such cases of polysemy can grade off into homonymy. In fact, it is interesting to note that the two meanings of *bank* frequently cited to illustrate homonymy, 'riverside' and 'financial institution', are believed to have a common historical origin in a form denoting a 'shelf, natural or artificial, of earth, rock, sand, or wood' (*Oxford English Dictionary, OED*).[3] The bank of a river is such a shelf. Regarding the 'financial institution' sense, the *OED* notes that 'The original meaning "shelf, bench"...was extended in Italian to that of "tradesman's stall, counter, money-changer's table",... whence "money-shop, bank", a use

---

[2] 'Frustrated by distracted workers so plugged in that they tune out in the middle of business meetings, a growing number of companies are going "topless," as in no laptops allowed. Also banned from some conference rooms: BlackBerrys, iPhones and other personal devices on which so many have come to depend...' (from 'When it's hard to stay focused, try going 'topless' to meetings': *San Jose Mercury News*, March 25, 2008).

[3] Thanks to Katrin Erk for pointing out this example to me.

of the word which passed, with the trade of banking, from Italy into other countries. This connection between the two senses of *bank* is probably unknown to the vast majority of contemporary speakers of English, so for them this is a case of homonymy, not polysemy. But since polysemy can gradually evolve into homonymy, the line between the two categories is fuzzy.

To take another example, the noun *dial* originally referred to a sundial (from Latin *dies* 'day'), from which it was generalized to other clocks, then to instruments resembling clocks ('An external plate or face on which revolutions, pressure, etc. are indicated by an index-finger or otherwise'—*OED*). The verb *dial* refers to various actions involving dials, including the manipulation of a telephone dial to initiate a connection. With dial telephones now virtually obsolete, the verb *dial* is currently used for any action that initiates a telephone connection, including the caller pushing buttons or even a computer establishing a connection. New generations of speakers need not know that throughout most of the 20th century, telephone connections were established by turning dials, so the connection between *dial* 'initiate telephone connection' and *dial* 'turn a dial' may be expected to disappear from the mental representation of the language.

While polysemy is ubiquitous, the number of senses of a word is sometimes overestimated due to the effects of context. In a classic critique of *Webster's Third* dictionary, Weinreich (1964) argued that the dictionary's criteria for distinct senses are inconsistent and that many of the putative senses are merely differences of interpretation determined by different linguistic contexts for the word. For example, of the many senses of the verb *turn*, *Webster's* listed 'to reverse or upset the order or disposition of', which was illustrated with the example '[They] found everything turned *topsy-turvy*'. Weinreich (1964: 407) argued that this 'reversal' meaning comes from *topsy-turvy* and not from *turn*, noting that it evaporates if the adjective is omitted, while omission of the verb leaves the meaning intact: '[They] found everything *topsy-turvy*'. Similarly, the verb *have* is sometimes assumed to have different senses (or 'readings') for various so-called 'inalienable possessions' such as medical conditions (*have a headache*), mental states (*have a good idea*), or kinship relations (*have a sister*). But it may be that the relations are supplied by the noun, while the verb *have* is, as Weinreich said about *turn*, 'a semantically depleted connector' that does not vary in meaning across these different contexts (Partee 2008; Tham 2005; Wechsler 2008a; Beavers et al. 2008).

The grammatical connection between senses of a polysemous word form can sometimes be seen in irregular inflectional morphology. For example, the many verb–particle constructions using *take*, such as *take off* 'become airborne', *take off NP* 'remove (clothing)', *take on* 'adopt', while varying in meaning in apparently unpredictable ways, are clearly related, since irregular past tense forms are parallel: *take/took off*, *take/took on*. Similarly, *shoot up* has the same past tense form across very different senses in *The stock price shot up* and *The heroin addict shot up* (Koenig 1999: 122–3). Forms with such widely differing meaning that we may consider them to be a case of homonymy rather than polysemy, according to our definition, can nonetheless have identical morphological paradigms, as a consequence of a common etymology. For example, consider: *She draws/drew pictures.* ~ *She draws/drew her hand across his face.* What is shared between senses in this case is a tense paradigm (*draw/drew*), which is somewhat more abstract than a phonological form.

2.2.2 Linguistic tests for distinguishing senses

Distinct from both polysemy and homonymy is 'generality', where a word is simply general in its application. The word *sweater* can apply equally to red and black sweaters, for example, but 'red sweater' and 'black sweater' are not two different senses of the word *sweater* (Zwicky and Sadock 1975). Instead of 'generality' the term 'vagueness' is sometimes used, but I will reserve the latter term for the problem of boundary cases discussed in Section 2.4. This section looks at tests for distinguishing generality (a single sense) from polysemy/homonymy (multiple senses).

There is a long tradition of applying linguistic tests to distinguish between senses (Cruse 1986; 1995; Pustejovsky 1995; Zwicky and Sadock 1975). We have identified three different cases: homonymy (multiple unrelated senses); polysemy (multiple related senses); and generality (one sense). Linguistic tests for distinguishing senses usually involve test sentences in which the word in question appears only once but is applied to more than one referent. Among the ways that it gets applied to multiple referents are through ellipsis, *one*-anaphora, coordination, and relative clause constructions.

We begin with 'identity tests'. It is assumed that one word token referring to two different entities cannot have with a different sense for each respective referent. Taking our earlier examples, we can attempt to mix the 'riverbank' and 'financial institution' senses of *bank*:

(3)   a. Mary is looking at a bank. John is (looking at one) too.
      b. Mary and John each visited a bank this morning.

(4)   a. Mary was wearing a sweater. John was (wearing one) too.
      b. John and Mary were each wearing a sweater.
      c. One of my teachers is pregnant and the other is a bachelor.

The examples in (3) are governed by a constraint that the two senses of *bank* must be identical. That is, it does not seem possible to give these sentences a 'crossed reading' in which Mary is looking at or visiting a riverbank while John looks at or visits a financial institution. This suggests that they are clearly distinct senses. In contrast, if we ask whether *sweater* is ambiguous or merely general with respect to color, (4a,b) shows that it is general, since there is no suggestion whatsoever that Mary's and John's sweaters match in color. The word sweater is just general, and not ambiguous, between 'black sweater', 'red sweater', and so on. Similarly, (4c) shows that *teacher* is general and not ambiguous between 'male teacher' and 'female teacher'.

Closely related to identity tests are zeugma tests. Zeugma is a metalinguistic trope that intentionally exploits polysemy, often for humorous effect, as in these examples (5a and b from Cruse 1986:13):

(5)   a. $\boxed{z}$ Arthur and his driving licence expired last Thursday.
      b. $\boxed{z}$ He was wearing a scarf, a pair of boots, and a look of considerable embarrassment.
      c. $\boxed{z}$ I heard a Californian student in Heidelberg say, in one of his calmest moods, that he would rather decline two drinks than one German adjective. (from Mark Twain, 'The Awful German Language')
      d. $\boxed{z}$ The Mad Hatter's riddle: 'Why is a raven like a writing desk?' Answer: 'Because Poe wrote on both.' (From Martin Gardner, *The Annotated Alice*, an answer attributed to Sam Loyd)

The symbol $\boxed{z}$ indicates an introspective judgment that the sentence is 'zeugmatic'. The traditional term for this figure of speech is 'zeugma' or, more accurately, 'syllepsis'. 'Zeugma' originally referred more generally to cases in which a word is shared between clauses, regardless of whether it has different senses in each context, while 'syllepsis' specifically refers to those cases of zeugma in which the word appears in construction with two clauses 'while properly applying to or agreeing with only one of them...or *applying to them in different senses* (e.g. literal and metaphorical)' (*OED* entry for *syllepsis*, emphasis added) The term 'zeugma' is now often used in this narrower sense, as equivalent to syllepsis, and more specifically, for the application of one word in different senses; that is how the term will be used here.

Clearly, for our tests to work our native speaker informants must be able to reliably distinguish zeugmatic from non-zeugmatic locutions (or, to use the older terminology, to distinguish syllepsis from mere zeugma); and indeed it seems plausible that speakers have such intuitions. Cruse (1986: 12), for example, includes zeugma among the 'principal varieties of semantic anomaly which can be easily recognised by direct intuition.' (Whether speakers make categorical judgments, or only judgments of degrees of similarity or zeugmaticity, is a question we turn to in Section 2.4.)

2.2.3 Caveats and complications

For the linguistic tests described in this section to yield insights requires well-designed test sentences and careful data collection methods. Certain methodological problems have plagued much of syntactic and semantic research, such as lack of controls and the potential for introducing bias in introspective judgments (Wasow and Arnold 2005). In addition there are pitfalls and complications from interactions with other aspects of semantic composition.

Cruse (1995) argued that we must distinguish 'discreteness', as indicated by identity tests, from 'antagonism', as indicated by zeugma tests. As evidence he cites the two putative senses of *book*, as text (the contents of the book) or as physical object (its 'cover design, typography, and so on'). These are called two facets of the word; see Section 2.2.4. He argues that the identity and zeugma tests give different results, based on the following examples:

(6)   a. Mary likes the book; so does Sue. (from Cruse 1995: 36, ex. 17)
      b. The book is difficult both to read and to carry around.

According to Cruse, (6a) abides by the identity constraint: Mary and Sue must both like the same facet of the book, either the text (the contents) or the physical object (its 'cover design, typography, and so on'). But the fact that (6b) is not zeugmatic shows that the two facets are, in Cruse's terms, non-antagonistic. Regarding (6a), I do not share

Cruse's judgment: for example, if Mary and Sue work for a publisher, Mary as book designer and Sue as editor, they could each like the book for a different reason, and (6a) would be perfectly felicitous in my opinion. The judgments are subtle, however.

On the basis of common theoretical assumptions, it would be surprising if discreteness and antagonism were independent. We should expect the identity and zeugma tests to give roughly consistent results. The idea behind both tests is that a single word is used in connection with predicates or modifiers that demand apparently different senses. The tests tell us whether a single token of the word can be general between the senses required by those predicates. But notice that the nature of the informant's task in the two tests differs. In the zeugma test we ask whether speakers judge the utterance to be a sort of pun, while in the identity test we ask how to interpret a sentence. Concerning the latter test, informants' interpretations are likely to vary depending on their proclivity for spinning imaginative scenarios and contexts that allow for a more liberal range of interpretations. Sensitivity to zeugma is a very different matter, probably subject to cross-speaker variation of a different sort, related to the speaker's sense of humor. So we might expect some divergence between the results of these tests, but it would be hasty to draw theoretical conclusions from that divergence. However, I am unaware of any careful, controlled study of such issues with a large sample of informants.

In general, indefinite NPs make for better identity constraint test sentences than definite ones. For example consider a clear case of nondistinct senses, such as our earlier example of *teacher*. Identity and zeugma tests clearly show that *teacher* is not ambiguous between 'male teacher' and 'female teacher'. See (7a), which shows that the putative senses 'male teacher' and 'female teacher' fail the identity test: the teachers liked by Mary and Sue respectively can be of different sexes, as expected. But in (7b), with a definite NP, the teacher liked by Mary and Sue are normally understood to be of the same sex, since they are referring to the same individual.[4]

(7)   a. Mary likes a teacher; so does Sue.
       b. Mary likes the teacher; so does Sue.

---

[4] Exceptions arise with definite NPs showing 'sloppy identity' as in *Mary likes her sister and so does John*, on the interpretation where John likes John's sister.

Thus (7a) gives the desired result while (7b) does not. In (8), *light* observes a strong identity constraint: either both coats are light in color or both are light in weight, but crossed readings are possible only as a pun.

(8) Mary was wearing a light coat; so was Sue.   (Cruse 1995: 36)

The indefinite *a light coat* is used in (8). Indefinites provide for a better identity test since we are interested in the *sense* of a predicate such as *book*, *teacher*, or *light*. Indefinites allow us to abstract away from the referent and look at the predicate as applied across two different referents. Definites evoke a discourse referent, so whatever is said about that referent in the first sentence carries over to the second, thus clouding the issue.[5]

2.2.4 Disjunctive and conjunctive senses; facets

Words can be defined by a cluster of properties that are not jointly necessary. For example, Jackendoff (1985) notes that *climbing* necessarily involves either 'moving upwards' or 'moving in a clambering manner', or both. Hence a person or other creature with appropriate appendages for clambering can climb *up* or *down* a ladder, but bicycles, trains, and other rolling vehicles can only climb *up*, not down:

(9) a. The cyclist climbed up/#down the hill (by bicycle).
     b. The monkey climbed up/down the ladder.

Interestingly, it seems possible to mix these readings without a zeugmatic effect:

(10) a. In this event, you climb up the hill by bicycle, then down using the rope ladder.
      b. Would you rather climb up the hill on a bike or down the ladder without one?

Based on this result, we conclude that there is a single lexical unit *climb* with a single disjunctive meaning of 'ascend or clamber'. In example (9a) the surrounding context effectively narrows this meaning to 'ascend', in example (9b) it is narrowed to 'clamber', and in (10) the 'clamber' subsense applies to one predicate and the 'ascend' sense to the other.

---

[5] On problems with zeugma tests, see also Geeraerts (1993).

Disjunctive senses have been distinguished from conjunctive senses such as the sense of *book* as physical object or 'tome' and as informational entity or 'text'. These two facets of the word's meaning, to borrow Cruse's term, are appropriate for different sorts of predicate (Cruse 1995):

(11)   a. *book* as [TOME]: The book weighs four pounds /has a red cover/etc.
       b. *book* as [TEXT]: The book is well written.

Pustejovsky's (1995: 31) examples include the following:

(12)   Count/Mass alternations: *lamb*
       a. The lamb is running in the field.
       b. John ate lamb for breakfast.

(13)   Container/Containee alternations: *bottle*
       a. Mary broke the bottle.
       b. The baby finished the bottle.

(14)   Figure/Ground reversal: *door, window*
       a. The window is rotting.
       b. Mary crawled through the window.

(15)   Product/producer alternation: *newspaper, Honda*
       a. The newspaper fired its editor.
       b. John spilled coffee on the newspaper.

Two observations about such cases have fueled some theoretical interest. First, at least some facets are non-antagonistic (Cruse 1995: 36ff.; Pustejovsky 1995; Pinkal and Kohlhase 2000). Thus examples like the following, which mix predicates that are suitable for physical and informational entities, are not zeugmatic (16a is from Cruse 1995; 16b and 16c are from Pinkal and Kohlhase 2000: 521):

(16)   a. Mary is reading a book. The book is difficult both to read and to carry around.
       b. Mary burned the amusing book.
       c. Mary understands the book on the shelf.

Second, each facet of a word may be independently involved in lexical relations such as hyponymy (type/subtype relations). For example, *book* qua TOME is a subtype of 'physical object' and a supertype of 'hardback', while *book* qua TEXT is a subtype of 'information' and a supertype of 'novel'.

(17)   hyponyms of different facets of book:
      a. book[TOME] < hardback
      b. book[TEXT] < novel

The combination of these two properties, namely being non-antagonistic and yet involved in independent hyponymy relations, brings about a problem of some theoretical interest, especially for theories of the lexicon such as Pustejovsky's, in which semantic inference is driven by semantic type hierarchies. Pustejovsky addressed this problem by introducing 'dotted types' (see Section 2.3.4).

2.3 Polysemy and sense extension

2.3.1 Systematic polysemy

The English systematic polysemy pattern *institution X ~ building that houses X* was noted earlier (example (2)). Some patterns of systematic polysemy (also called regular polysemy) are found across languages, while others vary from language to language. In a classic study of regular polysemy in Russian, Apresjan (1974: 18) notes that a Russian noun referring to a type of vessel can also designate 'the quantity of substance that the vessel is capable of containing.' The same applies to English nouns for vessels. While (18a) entails that there are three wheelbarrows, (18b) does not, since John could have made three trips with one wheelbarrow:

(18)   a. John hauled three wheelbarrows from the shed.
       b. John hauled three wheelbarrows of bricks from the shed.

In (18b), *wheelbarrow* designates the quantity of bricks contained in a wheelbarrow. Other Russian rules do not apply to English, as when the name of a bodily organ is used to refer to a disease of that organ. The Russian expression that translates literally as 'She has kidneys' (*počki* 'kidneys') can mean that she has a disease of the kidneys (Apresjan 1974: 24). A general English 'grinding' rule converts count nouns for objects to mass nouns referring to the stuff derived from the object: *There was too much apple in the cake.* But the English rule cannot apply to liquids: *???We fried the chicken in safflower/olive/corn*; *???I enjoyed a glass of orange.* French names of fruits can be used to refer to brandies made from them (*une prune* 'a prune', *une poire* 'a pear'), but not so in English (Nunberg 1995: 118).

More directly relevant to the present work are Apresjan's examples of verb polysemy. Many of them are diathesis alternations by another name. A Russian or English verb meaning 'to deform OBJ in a definite way' can alternatively be used to mean 'to cause (i.e. create) OBJ by deforming something in this way', where OBJ corresponds to the direct object: one can *drill the metal* or *drill the hole*, in the latter case causing the hole by drilling; *carve the wood* or *carve a notch*, in the latter case causing the notch by carving. Another rule relates 'action' to 'causation of action', e.g. *The meat has thawed* versus *We thawed the meat*. Such alternations are better known as diathesis alternations, or argument structure alternations (see Sections 3.2–3.5). As we review more recent theories of regular polysemy in this section, one question to keep in mind is whether or not such argument structure alternations should fall under a more general theory of regular polysemy.

2.3.2 Pragmatic roots of polysemy

Systematic polysemy is thought to be rooted in the pragmatic phenomena of 'reference transfer' and 'predicate transfer' (Nunberg 1979; 1995). In the right utterance context speakers can use any predicate *P* to refer to an entity *x*, even if *P* does not apply to *x* directly, but rather to an entity *y* that is related to *x*. The speaker uses *x* to mean *y*, where *y* bears a systematic relation to *x*; for example, *x* may be a part of *y*. In (19a) the speaker, a parking valet, utters the demonstrative *this*, where a key is the demonstratum but the referent is a car. In (19b) it is not the speaker but the speaker's car that is located out back (examples 19–21 are from Nunberg 1995: 110–11):

(19) a. This *(displaying a key)* is parked out back.
　　　 b. I am parked out back.

These two examples differ in an important respect. The subject *this* in (20a) actually refers to the car and not the key, as shown by the following:

(20) a. This is parked out back and may not start.
　　　 b. ???This fits only the left front door and is parked out back.

But the subject *I* in (21b) refers to the speaker, not the car:

(21) a. I am parked out back and have been waiting for 15 minutes.
　　　 b. *I am parked out back and may not start.

Both examples in (19) involve a meaning transfer: the speaker uses a predicate P to refer to an entity x, even if P does not apply to x directly, but rather to an entity y that is related to x. (It also must be obvious and "noteworthy" about x that it stands in this relation to a y with the property $P(y)$, within the given utterance context. See below.) In the first example the meaning transfer involves the subject NP, while in the second it involves the predicate *parked out back*:

(22) a. (19a): *this* (key) ⇒ 'the car that this key fits'
      b. (19b): *be parked out back* ⇒ 'be the driver of a car that is parked out back'

Note that the 1st person verb agreement in (19b) also suggests that the subject refers to the speaker, not the car: *I am/*is parked out back*. This can be contrasted with a different example that shows the agreement going the other way. In a restaurant context the server can refer to a customer by means of the dish he ordered, as when she says *The hash browns at table 20 wants(/*want) his(/*their) check*. Here the verb and pronoun show singular, not plural, agreement, suggesting a transfer from *the hash browns at table 20* (which is plural) to 'the person who ordered the hash browns at table 20' (which is singular).

The property contributed to the subject by the new predicate must be obvious or 'noteworthy', i.e. a useful classification in the context of utterance. A painter is more likely to say *I'm in the Whitney Museum* than *???I'm in the second crate from the right*, because when a painting goes to a museum the artist acquires a noteworthy property, but not so in the case of the crate (Nunberg 1995: 113–14). It's not clear that it is always the context of utterance that matters so much as the context of the described situation, as shown by contrasts in a past tense narrative:

(23) a. I was out back.
      b. I was idling.
      c. I was leaking oil.
      d. #I was for sale.
      e. #I was brand new at the time.

The predicates in (23a–c) allow a shift to predication on the car driven by me: 'I [drove a car that] was parked out back', and so on. It is not clear why (23d, e) do not allow such a shift, but the constraint, whatever it is, seems to apply to the past situation and not to the utterance context.

For Nunberg, such meaning shift is essentially a pragmatic phenomenon; these shifts are not instances of lexical polysemy. But when a usage becomes less context-dependent and more useful—that is, where the relation between *x* and *y* is obvious in many or most contexts for a given word—the result is systematic polysemy.

(24) Examples of systematic polysemy (Nunberg 1995)
   a. transmissions for cars: *4 speed, automatic*, etc.
   b. texts for inscriptions: a *Webster's Third*, a *Guide Bleu*, etc.
   c. painters for works: a *Picasso*, a *Derain*, etc.
   d. containers for volumes of stuff: *She drank two glasses*, etc.
   e. writer for oeuvre: *fifty pages of Wordsworth*
   f. place for inhabitants: *Indianapolis voted for the referendum*
   g. tree for wood: *The table is made of oak.*

Even these meaning shifts fall under a pragmatic theory for Nunberg, but he also claims that they can become 'idiomatic' or conventionalized, which thus allow for shifts that are less and less context-dependent. Importantly, these conventions vary from language to language, as noted already in the previous section. Next we look more closely at theories of how the mechanisms of meaning shift are represented in the synchronic grammar.

2.3.3 Sense extension in the grammar

Quite a few grammatical theories of regular polysemy have been developed, many of them formalized (Sag 1981; Pustejovsky 1993; 1995; Pustejovsky and Bouillon 1995; Copestake 1992a; 1995; Copestake and Briscoe 1995; Asher 2011). There are several issues facing such theories. A first question concerns the extent to which the rules of regular polysemy are lexicalized, as opposed to being general pragmatic processes that are not tied to particular words. A second issue is the role of the syntactic and semantic *context* of a polysemous word, and the process of semantic combination, as distinct from the role of the word meaning itself. The various theories offer different answers to those questions.

2.3.3.1 Sense enumeration   In a 'sense enumeration lexicon' the many senses are simply listed separately for each word, as in a traditional dictionary, and the syntax combines sense-specific words. Such sense enumeration accounts are inadequate for several reasons discussed by

Pustejovsky (1995: ch. 4). First, it conflates homonymy with polysemy. Two homophonous expressions are obviously different words that happen to have the same phonology. Using a feature notation, this suggests lexical entries like (25) for homphony, where "GENUS" refers to a semantic sort:

(25)
$$\begin{bmatrix} \text{PHON: } bank \\ \text{CAT: count noun} \\ \text{GENUS: financial institution} \end{bmatrix}, \quad \begin{bmatrix} \text{PHON: } bank \\ \text{CAT: count noun} \\ \text{GENUS: shore} \end{bmatrix}$$

But this format is inappropriate for polysemous expressions such as the following:

(26)
$$\begin{bmatrix} \text{PHON: } bank \\ \text{CAT: count noun} \\ \text{GENUS: financial institution} \end{bmatrix}, \quad \begin{bmatrix} \text{PHON: } bank \\ \text{CAT: count noun} \\ \text{GENUS: building} \end{bmatrix}$$

One problem with this representation is that the *institution ~ building* pattern is very general and productive, suggesting the application of a rule. The next question is the nature of that rule and where it applies.

2.3.3.2 Lexical rules   A first approach is to posit a lexical rule that operates within the lexicon and productively derives variant lexical entries from basic ones. Such systems for deriving words or word senses were worked out in some detail beginning in the 1990s, including Pustejovsky's (1993; 1995) theory of the Generative Lexicon, and related work by Copestake (1992a; 1992b; 1995) and colleagues. Copestake and Briscoe (1995) distinguish between 'constructional polysemy' and 'sense extensions'. In constructional polysemy, sense differences of a word are determined by the word's local syntactic and semantic context within the sentence (we postpone further discussion of this until Section 2.3.3.4). Sense extensions are genuine cases of systematic polysemy, where a class of words productively alternates between systematically related senses. The sense extensions are generated with productive lexical rules. For example, a 'grinding rule' takes a count noun as input and returns a mass noun; a 'portioning rule' applying to a mass term for a beverage and returns a single portion.

(27) 'grinding': count noun $\Rightarrow$ mass noun
    a. Bugs Bunny is eating a carrot.   (count)
    b. There's too much carrot in this cake. (mass)

(28)   'beverage portioning': mass noun ⇒ count noun
       a. I drank too much beer last night.   (mass)
       b. Would you like a beer?   (count)

One reason to assume that this process applies at the lexical level is that the mass/count distinction has a number of grammatical reflexes, and when a word is shifted then all of those properties change in lockstep. For example, English count nouns, but not mass nouns: (a) require a specifier when singular; (b) can appear with *a(n)* in singular; (c) have plural forms; (d) cannot appear with *too much*; (e) can be antecedents for *one*-anaphora:

(29)   a. Q: What do you want?
            A: Evidence! /*Clue!
       b. a clue /*an evidence
       c. clues /*evidences
       d. *too much clue /too much evidence
       e. John discovered the clue; Mary wants to discover one too.
          *John discovered the evidence; Mary wants to discover one too.

When a count noun is converted to a mass, it gets all of the mass noun properties: *too much carrot*; *Q: What did you put in the cake? A: Carrot.* Likewise, when a beverage mass is converted to the portion count noun, the noun is endowed with all of the count noun properties: *a beer*; *two beers*; *John liked the beer, so Mary wants one now.* This particular portioning rule applies only to beverages, so a derived count noun *water* must refer to a drink, not a puddle, for example. This can be seen in all of the above properties: The phrase *a water* must refer to a drink: cp. **You're dripping wet, and so now there's a water on the floor.* The phrase *two waters* must refer to two drinks, not two puddles. One-anaphora works for drinks but not for puddles: *John ordered the water; Mary wants one too;* but **John saw the water that dripped on the floor; Mary saw one too.* This suggests that the portioning rule applies to the words, and is not just a consequence of the syntactic environment (*pace* Borer 2005a). If portioning were a direct consequence of the local syntactic and semantic environment, then there would have to be multiple portioning rules, each with the same semantic effect and the same restriction to beverages: a beverage portioning rule for the article *a(n)*, another for plural morphology, another for *one*-anaphora, and so on.

2.3.3.3 Lexical licenses   Still, such lexical rules differ from more trad-itional cases of derivational or inflectional rules. Many polysemy rules are conventional but not tied to a particular lexical item or lexical type. For example, a rule takes us from a count noun for a tree of a certain genus (colloquially called 'species') to a mass noun for the wood derived from such a tree: an *oak* ⇒ too much *oak*; a *birch* ⇒ made of *birch*, etc. Nunberg and Zaenen (1992) refer to such rules as 'lexical licenses' that can be exploited to produce new lexical items, but are distinct from 'lexical rules' that can be subject to arbitrary syntactic or morphological conditions. Lexical licenses depend on background beliefs, not on strictly grammatical knowledge of words. They are 'conventions of use' that determine not what is grammatical but what is appropriate or in accordance with ordinary linguistic practice.

Nunberg and Zaenen assume that the principles or mechanisms permitting extended uses are based on general schemas of conceptual organization, which is why we see the same patterns recurring across many languages. What is conventionalized, and hence varies across languages, are not the mechanisms of transfer themselves but rather the semantic restrictions on the inputs or outputs of such mechanisms. For example, a very general rule of 'universal grinding' (Pelletier and Schubert 1989) takes us from a thing to the stuff derived from the thing; but lexical licenses restrict the application of this rule in lan-guage-specific ways. The English rule of grinding applies to names of animals to yield the meat or hide of the animal (*chicken, rabbit*), and applies to trees to yield the wood of the tree, but grinding in West Greenlandic Eskimo applies only to trees, not to animals (Nunberg and Zaenen 1992: 394, citing Jerrold Sadock, p.c.).

2.3.3.4 Coercion   While Nunberg and Zaenen distinguish their lex-ical licenses from lexical rules, the two mechanisms still share the function of deriving new lexical items from a stock of basic ones. Copestake and Briscoe (1995) contrast such lexical operations with 'constructional polysemy', where sense differences of a word are deter-mined by the word's local syntactic and semantic context within the sentence. The word *fast* seems to apply differently to different nouns, as in *a fast typist/motorway/car/driver*. Following Pustejovsky (1993; 1995), Copestake and Briscoe analyzed such cases by decomposing the semantics of the nouns being modified. The adjective *fast* selects an event argument to modify, but a typist or a motorway is not itself an event, so *fast* combines instead with an event variable that is found within the decomposition of the noun: with *typist* it is the typing event, with *motorway* it is an event of driving on the motorway, and so on. This yields the default interpretations, but other options are possible. For example, the default interpretation *a fast typist* is 'a typist who can type fast', but 'in the context of a race between typists and accountants, for example, a fast typist might be one who can run, ski or ride a motorbike quickly' (Copestake and Briscoe 1995: 33).

Pustejovsky analyzed the default interpretation of such modification in terms of 'selective binding' of an event variable within the decomposition of the noun. Pustejovksy posited, in addition to the standard argument structure of a word, a 'qualia structure' specifying certain ways in which the entity can interact with other entities. This qualia structure, which is based on Aristotle's 'modes of explanation', comprises four subtypes:

(30)   Qualia structure (Pustejovsky 1995)
     i. **Constitutive**: the relation between an object and its constituents, like material, weight, or parts and component elements.
    ii. **Formal**: that which distinguishes the object within a larger domain, like orientation, magnitude, shape, dimensionality, color, position.
   iii. **Telic**: the purpose and function of the object, in particular
        • the purpose that an agent has in performing an act;
        • the built-in function or aim which specifies certain activities.
    iv. **Agentive roles**: factors involved in the origin or bringing about of an object referring to the creater of an artefact or a cause.

The function of a typist is to type, so the TELIC qualia of the word *typist* contains a typing event:

(31) $\begin{bmatrix} \text{PHON: } \textit{typist} \\[1em] \text{ARGSTR:} \quad [\,\text{ARG1} \;\; \text{x:human} \quad] \\[1em] \text{QUALIA:} \quad \begin{bmatrix} \text{FORMAL} \quad \text{x} \\ \text{TELIC} \qquad \text{type(e,x)} \end{bmatrix} \end{bmatrix}$

An adjective like *fast*, when modifying this noun, selects the event variable e as its argument.

Pustejovsky treated constructional polysemy (which he calls 'logical metonymy') in terms of 'coercion', which he considered to be similar to the better-known semantic phenomenon of type-shifting. Like type-shifting, coercion is triggered by the linguistic context: a functor seeks an argument of a particular semantic type, but if it combines with a constituent of the wrong type, then coercion rules allow that type to be shifted or coerced to the right one. For example, aspectual verbs like *begin, start, finish, stop,* and *end* select an event-denoting complement. But they can combine with certain entity-denoting DPs to yield an event reading.

(32) a. Sam began a beer. ⇒ 'Sam began drinking a beer.'
      b. Sam began a cigarette. ⇒ 'Sam began smoking a cigarette.'
      c. Sam began a novel. ⇒ 'Sam began reading/writing a novel.'

Salient readings of these sentences involve the *telic* quale of the object noun: beers are for drinking, cigarettes are for smoking, and novels are for reading. Such sentences also have readings involving the object's *agent* quale: novels are made by writing, etc. The event variables are specified in the lexical entry of the nouns:

(33) $\begin{bmatrix} \text{PHON: } novel \\ \\ \text{QUALIA:} \quad \begin{bmatrix} \text{CONST} & \text{narrative(x)} \\ \text{FORMAL} & \text{book(x)} \\ \text{TELIC} & \text{reading(e1,x)} \\ \text{AGENT} & \text{writing(e2,x)} \end{bmatrix} \end{bmatrix}$

On Pustejovsky's analysis, the verb *begin* effectively coerces its complement into an event denotation, so that *a beer* in the context of a sentence like (32a) means 'drink a beer'; *a novel* in (32c) means either 'reading a novel' or 'writing a novel'. A statistical approach to logical metonymy is proposed by Lapata and Lascarides (2003).

2.3.3.5 Type presupposition accommodation   Pustejovsky's coercion account has been criticized on various grounds. In (33), coercion is driven by the qualia within the lexical entry of the noun, such as *book*. Asher (2011) notes that this gives the wrong truth-conditions for quantified nominals like *many books*, since it wrongly predicts coerced meanings like 'many novel readings'.

(34) George enjoyed many books last weekend.

Asher (2011: 80) argues that Pustejovsky's account predicts that (34) is true if there are many enjoyable events of reading one book over the weekend. The underlying problem is that the meaning shift does not seem to be occurring at the level of the noun, contrary to Pustejovsky's assumption. Also recall Nunberg's examples of meaning shifts involving indexicals rather than particular lexical elements. Pointing to a book, one can ask: *When did you begin this?* Despite the absence of any lexical item such as *novel* or *book*, the same range of event readings are possible. This suggests a pragmatic rather than a lexical approach— that is, it suggests that the process involves novels and not the word *novel* per se.

Of course, it could be that there are both lexical and pragmatic processes at work. Asher (2011: 90) cautions against eliminating the lexical component, noting that different aspectual verbs license different coercions:

(35) a. Mary finished/stopped eating the apple.
      b. Mary finished the apple.
      c. Mary stopped the apple.

The verbs *finish* and *stop* each accept event-denoting DP complements, but they coerce different events from the DPs: to *stop the apple* is to stop its physical motion, but *finish the apple* lacks the physical motion reading and instead normally suggests finishing an event of eating. Asher's analysis puts the meaning-shifting action in the verb rather than the noun, which also solves the problem with quantified DPs noted above. Hence Asher rejects a pan-pragmatic view, arguing instead that coercions are 'sensitive to actual lexical items' (Asher 2011: 90).

Asher emphasizes the lexical components of coercion, but his model of coercion treats that sensitivity to actual lexical items in terms of presupposition rather than truth-conditional meaning. This differs from the previous treatments by Pustejovsky (1993; 1995) and Copestake and Briscoe (1995). Like Pustejovsky, Asher sees coercion as a consequence of mismatches of semantic type. Asher treats such coercion not as shifting the truth-conditional content of words or phrases, but rather as a special case of the more general phenomenon of 'presupposition accommodation'. The presupposed content of an utterance often must be salient in the utterance context: the presupposition introduced by the word *too* makes it odd to hear *Kate lives in New York too,* unless information about someone other than Kate living in New York is salient in the discourse. In many cases presupposed content, if not already salient, can be accommodated: the phrase *Sylvain's son* presupposes that Sylvain has a son, but even if that information is not salient in the utterance context for the sentence *Sylvain's son is almost three years old*, that information is easily accommodated and added to the new updated context. Presuppositions introduced via the semantic types that a predicate specifies for its arguments are called 'type presuppositions' (Asher 2011: 8). Asher assumes that the lexical entries of words make simple contributions to truth-conditional content, but that they also introduce information about semantic types that results in type presuppositions. Formalized within a type composition logic, the process of predication allows for type adjustments corresponding to the accommodation of type presuppositions. Asher also allows type assignments to depend on discourse context. Instead of lexical rules that change the truth-conditional content of words, this theory places coercion effects within the presuppositional component of the system of semantic combination.

2.3.4 Copredication and dotted types

Copestake and Briscoe (1995) distinguish between 'constructional polysemy', where sense differences are determined by the local syntactic and semantic context, and 'sense extensions', where a class of words productively alternates between systematically related senses. They support this distinction with evidence from zeugma tests. If the compositional semantics is set up properly, then constructional polysemy is predicted to allow copredication by two different predicates, each forcing a different sense. But sense extension is predicted to fail the zeugma test, disallowing copredication, since the word or phrase as it appears in a sentence has either one sense or the other, depending on whether the meaning shift rule has applied or not.

An example of sense extension is the grinding rule. The grinding rule takes the name of an animal (genus), as in (36a) to the meat of that animal, as in (36b) (example from Copestake and Briscoe 1995: 38):

(36)   a. Sam fed the lamb.
      b. Sam enjoyed/carved the lamb. ('lamb meat')
      c. ?Sam fed and carved the lamb.
      d. ??Sam fed and enjoyed the lamb.

As shown in (36c,d), attempts at copredication fail. This suggests that *lamb* is genuinely polysemous and not vague between the two readings. Similarly, Nunberg's reference transfer examples clearly disallow such crossed readings (example from Copestake and Briscoe 1995: 43):

(37) a. The ham sandwich is getting stale.
      b. The ham sandwich wants a coke. ('customer who ordered the ham sandwich')
      c. ??The ham sandwich wants a coke and has gone stale.

Neither *lamb* nor *the ham sandwich* is a case of homonymy or 'accidental polysemy'. These are genuine instances of rule-generated meaning shifts, at least according to Copestake and Briscoe.

In contrast, such readings are fine in example (38) (from Copestake and Briscoe 1995: 32):

(38) a. Sam picked up his beer.   (*his beer* = physical object)
      b. Sam finished his beer.   (*his beer* = beer-drinking event?)
      c. Sam picked up and finished his beer.

Copestake and Briscoe analyze such cases as polysemy in the verb, not the DP (recall that there are other reasons to favor such an analysis). On that view, the DP *his beer* has the same meaning in (38a), (38b), and (38c). But the lexical entry for a verb such as *finish*, which selects an event-denoting complement, gives this verb the option of combining semantically with the eventive predicate in the TELIC quale of its object DP (Copestake and Briscoe 1995: 35 actually illustrate with the verb *enjoy*). On this view the phrase *his beer* is not polysemous at all, and so the so-called constructional polysemy (of the item passing the zeugma test) is only apparent.

Words with multiple facets seem to represent another sort of case (Cruse 1995). While a physical object and an event are clearly different types of thing, the two facets of the word's meaning intuitively pick out dual aspects of a single thing. A book has an informational aspect and a physical aspect, each one appropriate for a different sort of predicate:

(39) a. The book is interesting.
      b. The book weighs five pounds.

This case poses little or no problem for copredication (example from Asher 2011):

(40)　a. The book is interesting but very heavy to carry around.

　　　b. John's mom burned the book on magic before he could master it.

According to both Pustejovsky and Asher, these are ontologically complex or 'polymorphic' word meanings that require us to allow for 'complex types' that inherit from multiple supertypes. To this end Pustejovsky develops a theory of productive type construction, allowing for 'dotted types' such as PHYSICAL.OBJECT•INFORMATION (1995: 93). Pinkal and Kohlhase (2000) propose an alternative formalization and show in greater detail how the compositional semantics works.

The essence of such proposals is that the formal representation of the word meaning incorporates some internal structure representing the meaning facets, and this structure is visible to the compositional semantics of the sentence. In the analysis of (40a), for example, *very heavy to carry around* is predicated of the physical aspect of the book, while *interesting* applies to the informational aspect of the book. Pinkal and Kohlhase (2000: 522) note that quantifiers lead to ambiguities, with different interpretations depending on which facet they apply to. Hence *every book in the library* has a different cardinality depending on which of these sentences it appear in:

(41)　a. Mary burned every book in the library.　　(= every copy)

　　　b. Mary understood every book in the library.　(= every title)

However, dotted types are controversial. Many, including the last example, could be seen as cases of the much more general kind/token distinction observed with common nouns generally (e.g. Carlson 1977), as noted also by Asher (2011: 131). For example, *Mary has expertise on every animal in the zoo* involves the number of animal species while in *Mary fed every animal in the zoo* we count individual organisms. One possibility is that the semantics of the kind/individual ambiguity is a consequence of general semantic principles, but what counts as a kind for a particular noun depends on pragmatic properties of the noun: book kinds are individuated by their informational content (book 'titles'), animal kinds by species, and so on.

Another question is whether such putatively 'conjunctive' word meanings are really different in kind from the 'disjunctive' senses of words such as *climb* discussed in Section 2.2.4. It is not clear that all of them are. It is true that the typical book is both a physical and informational entity, but a book can have one such property without the other, as noted by Cruse (1995). He observes that a blank book has the physical but not the informational aspect. For the opposite, we can point to e-books, books on tape, or the books committed to memory by the 'bookpeople' in the novel *Fahrenheit 451*, which lack the usual physical manifestation as a tome. Just as climbing normally involves both clambering and ascending, a book is normally both informational and physical. But either property alone is sufficient.

2.4 Vagueness and related problems

Much of the above discussion idealizes each word sense to a fixed entity that picks out a clear set of referents in a given context. But there is a great deal of evidence that word meanings have rather vague boundaries. Typically there are situations to which a predicate such as *walk* clearly applies, but there are also unclear borderline cases, such as a child's first steps or a drunken stumble. There are clear instances of a *tree* and *bush* but there are also many plants in the grey area between *tree* and *bush*. Labov (1973) showed experimentally that there is no fixed boundary between what counts as a *cup*, as opposed to a *mug* or *bowl*. He presented subjects with simple line drawings, first of a receptical with equal height and width, with a handle, and roughly cylindrical but tapering towards the bottom. He asked what to call it, and all subjects called it a 'cup.' Other pictures were presented, with various dimensions and other properties. As the ratio of width to depth increased, more and more subjects called it a 'bowl' instead. But there was not a unique dividing line between cup and bowl. This indeterminacy also arises when we try to determine the boundaries between related senses of a single word, as discussed in Section 2.4.6, 'Sense spectra and gradient senses'.

This problem of vagueness has been studied and discussed widely from many perspectives. I will not attempt to cover this vast area here, but I hope to give enough of an overview to address those aspects that are relevant to the goals of this book. We begin with a brief look at the linguistics and philosophy literature, then turn to cognitive psychology.

2.4.1 Aristotle and Eubulides

In the *Metaphysics* Aristotle argued that the essence of a concept, and the meaning of a word referring to a concept, is characterized by a set of defining conditions that an object must meet. Each condition is individually necessary, and all the conditions taken together are jointly sufficient, to characterize the predicate. To be a *man*, something must satisfy the two conditions of being *two-footed* and an *animal*. Anything that satisfies all the necessary and sufficient conditions for being a man is ipso facto a man. Aristotle distinguished these two essential properties of men from accidental or optional properties such as being cultured or having a certain skin color.

The Aristotelian view is sometimes dubbed the 'classical' theory, conterposed to the observation that word meanings have vague boundaries (Murphy 2002; Smith and Medin 1981; Taylor 1989: 1; Lakoff 1987: chs 1 and 2). But in fact discussion of vagueness in meaning is equally ancient and has been extremely influential in western thought. It is discussed in connection with two puzzles that are usually attributed to a contemporary of Aristotle, the logician Eubulides of Miletus: the 'sorites paradox' and the puzzle of the bald man. The name *sorites* derives from the Greek word *soros* 'heap'. The original puzzle goes as follows. 'Would you describe a single grain of wheat as a heap?' No. 'Would you describe two grains of wheat as a heap?' No. And so on. You must admit the presence of a heap sooner or later, but where do you draw the line?[6] More precisely the puzzle is often posed as the following apparently valid deduction:

(42)   a. A single grain of wheat is not a heap.
      b. Inductive premise: There is no non-heap such that adding a single grain of wheat would transform it into a heap.
      c. Conclusion: Therefore, no amount of wheat is a heap.

There seems to be no definitive criterion for distinguishing a heap from a non-heap. The puzzle of the bald man is similar but starts at a yes answer: 'Would you describe a man with one hair on his head as bald?' Yes. 'Would you describe a man with two hairs on his head as bald?' Yes. 'Three hairs,' etc. You must refrain from describing a man with ten thousand hairs on his head as bald, so where do you draw the line? (Hyde 2011) Strikingly, this paradox arises with a great many content words.

Eubulides' sorites puzzles were passed from teacher to pupil, playing an important role in the philosophical debates of antiquity (Williamson 1994). Sorites arguments were the chief weapons used by the sceptics of Plato's Academy, to attack the perceived dogmatism of the Stoics.

---

[6] This presentation draws heavily from Hyde (2011).

Propositions are said to be 'vague' if there are borderline cases for which no amount of further inquiry will help us determine its truth or falsity (Sorensen 2012). No amount of analysis or investigation will settle whether a 6-foot man is 'tall'. Speakers can stipulate a precise threshold, but that is clearly a departure from ordinary usage of the word *tall*. Vague predicates are context-dependent, but that is just one factor. The interpretation of a vague predicate often depends on a comparison set: the interpretation of a term like *tall* depends on the comparison class provided by the context, such as *tall* (for a professional basketball player) versus *tall* (for a 10-year old child). But the term remains vague even if the comparison class is fully determined. On one view this is taken as indicating that the word *tall* is vague because the concept (or perhaps the sense) of tallness is itself vague.

2.4.2 Semantics of gradable predicates

Most content words are vague to some extent, although to different degrees and in different ways. Mathematical terms such as *odd (number)* or *prime (number)* lie at the extreme of sharp categoricity. At the other extreme are gradable predicates like *tall* or *hot*. Especially as applied to adjectives, a traditional distinction is recognized between gradable (also called scalar) adjectives like *hot, tall, wet,* and *dry,* versus non-gradable (non-scalar) adjectives like *prime (number)* and *pregnant* (Sapir 1944; Klein 1980; Kennedy 1999). The key test for gradability is the felicity of comparative forms and degree modifiers. For example, the gradable adjectives *fine* and *ominous* contrast with non-gradable ones *prime* (as in prime numbers) and *unanimous: finer, finest, extremely fine; more/most/very ominous;* but **primer/*primest/*more prime/*most prime/*extremely prime numbers; *more/*most/*very unanimous.*

Gradable adjectives have long been modeled with 'scales', i.e. ordered sets with a measure function.[7] The adjective is interpreted relative to a standard degree on that scale: *Michael Jordan is tall* means that Jordan's height is greater than some contextually determined standard (Kennedy 1999). The adjective *tall,* on this view, denotes the relation shown in (43), which holds of an object x and a degree of height d just in case x's height is at least as great as d (from Kennedy 1999):

---

[7] Measure functions are functions from individuals to numbers; for any measure function (e.g. age) there must be a 'preorder' (e.g. 'is at least as old as') such that this order is reflected in the $\leq$-order of the real numbers. A preorder is a relation which satisfies transitivity and reflexivity.

(43) $[\mid tall \mid] = \lambda d \lambda x.\text{HEIGHT}(x) \geq d$

A special assignment function evaluates d in the context. This analysis explains why, for a given utterance context, if we accept *Mary is tall* as true for someone named Mary who measures 6 feet in height, then we are compelled to accept it as true if she is 6 feet 2 inches tall, 6 feet 3 inches tall, and so on. Conversely, if Mary is deemed to be *short* at 6 feet, for example by an unusually tall speaker, then the speaker is compelled to accept someone under 6 feet in height as also *short* (again, we must keep the utterance context otherwise identical). In short, the standard is determined by the context, but the direction of entailment is built into the semantics of the gradable predicate itself.

Such analyses help to explain such entailments and also show how certain vague predicates are integrated into the compositional semantics. But they do not directly address the question of why we feel uncertain about the truth of borderline statements—an uncertainty that is resistant to further inquiry, as noted (see Kennedy 2011). Nor do they address the question of how communication is possible despite this uncertainty. Next we review some approaches to these questions, mainly within the philosophical literature.

2.4.3 Approaches to vagueness

For borderline cases, a vague statement is neither clearly true nor clearly false. So one approach to vagueness is to modify our notion of truth by devising logics with more truth values than the usual two, true and false. A popular version assigns to the sorites series an infinite set of truth values between 0 (fully false) and 1 (fully true). But this has been criticized as exacerbating the problem of overprecision that we started with. Now we need a threshold for each degree of truth, so instead of one overly precise line we have many (Sainsbury 1996: 255, cited in Sorensen 2012). Also it fails to explain a key observation: a simple vague statement can play a role in a complex statement that is precise. Intuitively *John is bald and John is not bald* should be false, as it is in classical logic (the Law of the Excluded Middle), but on an infinite value model it receives a positive truth value, e.g. 0.5, if each conjunct has that value (Kamp 1975). However, more recently Hampton (2007) has proposed a theory involving 'degrees of membership' that is claimed to avoid those problems, as discussed below.

The problems with many-valued logics seem to suggest that with borderline cases one faces ignorance or uncertainty, rather than certainty about a fractional truth. Such ignorance-based accounts date to the logician Chrysippus, the head of Plato's Academy from about 232 BC who was responsible for the systematic construction of Stoic logical theory. Chrysippus is believed to have written extensively on the sorites arguments but his views are not known with certainty because few of the papyrus scrolls survive. He is thought to have written that the wise man's answer to the repeated question 'Is it a heap?', posed after each addition of a grain, should start at 'No' for small numbers. Then at some point one should fall silent, and only much later, for large numbers of grains, answer 'Yes.' There are two main variants of this position, depending on what we assume to be the reason for the wise man's silence on borderline cases: on the 'supervaluation' approach, he is silent because the proposition 'It is a heap' lacks a truth-value; on the 'epistemic' approach, it has a truth-value, but he is silent because that truth-value is unknowable.[8] These two approaches are reviewed next.

For 'supervaluationists', we are uncertain about borderline cases because simple statements about them lack a truth-value.[9] Assuming truth-value gaps would seem to encounter the problem with a phenomenon noted above in connection with many-valued logics: some complex statements that contain vague simple statements seem to be clearly true or clearly false. For example, *John is bald* and *John is not bald* are each vague statements, but *John is bald or John is not bald* seems to be clearly true (by the Law of Bivalence), and *John is bald and John is not bald* seems false (by the Law of the Excluded Middle). Intuitively these follow because no matter where we set the threshold for baldness (say, at 50 hairs), the disjunctive statement above comes out as true and the conjunctive one as false. This intuition is modeled by allowing truth-values of complex propositions to be built out of a space of interpretations in which all the truth-gaps of the simple component propositions have been filled, that is, so-called supervaluations (as opposed to the usual valuations of truth in the context). The complex statement is true (it is said to be 'supertrue') if it would come out as true for every possible threshold we could specify. (Making a vague predicate precise in this way is called 'precisification': specifying an exact threshold is a way to 'precisify' the vague predicate.)

---

[8] Which of these two positions Chrysippus took, and whether he even claimed to have solved the sorites problem, are matters of controversy (Bobzien 2002).

[9] Subvaluationists take such statements to be both true and false, replacing the supervaluationist's truth-value *gap* with a truth-value *glut*.

Conversely, while a patch of uniform color on the red/pink borderline might be considered 'red' on one occasion and 'pink' on another, it is always false to say that *It is red and pink*: there is no way to make these terms precise that would make the uniform color patch a clear case of both the predicates 'pink' and 'red' (Fine 1975: 271). As Fine (p. 277) puts it, 'how an expression can be made more precise is already part of its meaning.'

On the *epistemic* view there is a precise threshold but it is unknowable (Williamson and Simons 1992; Williamson 1994). Williamson and Simons (1992: 159–62) attribute our ignorance of the exact boundary to its instability. The boundary is unstable, even for the same speaker, because it is continually affected by uses of the word. Williamson did not see the meaning of the vague term as changing with each use as a consequence of the context of use (that would be closer to the *context-ualist* view described below); rather, the extension of the term in a given idiolect depends on the whole pattern of that person's past and present use of the term in a variety of circumstances and moods. Our ignorance results from the fact that we have no way of surveying that entire pattern (Williamson and Simons 1992: 160). Since the border keeps shifting, speakers must allow a margin for error: for any object that is too close to the border, one cannot be certain which side it is on. For the epistemicist, the vagueness of a predicate results from our ignorance of the totality of factors that determine its extension.

In a linguistic study of the instability of the boundary of a vague predicate, Barker (2002) considered the effects of the use of vague expressions upon the standards adopted for later uses within the same discourse. He observed that uttering a vague sentence like *Feynman is tall*, in addition to informing the hearers about Feynman's height, can serve the metalinguistic function of 'sharpening' the standard of tallness for the purpose of the conversation. This aspect of the interpretation can be paraphrased as something like 'Around here Feynman is considered tall.' It effectively narrows the standard for tallness to be at Feynman's height or lower. Barker argues that this updating function is present to some degree in most uses of vague predicates.

Some critics of epistemic approaches find it implausible that people could effectively communicate with words while remaining ignorant about a core aspect of their meaning. Also, one normally can have various attitudes, such as fear, hope, and wonder, about a proposition even when one does not know whether it is true, but the putative sharp boundary does not seem to play a role in such other attitudes. For example, Field (2010: 203) denies that a rational man can even *fear* that he has just passed the threshold into being old (cited in Sorensen 2012). A related problem with this approach is that the borders between the area of certainty and doubt is itself vague. This compounds the problem by giving rise to 'higher-order vagueness', or vagueness about what counts as 'vague'.

Both the supervaluation and epistemic approaches deny the inductive premise (47b). The epistemicist explicitly claims that there is a sharp boundary, in contradiction to the inductive premise; and for the supervaluationist the inductive premise comes out as superfalse, since it is false for every precisification (Kennedy 2011). Critics of such theories ask why, if the inductive premise is actually false, people are apparently so inclined to accept it as true.[10] Delia Graff Fara calls this 'the psychological question' (Fara 2000; 2008). Why do vague predicates seem to lack clear boundaries?

Some recent approaches to vagueness address the psychological question, focusing on explaining speakers' judgments, both about the extension of vague statements and the inductive premise itself. The goal is to explain speakers' judgments in psychological terms. 'Contextualists' emphasize that whether a speaker judges a predicate to apply to a given object is variable and context-dependent. A speaker may call the same object 'orange' on one test run and 'red' on another, but still accept the inductive premise. Raffman's (1994) notion of context includes not only the external discourse factors such as those affecting the comparison class for a vague term, but also the internal context— aspects of the speaker's psychological state that affect categorization and discrimination. Raffman (1994: 47) notes that two adjacent items in a sorites series may be judged as category-identical when judged pair-wise, while the same two items, when judged one at a time, might be judged to be category-different. The reason is that people tend to categorize saliently similar objects in the same way. Raffman attributes this 'similarity contraint' to the shifts in internal context. Fara (2000) also emphasizes this constraint but explains it in terms of the speaker's interest in efficiency: the cost of discriminating between two similar

---

[10] Moreover, Kennedy (2007) argues that even when the context implicitly specifies a crisp threshold for a vague predicate, the inductive premise still seems valid. A sentence like *You review the short paper and I'll review the long one* is fine if the two papers are respectively 15 and 25 pages long, but it is odd if they are 24 and 25 pages long.

objects outweighs the benefit, so they count as the same for the present purposes. On these approaches a vague predicate has a boundary, hence the inductive premise is false, but Fara (2000) prefers not to call it a 'sharp' boundary because any attempt to bring it into focus causes it to shift somewhere else.

Summarizing this section, theories of vagueness can be broadly divided into two camps. One approach is to modify our notion of truth by allowing other truth-values besides true and false, or allowing truth-gaps. The other view maintains bivalence but sees uncertainty or ignorance. Recent versions of the latter view seem to be informed by two different tendencies. One is a move towards seeking explanation from the psychology of categorization and discrimination, and attempting to dissolve the sorites paradox by considering how different contexts affect judgments differently (Raffman 1994; 1996; Fara 2008). The other emphasizes the role of communication as speaker and hearer seek to expand the common ground (Barker 2002; Frazee and Beaver 2010).

2.4.4 Prototypes and their relation to vagueness

Related to vagueness is the observation that for many concepts people distinguish between better and worse instances. The best instances are called the 'prototypes' of a concept. Prototype effects have been demonstrated in experiments beginning in the 1970s (Rosch and Mervis 1975; Rosch et al. 1976; Rosch 1978). Much of that work concerns concepts, which raises the question of the relation between words meanings and concepts. The concept of 'heap' is an important part of the meaning of the word *heap*, and in fact many of the prototype experiments use words to evoke the corresponding concepts. But it should be kept in mind that word meaning involves more than concepts, and the two cannot be equated; see Section 2.4.5 'Normative aspects of words meaning' for discussion.

Prototype effects were originally taken to undercut the so-called 'classical' Aristotelian view of a concept as a set of defining criteria, which does not allow for fuzzy boundaries. But the problem of vagueness concerns *membership* in a category, while prototypes are concerned with the goodness or *typicality* of an example (Hampton 2007). The complex relation between these two distinct measures is discussed below.

A number of different forms of evidence support prototype theory (for an overview see Murphy 2002). One piece of evidence for prototypes is the high rate of agreement between subjects about which things are good examples of a category. For example, when asked to rank given items in terms of how good examples of *furniture* they are, the following order emerges, from best to worst (Rosch 1975):

(44)   *chair > sofa > table > dresser > desk > bed > bookcase > footstool >*
        lamp > piano > cushion > mirror > rug > stove > clock > picture >
        closet > vase > telephone

Similarly, when asked to enumerate instances of a concept, subjects in general start with the better examples and name less good examples only later. Also, subjects can verify category statements of the form *An X is a Y* (e.g. *A dog is an animal*) more quickly if *X* is a good instance of a category *Y*. Priming effects are sensitive to prototypes. Subjects performing a word discrimination task, when primed with a superordinate category, decide more quickly if the words are good instances of the superordinate category (Rosch 1975). Thus people are aware of how good a category instance a particular object is.

We said that a term is vague if it induces inquiry-resistant uncertainty: speakers are uncertain about whether the term applies to an object even when they have all the relevant knowledge, and no further inquiry will remove the uncertainty. Most of the examples of vague terms in the previous section are terms associated with a scale that gives rise to a sorites series, i.e. an ordered set with a measure function: *tall* (the height scale), *bald* (number of hairs), *child* (chronological age), and so on. But terms can be vague with respect to non-scalar properties. The line between cup and bowl is affected not only by the ratio of height to width, which is scalar, but also by whether or not it has a handle (Labov 1973). Whether something counts as a *heap* of grain depends not only on the number of grains but also on their physical configuration: they need to be piled up. These properties contribute to the inquiry-resistant uncertainty. The formal supervaluation account of vagueness has been extended to prototypes (Kamp and Partee 1995).

Some prototype theorizing in psychology is concerned with basically developing measure functions for properties that would otherwise lack an inherent scale, that is, algorithms to assign a score to an item to indicate how good an instance of some category it is. On the 'family resemblance' view (Rosch and Mervis 1975; the term comes from Wittgenstein), a category is associated with a set of features. Unlike the classical view, these features are not all necessary, nor are they jointly sufficient, but rather are weighted according to their importance. The category 'dog' might be characterized by the features 'eats meat', 'has four legs', 'wears a collar', 'is a pet', 'barks', and so on, some of them weighted more than others (example from Murphy 2002: 44). An item gets weighted credit for features it has, and similar credit is deducted for features it lacks. If the total score exceeds the 'categorization criterion', then it is judged to be in the category; if not, then it is not (Murphy 2002: 44). In some versions the features are not simply an unstructured set but rather are organized into schemata that capture dependencies between features, such as the features 'have wings' and 'able to fly', for birds. Such a theory is claimed to be superior to the classical view. Unlike the classical view, there need not be any absolutely essential features. It also explains why items with more features will be easier to categorize quickly because subjects reach the categorization criterion more quickly (Murphy 2002: 44).

An alternative to the prototype approach is the 'exemplar' model. The basic idea is that concepts are represented by memories of past examplars, not by an abstract description in terms of features. More specifically, a concept is represented (perhaps it is better to say that it is replaced) by all exemplars encountered and classified so far, or else at least the prominent cases. Speakers classify new instances by performing a global comparison of the new instance with the exemplars. Given some new item, if most of the things it is similar to are dogs, then that item is a dog. The fact that some new items are judged to be more typical than others is said to follow from this theory, since the greater the number of similar exemplars, the more typical. If previous typical exemplars are used first for comparison with a new instance, then judgment of new typical items should be faster. The exemplar view is a radical approach; as Murphy (2002: 49) observes, in some sense there is no real 'concept' at all on this view, since there is no abstraction of features from the set of exemplars. This model is problematic as well for several reasons. In particular, it leaves unspecified which properties similarity judgments are based on, and it does not mention possible relations between features (like being winged and being able to fly).

Whichever model is adopted, it seems clear that it must have a probabilistic component if it is to account for the uncertainty felt when one approaches the borderline. For example, Murphy (2002: 44) suggests that that an algorithm with weighted features as described above could explain the borderline effects, since 'If an item has about equal similarity to two categories (as tomatoes do to fruit and vegetable), then people may well be uncertain and change their mind about it.' But if the algorithm is deterministic, then it is unclear why the uncertainty persists even after thorough inquiry and reflection. If speakers are equipped with a precise algorithm and sharp categorization criterion, then they should become certain as soon as they have all the relevant information needed for the putative algorithm. Recall that on the super-valuation view there is no unique boundary, and on the epistemicist view the boundary is sharp but speakers cannot know where it is. In effect both views deny the existence of a 'categorization criterion' of the sort discussed by Murphy. Any deterministic psychological theory of categorization would seem to run into the same problem with inquiry-resistant uncertainty. Hampton (2007) proposes that the algorithm produces a probability distribution instead, corresponding to a speaker's estimate of the probability that others in the speech community would accept the categorization. He allows for probabilities of 0 and 1 at the two extremes: one may be entirely certain that a robin is a bird and that a mountain is not a bird. He points out that a (sigmoid) function indicating probabilities in the boundary region could still approach 0 and 1 smoothly (Hampton 2007: 364–5).

A remaining question is the relation between 'typicality' and 'mem-bership' in a category. Osherson and Smith (1997) note that one may feel that a robin is a more prototypical case of a bird than a penguin is, but still know with certainty that both are birds. They argue that typicality and membership reflect different underlying psychological processes. People have been shown to exhibit 'prototype effects' even for exact terms like *odd number* or *triangle*, and even when subjects know how the term is precisely defined (Armstrong et al. 1983). Arm-strong et al replicated Rosch's findings with such terms. For example, they find the prototypicality ranking shown in (45) for odd and even numbers of two sets each, where subjects where asked how good an example of an odd of even number each number is.

(45)　a. Even numbers:　$4 > 8 > 10 > 18 > 34 > 106$

　　　　　　　　　　　　$2 > 6 > 42 > 1000 > 34 > 806$

　　　b. Odd numbers:　$3 > 7 > 23 > 57 > 501 > 447$

　　　　　　　　　　　　$7 > 11 > 13 > 9 > 57 > 91$

Some relevant factors that emerged are: that high numbers are con-sidered less typical for either concept; that factors of 10 are considered good examples for even numbers; that numbers that contain more even digits are considered better examples for even numbers than numbers that also contain odd digits, hence 42 is a 'better' even number than 34. But terms like 'odd number' are not vague for the subjects in the experiments: any uncertainty is temporary and quickly yields to certainty after a little reflection.

These findings suggest that typicality and membership are distinct, which raises the question of how they relate to one another. Armstrong et al. (1983) reintroduce aspects of the classical theory, distinguishing between 'defining features' (the definitional criteria of the classical analysis) and 'identificational features' used by subjects to identify whether an instance belongs to a concept. Even if the defining features are strict, prototypicality effects can still arise from variation in the identificational features. More recently, Hampton (2007) proposed that membership judgments and typicality judgments are both sensitive to the same underlying psychological measure of similarity to a prototype, but they are governed by different functions on that similarity variable. The degree of membership is a sigmoid probability distribution representing the subject's estimation of the likelihood that other speakers would deem the item to belong to the category (this was mentioned above; see also Section 2.4.5). The degree of typicality is a different function on the same variable, similarity to the prototype. But on this view, the notion of the prototype still plays a crucial role in the understanding of vagueness. Boundaries around concepts are difficult to establish, and so people adopt a strategy of learning the conceptual cores instead. Hampton (2007: 380) concludes: 'Vagueness is the inevitable result of a knowledge system that stores the centers rather than the boundaries of conceptual categories.'

2.4.5 Normative aspects of word meaning

According to the approaches from cognitive psychology outlined in the previous section, word meanings consist of concepts or more complex 'pieces of conceptual structure' (Murphy 2002: 391). On that view, each language user associates a word with her own private concept or piece of conceptual structure. The speaker A uttering a word associates it with A's lexical conceptual structure and the hearer B retrieves B's lexical conceptual structure. Communication is possible because different people's concepts are sufficiently similar for a given word (Murphy 2002: 392).

But arguably many such views are inadequate if they ignore the *normative* aspect of words that arises as a consequence of their communicative function. Our intuitions about gradedness are based on meta-beliefs about how other speakers categorize things, and about variability in one's own categorizations (Hampton 2007). Moreover, these meta-beliefs can vary depending on what one believes (or fails to believe) about one's audience. For example, suppose a speaker and hearer have had very different past experiences with items they identified as *armadillos*, and neither of them knows much about what the other has experienced. Then it would be irrational for the hearer to interpret the speaker's use of the word *armadillo* by consulting the rich details of her (the hearer's) own private past experiences with armadillos.[11] Such an interpretation strategy would be irrational regardless of whether the hearer consults a summary representation of previous armadillo experiences as in the prototype theory, or directly consults the previous armadillo experiences as in the exemplar theory. A rational person hearing a word for X being uttered does not merely consult her own previous experiences with X, but attempts to recover the speaker's intention; and a speaker, meanwhile, modulates her speech to accommodate the hearer's likely interpretation (Grice 1975; Clark 1996; Tomasello 2003; 2008).

Word meaning involves social norms in a few different ways (Geeraerts 2009: 249–58, sect. 5.5.2). Putnam (1975) argued that natural kind terms such as *water* (or *armadillo*) are 'rigid designators' whose extension is ultimately decided by societal experts. But even when the experts are not consulted, there is evidence for normativity in ordinary conversation. For example, there is experimental evidence that when people in conversation refer repeatedly to the same object, they come to use the same terms. In one experiment, subjects interacted with a confederate speaker, making repeated references to objects (Metzing and Brennan 2003). Then either the original speaker or a new speaker used either the original expression or a new one for the object. Addressees were told to look at and then touch the objects referred to by the expressions, an action that was timed. The result was that hearers took longer to interpret a word when the same speaker

---

[11] For example, armadillos live in my area (Texas). I have seen a number of dead armadillos in the road, and I saw a live one cross my path once while hiking. Those specific experiences would not affect my interpretation of the word as uttered by someone who is unlikely to have ever seen an armadillo.

changed to a new word, while this effect was not found if a new speaker used a new word. This phenomenon, called 'lexical entrainment', is an example of the cooperative nature of language use (Grice 1975). When there are multiple ways to refer to an object, cooperative speakers choose only one possible term during a conversation in order to ease processing. Hearers assume that speakers do this. Once the interlocutors have used a given term they are said to have implicitly agreed to a 'referential pact' (Brennan and Clark 1996).

Such studies suggest that language users pay close attention to each other's use and adjust their usage and interpretation accordingly. Word meanings are established and conventionalized by this process. If word meanings are subject to normative pressures, then they are not equivalent to the private concepts of the things to which the word refers. This is supported by some studies of children that suggest a disconnect between their non-verbal concepts of things and their categorizations via word meanings. Jaswal and Markman (2007) contrasted two different ways in which children categorize objects. On the one hand, categories can be formed on the basis of similarities the children detect themselves. On the other, children also form categories based on verbal testimony. Interestingly, categories formed from these two different sources, linguistic and perceptual, can be dissociated. A study of 2-year-olds found that when such categories come into conflict, the children tended to accept the linguistic category over the perceptual one (Jaswal and Markman 2007).

Geerarts (2009: 255) floats a proposal to reinterpret prototypes as involving social rather than psychological variation. A core reading of a word, corresponding to the prototypically structured concept, is shared by all speakers, while peripheral senses, generated by semantic extension rules, vary depending on the linguistic history of individual speakers.

2.4.6 Sense spectra and gradient senses

Related to the issue of vagueness is the question of whether there is a sharp dividing line between polysemy and generality. Cruse gave an interesting sorites-like argument against a sharp boundary and in favor of degrees of antagonism between senses. First he cited this zeugmatic example involving two senses of *mouth* (Cruse 1986: 72):

(46)   [z] The poisoned chocolate entered the Contessa's mouth at the same instant that the yacht entered that of the river.

While (46) is zeugmatic (Cruse assigned it a ?), we can get from the 'human mouth' sense to the 'river mouth' sense without encountering zeugmatic incompatibility, by combining senses that are contiguous along a spectrum of related senses (Cruse 1986: 72):

(47)   a. John keeps opening and shutting his mouth like a fish.
       b. This parasite attaches itself to the mouths of fishes, sea-squirts, etc.
       c. The mouth of the sea-squirt resembles that of a bottle.
       d. The mouth of the cave resembles that of a bottle.
       e. The mouth of the enormous cave was also that of the underground river.

Assuming that none of the sentences in (47) is zeugmatic, then the contrast between the zeugmatic jump from human mouth to river mouth, on the one hand, and incremental non-zeugmatic jumps, on the other, suggests that the status of the zeugma test needs to be reconsidered. Rather than showing whether two uses of a word represent the same or different senses categorically, the test measures the 'degree of antagonism' between two senses. Cruse concluded that senses are gradient and introduced the term *sense spectrum* for this apparently continuous spectrum of meanings. This implies a continuum from polysemy (distinct but related senses) to generality (not distinct senses).

    Some psycholinguistic and quantitative corpus research has addressed the distinctions between homonymy, polysemy and generality, and the question whether those distinctions are hard lines or a matter of degree. Reading time and eye-tracking studies seem to show, first of all, that polysemy and homonymy are processed differently (Frazier and Rayner 1990). Subjects read sentences that required them to disambiguate a noun based on other material in the sentence. The noun *pitcher* is homonymous ('baseball player' 48a versus 'water vessel' 48b), while the noun *newspaper* in (48c,d) is polysemous.

(48)   a. Of course the pitcher pleased Mary, throwing so many curveballs.
       b. Of course the pitcher pleased Mary, being so elegantly designed.
       c. Unfortunately the newspaper was destroyed, managing advertising so poorly.
       d. Unfortunately the newspaper was destroyed, lying in the rain.

Frazier and Rayner found that subjects read more slowly when the nouns were homonyms like *pitcher* than when the noun was polysemous, like *newspaper*. According to their explanation, the separate homonyms force the listener to commit to a preferred interpretation (e.g. the most likely or frequent one), and when that commitment must be abandoned, the reanalysis increases comprehension time. For the senses of a polysemous word no such change is necessary. Pickering and Frisson (2001) found a similar effect for verbs, and concluded that polysemy involves a single underspecified lexical entry.

However, Klein and Murphy (2001; 2002) reached the opposite conclusion on the basis of a range of experiments involving recall, sensicality judgments, priming, and other methods. Their stimuli included nouns disambiguated by a single modifier, such as *wrapping paper ~ shredded paper ~ liberal paper*. For example they considered the word *paper* in the first two to have the same sense (physical substance made from wood pulp), while the third has a different sense (a news-paper company). They found no significant difference in speed or accuracy in processing polysemous versus homonymous pairs. But their stimuli were such that the semantic distance between the poly-semous pairs was not so different from the semantic distance between homonymous pairs. For example, *wrapping paper* is in part function-ally defined, and so it can be made of plastic, while *shredded paper* is not. So these are not exactly the same sense. Klepousniotou et al. (2008) replicated part of Klein and Murphy's study, but controlled for the amount of semantic overlap between the senses of polysemous words, and the processing difference returned.

Brown (2008) carried out a priming study to see whether there are separate mental representations for each related word sense. Subjects were presented with a 'priming' verb phrase and were asked whether the phrase 'made sense' or was 'difficult to make sense of.' After a 300 ms pause, a 'target' verb phrase, containing the same verb as the first, appeared on the screen, and again the participant judged its semantic coherence. The two verb senses implied by a prime/target pair ranged from identical (*cleaned the shirt ~ cleaned the cup*), through a spectrum from closely to distantly related sense, to unrelated homonyms (*banked the plane ~ banked the money*) (see Table 2.1).

The speed and accuracy of the target responses were then plotted against the relative relatedness of the senses. The subjects' performance improved monotonically as a function of how closely related the senses were. The improvement was gradual, with no sudden drop in perform-ance as we go from 'same sense' (generality) to 'closely related senses' (polysemy), nor is there a radical break between distantly related and unrelated (homonymy). Brown (2008) interpreted these results as

TABLE 2.1   Stimuli for polysemy vs. generality study (Brown 2008)

	Prime	Target
Unrelated	*banked the plane*	*banked the money*
Distantly related	*ran the track*	*ran the shop*
Closely related	*broke the glass*	*broke the radio*
Same sense	*cleaned the shirt*	*cleaned the cup*

implying that related word senses are not discrete entities but form a continuum.

The difficulty of establishing boundaries between senses of a word has been demonstrated in recent research related to word sense disambiguation. Computational word-sense disambiguation systems are often trained on corpora that have been annotated by hand with an indication of the specific sense of each ambiguous word (McCarthy 2009). Inter-annotator agreement, a measure of accuracy, is typically no better than about 67% to 78% (Erk et al. 2012). A fundamental problem is that a single token may involve multiple senses to different degrees, while the task assigned to the annotators relies on the implicit assumption that any given word occurrence will be adequately described by one sense. Instead of asking annotators to choose between senses, Erk et al. (2012) asked them to provide judgments for all listed senses of the target word and indicate not only whether each sense (from WordNet) applied, but to what degree it did. The result was that annotators provided many more judgments of multiple dictionary senses applying to a given occurrence, and made extensive use of the intermediate values on the rating scale. For example, subjects were asked to rate the word *paper* from the corpus sentence (49) for the applicability of each of the WordNet definitions for *paper* in (50):

(49)   This can be justified thermodynamically in this case, and this will be done in a separate paper which is being prepared.
                                                    (Erk et al. 2012: 513, table 6)

(50)   (i) a material made of cellulose pulp; (ii) an essay (especially one written as an assignment); (iii) a daily or weekly publication on folded sheets; contains news and articles and advertisements; (iv) a medium for written communication; (v) a scholarly article describing the results of observations or stating hypotheses; (vi) a business firm that publishes newspapers; (vii) the physical object that is the product of a newspaper publisher.

Subjects were asked to rate each sense on a scale from 1 to 5, where 5 is the best fit. All annotators gave the highest rating (of 5) to sense (v), but they also gave relatively high ratings to other senses such as (ii) (ratings of 3, 3, and 5) and (iv) (ratings of 5, 3, and 1). One subject even gave a rating of 5 to sense (i) 'a material made of cellulose pulp.' Some of these senses may be hyponyms of others: (iv) 'a medium for written communication' includes (ii) 'an essay...' as a special case, and broadly interpreted, (ii) includes (v) 'a scholarly article...' as a special case. In still other cases a word token may actually be used in two distinct senses simultaneously, such as the word *dismiss* in this example:

(51)   Simply thank your Gremlin for his or her opinion, dismiss him or her, and ask your true inner voice to turn up its volume.

(Erk et al. 2012: 518)

Among the options were 'bar from attention or consideration' and 'cause or permit a person to leave.' Annotators chose both of them. Arguably the word *dismiss* is being used in both the former 'disregard' sense and the latter 'usher out' sense: the 'Gremlin', a metaphor for negative thoughts, is to be ushered out, while the thoughts he/she represents are to be disregarded. Overall the researchers found high rates of inter-annotator agreement, and concluded that meanings can be described in a graded fashion (Erk et al. 2012: 539).

2.4.7 Probabilistic grammar and mixed categories

It is generally agreed that word meaning is vague. More controversial is the view that not only semantic categories but syntactic categories can be vague as well. On the one hand the notion of syntactic category plays a powerful role in syntactic theory: a set of properties that all covary across different formatives can be attributed to a common category rather than being repeated for each formative. On the other hand there are two problems: (i) we find a great deal of variation among speakers and (ii) some elements show a mixture of properties from different categories. Addressing the problem of variation, certain models of grammar incorporate gradient and even non-deterministic components, which interact with the more traditional symbolic grammar (e.g. Manning 2003; Aarts 2004; Sorace and Keller 2005; Bresnan and Nikitina 2009). As for the second problem, some theories posit 'mixed categories' that allow a single token to combine, e.g. Verb and Noun properties (e.g. Malouf 2000; Croft 2001; Spencer 2005). In short, while the traditional category-based or 'symbolic' conception of grammar has proven very useful, there have been important challenges to it.

Labov (1969) proposed to incorporate systematic variation into linguistic description and theory by extending the concept of a rule of grammar to that of a variable rule. Phonological rules describing apparent free variation were annotated with probabilities reflecting various factors of a stylistic, socioeconomic, or dialectal nature (Cedergren and Sankoff 1974). In that way the fuzziness and variability commonly attributed to performance factors were directly incorporated into the competence grammar. Since the 1990s this controversial idea has gained ground within syntactic theory, primarily as a consequence of the growth of corpus methods and computational linguistics.

In promoting a program of 'probabilistic syntax', Manning (2003) advocates keeping the mainstream categorical symbolic grammar but running probabilities over the elements of the grammatical representation. The subcategorization frames of verbs, for example, would be weighted based on their observed distribution, instead of all-or-none. Manning (2003) cites the example of the verbs *consider* and *regard*. In some syntactic treatments (Manning cites Pollard and Sag 1994), *consider* is reported to allow the NP-NP frame and reject the NP-Infinitive frame, while *regard* has the opposite subcategorization:

(52) a. We consider Kim to be an acceptable candidate.
      b. *We consider Kim as an acceptable candidate.

(53) a. *We regard Kim to be an acceptable candidate.
      b. We regard Kim as an acceptable candidate.

But a study of a *New York Times* corpus supports these judgments only as a tendency, and also reveals exceptions in both directions:

(54) a. The boys consider her as family and she participates in every-
         thing we do.
      b. Conservatives argue that the Bible regards homosexuality to
         be a sin.

(Manning 2003: 299–300, exx. 6, 8)

More generally the acceptability judgments reported for decontextualized example sentences under-represent the variation found in naturally occurring texts and speech. Probabilistic grammar rules are meant to capture the gradient character of language use. Similarly, the argument/adjunct distinction need not be seen as categorical according to Manning

(2003). Some syntactic dependents lie on the borderline and are notoriously difficult to classify as argument or adjunct. On this view the choice need not be forced; instead the dependents of a word have a gradient classification. To take another example, Sorace (2000) gives a gradient account of the unaccusative/unergative distinction, focusing on auxiliary selection (see Section 3.6.2).

Grammaticality judgments themselves are gradient: example sentences are not always clearly good or bad, but show a range of accepability. Not only do we find variation across speakers, but individual speakers are often unsure of their own judgments (Wasow and Arnold 2005: 1483). This uncertainty raises both methodological and theoretical issues. Regarding methodology, one method of addressing that gradability is to use magnitude estimation studies. Instead of forcing a choice between good, bad, and perhaps one or two intermediate judgments, the researcher gives the informants a large scale of options, using their judgment of a particular item as a benchmark for relative judgment of other samples (Sorace and Keller 2005).

As for the theoretical implications of gradient judgments, views diverge. Chomsky posited a distinction between the 'competence' grammar, which licenses the set of grammatical sentences, and 'performance' factors, which can upgrade or downgrade intuitive judgments (Chomsky 1965). Challenging the competence/performance dichotomy are radical stochastic theories that question whether such a principled distinction can really be drawn. According to Bresnan and Nikitina (2009: 161) 'the boundaries between categoricity and gradience are fluid in both lexicon and grammar.' In their study of the dative alternation, Bresnan and Nikitina hypothesize that at least some grammaticality judgments do not reflect the grammar, but directly reflect the probability of the locution, given pragmatic plausibility and contextual factors. See Section 7.1 for examples and discussion.

Another alternative to traditional grammatical categories is to allow mixed categories for the in-between cases. Instead of (or in addition to) giving a quantitative coefficient to each category (say, an item is '62% noun-like, 38% verb-like'), one can identify the particular noun and verb features that are combined in an item. Under such analyses, a part-of-speech category such as Noun or Verb is not a primitive, but is instead defined as a particularly important cluster of properties.

Malouf (1996; 1998; 2000) proposes such an analysis of gerundive constructions that evince a mixture of verbal and nominal properties. Many languages have such constructions. English verbal forms in -*ing* can serve as full-fledged verbs as in *Pat keeps folding the napkins*, or as full-fledged nouns heading noun phrases, as in (55a). They also appear in gerundive constructions introduced (if at all) by either the possessive characteristic of nominals (*Pat's* in (55b)) or an accusative NP (*Pat* in (55c)).

(55)   *Nominal phrase*   *Type*

   a. { Pat's /the } artful folding of the napkins   of-ing/mixed nominal
   b. Pat's artfully folding the napkins   POSS-ing
   c. Pat artfully folding the napkins   ACC-ing

                                       (from Malouf 1996: ex. 1)

Gerundive constructions have the syntactic distribution of a nominal (an NP or DP depending on one's theory) rather than a clause. For example, the subject of a subordinate clause can be a nominal (56a) but not a clause (56b), and gerundives are permitted (56c):[12]

(56)   a. I wondered if the construction of a spaceship had upset you.
       b. *I wondered if that John built a spaceship had upset you.
       c. I wondered if John's building a spaceship had upset you.

                                             (Abney 1987: 15)

But the *-ing* word in a gerundive construction resembles a verb rather than a noun, with regard to its complements (e.g. DP objects) and modifiers (adverbs, not adjectives). A common analysis follows Abney (1987) in positing a lower VP and a higher DP:

(57)   [Pat's [D [artfully folding the napkins]$_{VP}$]$_{D'}$]$_{DP}$

In Abney's (1987) structure the VP is a complement of a typically null D head. Bresnan's (1997) LFG analysis adopts Abney's DP but dispenses with the null D head because endocentricity can be satisfied via the f-structure in that theory.

   Malouf disputes this syntactic account, proposing instead a lexical account in the HPSG framework. The *-ing* word itself is a mixed category incorporating features of verbs (taking NP complements; accepting adverbial modifiers) and nouns (possessive specifier; NP-like external syntax). A lexical rule derives gerunds from the present participle form of a verb, with the following effects on the lexical item:

---

[12] Malouf (1996: 3) (citing Jørgensen 1981 and Quirk et al. 1985: 1230) notes one case where the distributions diverge: *There's no use (you/your) telling him anything.* (cp. *There's no use your explanation to him.*)

its complement specifications are inherited from the verb; the head value changes from 'verb' to 'gerund'; and it allows the subject argument of the verb to be discharged as either a SUBJ (subject, for the ACC-ing type) or a SPR (specifier, for POSS-ing type) (Malouf 2000: 20). The category 'gerund' is a subtype of 'noun', so the gerundive construction as a whole is a nominal projection (NP), which explains its distribution.

Malouf defends the lexical mixed category analysis on the basis of VSO languages like Arabic. The Modern Standard Arabic *maṣdar* construction, like the English gerundive construction, combines the genitive specifiers typical of NPs with the adverbial modifiers typical of clauses. The order, reflecting the VSO order of clauses, is Noun-Subject-Object. But the adverbial modifiers (*bistimraarin* 'persistently') appear after the genitive subject (*rrajuli* 'the man's'):

(58) ʔaqlaqa-ni   [ntiqaad-u   r-rajul-i
      annoyed-me   criticizing-NOM   the-man-GEN
      bi-stimraar-in   haaḏaa   l-mašruuʕ-i].
      with-persistence-GEN   this   the-project-ACC
      'The man's persistent criticizing of the project annoyed me.'
                                          (Fassi-Fehri 1993: 240)

On the syntactic analysis, gerunds take adverbial modifiers because they contain a partial verbal projection. But in (58) there is no contiguous VP, as shown. The head and the 'verbal' type elements (underlined in (58)) are interleaved with the nominal element. This pattern is consistent with the cross-linguistic generalization that in deverbalization, the historical order in which syntax changes from verbal to nominal forms is first the tense/aspect/mood morphology, then the expression of subjects, and finally the expression of objects (Croft 1991: 83). (English gerundives and Arabic *maṣdar* have undergone the first two changes: finite inflection is lost and the subjects are in genitive rather than nominative case.) Malouf proposes that this generalization follows from the structure of the lexical hierarchy responsible for the head word inheriting its nouny and verby properties, and not from coherence in the phrase structure.

The more general theoretical proposal is that categories are defined in terms of their properties, rather than the other way around. The part-of-speech categories like Verb, Noun, Adjective, and Preposition are not all-or-none word classifications, but rather are relatively common nodes in a rich lexical hierarchy of types and subtypes that determine the distribution and morphology of a word. Malouf assumes an HPSG hierarchical lexicon in which a word inherits properties from all supertypes to which it belongs, and a word can inherit along multiple dimensions (see Section 5.2.2). Gerunds are words that inherit some properties normally associated with nouns and others normally associated with verbs. Notice that while it may seem that such a theory effectively rejects the standard notion of grammatical category, in fact the opposite is true. It allows the rules of grammar to deal in a richer set of categories governed by a more flexible theory.

2.5 World knowledge in word meaning

Many theories of word meaning, even those incorporating sophisticated analyses of polysemy and vagueness, still do not adequately capture the rich scenarios evoked by the use of a word. The 'frame semantics' research program represents an ambitious attempt to fill that gap, and moreover takes this evocation of background information as fundamental to word meaning itself (Fillmore and Baker 2010). Frame semantics belongs to a class of theories that approach semantics by classifying experience first, then seeking the various linguistic forms used for expressing those experiences, the so-called 'onomasiological' approach (Geeraerts 2009: 23–5). This contrasts with the more common 'semasiological' approach, in which natural language is analyzed by isolating linguistic forms and then decoding their meanings and determining the rules for their composition into complex meanings. Frame semantics starts from people's concepts and studies the varying ways they can be expressed in language (Fillmore and Baker 2010).

A fundamental unit in frame semantics is the (cognitive) frame, defined as 'any of the many organized packages of knowledge, beliefs, and patterns of practice that shape and allow humans to make sense of their experiences' (Fillmore and Baker 2010: 314). For example, one frame is constituted by the culturally prescribed events and participants involved in a typical visit to a restaurant. Others include: the stages and processes in the life cycle of a human being; the visual and physical properties of a cube; the organization of a human face; and so on (Fillmore and Baker 2010: 314). The observation that memory is organized into these sorts of psychological constructs is influential in cognitive science. It derives from the notion of 'schemata' introduced by the psychologist Sir Frederic Bartlett in his study of memory

(Bartlett 1932). Minsky (1975) developed this idea and introduced the term 'frames', essentially synonymous with 'schemata' except that Minsky applied his construct to artificial intelligence as well as psychology (Brewer 1999). Some authors continue to use the original term 'schema' (Rumelhart 1980). 'Scripts' are members of the subtype of schema (or frame) involving stereotyped sequences of actions, such as the 'restaurant script' mentioned above (Shank and Abelson 1977).

A linguistic form is said to *evoke* or activate one or more frames. We can see the necessity for this very clearly by considering technical terms that can be understood only within a network of specialized knowledge: consider the sailing terms *boom, jib, spinnaker, tacking, jibing, hard alee*, and *mast abeam*, or the terms *id, ego, superego*, and *transference* from Freudian psychoanalysis. Without some understanding of how sailing works one cannot understand the verb *jibe*, defined as 'to change a vessel's course when sailing with the wind so that as the stern passes through the eye of the wind, the boom swings to the opposite side.'[13] Frame semantics treats the semantics of all content words in that way, based on the view that the meaning of a content word can only be understood through an appeal to the background frames associated with the word. For example (from Fillmore and Baker 2010: 319), the expression *on land* is specifically understood as contrasting with *at sea*, as in *The men were happy to spend several hours on land this morning*. Hence the use of the expression *on land* in this sentence implies that the men's 'several hours' were time out from a sea voyage.

The Berkeley FrameNet Project is a large scale lexicographic implementation of the frame semantics program for English.[14] Similar projects are under way for German, Spanish, Japanese, Chinese, and Italian. In FrameNet, situation types for which the language provides rich linguistic expressive capabilities are identified as frames. By way of illustration, Fillmore and Baker (2010: 321) describe the 'Revenge' frame as 'the last phase of a scenario in which someone A (the Offender) has offended or injured someone B (the InjuredParty) and after and because of that, someone C (the Avenger) does something to punish A.' Given in parentheses are the names of the 'frame elements,' aspects and components of the frame that are likely to be mentioned in a description of an act of revenge. Listed in connection with the frame

---

[13] Definition from Merriam-Webster online dictionary (http://www.merriam-webster.com/dictionary/jibe).

[14] See https://framenet.icsi.berkeley.edu.

are the 'lexical units,' which are words and other formatives that evoke and depend upon the frame. Lexical units belonging to the Revenge frame include the verbs *avenge, retaliate, revenge*; the phrasal verbs *get back (at), get even (with), pay back*; the nouns *payback, reprisal, retaliation, retribution, revenge, vengeance*; and the adjectives *vengeful, vindictive*.

In FrameNet, sentences from a large corpus are annotated with relevant frames evoked by words contained in them, and the appropriate constituents of those sentences are labeled as frame elements. The word *avenge* in (59a) evokes the Revenge frame, and phrases are associated with its frame elements as shown in (59b).

(59) a. Hook tries to avenge himself on Peter Pan by becoming a second and better father.

   b. [AVENGER:SUBJECT:NP Hook] tries to [TARGET avenge] [INJURED-PARTY:OBJECT:NP himself] [OFFENDER:OBLIQUE:PP on Peter Pan] [PUNISHMENT:OBLIQUE:PP-GERUND by becoming a second and better father].

(Fillmore and Baker 2010: 322)

In this way it becomes possible to study the varied linguistic expressions of frame elements. This offers an explanatory basis for a theory of argument structure. Note however that the onomasiological approach taken by frame semantics does not naturally lend itself to a treatment of polysemy. The two entries for *short*, one contrasting with *tall* and the other with *long*, occur in two different frames, and the theory does not automatically connect them.

In frame semantics, word meaning involves larger slices of experience than what corresponds to the word's argument structure or syntactic dependents. This aspect of the theory is shared by Clark and Clark's (1979) account of denominal verbs, described in Section 3.8.2. According to Clark and Clark (1979), the meaning of a verb like *to blanket* or *to spice* is determined by prototypical 'predominant features' of the cognate nouns from whence they derive. The nouns *blanket* and *spice* are classified as Placeables, evoking a locative relation $Loc(e,x)$ ('e is located at x'), where e corresponds to the noun's referent: stereotypically, blankets are placed on beds and spice is placed in food. Another theory of this type is Pustejovsky's theory of qualia (see Section 2.3.3.4). However, frame semantics is crucially different in taking an onomasiological approach. As a consequence, there is no attempt to delimit the scope of a frame based on the properties of a single form such as a word. The cognitive frames are motivated by what amounts to ethnographic study, and can encompass human experiences on any scale.

Some experimental psycholinguistic research has attempted to address the role of such general domain knowledge in word meaning, and the question whether there is also evidence for the more schematic semantic information usually assumed to accompany a lexical item. Priming studies have shown that a reader's exposure to nouns activates general knowledge of the events that typically involve the entities they denote (Hare, Jones, et al. 2009). Reading times are also affected by the reader's expectations about likely fillers of argument positions: *the brick* is more plausible than *the glass* as the agent argument of the transitive verb *shatter*, while preferences reverse for the patient argument. Not surprisingly, slower reading times are observed for the abnormal combinations (Hare, Elman, et al. 2009).

While it is undeniable that comprehending a content word often involves accessing general knowledge, an interesting question is whether there is evidence that more schematic, context-independent lexical information is accessed first. That question has been addressed with speed–accuracy trade-off experiments, in which subjects are forced to answer a question at short, controlled time intervals after receiving the stimulus. The accuracy of their answers at different intervals gives a picture of how comprehension proceeds over time. McElree et al. (2006) used stimuli like those in Table 2.2, and asked subjects to judge the sentence 'true' or 'false.' They assume, for example, that *Water pistols are dangerous* is false (hence the predicate is 'false of the phrase') while *Pistols are dangerous* is true (the predicate is 'true of the noun'). They found that subjects misjudged sentences like *Water pistols are dangerous* as true given short processing delays (under about

TABLE 2.2   Sample stimuli from McElree et al. (2006: 850)

Sentence type	Sample sentence
TN	*Water pistols have triggers.*
TP	*Water pistols are harmless.*
FN	*Water pistols have string.*
FP	*Water pistols are dangerous.*

TN = true of the noun; TP = true of the phrase; FN = false of the noun; FP = false of the phrase.

1 second), with the false alarm rate falling off with greater delays. This contrasted with sentences like *Water pistols have triggers*, in which the predicate is true of both the phrase and the noun. McElree et al. (2006) see that result as showing that very early in the processing, rich contextual information has not yet been incorporated and the subjects are instead responding on the basis of lexical information associated with the word *pistols*.

Gaylord et al. (2012) and Gaylord (2013) performed similar speed–accuracy trade-off studies for verbs instead of nouns, using stimuli such as *The dawn broke* followed by a task of judging whether or not 'Something shattered.' They report early false alarms to such stimuli, consistent with what has previously been shown for nouns, which lends support to the claim that verbs may in fact carry such a default meaning. However, many questions remain about nature of this default, such as whether it is a unique default or a probability distribution over senses, and whether a prior discourse context would influence it.

2.6 Conclusion

The problems of polysemy and vagueness are central to the study of word meaning and therefore also important for understanding the interactions between word meaning and syntax. Words typically have multiple related senses, and even for a single sense there are many borderline cases about which speakers are incurably uncertain. Our understanding of these two phenomena, both very active areas of current research, has improved, but there remain many unanswered questions, as well as questions with multiple, conflicting, controversial answers.

Word meaning stands at one end of the syntax–lexicon interface. Regardless of the details of the formal model for mapping the arguments of a verb or other predicate onto the syntax, the buck always stops at the word meaning, with its attendant problems of polysemy and vagueness. Some of the putative problems with mapping theories, such as the difficulty with finding reliable diagnostics for thematic role types and other elements of lexical semantic representation, may actually be endemic in the polysemous and vague nature of the words themselves. Indeed, many examples of systematic polysemy in works such as Apresjan (1974) are actually argument alternations by a different name. A better understanding of those underlying issues could lead to important adjustments to the mapping theories.

3

Argument alternations and cognates

3.1 Introduction

Very little can be concluded about the syntax–lexicon interface from looking at sentences in isolation. A single sentence does not allow us to determine the constraints on the use of a word or to tease apart which aspects of the meaning are contributed by a word and which by the rules of syntactic combination. But by investigating the behavior of a single word or word root across many different syntactic contexts, we can discern the grammatical content of the word and its relation to the syntactic structure. Thus we must study two orthogonal relations, the 'syntagmatic' relation holding between a head word and its dependent phrases and the 'paradigmatic' relation between different uses of a word or between morphologically related words (Saussure 1916).

This chapter reviews several types of paradigmatic relation. In 'diathesis alternations' (also called 'argument alternations' or simply 'alternations') such as the dative, locative, and causative alternations, a single verb form can appear with a range of alternative complement possibilities. For example, the verb *clear* allows the same three participants to be expressed in two different ways:

(1)   a. Jonas is clearing the books from the table.
       b. Jonas is clearing the table of books.

'Morpholexical operations', such as the passive, antipassive, applicative, and causative, signal the alteration of the complementation possibilities of a verb with a morphological change to the verb form. The English passive voice, for example, uses the past participle form of the verb. The following passive sentences correspond to the respective active voice examples in (1):

(2) a. The books are being cleared from the table (by Jonas).
     b. The table is being cleared of books (by Jonas).

Sections 3.3–3.5 discuss alternations of both types, those with no change to the verb form and those marked by a morphological change to the verb. The sections are organized by the nature of the argument change. Section 3.3 reviews changes involving the omission (or demotion, i.e. conversion to an oblique) of an object; Section 3.4 looks at omission or demotion of the agent or other role that would otherwise have been expressed as the subject; and Section 3.5 is concerned with muliple complements. This way of organizing things should not imply that the corresponding morphologically marked and unmarked alternations should necessarily be analyzed in the same way. But they have some properties in common and are often discussed together and sometimes analyzed in the same way. Next we discuss unaccusativity (Section 3.6) and variation in the lexicalization of events (Section 3.7). Section 3.8 concerns category conversion between cognate forms such as noun–verb cognates, which are related by rules of derivation, often accompanied by a morphological change.

   The main focus of this chapter is descriptive, a summary of the main observations and generalizations noted in the linguistics literature. For now, grammatical theory is secondary and discussed mainly in so far as it aids the presentation of fact. The theoretical approaches are taken up in earnest in subsequent chapters.

3.2 Argument selection

3.2.1 Variable polyadicity and subject–object asymmetry

In an event or state as described by a verb, typically certain participants are ontologically necessary: any act of *selling* requires a seller, a buyer, a commodity, and currency or other payment. All four participants can be expressed in a clause headed by this verb, as in (3a). Alternatively, some can remain unmentioned as in (3b–d), even though we know they must exist (example from Wechsler 2005a).

(3) a. Sue sold a car to John for $500.
     b. Sue sold a car to John.
     c. Sue sold a car for $500.
     d. Sue sold a car.

The buyer (John) and payment ($500) are ontologically necessary for selling to be what it is, but the complements expressing those participants are syntactically optional. This is an illustration of 'variable polyadicity', i.e. variation in the number of the verb's arguments that are expressed in a clause.

Distinct from the ontologically necessary participants are (semantically) optional participants. Selling a car involves someone giving up ownership of the car, but it can also optionally involve a salesperson acting as a selling agent. In fact, the sentences in (4) are ambiguous as to which of these two roles Sue is playing, prior owner or salesperson. Similarly, various 'instruments' of a sale can be mentioned, such as the *with*-PP in (4a) or the subjects of (4b–d):

(4)   a. Sue sold this car with clever advertising.
      b. Clever advertising sold this car.
      c. Sex is what sells cars to college students.
      d. Hard work sells cars.

Summarizing so far, a verb comes with a set of semantically necessary participants, and also perhaps some optional ones. Some or all of these (semantically necessary and optional) participants are expressed in a sentence.

In addition to illustrating variable polyadicity, this example also illustrates prioritization in 'subject selection'. For concreteness let us assume these thematic role type definitions from Kroeger (2005: 54–5), at least when the roles in question fit one of these definitions:

(5)   Thematic role types (Kroeger 2005: 54–5)
      AGENT: causer or initiator of events
      EXPERIENCER: perceives a stimulus or registers mental or emotional
         process or state
      RECIPIENT: receives something
      BENEFICIARY: entity whom the action is intended to benefit
      INSTRUMENT: used by agent to perform action
      THEME: undergoes change of location or possession; its location is
         specified; or object of perception, cognition or emotion
      PATIENT: acted on, affected, or created; or undergoes change of
         state
      LOCATION: spatial reference point
         SOURCE: beginning point of motion
         GOAL: endpoint of motion
         PATH: trajectory

In the examples in (6), *John* plays the role of Agent, *the window* is the Patient, and *a hammer* is the Instrument:

(6)   a. John broke the window.
    b. A hammer broke the window.
    c. John broke the window (with a hammer).
    d. The window broke.

A relative (often partial) ordering is imposed on thematic role types and on grammatical relations:

(7)   a. agent > beneficiary > recipient/experiencer > instrument > theme/patient > location
    b. Subject > Object

Linking between these two hierarchies must respect both orders, so that, for example, in a transitive Agent–Theme verb, the Agent must link to Subject and Theme to Object, while in a transitive Instrument–Theme verb, the Instrument links to Subject and Theme to Object. It cannot link not the other way around (i.e. the mapping is an order isomorphism between substructures of the two hierarchies). Notice that it applies to the subject and object relations but is mute on the question of oblique complements such as PPs in English. This idea of a hierarchy for selecting the roles to be played by subject and object has been influential in several different syntactic frameworks (see Section 4.2).

    The picture that has emerged so far is that a verb comes with specific sets of obligatory and optional participants. Certain of these participants are expressed as subject and possibly object, subject to a hierarchy determining the relative preference of roles for each. Other roles are expressed as obliques (PPs, in English), or remain unexpressed. A lexical argument structure can be represented as a set of roles, ordered from left to right according to the thematic hierarchy, with parentheses for optional roles:

(8)   break ⟨(AGENT), (INST) , PAT ⟩

These arguments are linked to grammatical relations in keeping with the constraint on subject and object selection given above:

(9)   break ⟨ AGENT ,   PAT ⟩   (6a)
             | |
             SUBJ   OBJ

(10)   break ⟨ INST,   PAT   ⟩   (6b)
            | |
          SUBJ   OBJ

(11)   break ⟨ AGENT,   INST,   PAT ⟩   (6c)
            | | |
          SUBJ   OBL   OBJ

(12)   break ⟨   PAT   ⟩   (6d)
               |
             SUBJ

This descriptive framework is adequate for describing most of the alternations and other phenomena treated in this chapter. The problems with it, and alternatives to it, are discussed in Chapters 4, 5, and 6.

3.2.2 Object selection

Verbs typically allow some flexibility regarding which event participant is realized as subject and object. Systematic polysemy (Section 2.3.1), when observed in verbs, typically can be seen as diathesis alternation. Verbs like *draw* and *paint* take as object either the effected object (*a picture*) or the depicted object (*a sunset*):

(13)   a. Mary is drawing/painting a picture.
       b. Mary is drawing/painting a sunset.

If the verb meaning is viewed as a relation between the subject and object denoted individuals, then the verb must be seen as polysemous. Dictionaries often list these variants as distinct senses of a word. Alternatively, by abstracting away from the particular participant realized we may see the verb *draw* as simply a predicate on events, as suggested by intransitive uses (*Mary is drawing*) or eventive gerundives (*Drawing is fun*). If the verb's meaning is viewed as a predicate on events, then something other than verb meaning must be responsible for distinguishing the particular roles played by the object. For convenience we use the term 'polysemy' here (see Section 2.3 for discussion).

The polysemy rule can be stated in (14), where OBJ represents the object argument:

(14)   a. rule: 'depict OBJ' ∼ 'create OBJ by depicting something'
       b. verbs: *draw, paint, film*

c. examples:
   draw/paint a tree ~ draw/paint a portrait
   film a demonstration ~ film a movie

The options for object selection vary from verb to verb. Contrast (13) with (15):

(15) a. Mary depicted/photographed the sunset.
      b. (*)Mary depicted/photographed a picture.

A closely related alternation is *play Iago* ~ *play the role of Iago*, where the role is in one sense created by the actor. English has other 'image creation' verbs with similar but not identical polysemy rules (Levin 1993: 169–72):

(16) a. rule: 'create OBJ(image)' ~ 'alter OBJ by marking it with an image'
      b. verbs: *appliqué, emboss, embroider, engrave, etch, imprint, incise, inscribe, mark, paint, set, sign, stamp, tattoo*
      c. examples:
         inscribe his name on the ring ~ inscribe the ring (with his name)
         paint a toy ~ paint a design

                                          (Levin 1993: 169)

Verbs allowing only the first variant include *scribble* and *print*, those allowing only the second include *decorate* and *illustrate*:

(17) a. The jeweller scribbled his name on the contract.
      b. *The jeweller scribbled the contract with his name.
      c. *The jeweller decorated the name on the ring.
      d. The jeweller decorated the ring with the name.

                                          (Levin 1993: 170–71)

Similar object participant alternations are found in Russian:

(18) vyšit'   podušku ~ vyšit'   uzor
      embroider cushion   embroider design

                                          (Apresjan 1974: 25)

Similarly, the following example from Russian (from Apresjan 1974: 25) has parallels in English:

(19) a. 'to deform OBJ in a definite way' ~ 'to create OBJ by deforming in this way'

b. Russian *burit'* 'to bore, drill'
   | *burit'* | *zemlju* | ~ | *burit'* | *skvažinu* |
   | drill | earth | | drill | borehole |

c. English *drill, carve*
   | drill the wood | ~ | drill a hole |
   | carve the wood | ~ | carve a notch |

A related but distinct cross-linguistic pattern is shown here for Russian, English and Tamil:

(20) 'treat, process OBJ in a definite way' ~ 'eliminate OBJ by treating in this way'

a. Russian *konopatit'* 'to caulk'
   | *konopatit'* | *lodku* | ~ | *konopatit'* | *ščeli* |
   | caulk | boat | | caulk | chinks |

   (Apresjan 1974: 25)

b. English *repair, cure*
   | repair boots | ~ | repair a tear |
   | cure her | ~ | cure the disease |

c. Tamil *thekkuradhu* 'sew up'[1]
thuni	thekkuradhu	~	ottai	thekkuradhu
cloth	sew-up		tear	sew-up
'sew up the cloth'			'sew up the tear'	

(21) 'treat OBJ in a definite way' ~ 'cause a change in OBJ by treating in this way'

a. English: shave my beard ~ shave my face.

b. French[2]
   (i) | Elle | a | coiffé | ses longs cheveux. |
       | She | has | cut | her long hair. |

   (ii) | Elle | a | coiffé | l'enfant. |
        | She | has | coiffed | the child. |

English has no similar verb for cutting hair that participates in this pattern, except the French borrowing *to coiffe*, and perhaps the verb *to style*, in some circles. Verbs like 'close' can be used for either the aperture (the door) or the area being blocked off (the room), in Russian and French, but not as widely in English.

---

[1] Thanks to Ashwini Ganeshan for the Tamil examples.
[2] Thanks for Charles Mignon for the French examples.

(22) 'shut OBJ off' ~ block OBJ access by shutting something off'

  a. Russian *zakryt'* 'close'
     zakryt'   dver' ~ *zakryt'   komnatu*
     close   door   close   room

(Apresjan 1974, 27)

  b. French *fermer* 'close'
     Elle ferme la   porte.
     She   closes the door.
     Elle ferme la   chambre.
     She   closes the room.

  c. English
     close the door ~ ??close the room (but: close the shop; close up the room)
     lock the door ~ lock the room

The English verb *close* does not normally take as its object the area being blocked off, such as a room or car. But it allows some variants such as *close the shop* and *close up the room*.

  Summarizing, verbs typically allow some variation with regard to the participant expressed by the object argument. This variation falls into common semantic patterns, which can be considered to be systematic polysemy, if we take the verb meaning to be the semantic relation between subject and object arguments. Despite these common patterns, such alternations vary from verb to verb, and from language to language. See Levin (1993) for an annotated compendium of English verbs classed according to argument selection.

3.3 Object omission and demotion

3.3.1 Object drop

Many verbs optionally appear with a direct object. Whether the unexpressed argument is understood as indefinite or definite can depend upon the verb. For example, that argument is indefinite in the case of *eat* but definite for *find out* (Fillmore 1986):

(23) a. Jonas is eating all the sushi.
      b. Jonas is eating.

(24) a. Jonas found out the answer.
      b. Jonas found out.

Fillmore (1986: 2) refers to these two types as Indefinite Null Complements and Definite Null Complements, respectively. Sentence (23b) does not require a particular discourse context to identify the eaten thing, and means roughly 'Jonas is eating something'; while (24b) requires a context that identifies what was found out, and means roughly 'Jonas found it out' or 'Jonas found out about it.' Thus it is not at all odd to say 'Jonas is eating; I wonder what he is eating' but much odder to say 'Jonas found out; I wonder what he found out' (Fillmore 1986: 2). Also 'Jonas did not eat yesterday' entails that he did not eat anything, while 'Jonas did not find out yesterday' does not entail that he did not find out anything, but rather only that he did not find the contextually identified thing. In English and many other languages, transitive verbs vary as to whether an object may be omitted with an indefinite or definite interpretation, or not at all.

It has long been noted that the possibility of omitting the object varies from verb to verb. Omission of the object is much less acceptable with other verbs, even some with similar meaning:

(25) a. Jonas is devouring all the sushi.
      b. *Jonas is devouring.
(26) a. Jonas is dining (on the sushi).
      b. Jonas is dining.
      c. *Jonas is dining the sushi.

At the same time, some regularities have been noted. Next we consider the semantics of a dropped object more closely, and then look for semantic generalizations about which verbs allow omission.

Fillmore (1986: 2) noted that under Indefinite Null Complements one can distinguish two subtypes, one involving 'a semantic object of considerable generality, the other requiring the specification of various degrees of semantic specialization'. The unexpressed argument of *eat* and *drink* in (27a) is 'anything', while that of *eat* in (27b) is more specifically a meal, not merely something; and that of *drink* in (27c), under one common interpretation, is 'alcoholic beverages'. Fillmore notes that in example (27d) (attributed to James McCawley, lecture), 'the missing object is taken to include breads or pastries, not potatoes or hams.'

(27) a. When my tongue was paralyzed, I couldn't eat or drink.
      b. We've already eaten.
      c. I've tried to stop drinking.
      d. I spent the afternoon baking.

The specialization of the implicit argument in (27b–d) is one step along a path towards increasingly distinct polysemy of the verb (see Chapter 2). In the intended interpretation of (27b), it means something like 'we have dined on a meal', and would not be appropriate if, for example, we have just eaten a couple of peanuts. In a rich context this semantic default can be overridden. For example intransitive *eat* can be used to cancel a presupposition that eating is completely impossible or prohibited, as in (27a).

   These various readings are indefinite; indeed, *eat* does not seem to allow definite null complements at all. For example, (27b) cannot mean 'We've already eaten them.' The discourse in (28) is ill-formed:

(28)   A: What happened to the cookie that I was saving?
        B: #I ate already.

The notation introduced in Section 3.2 leaves open the question as to whether intransitive *eat* (23b) should be as shown in (29a) or (29b):

(29)   a. *eat* ⟨ AGENT,   PAT ⟩ $\exists y.$**eat**' (x,y)
                     | |
                   SUBJ   Ø

        b. *eat* ⟨ AGENT ⟩   **eat-a-meal**' (x)
                     |
                   SUBJ

On the former view, we have the same *eat*-relation as in transitive uses, but we existentially quantify one argument, as shown. On the latter view, transitive and intransitive *eat* express different relations.

   The sense specialization that accompanies theme omission is often more rigidly lexicalized. For example, the verb *draw* originally meant to pull or drag (30a), but was specialized for pulling a pencil, pen or charcoal across a surface, hence making an image or depicting.

(30)   a. Mary is drawing her finger across her forehead.
        b. Mary is drawing her finger.
        c. Mary is drawing a picture.
        d. Mary is drawing.

In current use the form lacking the PP complement allows only the newer artistic sense. Sentences (30b–d) can only mean that Mary is creating a drawing, not that she is dragging her finger or a picture somewhere in (30b,c) or that she is pulling some unspecified thing in

(30d). This covariation between sense specialization (*idiosyncratic poly-semy*; see Section 2.2.1) and restrictions on subcategorization frame is very typical for verbs.

The distribution of object drop across verb meanings is not entirely arbitrary, and there have been attempts to discover the semantic gen-eralizations. In a discussion of the causative alternation (see Section 3.4), Kiparsky (1997) proposes a constraint against omitting what he terms a *constitutive* argument, which he defines as 'An argu-ment which must participate in the entire event in a particular way.' Thus the agent of *splash* (*We splashed mud on the wall*) can be omitted (*Mud splashed on the wall*), since the splasher initiates the action but need not participate continuously throughout the splashing event. But the agent of *paint* (*We painted the wall*) cannot be omitted (*The wall painted) because painting requires direct initiation and continuous participation of the Agent. Applied to objects, Kiparsky contrasts verbs like *roll* or *bring*, which require continuous participation of the object argument in a particular way, with *push*, which does not:

(31)   a. John pushed/#rolled/#brought the cart, but it didn't move.
        b. John pushed/rolled/brought the cart
        c. John pushed/*rolled/*brought.

As shown in (31b,c), the object of *push* is omissible, while objects of *roll* and *bring* are not.

Some languages allow Definite Null Complements quite generally for all verbs, as long as the discourse context supports a definite, pronoun-like interpretation for the omitted object. This phenomenon is usually called 'null anaphora' or 'pro-drop' (pronoun drop). Japanese is an example:

(32)   Naoki-ga   mi-ta.
        Naoki-NOM   see-PAST
        'Naoki saw it/him/her/*himself.'

The missing object is interpreted like a pronoun, hence this sentence can be used if the referent of the pronoun is clear from the discourse context. Note that this null object has the binding properties of an ordinary (non-reflexive) pronoun, showing disjoint reference with the subject, as indicated by the translation.

Languages allowing object pro-drop fall into two subtypes: those in which head-marking morphology on the verb cross-references the person, number, and/or gender features of the object; and those lacking such head marking, like Japanese. When the verbs do cross-reference the object, the question arises as to whether the morpheme on the verb is an agreement marker or an incorporated object pronoun. Bresnan and Mchombo (1987) address this issue for the Bantu language Chichewa (see also Bresnan 2001: ch. 8). Chichewa verbs cross-reference both subject and object. (The numbers refer to noun classes.)

(33) *Njûchi zi-ná-wá-lum-a*   *a-lenje.*
      10.bee 10.SM-PST-2.OM-bite-FV   2-hunter
      'The bees bit them, the hunters.'

Bresnan and Mchombo argue that (i) the Chichewa object marker (OM) is an incorporated pronoun, as the translation of the above sentence is meant to suggest; and (ii) the subject marker (SM) alternatively functions as either an agreement marker, when cooccurring with an associated subject NP (*njûchi* 'bees'), or an incorporated pronoun, when no subject NP appears.

In contrast with Chichewa, the cross-referencing morphemes on verbs and auxiliaries in Warlpiri (Australian) are agreement markers and not incorporated pronouns, even when the NPs are dropped, according to Austin and Bresnan (1996) and Legate (2002). They note that NP arguments can be interpreted as either definite or indefinite depending on context (34a); in example (34b), the word order and context force an indefinite, existential interpretation. In contrast, the omission of an NP argument forces a specific interpretation, so that (34c) cannot mean 'Someone is spearing someone or something'.

(34) a. *Ngarrka-ngku =ka   wawirri   panti-rni.*
         man-ERG   PRS kangaroo.ABS   spear-NPAST
         'The/a man is spearing the/a kangaroo.' (Simpson 1991: 153)

      b. *Balgo   Mission-rla   ka-lu   Warlpiri-ji.*
         Balgo   Mission-Loc   PRS.IPFV-3pl   Warlpiri-TOP
         'At Balgo Mission there are Warlpiri people living.'

                                              (Legate 2002: 71)

      c. *Panti-rni   =ka.*
         spear-NPAST   PRS
         'He/she is spearing him/her/it.'   (Simpson 1991: 153)

This contrast in interpretation follows if the omission of Warlpiri argument NPs is pro-drop of the type found in agreement-poor languages like Japanese, which yields a pronoun-like interpretation. But this contrast is mysterious if *all* these sentences have incorporated pronominal arguments.

Finally, some languages have verbal morphology that is intermediate between agreement and pronoun incorporation. Person agreement markers derive historically from incorporated pronouns. An agreement marker can sometimes retain the restriction to specific reference as a semantic vestige of its pronominal pedigree. Hence it has been observed that certain agreement markers appear only under a condition of specificity or animacy in certain languages including some Bantu languages (Givón 1976; Wald 1979) and some Spanish dialects (Suñer 1988). Such cases are often discussed under the rubric of 'clitic-doubling' phenomena.

Such instances of pro-drop apply irrespective of the particular verb or verbal semantics, in contrast with object drop, which varies from verb to verb as in English. Only the verb-variable type is generally treated as directly relevant to argument structure. However, both types are relevant here. When a verbal morpheme covaries with object omission, it is not necessarily a cross-referencing marker as above, since it could be a marker of verb detransitivizing, a process described in the next section. It is not always obvious a priori how to analyze such a morpheme, and we will see cases of controversy.

3.3.2 Antipassive

Several types of morphological mechanism have a potential for removing an object from the complement structure of a verb, including antipassive voice, affixal reflexives and reciprocals, and noun incorporation. Here we discuss antipassive.

In many languages verbs can be marked with 'antipassive' voice to indicate that the object of an otherwise transitive verb has been suppressed or 'demoted' to oblique status. Such inflection tends to be found in languages where transitivity is important to the syntax. Hence it is most common among ergative languages, where the subject appears in ergative case (or determines ergative agreement) if the verb also takes a direct object, but absolutive case (or agreement) if the verb lacks an object. For example, the Greenlandic Eskimo verb *unatar-* 'beat' is transitive, with ergative subject and absolutive object (35a). But with the antipassive suffix -*a*, the theme argument is either expressed as an oblique as in (35b) or suppressed entirely as in (35c):

(35) Greenlandic Eskimo
a. Angut-up   arnaq   unatar-paa.
   man-ERG   woman(ABS)   beat-IND.3sgSb.3sgOb
   'The man beat the woman.'

b. Angut   arna-mik   unata-a-voq.
   man(ABS)   woman-INSTR   beat-ANTIP-IND.3sgSb
   'The man beat the woman.'

c. Angut   unata-a-voq.
   man(ABS)   beat-ANTIP-IND.3sgSb
   'The man beat someone.'

In Mam Mayan, a normally transitive verb, when appearing in anti-passive, takes an oblique complement introduced by a relational noun (RN) instead (England 1983: 4–5, exx. 7a, 9b).

(36) a. Ma   chi   kub'   t-tzyu-ʔn   šiinaq   qa-cheex.
         ASP   3pA   DIR   3sE-grab-DS   man   PL-horse
         'The man grabbed the horses.'

      b. Šiinaq   š-Ø-kub'   tzyuu-n   t-e   qa-cheex.
         man   ASP-3sA-DIR grab-ANTIP 3s-RN/PAT PL-horse
         'The man grabbed the horses.'

In Dyirbal (Australian), a gap can be coreferential with an argument in the preceding clause, if both the gap and antecedent are absolutive arguments, i.e. either the subject of intransitive (S) or object of transitive (O), but not the ergative subject of a transitive (A). Thus the antipassive is useful for converting the agent of a transitive, normally in ergative case, into the absolutive subject of an intransitive.

(37) a. yabu   ŋuma-ŋgu   bura-n.
         mother.ABS   father-ERG   see-NFUT
         'Father(A) saw mother(O)'

      b. ŋuma   banaga-nʸu   yabu-ŋgu   bura-n.
         father.ABS   returned-NFUT   mother-ERG   see-NFUT
         'Father(S) returned and mother(A) saw (him(O)).'

      c. ŋguma   bural-ŋa-nʸu   yabu-gu.
         Father.ABS   saw-ANTIP-NFUT   mother.DAT
         'Father(S) saw mother(OBLIQUE).'

      d. ŋuma   banaga-nʸu   bural-ŋa-nʸu   yabu-gu.
         Father.ABS return-NFUT   saw-ANTIP-NFUT   mother.DAT
         'Father(S) returned and (he(S)) saw mother(OBLIQUE).'
                                                    (Dixon 1994: 10–13)

Note that the complement of the antipassive verb appears in dative case. The antipassive can be summarized as an operation on argument structures that replaces OBJ with OBL or Ø (no expression), which converts a transitive into an intransitive clause. Antipassive is often semantically associated with a decrease in the 'affectedness' of the demoted object (see Section 3.3.3). Affixal reflexive morphology can also detransitivize a verb, according to some analyses (Sections 3.4.2.2 and 3.4.2.3).

3.3.3 The conative alternation

In the conative alternation an object argument alternates with expression as an oblique (Guerssel et al. 1985; Levin 1993; Van der Leek 1996; Beavers 2006):

(38) a. Pat hit the door.
      b. Pat hit at the door.

The English conative has a de-resultativizing effect that makes it incompatible with resultative secondary predicates:

(39) a. Joe kicked the box (flat).
      b. Joe kicked at the box (*flat).
      c. The box is being kicked (flat).
      d. The box was being kicked at (*flat).

There is a tendency for English predication subjects to be direct arguments (subjects and objects) rather than obliques (PPs) (Bresnan 1982a; Williams 1980), but the contrast between the passives in (39c) and (39d) show that this deresultativization effect is independent of that tendency. Moreover this effect explains the observation that the conative is not possible with inherently resultative verbs like *break* (40), and verbs lacking results altogether, like *touch* (41) (Levin 1993):

(40) a. John broke the machine (#but this had no effect on the machine).
      b. *John broke at the machine.

(41) a. Mary touched the glass (*dirty/*to pieces).
      b. *Mary touched at the glass.

More generally, Levin (1993) observes that the conative variant is possible with verbs involving both contact and motion, like *cut* (*hack, saw, scratch, slash,*...) and *hit* (*bash, kick, pound, tap, whack,*...), but

not *break* (*crack, rip, shatter, snap*...) or *touch* (*pat, stroke, tickle,*...).
Beavers (2006) notes that with creation or consumption verbs the
conative variant has the effect of leaving unspecified the 'complete'
creation or consumption reading normally found with such predicates.

(42) a. Caesar drank a glass of beer, #but didn't finish it.
      b. Caesar drank at a glass of beer (slowly), but didn't finish it.
      c. Caesar drank a glass of beer in/?for five minutes.
      d. Caesar drank at a glass of beer (slowly) for/??in an hour.

The *at*-PP variant suggests that some drinking occurred, but the drinking event was not necessarily completed. See Section 4.5 for more
discussion and analysis.

3.3.4 Dependencies between an object and its co-complement

A number of researchers have noted that in certain cases the presence
of a second complement, in addition to the direct object, seems to
protect an otherwise optional object from omission (Bresnan and
Zaenen 1990; Wechsler 1997a; Rappaport Hovav and Levin 1998).
First and perhaps least surprisingly, an object cannot be dropped if it
is also serving as the subject of a secondary predicate, whether that
predicate is resultative (43) or depictive (44) (Bresnan and Zaenen
1990; Wechsler 1997a; Rappaport Hovav and Levin 1998):

(43) a. They were pounding the metal (flat).
      b. They were pounding.
      c. *They were pounding flat.

(44) a. They were eating the fish (raw).
      b. They were eating.
      c. *They were eating raw.

This observation is reminiscent of Bach's Generalization, according to
which an English direct object controller cannot be omitted (Bach
1979). For example, the verb *promise* is a subject-control verb, hence
the object can be omitted, while *persuade* is an object-control verb so
that object argument must appear:

(45) a. John promised (Mary/Ø) to leave soon.
      b. John persuaded (Mary/*Ø) to leave soon.

The phenomenon is not limited to secondary predicates and infinitives,
but extends to various PPs that are not normally considered to be

predicates (Bresnan and Zaenen 1990; Wechsler 1997a; Rappaport Hovav and Levin 1998). With material-product alternation verbs like *carve*, an object NP expresses either the product of the carving (46b) or the source material (46c) (see Levin 1993: 56). With the NP–PP complement pattern, both product and source can be expressed, as shown in (46d,e). But when either PP appears, then the NP cannot be dropped, as shown in (46f,g).

(46)   a. Martha is carving.
       b. Martha is carving a toy.
       c. Martha is carving a piece of wood.
       d. Martha is carving a toy from a piece of wood.
       e. Martha is carving a piece of wood into a toy.
       f. ? Martha is carving from a piece of wood.
       g. *Martha is carving into a toy.   (Wechsler 1997a: 129)

Rappaport Hovav and Levin (1998) note similar facts, and further observe that with some verbs the PP is required, in order for the object to appear, as shown in (47d):

(47)   a. Phil swept (the floor).
       b. Phil swept the crumbs onto the floor.
       c. *Phil swept onto the floor.
       d. ?Phil swept the crumbs.

Wechsler (1997a) and Rappaport Hovav and Levin (1998) propose broadly similar analyses. For Wechsler (1997a) the preposition, like the resulative and depictive adjectives (43 and 44), selects the theme argument and places a syntactic restriction on its expression. For Rappaport Hovav and Levin (1998) *the crumbs* is not a lexical argument of *sweep*, but rather is an argument of the subevent (of the crumbs moving onto the floor). The preposition *onto* is the main predicate of that subevent, so on Rappaport Hovav and Levin's theory it must be expressed if *the crumbs* is to appear (see Section 4.4.4.3).

   A dependency between the appearance of co-complements has also been observed in ditransitives (Bresnan and Moshi 1990; Bresnan and Zaenen 1990). The object of *cook* allows indefinite object deletion, i.e. the theme argument (such as *turkey* in (48a)) can be omitted. A benefactive PP can be added to the clause with or without the object NP (48a,b). But if the benefactive is expressed as an inner object instead of a PP, as in (48c), then the theme becomes obligatory. Hence (48d) lacks the reading that (48b) has, i.e. 'Mary cooked the children something.'

(48) a. Mary cooked turkey (for the children).
      b. Mary cooked Ø (for the children).
      c. Mary cooked the children turkey.
      d. *Mary cooked the children Ø.

Bresnan and Moshi (1990) show that Bantu languages are split between those allowing and those disallowing locutions like (48d), in which the theme argument of a ditransitive is omitted in the presence of an applied benefactive object. In Kichaga the theme argument of the verb *lyi-* 'eat' can be omitted, as shown in (49a). The applicative morpheme *i-* shown in (49b) increases the valence of the verb, which therefore takes an extra applied object, interpreted in these cases as a benefactive ('for his wife') or malefactive ('on his wife'). The cognate sentences in Chichewa are also acceptable. Interestingly, while Kichaga also allows the theme to be dropped from the applied construction, as in (49c), the corresponding Chichewa sentence is not allowed.

(49) a. Kichaga (OK in Chichewa):
          N-a-i-lyi-a   (k-elya).
          FOC-1s-PRS-eat-FV   7-food
          'He/She is eating (food).'

      b. Kichaga (OK in Chichewa):
          N-a-i-lyi-i-a   m-ka   k-elya
          FOC-1s-PRS-eat-APPL-FV   1-wife   7-food
          'He is eating food for/on his wife.'

      c. Kichaga (* in Chichewa):
          N-a-i-lyi-i-a   m-ka.
          FOC-1s-PRS-eat-APPL-FV   1-wife
          'He/She is eating for/on the wife.' (Bresnan and Moshi 1990)

Thus Chichewa resembles English in that the theme cannot be omitted in the presence of an object benefactive. Across Bantu languages, the ability of the second object to undergo unspecified object deletion patterns with several other 'primary object' properties, including the ability to become the subject of a passive, to reciprocalize, and to be expressed as a verbal affix (Bresnan and Moshi 1990). See Section 5.2.1.3.

3.4 Causative, inchoative, and result state alternations

3.4.1 Introduction

The 'causative alternation' results from optionality of a causer or agent argument, as in (50):

(50)   a. Jonas dried the socks.   (causative)
       b. The socks dried.   (inchoative)

The causative sentence can be paraphrased with the corresponding inchoative sentence embedded under a verb of causation such as *cause*, *make*, or *bring about*. Hence (50a) means 'Jonas caused the socks to dry.' The causative alternation is very common in language. Levin (1993: 28–9) lists over 300 alternating verbs of English, and the list is not exhaustive. This alternation is found in a great many, perhaps all, languages of the world. Nedjalkov's (1969) typological study of the causative alternation covers 60 languages of diverse type, and Haspelmath (1993) looked at a different set of 21 languages. Languages vary in whether or how the alternation is marked morphologically (on which, see Section 3.4.2), but I am unaware of a language lacking this alternation entirely.

In an important subset of causative alternations, the intransitive alternant is an inchoative verb, that is, a verb expressing the coming about of some semantic state. This subtype is called the *causative-inchoative alternation*. The example (50b) is of this type; the state that comes about can be paraphrased as 'the socks are dry'. Often, as in that example, the verb (here, the verb *dry*) has a cognate adjective expressing that stative property (the adjective *dry*). English has many cognate triples of the form ⟨ causative verb, inchoative verb, stative adjective ⟩ such as *open*$_{CAUS}$, *open*$_{INCH}$, *open*$_{ADJ}$:

(51)   a. Joan opened the door.   'Joan caused the door to open$_{INCH}$.'
       b. The door opened.   'The door became open$_{ADJ}$.'
       c. The door is open.

Other causative alternations do not involve inchoate states, such as *Mary rolled the wagon down the hill.* ~ *The wagon rolled down the hill.* Summarizing the semantic relations between such sentences: A causative sentence can be paraphrased with the corresponding inchoative sentence embedded under a verb of causation (*cause*, *make*, *bring about*, etc.) An inchoative sentence can be paraphrased with the corresponding adjective (*open*$_{ADJ}$), plus a verb of becoming (*become, get, come to be*, etc.).

Those systematic semantic relationships between causative, inchoative, and stative adjective have inspired a long tradition of grammatical analysis in which the primitive semantic relations CAUSE and BECOME are formatives that combine with the state to give the verb meanings:

(52)   a. Joan opened the door.   CAUSE(j, BECOME(**open**'(d))
       b. The door opened.   BECOME(**open**'(d))
       c. The door is open.   **open**'(d)

This decomposition idea dates back at least to Lakoff (1965), who posited CAUSE and BECOME as silent word-like elements in the syntactic structure (see Section 4.4.3). Dowty (1979) refined the semantic analysis and argued that these primitive semantic operators belong in the lexical decompositions of verbs, not in the syntactic structure of sentences. Levin and Rappaport Hovav (1995) propose that in the inchoative form, the agent variable is still present, albeit existentially quantified (see Section 3.4.2.2).

Haspelmath (1993) observes that cross-linguistically the causative–inchoative verb alternation is particularly regular in verbs that are derived from adjectives. German and Russian deadjectival transitive verbs always allow inchoatives to be formed from the transitive, using the detransitivizer *sich* in German and *-sja* in Russian. The claim is that if the causative (the (a) examples) and the adjective (the (c) examples) are cognates, then the semantically intermediate inchoative form (the (b) examples) is also possible:

(53)   German (Haspelmath 1993: 94)
       a. *verflüssigen*   'make liquid'   (causative V)
       b. *sich verflüssigen* 'become liquid'   (inchoative V)
       c. *flüssig*   'liquid'   (adjective)

(54)   Russian (Haspelmath 1993: 95)
       a. *povysit'*   'raise' (causative V)
       b. *povysit'-sja*   'rise'   (inchoative V)
       c. *vysokij*   'high'   (adjective)

Many English verbs have adjective cognates. Deadjectival causative–inchoative verbs include at least these four types (Levin 1993): verbs with the same root form as the adjective (*blunt, clear, dry, open*); *-en* verbs (*awaken, brighten, widen*); *-ify* verbs (*acidify, purify*); and *-ize* verbs (*regularize, stabilize*). (Some of the *-ize* verbs may be denominal rather than deadjectival: *caramelize, pressurize, vaporize*, etc.)

In addition to causative alternation verbs related to adjectives, Levin (1993) distinguishes a second subtype of causative alternation which she calls the Induced Action Alternation, in which 'the causee is typically an animate volitional entity that is induced to act by the causer' (p. 31).

(55)   a. Sylvia jumped the horse over the fence.
        b. The horse jumped over the fence.

(56)   a. The scientist ran the rats through the maze.
        b. The rats ran through the maze.   (Levin 1993: 31)

This is sometimes called the 'accompanied causation' alternation, since the subject argument of the transitive is often understood as accompanying the object argument: if *Mary walked John home*, then not only did John go to his home, but also Mary accompanied him. But as Levin notes, not all of them have this property, citing the example of rats in the maze (56).

Some causative alternations fit into neither the causative-inchoative nor the induced action subtypes. These include verbs involving the emission of sound (*ring, beep, click, squeak*), light (*blink, flash, shine*), and substances (*bleed, squirt*), among others such as *burp, choke*, and *lodge* (Levin 1993: 31–2):

(57)   a. The visitor rang the bell.
        b. The bell rang.

The ringing of the bell could be a momentary event that does not bring about a state change.

3.4.2 Causativization and anti-causativization

Languages vary as to morphological marking of the verb in the causative alternation. The English verb normally has the same form irrespective of transitivity. Building on the work of Nedjalkov (1969), Haspelmath (1993) distinguishes five morphological patterns for this alternation, for which he adopts (translations of) Nedjalkov's Russian terms, namely 'causative,' 'anticausative,' 'equipollent,' 'suppletive,' and 'labile':

(58) Varieties of morphological marking for causative alternations
    a. **causative**: inchoative is basic, causative is derived
        ex. Georgian   *duɣ-s*   'cook (intransitive)'
                       a-duɣ-ebs 'cook (transitive)'

    b. **anticausative**: causative is basic, inchoative is derived
        ex. Russian   *katat'-sja* 'roll (intr.)'
                      katat'   'roll (trans.)'

    c. **non-directed**: neither is derived from the other. Three
        subtypes:

        (i) **equipollent**: both derived from the same stem with dif-
            ferent morphology:
            ex. Japanese   *atum-aru* 'gather (intr.)'
                           atum-eru 'gather (trans.)'
        (ii) **suppletive**: different roots. ex. English *kill* ~ *die*
        (iii) **labile**: same form for both. ex. English *He dried them.*
            ~*They dried.*

The semantic conditions on the causative alternation seem to depend
upon the direction of the morphological derivation. Non-directed
alternations are discussed in Section 3.4.2.1 with a focus on English.
Anticausativization and the related phenomena of middles and passives
are discussed in Sections 3.4.2.2 and 3.4.2.3 respectively, and morphological causativization is discussed in Section 3.4.2.4.

3.4.2.1 Non-directed causative alternations in English English
causative alternations are non-directed. They are mainly labile, apart
from some possibly suppletive pairs like *kill~die, take~go, bring~come.*
The determination of which verbs alternate can be split into two questions:
First, why do many transitives (*cut, shelve, write, eat,* and many others; see
(59a)) refuse to decausativize? Second, why do many intransitives (*laugh,*
cry, smile, appear, and many others; see (59b)) refuse to causativize?

(59) a. John cut the rope./*The rope cut.
      b. *The comedian laughed us./We laughed.

On the face of it, it seems clear that the causative alternation is a lexical
property, at least in English. Some verbs alternate while others permit
only the transitive or only the intransitive variant:

(60) a. John dissolved the company./The company dissolved.
      b. John eliminated the company./*The company eliminated.
      c. *John disappeared the rabbit./The rabbit disappeared.

But it is equally clear that there are semantic restrictions, or at least strong tendencies, governing the distribution of this alternation among verbs.

An early observation that remains influential revolves around the distinction between 'internal' and 'external' causation (Smith 1970; McKoon and Macfarland 2000). The issue is whether the cause is internal or external to the theme argument, i.e. the argument that undergoes a change, expressed as object of the causative verb and subject of the intransitive. In the intransitive sentences, 'the activity or change can be said to occur without an external agent', but if the action is such that 'external control of the change can be assumed by an agent,' then the transitive variant is also possible (Smith 1970: 101). Hence a verb alternates if the action it describes can occur either with or without a cause that is external to the theme. With the non-alternating transitive verbs *destroy, build, cut, slice, draw*, etc., 'activity or motive force can be attributed only to the agent, the subject of the transitive verb' (Smith 1970).

Essentially the same idea is also expressed in terms of the notion of 'spontaneity' (Haspelmath 1993). An inchoative verb describes an event as spontaneous, meaning that it occurs without any cause or else the causes are so obscure that the event is perceived as lacking a cause. The non-alternating transitive verbs describe events as not occurring spontaneously, but rather requiring some external cause. Summarizing:

(61)   Spontaneity Condition. If an event is described as resulting from a theme-external cause then that cause must be expressed, so the clause must be transitive (causative); while if the event is not described as resulting from a theme-external cause, but instead is described as a spontaneous occurrence or as resulting from a theme-internal cause, then the clause must be intransitive (inchoative).

Haspelmath (1993) posits a condition of this kind as a functionally motivated influence on lexicalization patterns. Events that are 'common in nature' (*freeze, dry, sink, go out, melt*) tend to be lexicalized as inchoatives. Either they are strictly intransitive and do not alternate or, if they do alternate, then the inchoative form is basic and the causative form is morphologically marked. Events that are 'typical of things humans do' (*split, break, close, open, gather, connect*) tend to be lexicalized as causatives: either they are strictly transitive and do not alternate or, if they do alternate, then the causative form is basic and the inchoative is morphologically marked. Haspelmath illustrates the basic idea with this scale of increasing likelihood of spontaneous occurrence, with 'wash' as least and 'laugh' as most likely to occur spontaneously:

(62)   Spontaneity hierarchy

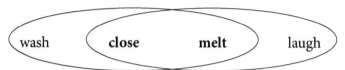

The ovals on the left and right represent lexically transitive and lexically intransitive verbs, respectively. Across languages we find that 'wash' tends to be lexically transitive (only); 'laugh' tends to be lexically intransitive (only); and 'close' and 'melt' tend to alternate.

Spontaneity is not a property of events but of descriptions: a single event can be depicted without contradiction as both spontaneous and unspontaneous. In fact for alternating verbs the causative entails the intransitive: if *Jonas dried the socks*, then *the socks dried*. Thus the intransitive sentence does not entail that there is no external cause. The speaker can also use it when she disregards an external cause. So the explanation for the badness of *The pizza is cutting* cannot be a rule to the effect that known external causes must be expressed. Apparently no such rule is operative in English. Instead our judgments of such sentences may be influenced by imageability: one can readily imagine a scene of socks drying with no agent present, but one cannot imagine pizza being cut unless the image contains an agent who is doing the cutting.

A second semantic condition involves 'agent-oriented meaning components.' Several scholars have observed that a transitive verb specifying that the agent participates in the event in a specific way generally does not allow an inchoative variant (Guerssel et al. 1985; Levin 1993; Haspelmath 1993; Hale and Keyser 1993; 1997; Kiparsky 1997). That is, *a causative–inchoative verb pair must lack an agent-oriented meaning component.*

(63)   Agent-Manner Condition. A verb meaning that refers to a change of state or a going-on may appear in an inchoative–causative alternation unless the verb contains agent-oriented meaning components.   (part of Haspelmath 1993: 94, ex. 16)

Haspelmath (1993: 93) illustrates with the contrast between *cut* and *tear*: to *cut* something requires that the agent use a sharp instrument such as a knife or scissors, but *tear* places no such condition on the manner in which the agent participates in the event. Hence *tear* is a good candidate for omission of the agent, while *cut* is not (examples from Haspelmath 1993: 93):

(64)   a. The girl tore her pants./The pants tore.
       b. The tailor cut the cloth./*The cloth cut.

Levin (1993: 9–10) makes the same point with reference to *cut* and *break*.[3] Similarly, *washing* differs minimally from *cleaning* in requiring the use of soap and/or washing instruments. In keeping with this generalization, only 'clean' and not 'wash' alternates in Russian: *očiščat'* 'clean (transitive)' ~ *očiščat'-sja* 'become clean' (Haspelmath 1993: 93).

Haspelmath (1993: 94) attempted to explain the Agent–Manner condition as a consequence of a version of the Spontaneity condition: in order for the agent to be omitted, spontaneous occurrence of the event type must be likely. Agent-oriented meaning components would make spontaneous occurrence unlikely, so verbs expressing such meaning components would tend not to allow omission of the agent. He notes that the verb *decapitate* fails to alternate (**The heretic decapitated at noon*) although the specific meaning component 'by severing the head from the body' is clearly patient-oriented and not agent-oriented, so the agent manner condition per se fails to explain its lack of an inchoative use. Instead he attributes that to a strict transitive lexicalization due to the rarity of spontaneous decapitation.

Interestingly, in precisely such unlikely circumstances the verb *decapitate* can be inchoativized, as shown by these web examples (search string: *spontaneously decapitate*):

(65)   a. (from a film synopsis) Jeff has a problem: his best friend Carl has spontaneously decapitated. So what does Joe do but drag his headless friend to their favorite topless bar, sets him in a corner booth, and watch dancing strippers.

       b. (dermatology) Granulomas should be managed medically as they nearly always spontaneously decapitate in 4 to 6 months. They tend to recur.

---

[3] Levin cites Guerssel et al. (1985) for this observation.

c. Packed with 70+ minutes of songs about bunnies, squid, aard-
varks, and classmates, this collection is certain to make you wish
you could spontaneously decapitate.

Apparently this verb need not be lexically specified for transitivity.
Instead the spontaneity condition can be taken as a condition on
interpretation. Such a condition would explain why intransitive *decapitate* sounds rather bad under normal circumstances (e.g. *The heretic
decapitated at noon*), while still allowing it to describe an event where
the cause is internal to the theme.

Many other supposedly disallowed inchoative verbs improve dra-
matically under interpretations in which the agent–manner specification disappears or shifts from the agent to another argument. For
example, Hale and Keyser (1993) illustrate the Agent–Manner generalization with the following contrast (their examples 40 and 41):

(66) *splash, drip, dribble, pour, squirt, ...*
    a. The pigs splashed mud on the wall.
    b. Mud splashed on the wall.

(67) *smear, daub, rub, wipe, ...*
    a. We smeared mud on the wall.
    b. *Mud smeared on the wall. (Hale and Keyser's judgment; but
       see below)

In the *splash*-type verbs, the manner component is primarily internal in
orientation. The verb *splash* describes the configuration and motion of
the liquid but not the external cause of that configuration and motion.
In the *smear*-type the manner component relates to the external agent
(Hale and Keyser 1993: 90).

But a web search for the string *it smears on* revealed many examples
of inchoative *smear*:

(68) a. Maggie feeds it to him. He takes a bite of it, and it smears on
      his nose a bit.
    b. Bell said the problem stems from the plastic plate. After paint
      gets on it, it smears on the abutting wall.
    c. Mud is part of life on the farm—it smears on jeans and sticks
      under fingernails.
    d. Her hands were already covered in his blood, and it was
      smearing on the white shift she wore.
    e. In that case, re-align your efforts into (a) making the sunblock
      last longer without reapplication...and (b) making it smear
      on less goopily.

Actually the verb *smear* has both an agent-oriented and theme-oriented manner. To *smear* is 'to spread or daub with a sticky, greasy, or dirty substance' (Oxford English Dictionary on-line). The specialized aspects of this action involve both the manner employed by the agent (spreading or daubing), and the inherent quality of the theme substance (a 'sticky, greasy, or dirty substance'). Even without syntactically expressing an external agent, specifying a 'sticky, greasy, or dirty' theme can be sufficient for an event to qualify as smearing. Hale and Keyser's causative example (67a) evokes a scene of people spreading or daubing mud on a wall, strengthened by the pragmatic bias to interpret it as a volitional act. One naturally attempts to interpret (67b) as a description of the same scene, since the sentences are paired. But a scene of intentional smearing cannot be imagined without anyone doing the smearing, so the sentence is judged unacceptable. Changing the pragmatic bias to a non-volitional act improves the judgment: *We were covered with mud. Some mud smeared on the wall, as we squeezed through the narrow hallway.*

Assuming the Agent Manner condition, this double-manner account predicts degraded judgments if neither agent nor theme is expressed. The verb *smear* is a locative alternation verb (Section 3.5.2), but only one alternant can be decausativized:

(69)   a. She smeared sunscreen on his nose.
    b. She smeared his nose with sunscreen.
    c. The sunscreen smeared on his nose.
    d. *His nose smeared with sunscreen.

The contrast between (69c) and (69d) is supported by corpus data. While web searches for *it smeared on* produced many hits, including those in (68), a search for *it smeared with* turned up no results. The operative condition on *smear* appears to be that a constitutive argument, i.e. one involving a spreading or daubing agent or a smearworthy substance, must be expressed as a direct argument (subject or object). Example (69d) is ruled out since neither participant is expressed as a direct argument.

In a refinement of the Spontaneity Condition, Kiparsky (1997) observes that agents cannot be omitted if the actions they carry out require the continuous participation of a causing Agent throughout the event. On the other hand, inchoatives can describe event with external causes, as long as the event is of the type that can continue after the external cause ceases to participate (Kiparsky 1997: 495). Obligatorily transitive verbs (Kiparsky cites *shelve, paint, bring, put, drag, tow, haul, push, kick, press*) 'denote processes requiring the direct initiation and continuous participation of a causing Agent. When John stops painting the wall, the painting stops. (...) When John stops pushing the cart, the pushing stops, even though the cart may continue to move.' In contrast, alternating verbs (Kiparsky cites *redden, thin, hang, roll, slide, sink*) 'denote processes which can be initiated without the participation of a causing Agent (e.g. *The sky is reddening, Fred's hair is thinning, The branch is hanging*), and which, once initiated, can continue without it.'

Kiparsky's account is meant to cover object drop as well (see Section 3.3.1). He hypothesizes that *an argument which must partici- pate in the entire event in a particular way* cannot be omitted (Kiparsky 1997: 497). Applying this idea to Theme arguments, Kiparsky notes that *movement* of a theme X is entailed by *roll X* and *bring X* but not *push X*:

(70) a. John pushed/#rolled/#brought the cart, but it didn't move.
      b. John pushed/#rolled/#brought.

Example (70a) shows that the theme arguments of *roll* and *bring* must participate in the entire event in a particular way. By Kiparsky's hypothesis they cannot be omitted, which is supported by (70b).

So far we have focused on detransitivization, starting with transitive verbs and asking why only some of them allow the anticausative. We must also ask why many English intransitives cannot be causativized:

(71) a. Mary laughed.
      b. *John laughed Mary. ('John made Mary laugh.')

As discussed above, according to Haspelmath verbs like *laugh, cry, smile* tend to be lexicalized as intransitive because they are usually spontaneous activities, in the sense that the event lacks a salient exter- nal cause. The lexically idiosyncratic nature of causativization in English—albeit governed by lexicalization tendencies, as noted—can be further illustrated with verbs like *grow* and *learn*. The verb *grow* existed exclusively as an inchoative for over 1,000 years in the history of English, before transitive *grow* was coined (*c.*1774). Many English verbs underwent the causative alternation before and after that innovation took place. As for *learn*, it lacks a causative in standard English, but some dialects permit it: %*She learned me how to knit.* I am unaware of any general principle that would explain the difference between English before and after 1774, or between the two dialects with respect to *learn*.

Instead the lexical representations of the verbs simply differ as a result of convention.

3.4.2.2 Anticausatives

In languages where anticausativization is morphologically marked, the addition of a morpheme has the effect of removing the cause argument. A common strategy is for a reflexive morpheme to be pressed into service for forming the anticausative (these are sometimes called middles; see Section 3.4.2.3). For example, from Spanish transitive *romper* 'break' (72a) we derive the inchoative *romperse* (72b):

(72) a. Juan rompió el vaso.
         Juan broke   the cup
         'Juan broke the cup.'

      b. El   vaso se   rompió.
         the   cup   REFL   broke
         'The cup broke.'

According to a common analysis, the clitic (*se* in 72b) detransitivizes the verb, removing the causer argument (e.g. Grimshaw 1982). On that view, while the clitic is historically related to the reflexive, it has a different function in such inchoatives. Van Valin and LaPolla (1997: sect. 7.5.3) propose an analysis of that type on the basis of data from Italian. They connect such *si*-marked inchoatives to reflexives by applying the same causer-removing analysis to both. That is, the clitic *si* has the effect of suppressing the agent argument not only in the inchoatives, but also in 'true' reflexives like *Maria si è tagliata* 'Maria cut herself' (Van Valin and LaPolla 1997: 407, ex. 7.111). For the latter type an interpretive principle allows for the privileged syntactic argument to be both actor and undergoer.

Alternatively such inchoatives can be seen not as lacking a causer argument, but rather as having an *internal* causer: the cause of the breaking in (72b) is the cup itself. Koontz-Garboden (2009) has argued that anticausatives, at least those expressed by reflexive morphology, are literally reflexive. On that view the Spanish example (72b) means 'the cup broke itself.' Following Rappaport Hovav and Levin (1998) he assumes the Monotonicity Hypothesis, which he expresses as follows:

(73)   Word formation operations do not remove operators from lexical
       semantic representations.   (Koontz-Garboden 2009: 80)

For causative (transitive) *romper* 'break' he assumes this logical form:

(74) [[*romper*]] =
$\lambda x \lambda y \lambda s \lambda e[\exists v[CAUSE(v, e) \wedge EFFECTOR(v, \boxed{y}) \wedge BECOME(e, s)$
$\wedge THEME(s, x) \wedge \textit{not-whole}(s)]]$

(Koontz-Garboden 2009: 85, ex. 17)

CAUSE is a relation between events *v* and *e*, and EFFECTOR is a highly generalized agentive role played by some participant (*y*) in the causing event (*v*). The effector can be an instrument, an animate entity, or inanimate entity (Van Valin and Wilkins 1996). In the intransitive *romperse* 'break', the *x* variable of the theme replaces that of the subject, resulting in a reflexive:

(75) [[*romperse*]] =
$\lambda x \lambda s \lambda e[\exists v[CAUSE(v, e) \wedge EFFECTOR(v, \boxed{x}) \wedge BECOME(e, s)$
$\wedge THEME(s, x) \wedge \textit{not-whole}(s)]]$

So this is identical to transitive *romper*, except that a single variable, for the subject, fills the role of both 'effector' and 'theme'.

The challenge for such an account is to motivate the existence of CAUSE for the inchoative, despite some facts suggesting the anti-causative entirely lacks an external cause (see (81)). Paralleling the English contrast between (81b) and (81b'), Spanish *se*-intransitives do not allow purpose clauses, while Spanish passives do (Koontz-Garboden 2009: ex. 45). However, the theme is usually inanimate, hence unsuited to be the controller of the purpose clause. Verbs with an animate theme can control into purpose clauses :

(76) Y   aquel día, hace tres   años, cuando Phil se
      and   that   day   from three years when   Phil REFL
      ahogó   para salvarle   la   vida   a Jim...
      drowned   to   save.3SG   the   life   to Jim
      'And on that day, three years ago, when Phil drowned (him-
      self) to save Jim's life...'

This resembles English verbs like intransitive *move* and *change*:

(77) a. We moved the rock.
      b. John moved (in order to get out of the way).

These verbs allow readings where a single subject fills both the agent and theme roles, making a semantic form like (75) very plausible. Koontz-Garboden treats all reflexive-marked inchoatives as similar to such verbs in semantic form, but sees the inanimacy of some effectors as the reason for their failure to exhibit agent properties such as control into purpose clauses.

3.4.2.3 Middles and passives

In the 'middle construction,' transitive verbs allow omission of the agent under certain special semantic conditions (Fagan 1992; Ackema and Schoorlemmer 2005):

(78)   a. This cheese cuts easily.
         (cp *The cheese is cutting./*The cheese cuts.)
       b. Bureaucrats bribe easily.
         (cp *The bureaucrat is bribing./*Bureacrats bribe.)

The middle construction normally has a generic rather than episodic interpretation. These examples do not describe specific episodes of cutting and bribing, but rather general properties. On one view they express a general property of events of cutting this cheese or bribing bureaucrats, namely that such actions are carried out with ease (Condoravdi 1989). Being non-episodic sentences, they are stative, as shown by the use of the simple present rather than the progressive, when in present tense. An adverb like *easily* is normally required, since it expresses the general property being predicated of the event type. However, a modal can also be used, expressing the possibility of such an event: *This meat may cut, but you never know.* The modality can even be implicit, as in *This dress buttons*, which expresses 'the fact that anybody can do it' (Ackema and Schoorlemmer 2005: 142, exx. 34 and 35).

The term 'middle' is used here for a construction formed with a normally transitive verb, used intransitively with the patient as subject, and with a special generic interpretation. Somewhat confusingly, the term 'middle' is used for two other related phenomena. 'Middle voice' refers to verb forms that are formally but not semantically reflexive, as in Ancient Greek *eklegomai* (choose.REFL), which means 'choose for oneself' and not 'choose oneself' or 'be chosen' (Ackema and Schoorlemmer 2005: 134, ex. 3). Note that the subject is the agent and not the patient of 'choose.' We put this type aside, as it does not relate to the causative alternation. In addition, the term 'middle' is sometimes used for the morphologically marked anticausatives as discussed in the previous section.

Unlike the English middles, reflexive-marked anticausatives allow episodic readings, as in the Spanish example (137b), or this French example:

(79) La question se traite actuellement à l'Assemblée.
      the issue REFL discusses now in Parliament
      'The issue is being discussed now in the National Assembly.'
      (Zribi-Hertz 1982: 349, cited in Ackema and Schoorlemmer
      2005: 152)

Since the relation denoted by the transitive verb requires an external agent (even if covert), the sentence can have a passive-like reading, so it is sometimes called a 'reflexive-marked passive' (Ackema and Schoorlemmer 2005).

Middles, passives, and anticausatives have in common that the agent argument of a verb, normally expressed as the subject of a transitive, is instead left unexpressed. This is shown schematically in (80):

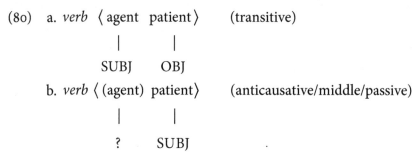

(80) a. *verb* ⟨ agent patient ⟩   (transitive)

           | |

         SUBJ   OBJ

     b. *verb* ⟨ (agent) patient ⟩   (anticausative/middle/passive)

           | |

         ?   SUBJ

What distinguishes these various types is the status of the agent argument. This is a complex issue, to which we turn next.

It is usually assumed that an intransitive like *The cookies baked* lacks an agent entirely. This contrasts with the passive *The cookies were baked*, which contains an implicit, existentially bound agent argument. The implicit agent of the passive, in contrast to the inchoatives that lack one, can be seen in various contrasts. Most obviously, the passive allows expression of the agent in a *by*-phrase (81a), while the inchoative does not (81a'). The implicit agent can license an instrumental phrase (81a) while the *with*-PP in (81a') lacks the instrumental reading. Also, the agent can control a purpose clause as in (81b); the agent licenses a comitative co-agent (81c); and temporal modifiers can include the agent's preparation phase of the event (81d) (examples from Wechsler 1995: 97):

(81)   a. The cookies were baked (with an oven) (by John).
        a'. The cookies baked (*with an oven) (*by John).
        b. The cookies were baked in order to bribe the teacher.
        b'. The cookies baked (*in order to bribe the teacher).
        c. These cookies were baked with a friend.
        c'. The cookies were baking (*with a friend).
        d. It took 30 minutes for the cookies to be baked.
            (can include time of agent's preparations as well)
        d'. It took 30 minutes for the cookies to bake.
            (includes only the time in the oven)

So a common view is that the inchoative has just one argument, and lacks an agent both syntactically and semantically. In contrast, the passive has an agent semantic argument that can remain unexpressed.

It should be noted, however, that Levin and Rappaport Hovav (1995) suggested that some alternating verbs still have an existentially quantified agent argument even in the inchoative variant. On their view the verb *break* is dyadic in both (82a) and (82b). In the latter the causer is existentially bound:

(82)   a. Mary broke the stick.
            transitive *break*:   [x DO-SOMETHING] CAUSE
                                  [y BECOME *BROKEN*]

        b. The stick broke.
            intransitive *break*: $\exists x[[x$ DO-SOMETHING] CAUSE
                                    [y BECOME *BROKEN*]]

Levin and Rappaport Hovav (1995: 86) argue, first of all, that in English the transitive is basic and the intransitive is derived through anti-causativization, and not the reverse. The transitive has 'looser selectional restrictions':

(83)   a. He broke his promise./*His promise broke.
        b. The wind cleared the sky./The sky cleared.
        c. The waiter cleared the table./*The table cleared.

Assuming that derivations can be semantically restricted then this possibility is expected. But if intransitive *clear* were basic and transitive *clear* derived from it, there would be no source for transitive *clear* in (83c). Levin and Rappaport Hovav assume that operations can only add and not subtract semantic structure (the Monotonicity Hypothesis; see

(73)), so deriving the intransitive cannot strip away the agent, but only bind it.

In English middles the covert agent's behavior is intermediate between that of the inchoative and the passive. Such middles do not allow *by*-phrases, but instrumental phrases are acceptable: *Styrofoam cuts easily with a hot wire*. In Condoravdi's neo-Davidsonian analysis the existence of the agent in the middle is an entailment of the lexical meaning of the verb. The agent variable appears in the restrictor of a generic operator, and is not part of the argument structure in the usual sense (Condoravdi 1989). Like the English style middles, reflexive-marked anticausatives also have an intermediate status with respect to their agent arguments. In some languages such anticausatives allow the agent to be expressed in an oblique phrase, as in the Greek example (84a). In Italian they can control into a purpose clause (84b).

(84)   a. Afto to psomi kovete   efkola akoma ki apo pedia.
          this   the bread cut.MID3sg easily still   and by children
          'This bread can be cut easily even by children.'
                                          (Condoravdi 1989: ex. 15a)

       b. Quell'uomo politico   si   può corrompere (facilemente)
          that   politician REFL can bribe   easily
          per dimostrare   la propria   influenza.
          to   show   one's   influence
          'It is easy to bribe that politician to show one's influence.'
                                          (Cinque 1988: 562)

The grammatical representation of the covert agent argument remains controversial for the constructions discussed here.

3.4.2.4 Morphological causativization

In causativization, a verb is morphologically derived in a process that adds a causer argument. Cuzco Quechua *wirayay* means 'become fat', and the addition of the causative morpheme *chi* yields *wiraya-chi-y* 'cause to become fat' (Koontz-Garboden 2009: 78, ex. 4). Morphological causativization typically occurs more freely than morphologically unmarked causativization, applying to intransitive verbs from a wide range of semantic types, as well as transitive verbs. For example, the Chichewa morpheme *-ets* can be suffixed to an intransitive like *gw* 'fall' to give a causative verbs (example from Baker 1988):

(85) mtiskana anau-gw-ets-a   mtsuko.
        girl   SM-fall-CAUS-FV waterpot
        'The girl made the waterpot fall.'

When applied to transitive *phik* 'cook' the result is a three-argument verb with either two objects as in (86a) or an object and an oblique as in (86b) (example from Alsina 1992):

(86) a. Nungu   i-na-phik-ets-a   kadzidzi maungu.
          porcupine SM-PAST-cook-CAUS-FV owl   pumpkins
          'The porcupine made the owl cook the pumpkins.'

      b. Nungu   i-na-phik-ets-a   maungu kwa kadzidzi.
          porcupine SM-PAST-cook-CAUS-FV pumpkins to   owl
          'The porcupine made the owl cook the pumpkins.'
          (or 'The porcupine had the pumpkins cooked by the owl.')

Cross-linguistically, causativized intransitives tend to be transitives as in (85). Causatives formed on transitives vary across languages, being expressed as ditransitives like (86a) in some languages and as object-oblique structures like (86b) in others, while still others are like Chichewa in allowing either expression. The ditransitive is generally an option only if the language independently allows lexical ditransitives, for example for verbs of possession transfer like 'give'.

In the argument structure of a morphologically causative verb, the argument corresponding to the subject of the underlying verb stem is called the 'causee.' In many languages the causee retains some apparent subject properties, i.e. syntactic properties normally found to characterize only subjects and not complements. For example, reflexives in Turkish normally require a subject antecedent but can take the dative causee as antecedent in causatives:

(87) Hasan   ban-a   kendi-m-i   yika-t-ti.
        Hasan   me-DAT   self-1SG-ACC   wash-CAUS-PST
        'Hasan made me wash myself.'   (Aissen and Hankamer 1980)

Such facts have inspired different analyses of causatives in transformational and lexicalist theories. To the transformationalist they suggest a complex clause structure in which the causee is in a chain with an empty category in an embedded subject position, or is a 'subject' at some other level of structure such as d-structure (Baker 1988). The reflexive binding rule is sensitive to such underlying subjects. In lexicalist accounts, this indicates the presence of some internal structure

within the argument structure of the causative (Manning et al. 1999).
Applied to the Turkish example, the idea is that, instead of the simple
structure (88a), the structure of the causativized Turkish verb in (87)
would be either (88b) or (88c).

(88)   a. **cause-to-wash** ⟨ causer,   washer,   washee ⟩
                        SUBJ   OBL   OBJ

   b. **cause** ⟨ causer, **wash** ⟨ washer, washee ⟩⟩
                 SUBJ   OBL   OBJ

   c. **cause** ⟨ causer, causee$_i$, **wash** ⟨ washer$_i$, washee ⟩⟩
                 SUBJ   OBL   OBJ

The rule for the Turkish reflexive is that its antecedent must be an
'a-subject' (sometimes called the logical subject), the highest argument
in its local argument structure. As the highest argument of **wash**, the
dative causee is an a-subject, so it can bind the reflexive in (87).
Another question is whether the causee is an argument of the cause
predicate, as in (88c), or not, as in (88b). For example, Alsina (1992)
argues that in the Chichewa alternation in (86), the object NP is a
causee argument of the higher cause predicate, regardless of whether it
is the agent (as in 86a) or patient (as in 86b) of the base predicate.

3.4.3 Inchoatives and statives

We saw that in the causative alternation a morphological change can go
in the direction of either anticausativization or causativization. Similarly, words denoting a state and inchoative cognates denoting a change
into that state can be related by morphological derivation in either
direction. English has examples of both (from Koontz-Garboden 2005):

(89)   Inchoative Verb ⇒ Adjective
       a. Sandy broke the glass. (causative change of state)
       b. The glass broke. (non-causative change of state)
       c. The glass is broken. (state predicate is deverbal)

(90)   Adjective ⇒ Inchoative Verb
       a. The knot loosened. (non-causative change of state)
       b. Sandy loosened the knot. (causative change of state)
       c. The knot is loose. (state predicate is morphologically basic
          adjective)

The direction of derivation falls into a typological pattern that Koontz-Garboden (2005) explains in terms of Dixon's (1982) distinction between 'result states' and 'property concepts.' Result states expressed by adjectives like *broken* and *ruined* are the result of some action. They entail that there was an event giving rise to the resulting state; hence #*The glass is broken, but it never broke* is a contradiction. Property concepts states like *red* and *big* do not presuppose a prior event, so *The dirt is red, but nobody reddened it* is not contradictory. Such concepts are naturally described by adjectives in languages that have that lexical category. These are predicates denoting properties like speed, age, dimension, color, or value.

The cross-linguistic generalization is that 'result state adjectives' tend to be derived from the verb denoting the causing event, as in *break/broken*. 'Property concepts,' for example *red*, are morphologically basic, whether lexicalized as nouns, verbs, or adjectives (Koontz-Garboden 2005). They are never derived from the corresponding change-of-state verb. Instead, the inchoative verb is derived from the word denoting the state (e.g. *redden*). Some English adjectival passives like *closed* are polysemous between the property concept and result state meaning: *We hung the door closed* does not presuppose any closing event. For those that distinguish between the property concept (*open*) and the corresponding result state (*opened*), the prediction is that the morphologically marked form will denote the result state.

3.5 Alternations involving multiple arguments

3.5.1 Direct and oblique arguments

We have seen that verbs often allow their objects to express alternative event participants. At the same time, languages often have other means for expressing the participants that are not selected for objecthood, using oblique morphology such as prepositions or oblique case. Either the material (91a) or the location (91b) can be selected as the object of *spray*.

(91) a. Mary sprayed the water.
      b. Mary sprayed the plants.

The participant not selected as object can still be expressed by an oblique phrase:

(92) a. Mary sprayed the water (on the plants).
      b. Mary sprayed the plants (with the water).

An apparent functional motivation for oblique grammatical expressions is simply that speakers often want to express both participants in a single clause. When two participants are competing for the same object position, then the one that loses the competition must be expressed in a different way. Given the flexibility in object selection, together with the possibility of oblique expression of either event participant, the result is a diathesis alternation: two different possible grammatical expressions of roughly the same event, as in (92).

The study of alternations has provided fertile ground for investigating the theoretical question of the lexical representation of the verb (this issue is discussed in Chapter 6). It is not clear that the issue is really any different for alternations in which *two* arguments can be expressed in two different ways, as opposed to the simple alternation in the participant roles of a single complement, discussed in Section 3.2.2. We saw that verbs like *paint* allow either the effected representation or the depicted entity as their object. But only one of the two can be expressed in a given clause:

(93) a. (As for Mary's latest work of art,) *she painted it of (from/
         etc.) the sunset.
      b. (To remember the beautiful sunset,) *Mary painted it into
         (at/etc.) a picture.

It may be that English happens to lack prepositions for expressing such event participants. Verbs that allow alternative expression such as locative alternation verbs may not be so different in principle; there just happen to be prepositions available for their arguments. But they nonetheless provide an opportunity to bring together evidence from two sources: the comparison of the meanings of the two alternates, and the observation of which semantic classes of verbs participate in the alternation, as opposed to those allowing only one alternative. These two approaches will be illustrated with a look at locative alternations, i.e. the diathesis alternations involving a theme and location, like (92).

3.5.2 Locative alternations

Locative alternation clauses express events in which some entity (the 'locatum') moves to a location (e.g. Anderson 1971; Pinker 1989; Levin 1993; Dowty 1991; Beavers 2010). They alternate between direct object expression of the location or the locatum. In the common variety that is also called the '*spray–load* alternation', the locatum may alternatively appear in a *with*-PP, while oblique expression of the location can be in any of a variety of locative PPs:

(94)   a. John loaded the wagon with the hay.   (*with* variant)
       b. John loaded the hay on the wagon.   (locative variant)

(95)   a. Mary sprayed the wall with the paint.   (*with* variant)
       b. Mary sprayed the paint on the wall.   (locative variant)

In a related construction the entity is removed rather than added, and an *of*-PP can be used for that entity:

(96)   a. John cleared the table of dishes.   (*of* variant)
       b. John cleared the dishes from the table.   (locative variant)

The closely related *swarm* alternation is an intransitive variant with its own special semantic properties (Dowty 2000):

(97)   a. Bees are swarming in the garden.
       b. The garden is swarming with bees.

The '*swarm* alternation' will not be covered here. The difference in meaning between the locative alternation variants will be covered next, followed by discussion of the verbs that undergo the alternation.

The two variants carry a subtle difference in meaning that has been called the 'holistic effect': the event involves the direct object participant taken as a whole, while the other participant need not be taken in this way (Anderson 1971). Sentence (94a) suggests that the wagon is full while perhaps some hay remains unloaded, while the result of (94b) is that the hay has all been loaded while perhaps there is room left in the wagon. This effect is not literally entailed, however. The holistic effect is strengthened (or made more salient) through modification with *completely* or *partly*, as noted by Dowty (1991: 590). Example (98a) suggests that no hay remains unloaded, although space may remain in the wagon. In contrast, (98b) suggests that the wagon is full, while some hay may remain unloaded. Finally (98c) is decidedly odd, since the bare mass nominal *hay* is non-quantized, so there is no inherent endpoint to the hay-loading event:

(98)   a. John completely loaded the hay on the wagon.
       b. John completely loaded the wagon with hay.
       c. #John completely loaded hay on the wagon.

While nearly everyone agrees that there is a meaning difference, views vary on the proper characterization of that difference as well as the explanation for it.

According to the aspectual view, the direct object is responsible for the telic event structure (Anderson 1971; Tenny 1987; 1994; Dowty 1991; Wechsler and Lee 1996). The event is delimited through the transfer of quantification from the incremental theme argument, which can be either the location or the locatum (see Section 4.5). Referring to example (94), the extent of either the wagon or the hay determines the end of the event.

There are various proposals for how and why the 'holistic' meaning correlates with direct object expression. Tenny (1987; 1994) stipulated a universal principle that the direct object has a privileged role in 'measuring out' the event. Thus the incremental theme (see Section 4.5) appears in direct object position. Wechsler and Lee (1996: 648–51) posited that accusative Case, not objecthood per se, is the syntactic side of this relationship. In effect, event delimitation is associated with a DP position governed by the verb, hence very local to the verb position. This allowed Wechsler and Lee to connect the holistic effect to the assignment of accusative case to event-delimiting adverbials in some languages (see Section 4.5).

In constructional and templatic approaches, the locative alternation arises when a single verb is combined with two different constructions or templates. Following Rappaport and Levin (1988), Pinker (1989: 77ff.) assumed two different structures, one for movement verbs like *put* (99a), and one for change-of-state verbs like *cover* and *fill* (99b).

(99) a. X moves Y into/onto/etc. Z
      b. X causes Y to change its state (by means of moving Z to Y).

In both structures the *Y* argument maps to the direct object. Some verbs can be inserted into either structure, resulting in the locative alternation. This participant undergoes a change of location or state, which becomes clearer if the change is 'complete', resulting in the holistic effect.

For Dowty (1991: 590), the semantics of incremental themehood is not directly associated with a position, case, or grammatical function. Rather, it is one of several properties contributing to the Patient Proto-role, which in turn is associated with direct object selection (see Section 4.3). The incremental theme is therefore selected as the direct object of the verb.

Beavers (2010) treats the holistic effect within the context of a broader theory of affectedness and its influence on the choice between direct and oblique encoding of arguments. Beavers defines a hierarchy of affectedness ranked according to the relative strength of the truth conditions (see Section 4.5). Given a choice between direct and oblique expression of a given event participant, the direct will always be at least as strongly affected as the oblque. The candidates under comparison are not the coarguments competing for direct object expression, but rather the different syntactic expressions of a given semantic argument. As Beavers points out, this approach explains why we find the same (or similar) semantic conditions on direct/oblique alternations, even when the alternation involves only a single argument. In the conative alternation the direct argument is more strongly affected than the oblique, hence in *John cut the rope*, the rope is more affected than in *John cut at the rope* (Section 3.3.3).

Pinker (1989) considers which verb classes do or do not alternate. Pinker's proposal, at the most general level, is that types of actions that can be construed as something that can happen to the location are more likely construed with the location as direct object. (Recall that the direct object has patient-like properties). Types of actions that can be construed as something that can happen to the locatum are more likely construed with the locatum as the direct object, e.g. if they specify a particular state of the locatum. Next we review some of the verb classes noted by Pinker.[4]

Verbs expressing simultaneous forceful contact and motion of a mass against a surface do alternate (100). But if the mass moves by the force of gravity then the verb allows only the locative form (101).

(100)   forceful contact and motion: *brush, dab, plaster, rub, smear, smudge, spread*, etc.
    a. Mary brushed the paint on the wall.
    b. Mary brushed the wall with paint.

(101)   gravity-induced motion: *dribble, drip, dump, pour, spill*, etc.
    a. John poured the milk into the glass.
    b. *John poured the glass with the milk.

This contrast might be related to the meaning difference in various ways. The former type of action leads to a definite change in the

---

[4] This discussion draws upon lecture notes by Manfred Krifka.

location, while the latter specifies only the particular manner of a movement and hence can be applied only to the movement verb pattern. Other alternating verbs include those involving ballistic motion (102) and spatial arrangement (103).

(102)   *inject, splash, splatter, spray, sprinkle, squirt*
        a. Mary splashed water on the dog.
        b. Mary splashed the dog with water.

(103)   *heap, pile, stack*
        a. John stacked books onto the shelf.
        b. John stacked the shelf with books.

The *with*-form is presumably possible because in the former type the imparting of force leads to a specific change of the object, while in the latter type they specify the resulting configuration of the objects and that is seen as changing the state of the location in a particular way.

Verbs of forcing objects into a container against the limits of its capacity alternate (104). To be affected to its limits is mainly a property of the container, hence the *with*-form.

(104)   *pack, cram, crowd, jam, stuff, wad*
        a. John packed the books into the suitcase.
        b. John packed the suitcase with books.

Verbs of expulsion of a mass do not alternate. They indicate the cause of the movement but nothing specific about the locative goal.

(105)   *emit, excrete, expel, secrete, spit, vomit*
        a. John spat tobacco juice onto the table.
        b. *John spat the table with tobacco juice.

Verbs of attachment do not alternate either. Presumably, the type of attachment of another object does not constitute a specific state change for an object.

(106)   *attach, fasten, glue, nail, paste, pin, staple, stick, tape*
        a. John taped the note on the letter.
        b. *John taped the letter with the note.

Verbs that express a qualitative change of an object that arises with the addition of another object only show the *with*-form, as predictable.

(107)   *adorn, burden, clutter, endow, enrich, litter, soil, stain, taint*
      a. Mary stained the carpet with wine.
      b. *Mary stained wine onto the carpet.

Verbs that express that a surface or volume is completely covered or filled do not alternate.

(108)   *flood, coat, cover, pad, pave, tile, soak, drench, saturate*
      a. John covered the baby with a blanket.
      b. *John covered the blanket on the baby.

They come only in the *with*-form, the reason being that it depends on the locatum whether it is completely affected, and hence this can be construed as a property of the locatum.

3.6 Unaccusativity

Intransitive clauses in many languages appear to split into two classes. According to the Unaccusative Hypothesis, the two intransitive types are distinguished according to the whether its subject resembles the subject or object of a transitive clause (Perlmutter 1978). In 'unaccusative' intransitive clauses, the subjects share some properties with the objects of transitives. In 'unergative' intransitive clauses, the subjects do not share special properties with objects, but behave like other subjects. This split raises a number of questions. Is unaccusativity encoded in the discrete, combinatorial syntax? On the unified, categorial view, the two classes differ in category, and the various properties that distinguish the two types reflect sensitivity to that category difference. Assuming that view, another question concerns the particular nature of that grammatical encoding (see Section 3.6.4).

Alternatively, on the non-unified view, each putative 'diagnostic' for the unaccusative/unergative distinction has its own independent explanation, due to the semantics of the specific construction or morpheme in question. To the extent that the semantic content of certain constructions and morphemes is similar, they tend to cluster together. Also, the clustering of properties may be rooted in a shared or related historical origin. Whether due to a semantic or historical relationship, that similarity is not directly encoded in a common representation in the synchronic competence grammar.

First we will review some of the phenomena that have been atttributed to the unaccusativity split. Syntactic accounts of unaccusativity usually assimilate unaccusative subjects to transitive objects by giving them the same representation at some underlying level, but we postpone description of these systems until Section 3.6.4. In this section we will look at semantic factors, and a brief consideration of some historical factors with a focus on the historical roots of auxiliary selection and split ergativity.

3.6.1 Properties of unaccusatives

In many languages, transitive verbs have an intransitive variant in which the semantic role of the subject is the same as that of the object of the transitive, as in this French example (Alexiadou et al. 2004: 2–3)

(109) a. Jean   brisera   le   verre.
        John   break.FUT   the   glass
        'John will break the glass.'

   b. Le verre   se   brisera.
       the glass   REFL   break.FUT
       'The glass will break.'

   c. Jean   se   défend.
       John   REFL   defends
       'John defends himself.'

Assuming true reflexives like (109c) are transitive, Perlmutter (1978; 1989) suggested the reflexive morpheme in an anticausative like (109b) is a grammatical reflex of underlying transitivity, that is, the underlying objecthood of the surface subject. More recently, Koontz-Garboden (2009) has argued that reflexive-marked anticausatives like (109b) are literally reflexive, given the appropriate semantics of reflexives (for discussion see Section 3.4.2.2). Burzio (1986) argued in detail that certain Italian subjects are underlying objects, such as subjects of inherent reflexives as in (110).

(110) a. Giovanni   si   vergognava.
        Giovanni   REFL   ashamed
        'Giovanni is ashamed.'

   b. [__ [si vergognara Giovanni]$_{VP}$]$_S$

Some cases like this lack a corresponding transitive, but the tell-tale reflexive morphology is still evident, and Burzio provided further evidence of underlying objecthood.

The way to demonstrate unaccusativity is to identify some property of transitives verbs or clauses, and then observe that same property in a proper subset of the intransitives. The European languages with two auxiliary verbs for perfect aspect, corresponding to *be* and *have*, generally use the *have* auxiliary for all active transitives and *be* for passives. Most intransitive actives use the *have* auxiliary, but some use the *be* auxiliary, suggesting that, like passives, they take an underlying object as their subject. The auxiliary split is discussed further in Section 3.6.2.

Some other phenomena that vary in similar ways depending on the intransitive verb include English resultative constructions (but see Section 7.2 for other views), prenominal perfect or passive participles (various languages; see below), *ne*-cliticization (Italian); *was-für* split (German, Dutch), impersonal passives, Russian *po*-phrases, Russian genitive of negation, and split ergativity in many languages (see Alexiadou et al. 2004). When several phenomena correlate within a single language this is taken as evidence for a grammatical distinction to which the various processes are sensitive.

However, closer inspection often reveals that the properties only partially correlate. Zaenen (1988; 1993) examined three putative diagnostics distinguishing unaccusatives from unergatives in Dutch: auxiliary selection, impersonal passive formation, and prenominal participial modifiers. She found that they depend on different semantic properties, and moreover the criterial properties apply to different sorts of entities: while the criteria for auxiliary selection applies to verbs, the criteria for impersonal passive apply to whole sentences in context. Dutch intransitive verbs split into two groups with respect whether they select *hebben* 'have' or *zijn* 'be' as the auxiliary in the perfect aspect. Developing an idea from traditional grammar, Zaenen identified the semantic basis for these groups as lexical telicity: telic verbs use *zijn* (see also Van Valin 1987; 1990; Van Hout 2004). She tested for telicity with a durative adverbial *urenlang* 'for hours', which modify atelic predicates only. According to a closely related view, the 'be' auxiliary is used when the result state of the denoted event involves a property of the subject referent (see Section 3.6.2).

Auxiliary selection in Dutch is a lexical property of verbs, largely insensitive to modifiers and context. Hence the relevant notion of 'telicity' is sensitive to the 'basic' event denoted by the verb (Aktionsart), but insensitive to the complex aspect of the sentence as a whole. Auxiliary selection is usually fixed by the verb. Sometimes a verb alternates in auxiliary selection, but then it is due to variable polyadicity of the verb: *lopen* 'run' (atelic, hence uses *hebben*), but *naar huis lopen* 'run home' (telic, hence uses *zijn*) (Zaenen 1993: 136ff.). Also, Sorace (2000: 866) points out exceptional participles like *gestegen* 'risen', which is normally telic and takes BE, but can be detelicized by modifying with durative adverbials like *3 uurlang* 'for 3 hours', in which case it takes HAVE. But on the whole auxiliary selection tends to be fixed for a given verb regardless of the semantic contribution of other elements of the sentence or the utterance context.

The ability to form impersonal passives, held as another unaccusativity test, is dependent on a different semantic criterion—controllability by an agent. Zaenen tested for controllability by embedding under *dwingen* 'force' and modifying with *opzettelijk* 'on purpose'. For example, 'work' and 'bleed' are both atelic and thus take *hebben* as auxiliary, but the former is controllable while the latter is not, which affects impersonal passives (Zaenen 1993: 136–7):

(111)   a. De meisjes hebben hard gewerkt.
           the girls   have   hard worked
           'The girls have worked hard.'

      b. Er   werd hard gewerkt (door de   meisjes).
           there was   hard worked   by   the   girls
           lit. There was worked hard (by the girls).

      c. De   man   heeft gebloed.
           the   man   has   bled
           'The man bled.'

      d. *Er   werd (door de   man) gebloed.
           there was   (by   the   man) bled
           lit. There was bled (by the man).

Significantly, for the determination of auxiliary selection, atelic aspect classifies lexical items (verbs). But controllability is a feature of the impersonal construction, not of the verb per se. A normally uncontrollable action such as falling can be used in the impersonal passive in a context such as actors falling on cue (Zaenen 1993: 139). Similarly, telicity is required for prenominal modifiers like *de gevallen jongen* 'the fallen boy', but this involves sentence aspect, not lexical aspect. Table 3.1 summarizes the data. But note that the [±control] feature does not really classify verbs but rather whole sentences in context.

Zaenen gives a standard unaccusativity analysis to auxiliary selection, using LFG Lexical Mapping Theory (see Section 5.2.1). The [−r]

TABLE 3.1   Dutch intransitive verbs (based on Zaenen 1993: 132)

	Atelic [aux: *hebben*]	Telic [aux: *zijn*]
+ control [impersonal passive better]	*telefoneren* 'phone'	*aankomen* 'arrive'
– control [impersonal passive worse]	*stinken* 'stink'	*sterven* 'die'

intrinsic classification is the equivalent of an 'internal argument' or underlying object in transformational theories. Zaenen's rule states that the auxiliary *zijn* is used when an intrinsically [–r] role is expressed as the subject. She analyzes the semantics of this lexical distinction using Dowty's (1991) proto-role theory (Section 4.3).

3.6.2 Auxiliary selection

Why does *have/be* auxiliary selection reflect unaccusativity? First consider the origin of the BE auxiliary in Latin. Originally classical Latin had, in addition to its synthetic tense forms, analytic (periphrastic) forms using *esse* 'be' as auxiliary. These included the passive perfect, such as *laudatus eram* 'I had been praised' and the so-called deponent perfects, that is, morphologically passive forms that lack active counterparts, as in *profectus eram* 'I had left'. These periphrastics are thought to have been stative: they indicate a property of the subject at reference time. More specifically they were stative resultatives, which indicate a state obtains at reference time as a result of a previous event. These are like English *She is gone*, except that the Latin construction was more general. Schwarze (2001: 161–2) notes that the tense of the participle and the *esse* 'be' auxiliary were independent. Eventually the periphrastic came to be used for the 'perfect passive', allowing non-resultative interpretations like passive *Amatus est* 'he was loved', as well as some deponents such as *Locutus est* 'He spoke.' The deponents included both agentive (*loqui* 'speak', *minari* 'threaten') and non-agentive (*mori* 'die', *nasci* 'be born') verbs. The agentive deponents dropped out, so that 'all Latin verbs in the context of which *essere* [Italian 'be'—S.W.] started its career as a tense auxiliary are non-agentive' (Schwarze 2001: 163).

The verb *habere* 'have' is thought to have developed into a new auxiliary through a reanalysis. Secondary predicates with passive participle, as in (112), were common:

(112) Habeo   cibum   coctum.
       have.1SG.PRS food(M.SG).ACC cook.past.passive.M.SG.ACC
       'I have food, cooked.'   (Schwarze 2001: 164, ex. 36)

The secondary predicates were reanalyzed as primary predicates, so
that (112) became 'I have cooked food.' As a consequence of this
reanalysis, the NP (here *cibum* 'food'), which was previously the subject
of the participle, became its object instead. This is thought to be the
origin of participle agreement with some objects in modern Romance.
Later it became possible to drop the object, yielding certain intransitives
(so-called 'unergatives') with *habere* 'have', as in *Habeo intellectum* 'I
have understood' (Schwarze 2001: 166).

The *have/be* plus participle periphrastics followed a common devel-
opmental trajectory from resultative to perfect to perfective interpretations (Bybee et al. 1994).

(113)   a. resultative: state exists as a result of past action.
           He is gone. My hat is ruined.

        b. perfect: situation occurred prior to reference time and is
           relevant at reference time
           He has left.

        c. perfective: situation viewed as bounded (hence normally in
           the past); used for narrative sequences.
           *Suddenly a shot rang out. Then the maid screamed. A door
           slammed.*
           (cp. *Suddenly a shot rang out. ??Then a maid has screamed.
           ??A door has slammed.*)

Both *esse* and *habere* periphrastics had resultative interpretations originally. The perfect-to-perfective shift in the interpretation of these
periphrastic constructions has happened to various degrees in the
European languages. English retained the perfect interpretation,
hence the contrast in (113c). French passé composé is now simply
interpreted as perfective, without the suggestion of present relevance;
German is similar (Bybee et al. 1994: 85).

The implications for auxiliary selection in modern Italian are as
follows. Transitives always get HAVE (*avere*), because only the *habere*
periphrastic had an object NP. Intransitives resulting from transitives
dropping their object also take HAVE. Passives and deponents always
take BE (*essere*) or some other auxiliary, because they derived from the
Classical Latin passive perfect, the stative construction that used *esse*.

So both auxiliaries came from stative resultatives. But the crucial part of the story that explains the semantic reflexes of split intransitivity is that *only in the BE type is the result predicated of the subject*. Hence intransitive verbs entailing a linguistically salient result state take BE. These include verbs indicating a change of location, change of state, and so on. Indeed, across the auxiliary split languages, the BE auxiliary tends to be used when the result of the denoted event involves a property of the subject referent that is linguistically salient and inferrable from the clause. Consider this hierarchy of semantic properties of verbs in the European auxiliary split languages, listed from those most likely to select BE to those most likely to select HAVE:

(114)   [BE] change of location > change of state > continuation of a pre-existing state > existence of state > uncontrolled process > controlled process (motional) > controlled process (non-motional) [HAVE] (Sorace 2000)

Starting from the 'BE' end of Sorace's (2000) list, change of location verbs with meanings like 'come' and 'arrive' consistently select the BE verb in all of the languages. Change of state verbs almost always take BE, with a few exceptions: for example, the Dutch participle *gestegen* 'risen' normally takes BE, but it can be detelicized by modifying with durative adverbials like *3 uurlang* 'for 3 hours', in which case it takes HAVE (Sorace 2000: 866). The third property, 'continuation of a pre-existing state', covers verbs with meanings like 'remain'. The event types denoted by all three of the most BE-friendly verb classes have result states involving a salient property of the subject referent. This usually correlates with telicity (recall Zaenen's analysis of Dutch), but not always. Consider the third type: *X remained in Holland* has a result—namely, that *X* is in Holland—but it is not telic. Conversely, some telic predicates such as *run a lap* lack salient results. Many of the properties in this hierarchy follow from the historical origin of BE periphrastics from stative resultatives in which the result state is predicated of the subject.

3.6.3 Split ergativity

In ergative case and agreement systems, absolutive marking appears on the objects of transitives and the subjects of intansitives, which is a kind of unaccusative property. West Greenlandic (115) and Sacapultec Maya (116) illustrate ergative case and agreement systems, respectively (CA = completive aspect).

(115) a. Oli-p   neqi   neri-vaa
           Oli-ERG   meat.ABS   eat-IND.TR.3sg.3sg
           'Oli eats meat.'

       b. Oli   sinippoq
           Oli.ABS   sleep-IND.INTR.3sg
           'Oli sleeps.'

(116) a. š-at-ak-ek
           COMPL-2p-enter-INTR
           'you entered'

       b. š-Ø-ak-ek
           COMPL-3p-enter-INTR
           'he/she entered'

       c. š-at-ri-č'iy-aŋ
           COMPL-2p-3p-hit-TR
           'he/she hit you'

       d. š-Ø-a:-č'iy-aŋ
           COMPL-3p-2p-hit-TR
           'you hit him/her'

In the characteristic ergative pattern, S (subject of intransitive) and O (object) are marked the same, and distinguished from A (subject of transitive):

(117) West Greenlandic case endings

	3p (he/she)
A	-p
S	ø
O	ø

(118) Sacapultec Maya person markers

	2p (you)	3p (he/she)
A	a:	ri
S	at	ø
O	at	ø

Absolutive marking satisfies the definition of an unaccusative property, since it is shared between objects and intransitive subjects.

In split ergative systems called 'active' alignment systems, intransitives are split between ergative and accusative alignment depending on the verb meaning (Merlan 1985; Mithun 1991). In a study of active splits in subject person markers on verbs, Merlan (1985) refers to the two forms as 'subjective' and 'objective', depending on whether the verb form corresponds to subjects or objects of transitives. From a study of eight languages, she observes that in every language, one of the two forms is used on a smaller set of verbs, and that same form is the more semantically specialized and distributionally limited—that is, it is the marked form. But which one is marked varies from language to language. Interestingly, Merlan found that the specialized class of intransitive verbs, regardless of whether it uses the subjective or objective form, 'contains, with few or no exceptions, verbs which require animate subjects' (Merlan 1985: 347). The other form (the unmarked one) favors inanimates but also has some animate-only verbs. Also, that specialized class of intransitives (again, regardless of whether it is the subjective or objective class) always includes verbs related to body functions and processes such as 'cough,' 'sneeze,' 'breathe,' and 'shout.'

In addition to such correlations with markedness, the lexical meaning also tends to correlate with the particular inflectional form, subjective or objective, in ways that resemble the unaccusative splits discussed above. The semantics of active splits can involve either patient-related properties (affectedness, telicity, result state) or agent-related properties (agency, control, non-stativity). Mithun (1991) elucidated the parameters of cross-linguistic variation with active splits in Guaraní, Lakhota, Central Pomo, and other languages. In Guaraní it depends on stativity, according to Mithun: events use Agent case, states use the objective form. For Lakhota the key condition for the subjective form is agency, defined as 'performing, effecting, or instigating' the action. This includes the performance of uncontrollable actions like sneezing. Central Pomo employs the objective form when the subject either is 'significantly affected' or lacks control over the situation, such as in sneezing. The subjective form is used elsewhere. Active languages vary according to the particular semantic properties that condition the split. Mithun also observes that each language has lexical exceptions due to semantic drift and borrowing. Guaraní, as noted, reserves the objective form for stative verbs. Despite being non-stative, *esaví* 'to wink' takes

Patient case on its subject because it literally means 'to have defective eyes' (*esá* 'eye'), which is stative (Mithun 1991: 513).

Active splits are often cited as diagnostics for unaccusativity (Alexiadou et al. 2004: 7, citing Harris 1981 on Georgian). However, in some instances of split ergativity where the subjective form is semantically marked, it is questionable whether the objective form really reflects an underlying grammatical unity between objects and some subjects. It may merely be the elsewhere case. Hindi/Urdu case marking provides an example. In transitive Hindi/Urdu clauses in perfective aspect, the subject gets *-ne*, an ergative case since it need not appear on subjects of intransitives (except as noted below). The verb agrees with the object, which takes the accusative *-ko* when it is definite (119b):

(119) a. Laṛkā-ne   kutte   dekhe   hai.
           boy-ERG   dogs   seen.PL   AUX
           'The boy has seen some dogs.'

       b. Laṛkā-ne   kutte-ko   dekhe   hai.
           boy-ERG   dogs-ACC   seen.PL   AUX
           'The boy has seen the dogs.'

The Hindi/Urdu ergative case marker *-ne* can be used on intransitive subjects, correlated with volitionality. Unergatives systematically allow this case alternation (Butt 2001: 122):

(120) a. Ram   khãs-a.
           Ram[M].NOM   cough-PFV.M.SG
           'Ram coughed.'

       b. Ram-ne   khãs-a.
           Ram[M].ERG   cough-PFV.M.SG
           'Ram coughed (purposefully).'

Let us contrast this situation with auxiliary selection in Romance and Germanic. While Hindi/Urdu ergative case indicates volitionality in intransitives, it is not clear that Romance and Germanic HAVE auxiliaries have any semantic value related to an agent argument. Instead, the BE auxiliary indicates the marked property, namely that a result state applies exceptionally to the subject—rather than the object, which is the normal grammatical function for affected themes. In contrast, the semantic content of this Hindi–Urdu case pattern is not patient-oriented content but rather agent-oriented content (volitionality).

There seems to be very little motivation for representing nominative subjects such as the one in (120a) as related to objects in any way.

Hindi/Urdu ergative case shows up only in perfective clauses. This is consistent with a typological correlation between ergative morphology and perfective aspect—a correlation reminiscent of the HAVE/BE split. However, Anderson (1988: 344–8) and Garrett (1990: 264) caution against assuming a direct grammatical connection between ergative case morphology and perfective aspect. They argue that the connection is an indirect side-effect of the historical origin of ergativity. The ergative system of Hindi/Urdu can be traced to the Sanskrit periphrastic passive/adjectival participle construction (Anderson 1977; 1988). The gloss for the (invented) Sanskrit passive clause in (121) is given in (121a) (taken from Garrett 1990). This is argued to be have been reanalyzed to yield the ergative clause in the Middle Indo-Iranian shown by the gloss in (121b):

(121)   ahi-r   indr-eṇa   ha-ta-ḥ.
    a. serpent-NOM.SG   Indra-INS.SG   kill-PTCP-NOM.SG
       'The serpent has been killed by Indra.'

    b. serpent-ABS.SG   Indra-ERG.SG   kill-PFV-NOM.SG
       'Indra has killed the serpent.'

(PTCP = participle; PFV = perfective aspect) The following reanalyses are posited as part of this syntactic change: NOM ⇒ ABS; INS ⇒ ERG; passive voice ⇒ active voice (in transitive clauses). In modern Hindi/Urdu (and perhaps already in Middle Indic), deeper subject properties such as subject-oriented reflexives pick out the ergative NP:

(122)   mẽ-ne   apne-ko   dekhā.   (Anderson 1977: 335)
    I-ERG   self-ACC   saw
    'I saw myself.'

The ergative argument that decends from an oblique has become a full-fledged grammatical subject. The result is a morphologically ergative case system.

The Hindi/Urdu ergative split resembles the HAVE/BE auxiliary split in Romance and Germanic in that they show up only in the perfect aspect. However, Anderson (1988: 344–8) and Garrett (1990: 264) argue that the typological correlation between ergative morphology and perfective aspect is not in itself significant. That is, perfectivity is not in itself associated with ergativity in the synchronic grammar. The source of the correlation is the fact that perfectives are a very common source for passives. Passives are both the source of tense/aspect splits and of ergative structures via reanalysis as active, transitive verbs.

3.6.4 Syntactic accounts of unaccusativity

Syntactic accounts of unaccusativity usually assimilate unaccusative subjects to transitive objects by giving them the same representation at some underlying level. In Relational Grammar the grammatical relations were numbered, 1 for subject, 2 for object (Perlmutter 1983; Perlmutter and Rosen 1984). Grammatical relations were defined at various strata, from an initial stratum corresponding roughly to 'thematic prominence' (see Rosen 1984) to the final stratum, corresponding to surface relations. Unaccusative subjects, like objects, were assumed to be have the 2 function at the initial stratum, from which they advance to 1 (Perlmutter 1978; 1989). Similarly, in Government/ Binding the unaccusative subject is analyzed as a deep object (Burzio 1986):

(123)   Transformational representation
      Transitive: [Mary [dropped the glass]$_{VP}$]
      Unergative: [Mary [screamed]$_{VP}$]
      Unaccusative: [__ [fell the ball]$_{VP}$] $\Rightarrow$ [The ball$_i$ [fell e_i]$_{VP}$]

Turning next to LFG, the 'underlying level' in Lexical Mapping Theory is the intrinsic classification of the argument roles of a verb (Section 5.2.1). Subject and object are the two thematically unrestricted [−r] grammatical functions. So a [−r] intrinsic classification is posited for arguments that alternate between subject and object:

(124)   Lexical Mapping Theory (LFG) intrinsic classifications
      Transitive: *drop*   <   agt   th   >
                                      [-o]   [-r]
      Unergative: *scream* <   agt   >
                                      [-o]
      Unaccusative: *fall*   <   th   >
                                      [-r]

The theme of the transitive surfaces as object (in active voice) or subject (in passive voice). The sole argument of an unaccusative like *fall* receives the same classification. It can only surface as subject in English, but has certain object-like properties, a phenomenon Bresnan and Zaenen (1990) call 'deep unaccusativity.'

The Role and Reference Grammar notion of the Undergoer macro-role is similar but not identical to the 'deep object'. Canonical unaccusative subjects are Undergoers, as are transitive objects, but some unaccusative subjects are analyzed differently (Van Valin 1990). In a related proposal, Dowty (1991) floats the idea that an unaccusative subject has more Patient proto-role properties than Agent proto-role properties, while an unergative subject has more Agent than Patient proto-role properties.

3.7 Lexicalization of events

3.7.1 Typology of motion and manner lexicalization

Talmy (1985; 2000) analyzed motion events into several semantic components and studied the way languages vary typologically in their syntactic expression of those components. What are the components of a motion event? First, the very fact of motion itself can be indicated. A 'motion event' involves a moved object and the medium or reference point with respect to which the position of the object is gauged. Talmy called these the 'figure' and 'ground,' respectively. The trajectory of the movement, for which Talmy used the term *path* in its general sense, includes as subcomponents the source, (intermediate) path, and goal. The component of 'deixis', the specification of whether motion is towards or away from the speaker, hearer, or other deictic center, is a subtype of the path component. In addition, descriptions of motion can specify the manner of motion, and its cause. Various combinations of these components can be conflated in the meaning of the verb, or alternatively encoded in the adpositions or other dependents of the verb.

Talmy's typology distinguished 'verb-framed' from 'satellite-framed' languages, depending on whether the 'path of motion' is encoded in the verb root or in its 'satellites' such as prepositions, particles, or affixes. In satellite-framed languages, the path of motion is expressed by the satellites while the manner of motion is in the verb root. The typical movement verbs of English are of this type (125a,b). German (125c) and Russian (125d) illustrate affixal path encoding.

(125) a. John walked [motion+manner] into [path] the room.

  b. Mary climbed [motion+manner] down [path].

  c. weil   da   eine   Eule   plötzlich   raus-flattert
     because there   an   owl   suddenly   out-flaps
     'because an owl suddenly flaps out.'

  d. Tam   vy-skočila   sova.
     there out-jumped   owl
     'An owl jumped out.'
     (Slobin 2004: 224, ex. 5, cited in Beavers et al. 2010: 339, ex. 11)

In verb-framed languages, the main verb in a clause expressing motion does not encode manner, but rather its trajectory (or path). Examples include Spanish, French, Turkish, Japanese, and Hebrew. Any specification of manner must come from a subordinate adjunct. These Spanish examples illustrate a range of motion+path conflations (Talmy 1985).

(126) a. La botella   entró [motion + path]   a la   cueva (flotando)
        the bottle   moved-in   to the cave   floating
        'The bottle floated into the cave.'

  b. La   botella   pasó   por   la   piedra   (flotando).
     the   bottle   moved-by   for   the rock   floating
     'The bottle floated past the rock.'

  c. El   globo   subió   por la chimenea (flotando).
     the   balloon moved-up   for the chimney floating
     'The balloon floated up the chimney.'

  d. La   botella iba   por   el   canal   (flotando).
     the   bottle   moved-along   for   the canal   floating
     'The bottle floated along the canal.'

It is difficult to express motion and manner in a single verb in Spanish:

(127) a. ??La botella   flotó   a   la   cueva.
        the bottle   floated   to   the   cave
        'The bottle floated to the cave.'
        (Beavers et al. 2010: 11, ex. 18b)

  b. The bottle floated (in)to the cave.

In contrast, English allows conflation of motion and manner on the verb, as shown in (127b). However, English also has many movement verbs of the 'Romance' type in (127), having borrowed many verbs of this type from French, such as *enter, exit, pass, descent, return, cross, traverse, ascend, escape,* and *recede* (Wienold 1995). There are also a few Germanic verbs of this kind, such as *rise* and *leave*.

Slobin (2004) and Zlatev and Yangklang (2004) supplemented Talmy's verb-framed and satellite-framed types with a third type, 'equipollently framed' languages, in which multiple serialized main verbs encode manner and path. An example of such a serial verb language is Thai. In Thai, serial verb constructions are very common and serve a wide variety of semantic functions (Kanchanawan 1978; Muansuwan 2001; 2002; Sudmuk 2005). Thai has few prepositions, and many of the functions of prepositions in preposition-rich languages are taken over by verbs in Thai. Focusing on words expressing motion, the forms *den* 'walk', *khâw* 'enter', and *thǔŋ* 'arrive' are all verbs. Each of these words can head an independent sentence:

(128)   a. Piti   den.
             Piti   walk
             'Piti walked.'

         b. Piti   khâw   rooŋrian.
             Piti   enter   school
             'Piti entered the school.'

Combinations of these verbs can also be serialized as shown in (129) and (130) subject to certain constraints on combination and ordering (Muansuwan 2002; Sudmuk 2005). The deictic component of motion semantics is illustrated by the Thai verbs *maa* 'come' and *pay* 'go'. More complex combinations are possible as in (130b) where three verbs are serialized:

(129)   Piti   den   khâw   rooŋrian.
         Piti   walk   enter   school
         'Piti walked into the school.'
         (Wechsler 2003: ex. 2a; 2008b: ex. 1a)

(130)   a. Piti   (maa/pay)   thǔŋ   rooŋrian.
             Piti   (come/go)   arrive school
             'Piti arrived (here/there) at school.'

         b. Piti   den   pay   thǔŋ   rooŋrian   mǔɨawaanníi.
             Piti   walk   go   arrive school   yesterday
             'Piti walked to school yesterday.'
             (Wechsler 2003: exx. 2b, 3c; 2008b: exx. 1b, 4)

Each of these Thai sentences expresses a single event. For example, while the Thai form *khaŵ* in (129) is categorially a verb, glossed here as 'enter', its meaning is closer to the English preposition *into*.

Korean further illustrates the fine line between verb and preposition meaning. Certain serialized elements in Korean motion constructions are generally analyzed as verbs, roughly as in Thai, but resemble prepositions in some respects. Korean has four basic directional verbs: *na* '(move) out', *tul-e* '(move) in', *oll-a* '(move) up', and *nayly-e* '(move) down'. The forms *tul-* '(move) in' and *na-* '(move) out' cannot be used alone to represent motion in modern Korean, but require the support of a deictic verb *ka* 'go' or *o* 'come'. This is illustrated for *na-* '(move) out' in (131) and for *tul-* '(move) in' in (132).

(131) a. ku-ka   wuntongcang-ey na   ka-ss-ta.
          he-NOM   playground-to   out   go-PST-DEC
          'He went out to the playground.'

       b. *ku-ka   wuntongcang-ey na-ss-ta.
          he-NOM   playground-to   out-PST-DEC
          'He went out to the playground.'

(132) a. ku-ka   kyosil-ey   tul-e   o-ss-ta.
          he-NOM   classroom-to   into-C   come-PST-DEC
          'He came into the classroom.'

       b. *ku-ka   kyosil-ey   tul-ss-ta.
          he-NOM   classroom-to   enter-PST-DEC
          'He came into the classroom.'

The forms *tul-* '(move) in' and *na-* '(move) out' were main verbs in earlier forms of Korean, but are in transition to becoming path satellites when they precede a deictic verb, according to Im (Im 2001: 113). Im cites this example from the Korean of 1445, where *na-* 'go' is used as a main verb:

(133) ptut   moll-a   mot   na-ni.
        meaning   not.know-C   not   go.out-C
        'Since I don't know the meaning, I don't go out...'
        (from *Yongpiechenka*, cited in Im 2001: 113)

At that time, the Korean construction resembled Thai as described above: the directional forms were full-fledged, stand-alone verbs. This main verb use of *na-* is no longer productive in modern Korean, although it is preserved in some relics (Im 2001: 114, fn. 67):

(134) a. namwu-uy ssak-i   na-ss-ta.
          tree-GEN   bud-N   exit-PST-DEC
          'Trees have budded.'

      b. hay-ka   na-ss-ta.
          sun-NOM   exit-PST-DEC
          roughly 'The sun has risen/appeared.'

But in normal, non-idiomatic motion constructions, *na-* and *tul-* require deictic verbs in contemporary Korean. According to one view, the path verbs have lost the motion component and now serve as modifiers, so the deictic verb is needed in order to express motion (Choi and Bowerman 1991; Talmy 2000; Im 2001; 2002). See also Wechsler (2008b: fn. 1) on this specific issue, and Wienold (1995) and Zlatev and Yangklang (2004) for further Talmyesque analyses of Korean.

Talmy saw the observed differences between languages as evidence for parametric variation among a set of typological alternatives from which individual languages choose. Much subsequent work followed suit. But some of the more recent work has emphasized the fact that languages are not monolithic in their choice of conflation pattern. Patterns can vary within a language depending on word choice. Consider French. In keeping with Talmy's typology, French verbs expressing manner, such as *courir* 'run', generally disallow a path reading of a PP complement.

(135) La souris   court   sous   la   table.
        the mouse   runs   under   the   table
        'A mouse-running event is taking place under the table.'
        (non-PATH)
        (Not: 'The mouse is running to a position under the table.'
        (PATH))

However, Fong and Poulin (1998) observed that some French verbs allow the path reading. These include *rouler* 'roll', *basculer* 'topple over'/'tip over', *débouler* 'roll down', and *dégringoler* 'tumble down'.

(136) La   balle   a   roulé   dans   la   boîte.
        the   ball   has   rolled   in   the   box
        (i) The ball-rolling event took place in the box. (non-PATH)
        (ii) The ball rolled into the box. (PATH)

Also some French prepositions force the path reading: *vers* 'toward', *à travers* 'through':

(137) a. Le   poisson a   nagé   vers   la   rive.
          the   fish   has   swum   towards the   river.bank
          'The fish swam towards the river bank.'
       b. L'enfant a   couru vers   sa   mère.
          the'child has   run   towards her   mother
          'The child ran towards her mother.'

Resultatives illustrate this point too. Unlike English, which allows resultative secondary predicate APs as in *Claude wiped the table clean* (see Section 7.2), French generally does not allow them :

(138) Claude a   essuyé la   table (*propre).
       Claude has   wiped   the table clean
       'Claude wiped the table (clean).'

But Fong and Poulin (1998) observe that certain lexical causatives allow such APs: *render* 'render', *changer* 'change', *métamorphoser*, *transformer* 'transform'.

(139) Claude a   rendu   les   enfants   heureux/célèbres.
       Claude has   rendered the   children   happy/famous
       'Claude made the children happy/famous.'

Fong and Poulin analyze this interaction between word choice and language typology using Rappaport Hovav and Levin's (1998) templatic approach (see Section 4.4.4.3). English verbs are associated with basic aspectual templates that can be freely augmented through the application of a productive rule. For example, *wipe* is an activity verb (*Mary wiped the table for a while*), but its template (shown in (140a)) can be augmented to form an accomplishment predicate (*Mary wiped the table clean*), as in (140b).

(140) a. [x ACT]$_{< MANNER >}$ (activity)
       b. [[x ACT]$_{< MANNER >}$ CAUSE [y BECOME < STATE >]]
                                                    (accomplishment)

French verbs and prepositions inherently encode parts of the accomplishment structure. But if French lacks this English-style productive rule for free augmentation of templates, then any accomplishment formation in French must be inherent in the lexical meaning of the verb or preposition. An important implication of this analysis is that it requires a distinction between two types of lexical meaning: inherent lexical meaning of particular verbs, prepositions, etc. and the constructional meaning arising through template augmentation.

Beavers et al. (2010) developed this approach into a full-fledged theory (they cite Song and Levin 1998 as a precursor). They derive the patterns of cross-linguistic variation in motion event encoding from interactions between universal constraints, on the one hand, and the syntactic, lexical, and morphological inventories of particular languages, on the other. They make two key assumptions: that the verb is the only clause-obligatory lexical category; and that a single verb may lexicalize manner or path but not both (Beavers et al. 2010: 4). The latter assumption is a species of 'manner–result complementarity,' which is discussed next (Section 3.7.2).

3.7.2 Manner–result complementarity

A recurring question in lexical semantics scholarship is whether there are universal limits on the complexity of word meanings. Rappaport Hovav and Levin (2010), building on their earlier proposals for a templatic approach to lexically encoded event structure (Rappaport Hovav and Levin 1998), proposed a constraint to the effect that a verb may encode either the specific manner or the specific result of an event, but *a single verb cannot encode both manner and result.* Rappaport Hovav and Levin (1998) posited these lexico-semantic event structure templates (see Section 4.4.4):

(141)   Event structure templates
   a. $[\text{x ACT}_{\langle \text{MANNER} \rangle}]$ (activity)
   b. $[\text{x } \langle \text{STATE} \rangle]$ (state)
   c. $[\text{BECOME } [\text{x } \langle \text{STATE} \rangle]]$ (achievement)
   d. $[[\text{x ACT}_{\langle \text{MANNER} \rangle}] \text{ CAUSE } [\text{BECOME } [\text{y } \langle \text{STATE} \rangle]]]$ (accomplishment 1)
   e. $[\text{x CAUSE } [\text{BECOME } [\text{y } \langle \text{STATE} \rangle]]]$ (accomplishment 2)

The idiosyncratic aspect of a word is represented by filling out the positions given in angle brackets by non-logical constants. The constants subscripted to ACT in (141a,d) are modifiers indicating the manner of an action. The constants indicated by STATE in (141c,d,e) are arguments of the BECOME operator, and indicate the result state.

(142)   a. Activities
        MANNER specified: e.g. *jog, run, creak, whistle* …
        INSTRUMENT specified: e.g., *brush, hammer, saw, shovel* …
    b. Accomplishment 1:
        STATE specified as PLACE:
          bag, box, cage, crate, garage, pocket … (location verbs)
        STATE specified as WITH ⟨PLACEABLE OBJECT⟩, OBJECT specified:
          butter, oil, paper, tile, wax (locatum verbs)
    c. State (internally caused):
        STATE specified, e.g. *bloom, blossom, decay, rot, rust, sprout* …
    d. Accomplishment 2 (externally caused state):
        STATE specified, e.g. *break, dry, harden, melt, open* …

Complementarity between manner and result is implicit in the templates in (142), assuming that only one constant can be specified per verb root. Referring to the arguments (of BECOME) and the modifiers (of ACT), Rappaport Hovav and Levin (2010: ex. 10) state the generalization:

(143)   The lexicalization constraint: A root can only be associated with one primitive predicate in an event schema, as either an argument or a modifier.

In a sense all events have both manner and result, so more precise definitions are needed. Rappaport Hovav and Levin (2010) establish the following distinction.

    They suggest that 'result' roots specify scalar changes, i.e. directed change in the value of a single attribute (see Section 4.5). This typically involves motion or other change in some partipant. The scale can be a many-point scale (*advance, descend, fall, recede, rise, flatten, lengthen*) or a 'two-point scale' measuring only a binary change (*crack, arrive, reach*).

    In contrast, 'manner' roots specify nonscalar changes. These typically are complex changes, i.e. combinations of different types of change. This complexity means that there is no privileged scale measuring a single change. For example, the verb *jog* involves a specific pattern of movements of the legs—one that is different, for example, from the pattern associated with *walk*. Other manner distinctions are involved in *flap, flutter, rumble, sweep*, and so on.

    Rappaport Hovav and Levin (2010) claim that no verb lexicalizes both result and manner. The verbs in the preceding paragraph and in (142) can be seen to abide by that constraint, encoding either manner or result but not both. But there are apparent exceptions, such as the verb *cut*. To cut something is to sever it using a sharp instrument, which thus involves a specific manner. Moreover, *cut* passes the two tests for manner verbs proposed by Rappaport Hovav and Levin: it undergoes the conative alternation (144a–c), and it fails to undergo the causative alternation (144d).

(144)   a. Margaret cut the bread.
        b. Margaret cut at the bread.
        c. She got the blade pulled out and started cutting at the tape on Alex.[5]
        d. *The bread cut.

But *cut* also seems to entail a specific result. A general test for result is that appending *but nothing is different about it* yields a contradiction for result verbs (145) but not for others (146) (Beavers and Koontz-Garboden 2012):

(145)   a. #Shane just broke the vase, but nothing is different about it.
        b. #Shane just shattered the bottle, but nothing is different about it.
        c. #Shane just destroyed his house, but nothing is different about it.

(146)   a. Tracy just swept the floor, but nothing is different about it.
        b. Tracy just wiped the floor, but nothing is different about it.
        c. Bob just yelled, but nothing is different about him.
        d. Bob just ran quickly, but nothing is different about him.

Applying this test to *cut* yields a contradiction, suggesting it is a result verb:

(147)   #Dana cut the rope/paper/cake, but nothing is different about it.

Hence *cut* encodes both manner and result. Rappaport Hovav and Levin (2010) reply that *cut* does not lexicalize a specific manner, since it is rather flexible about the action performed and the instrument used. This shows the somewhat subjective nature of the categories.

A revised version of the manner–result complementarity constraint is proposed by Beavers and Koontz-Garboden (2012). They note a number of prima facie counterexamples. These include verbs indicating

---

[5] www.authorhouse.com/BookStore/ItemDetail?bookid=28127.aspx

methods of killing (*crucify, drown, electrocute, guillotine, hang*) and cooking (*barbecue, blanch, braise, broil, deep-fry, fry, grill, hardboil, microwave, poach, roast, sauté, stew, toast*). The manner is rather specific but the verbs also entail results:

(148) a. #Jane just drowned Joe, but nothing is different about him.
     b. #Shane just braised the chicken, but nothing is different about it.

However, Beavers and Koontz-Garboden (2012) claim that for these exceptional verbs the result state is not decomposable. They support this with the further claim that the adverb *again* cannot take scope over just the result state of *drown* (see Section 4.4.3). The sentence *John drowned the zombie again* presupposes that the zombie died specifically by drowning before, and not by just any method. With respect to the template theory, this means that *drown*, and other verbs like it, lack the elaborated accomplishment structure shown in (141d,e). Instead they have simpler structures like (141a).[6]

3.8 Category conversion

In most if not all languages, verbs can be converted to nouns, and nouns and other categories can be converted to verbs. By investigating which properties of a word are inherited under conversion, we are able to separate the lexical representation from the effects of the syntax proper, and see how the two interact. Lexical conversions from verbs to other categories and vice versa are discussed in Sections 3.8.1 and 3.8.2, respectively.

3.8.1 Deverbal nominals

In most languages, verbs have nominal cognates that are traditionally assumed to result from a morphological process in which verbs are converted to nouns. The phenomenon of nominalization has played a major role in the history of linguistic theorizing, some highlights of which are reviewed next.

---

[6] Since *drown* undergoes the causative alternation, a structure lacking CAUSE such as (141a) will not quite do for that verb (as pointed out to me by Robert Van Valin, p.c.). What is needed is a structure containing CAUSE with a resulting *event* ('The zombie drowned') but no result *state* ('The zombie is dead').

There is a systematic relation between sentences like (149a), gerund-ive nominals (GNs) like (149b) and derived nominals (DNs) like (149c). In early transformational grammar, the transformation was the only mechanism for capturing such systematic relations. This led early transformationalists to assume that a single deep structure under-lies all three and that transformations derive the different surface expressions.

(149)   a. The enemy destroyed the city.   (Sentence)
        b. [the enemy's destroying the city]$_{NP}$
           (was unfortunate).   (Gerundive Nominal)
        c. [the enemy's destruction of the city]$_{NP}$ (Derived Nominal)

Lees (1960) and Chomsky (1964: 47) posited transformational analyses in which virtually the same deep structure underlies all three (the only difference is that the structures for the nominals lack Tense). Trans-formations like (150) were responsible for deriving the nominals:

(150)   a. Gerundive Nominal transformation:
           NP – Aux1 (Aux2) VP1 $\Rightarrow$ NP+Possessive – ing (Aux2) VP1
        b. Derived Nominal transformation:
           NP – Aux – V – (NP) $\Rightarrow$ NP+Possessive – nom+V – (of+NP)

The gerundive nominalization transformation applies:

(151)   [the enemy]$_{NP}$ Aux [destroy the city]$_{VP}$ $\Rightarrow$
        [the enemy]$_{NP}$ +Possessive – ing [destroy the city]$_{VP}$

[Possessive] is spelled out as the 's clitic so [the enemy]NP +Possessive becomes *the enemy's*. A minor 'affix-hopping' transformation moves the *-ing* affix onto the following verb, to form *destroying*. The category of the whole gerundive is S, while it should be NP, so a special 'generalized transformation' allows the resulting S to be substituted for an NP within a larger construction.

The nominal in (149c) was derived by applying the derived nominal transformation:

(152)   [the enemy]$_{NP}$ Aux [destroy the city]$_{VP}$ $\Rightarrow$
        [the enemy]$_{NP}$ +Possessive nom+destroy of the city

The symbol 'nom' is a nominalizing feature which turns verbs or adjectives into nouns: nom+destroy is spelled out as *destruction*. As with the GNs, a 'generalized transformation' places the derived nominal in an NP position within a larger sentence. However, in the case of the DN it is more complicated. Chomsky (1964) noted that derived nominals allow determiners and adjectives while gerundive nominals do not:

(153)   a. the destruction of the city
        b. the enemy's wanton destruction of the city

(154)   a. *the destroying the city
        b. *the enemy's wanton destroying the city

But there were problems. To derive (153b) the DN must be allowed to substitute for only part of the NP, namely the N, leaving the Det slot open for *the* to appear. Adjectives modify only nouns, so it must be the category N, not V, that appears to the right of the adjective *wanton*. Chomsky (1965: 185) attempted to solve these problems with a more complex structure, but admitted that it was not an adequate solution.

In the classic paper 'Remarks on nominalization' Chomsky (1970) completely abandoned the earlier approach. There he argued that DNs are not derived by transformation at all, but rather are directly generated by the phrase structure rules for the NP. He showed that DNs contrast with GNs, which he continued to derive transformationally from clause-like deep structures as before.

Gerundive nominals can be formed with every verb in the language (except modals which do not inflect, hence lack the necessary *-ing* form). The complement possibilities of the gerundive precisely match the cognate verbs, whether transitive (see 149b), ditransitive (*his giving the girl a rose*), or patterns involving obliques, infinitives, or clausal complements. They permit the same sequences of auxiliaries as in clauses (*his having seen her*; *his being seen*), and take adverbial rather than adjectival modifiers (*his having recently fled*). The gerundive nominal bears a regular semantic relation to the proposition denoted by the corresponding clause. In short, apart from the genitive specifier and the nominal-like distribution of the GN as a whole, the internal structure of the GN is entirely clause-like.

Taking it a step further in the later setting of Government and Binding theory, Abney (1987) posited that the gerundive nominals simply contain a (base-generated) VP, thereby dispensing with a transformation to relate it to clausal syntax. Nominals became functional projections of the determiner, hence DPs. The head D, which can be a silent functional head, takes a VP as complement in the GN ([his D [liking her]$_{VP}$]$_{DP}$), and takes an NP as complement in ordinary nominals ([his D [picture of her]$_{NP}$]$_{DP}$). Bresnan (1997; 2001: ch. 13) adopted a lexicalist version of Abney's DP structure, but without the silent D head. The GN has the structure of a DP containing a VP and an optional possessive to its left.[7]

Derived nominals like *destruction* contrast sharply with gerundives like *destroying* in all of those respects. They are not fully productive: *shoot* ~ **shootation*. The complement possibilities are characteristic of nouns, not verbs, hence there are no NP objects or double objects (**the destruction the city*; **the gift Mary a Fiat*). They reject auxiliaries. The semantic relation to the cognate verb is highly idiosyncratic, varying from one word to the next:

The idiosyncratic character of the relation between the derived nominal and the associated verb has been so often remarked that discussion is superfluous. Consider, for example, such nominals as *laughter, marriage, construction, actions, activities, revolution, belief, doubt, conversion, permutation, trial, residence, qualifications, specifications*, and so on, with their individual ranges of meaning and varied semantic relations to the base forms. There are a few subregularities that have frequently been noted, but the range of variation and its rather accidental character are typical of lexical structure.   (Chomsky 1970: 19)

Chomsky therefore proposed that such nominals are derived from their base verbs in the lexicon prior to insertion into the syntactic structure. He called this the Lexicalist Hypothesis. The nominal inherits the subcategorization frame from the source verb, and minor transformations adjust the form of the nominal, e.g. inserting *of* before an object NP.

To strengthen his case against a transformational origin for DNs, Chomsky noted that certain clause types lack corresponding nominals:

(155)   a. John is easy to please.
　　　　b. John's being easy to please (delights Mary).　　　　GN
　　　　c. *John's easiness to please　　　　　　　　　　　　DN

(This example involves deadjectival rather than deverbal nominalization.) This is explained on the lexicalist hypothesis, assuming that (155a) is itself derived by transformation. Lexically the adjective *easy* takes a clausal subject: *(for us) to please John is easy*. Extraposition derives forms like *It is easy (for us) to please John*, and tough-movement raises the NP *John* to give (155a). Since *easy* does not directly subcategorize for the form in (155a), it is not available for *easiness* to inherit in the lexical derivation.

---

[7] But see Section 2.4.6 for Malouf's (2000) alternative.

. However, not all transformationally derived clauses lack corresponding nominalizations. There are nominalizations akin to a passive clause:

(156) a. The enemy destroyed the city.   (=149a)
       b. The city was destroyed (by the enemy).
       c. the city's destruction (by the enemy)   DN

For this Chomsky posited a distinct passive-like transformation applying within the NP, along with the passive transformation he assumed
for clauses. But Chomsky (1970) did not attempt a principled explanation of why certain transformations apply in only the verbal domain
and others apply in parallel in both the verbal and nominal domains.

    Rappaport (1983) did address that question. The generalization she
observed is that for a derived nominal to be acceptable the pre- and
post-nominal NPs must be thematic, that is, they must receive thematic
roles from the noun. There can be no raising to subject, as in tough
movement (155); there can be no raising to object (157a'); and no
expletives (157b',c'):

(157) a.   Herbie believed Louise to be a great singer.
       a'. *Herbie's belief of Louise to be a great singer
       b.   There arrived a young girl.
       b'. *there's arrival of a young girl
       c.   It annoys him that people are cruel.
       c'. *its annoyance of him that people are cruel

Rappaport concluded that what the noun inherits from the verb in the
lexical derivation is not its syntactic subcategorization frame (as in
158a) but its argument structure (as in 158b):

(158) a. *destroy* [__ NP]
       b. **destroy** ⟨ agent, theme ⟩

As further evidence, Rappaport observed that the prepositions selected
to mark arguments of the deverbal nominal are largely predictable
from the thematic role type, but not from the subcategorization. For
example, goal arguments can be direct objects of verbs, but in nominals
they are marked by *to*-PPs:

(159) a. Herbie promised Louise to write.
       b. Herbie's promise {to/*of} Louise to write

                                   (Rappaport 1983: 119, ex. 16)

Thus argument structures, not subcategorization frames, provide the necessary information to the syntactic rules for argument expression within nominals. Rappaport proposed that the argument structure associated with the root is held in common between the verb and its nominalization, and different rules specify the expression of those arguments in verbal and nominal domains.

Vestiges of both Chomsky's subcategorization view and Rappaport's argument structure view can be seen in the later non-transformational lexicalist models of lexical rules.[8] HPSG tends to favor the former, while LFG favors the latter (see Section 5.2). The HPSG rule for passive, for example, involves manipulating the subcategorization list of the active verb. In contrast, LFG's Lexical Mapping Theory assumes a single underspecified argument structure underlying both the active and passive.

Grimshaw (1990) argued that only some nouns have a thematic argument structure. Nouns with argument structure denote complex events, i.e. events with some internal structure; while nouns without argument structure denote simple events, hence lack event structure:

(160)   a. complex event (process):
            The doctor's examination (of the patient) was successful.
        b. simple event:
            (i) result nominals: denote the result of the corresponding event nominal
                 The examination/exam was on the table.
            (ii) other nouns denoting simple events: *trip, event, race, exam,...*
                 **The examination of the patients was on the table*
                 **the exam of the patients*
                                            (Grimshaw 1990: 47, 49)

Grimshaw's central claim is that nouns that are ambiguous between denoting simple and complex event have an argument structure only on the complex event reading. As a result, complements of such nouns appear to be optional.

When we force the complex event reading (also called the 'process reading') by adding certain types of adjective like *constant*, then often the internal argument becomes obligatory:

---

[8] Nunes (1993) presents a Role and Reference Grammar analysis of argument inheritance in derived nominals.

(161)   a. The assignment is to be avoided.
        b. The constant assignment of unsolvable problems is to be
           avoided.
        c. *The constant assignment is to be avoided.

(Grimshaw 1990: 50)

Similarly, the expression of an agent, whether as possessive or *by*-phrase,
can force the presence of an internal coargument:

(162)   a. the expression (of aggressive feelings)
        b. the expression of aggressive feelings by patients
        c. *the expression by patients

(Grimshaw 1990: 52)

Mixed nominals (*of-ing* nominals), i.e. true nouns formed with *-ing* and
taking the sort of complements nouns take (unlike gerundives), are
unambiguously complex, according to Grimshaw, taking obligatory
arguments, parallel to verbs:

(163)   a. the felling of the trees   (cp. they felled the trees)
        b. *the felling   (cp. *they felled)

(Grimshaw 1990: 50)

Process nominals have properties suggestive of mass nouns. According
to Grimshaw they reject *one* and *a(n)* and lack plurals (recall that for
Grimshaw gerundives are unambiguously process nominals):[9]

(164)   a. The shooting of rabbits is illegal.
        b. *A/*One/*That shooting of rabbits is illegal.
        c. *The shootings of rabbits are illegal.   (Grimshaw 1990: 56)

Grimshaw also noted that only process nominals can control into purpose clauses (165a) and allow clause-like temporal modifiers (165b):

(165)   a. the translation of the book (in order) to make it available to a
           wider readership
        a'. *the translations of the book (in order) to make it available
           to a wider readership
        b. the total destruction of the city in/*for two days
        b'. *Jack's trip in/for five hours   (Grimshaw 1990: 58)

---

[9] The word *shooting* can be used as a count noun when the victim is human: *the specific
guns used in the shootings of Andrew Young, Salada Smith, and Michael Ceriale* and *a
shooting of a 7-year-old girl.*

In short, the process nominals are more clause-like in their behavior. Grimshaw proposed that only process nominals have true argument structure, while the other nominals have only a referential argument.

An important difference between (non-gerundive) nominals and clauses is that the former denote events while the latter denote propositions (Vendler 1967; Zucchi 1993: 25). Only the former take place in time:

(166)   Nominals denote events
      a. John's looting of the house was slow/was sudden/took a long time.
      b. John's destruction of the house was slow/was sudden/took a long time.

(167)   Gerundives and clauses denote propositions
      a. #John's looting the house was slow/was sudden/took a long time.
      b. #That John looted the house was slow/was sudden/took a long time.

Propositions have a truth value, so to be suprised about a proposition is to be surprised that it is true. But our surprise about an event could involve any aspect of the event:

(168)   a. That he performed the song surprised us.
      b. His performing the song surprised us.
         ($\Rightarrow$ We were surprised by the fact that it happened at all.)

(169)   a. His performing of the song surprised us.
      b. His performance of the song surprised us.
         ($\Rightarrow$ could be surprised by some aspect of the event: how it was done, etc.)

Note that this semantic distinction depends upon the syntactic category of the head word: projections of verbs denote propositions, while projections of (event) nouns denote events. It is unclear how this correlation is explained on theories that attempt to do away with lexical categories (e.g. Borer 2005a; Marantz 1997).

More recent work on event nominals, especially within the Minimalist program, has built upon Grimshaw's distinction between process (or complex event) nominals and simple event nominals (see e.g. Borer 2003; Alexiadou 2001; 2009; Alexiadou et al. 2007). Borer (2003) claims, *contra* Grimshaw, that some nouns derived from adjectives and stative verbs seem to have an argument structure, citing examples like *The court's awareness of the problem* and *The party's satisfaction with the counting results*. Finer semantic distinctions among the result nominals have been drawn, with attempts to derive them from the process reading, which is usually taken as basic. Some result nominalizations like *creation* and *translation* can refer to a physical or abstract entity created in the verb-denoted event. Bisetto and Melloni (2005) claim that verbs of creation that imply the realization of an entity all have that property. They cite Italian *creare* 'to create'. Its nominalization *creazione* 'creation' can refer either to the event (the process reading, as in 170a) or to the concrete effected object (170b):

(170) a. La creazione di quella scultura (da parte dell'artista) fu lunga
          e difficoltosa.
          'The creation of that sculpture (by the artist) was long and
          troubled.'
       b. La creazione (*della scultura) è bella.
          'The creation (*of the sculpture) is beautiful.'
                                         (Bisetto and Melloni 2005: 397–8)

On the entity result reading, the nominal rejects an 'of'-phrase complement, as shown in (170b). Such 'object result' nominals absorb the verb's internal argument, since the nominal refers to the entity filling that role (Bisetto and Melloni 2005: 398). While these readings fall into recognizable patterns, there appears to be considerable idiosyncratic variation across verbs and languages. For example, Italian *costruzione* 'construction' can only refer to an entity such as a building or edifice, but not a table, for example. English *construction* is similar, for some but not all speakers: Pustejovsky (1995: 94) gives the example *The construction is standing on the next street*, but for the present author *construction* cannot refer to a building so the example sounds odd. The noun *obstruction* can refer to the result state (*The obstruction may be temporary or permanent*) or a physical object (*We extracted the obstruction and disposed of it*). As noted in the quotation from Chomsky preceding example (155), the semantic relation between derived nominals and the cognate verb is characterized by considerable idiosyncratic variation with various subregularities.

English nominalizations in -er (*talker*) and -ee (*payee*) are used to refer to participants in the verb-denoted event. Rough equivalents of -er nominals are found in many languages, while morphology corresponding to -ee is typologically rarer (Alexiadou 2014). English -er nominalization is highly productive for subject arguments, whether in the role of agents (*writer, driver, speaker*), instruments (*opener, paper-cutter*), experiencers (*hearer*), or other roles that subjects have. In addition some correspond to complement arguments, but this is not productive: *fryers, keepers* (things one fries or keeps), *diners* (places where one dines), *sleeper* (train car where one sleeps), and so on (examples from Alexiadou 2014).

Zero derivation of nouns from verbs is quite common in English: *cut, bend, break, burn, moan, laugh*, and so on. Many of them denote the result state of the event denoted by the cognate verb, while others seem to refer to the event itself. Particular deverbal nouns have gone in and out of fashion throughout the history of the language. The *Oxford English Dictionary* lists uses of *distroie* (*destroy*) as a noun:

(171)   The sweete boy, wailinge most rufullie his frendes distroie.[10]
          (1616)

This is not grammatical in present-day English. Newer or less well-accepted uses are sometimes prescriptively stigmatized by language pundits. In a *New York Times* blog entitled 'Those irritating verbs as nouns', Hitchings (2013) discusses 'irritating' locutions like *I have a solve, the magician's reveal, Let's all focus on the build, That's the take-away from today's seminar*, and *an epic fail*.

3.8.2 Denominal verbs

A key issue addressed in the previous section is what kind of lexical information associated with the verb, such as its argument structure, is inherited by the deverbal noun. When nouns (*a saddle, a bench*) are converted to verbs (*saddle the horse, bench the player*) the opposite question arises: how does the verb acquire an argument structure that is absent from the source noun? In the common type considered here, the source noun denotes an entity that normally participates in actions of the type denoted by the verb, as in these examples and their para-phrases (from Clark and Clark 1979):

(172)   a. Jane blanketed the bed.
          b. Jane did something to cause it to come about that [the bed had one or more blankets on it].

---

[10] From John Lane (1616), *Continuation of Chaucer's Squire's Tale*, Part IX, p. 476 (Chaucer Society, 1887–90).

(173)   a. Kenneth kenneled the dog.
        b. Kenneth did something to cause it to come about that [the dog was in a kennel].

Some of the deverbal nouns have become common and conventional-ized, while others are formed on the fly, suggesting a highly productive process at work.

In the earlier Generative Semantics tradition, James McCawley pro-posed to literally derive denominals from sentences with the corres-ponding verb, for example, deriving (174a) from (174b) (McCawley 1971: 28–9, cited in Clark and Clark 1979):

(174)   a. John nailed the note to the door.
        b. John CAUSED a NAIL to HOLD the note ON the door.

But Clark and Clark rejected syntactic derivations of this kind. For common, conventionalized denominal verbs there are several prob-lems. First, the noun origins of many such verbs have been lost. People do not think of Captain Boycott or Judge Lynch when they interpret *boycott the store* or *lynch the prisoner*. Even transparent denominals often do not contain the noun's meaning: *land* does not mean 'put onto land' since one can land on a lake. See Kiparsky (1997) for more examples of such semantic 'bleaching' in denominal verbs. Also denominal verbs usually exhibit semantic idiosyncrasies: *land (the plane)* means 'put down', while *ground (the plane)* means 'keep down', rather than the reverse. Clark and Clark conclude that most common denominal verbs have become fully or partially specialized, and are not fully predictable by derivations.

Other denominal verbs are clearly innovations, and as noted by Clark and Clark (1979), even the common, conventionalized forms were once innovations. So the theory needed for the innovative process should form the basis for a theory of the conventionalized forms as well. We will review Clark and Clark's proposal and then reconsider a syntactic account.

Clark and Clark propose a pragmatic account of innovative denom-inal verbs based on Grice's cooperative principle (Grice 1975). Innova-tive denominal verbs have an indefinitely large number of potential senses, and their interpretation depends on the context, especially the cooperation of the speaker and listener. Innovative denominal verbs are governed by the following convention set out in (175):

(175)   The innovative denominal verb convention
        Using an innovative denominal verb sincerely, the speaker
        means to denote the kind of situation that he has good reason
        to believe that on this occasion the listener can readily compute
        uniquely on the basis of their mutual knowledge in such a way
        that the parent noun denotes one role in the situation, and the
        remaining surface arguments of the denominal verb denote
        other roles in the situation.   (Clark and Clark 1979: 787)

Many contextual factors influence whether the speaker 'has good reason to believe that on this occasion the listener can readily compute' the
right situation. Obviously a key factor is the listener's presumed knowledge of the meaning of the noun. Clark and Clark therefore base their
theory on an investigation of noun meanings, drawing on prototype
theory (see Section 2.4.4).

Nouns are classified according to the prototypical predominant
features of the entities they denote. These can involve (i) their physical
characteristics (color, shape, weight, breakability, etc.); (ii) their normal
ontogeny, e.g. *bricks* are molded from clay, baked in ovens, and sold by
building-supply firms; and (iii) their potential roles, e.g. *bricks* are
ordinarily cemented with mortar in horizontal rows to form walls,
among other uses. (These three dimensions prefigure Pustejovsky's
later qualia; see Section 2.3.3.4).

Some examples: (a) *Placeables* are things whose conventional role is
to be placed with respect to other objects: *carpets* go on floors. Clark
and Clark note that carpets depend for their characterization on floors,
not the reverse. Hence carpets are placeables (carpets go on floors), and
not places (floors do not inherently or typically 'go under carpets').
(b) *Places* are things with respect to which other objects are conventionally placed: *kennels* are places where one ordinarily keeps dogs.
(c) *Time intervals* like *summer* are temporal locations for events and
processes. (d) *Agents* are things whose predominant feature is that they
do certain things: *butchers* cut meat professionally. (e) *Receivers* are
things picked out for their role in receiving or experiencing things, e.g.
witnesses. (f) With *result* nouns, ontogeny is important: they denote
end-products of some action or transformation: *widows* result from the
loss of their husbands. (g) *Antecedents* characterize the beginnings of
some actions or transformations, such as materials out of which some
products can be made. (h) *Instruments* must be physically present for
certain actions to take place.

(176) Principal categories and their predominant features. The e variable corresponds to the entity denoted by the noun (Clark and Clark 1979: 792, table 1)

	Category	Examples	Predominant feature
a.	Placeables	*blankets, spice*	$Loc(e,x)$
b.	Places	*kennel, bench*	$Loc(x,e)$
c.	Time intervals	*summer, weekend*	$During(x,e)$
d.	Agents	*butcher, usher*	$Do(e,x)$
e.	Receivers	*witness, boycott*	$Happen\text{-}to(x,e)$
f.	Results	*group, powder*	$Become(x,e)$
g.	Antecedents	*piece together*	$Become(e,x)$
h.	Instruments	*handcuff, autoclave*	$With(Do(x,y),e)$

The situation denoted by a denominal verb is projected from the predominant features of the source noun. Location verbs like *to bench* take their form from the name of the locative goal of the action, as in *bench the player*, which means roughly 'put the player on the bench'. Locatum verbs like *to paint* take their form from the name of the item being located, as in *paint the house*, which means roughly 'put paint on the house'. Some nouns like *shelf* have at least two predominant features: they are places that things are put on, and placeables that are put on walls. This has allowed *shelf* to establish two meanings, in *shelve the books* and *shelve the closet* (Clark and Clark 1979: 793).

Turning now to syntactic accounts, an influential proposal by Hale and Keyser (1993) revives the older generative semantics approach (recall (174)). Hale and Keyser derive denominal verbs such as *paint* and *shelve* from a syntactic structure containing the cognate nouns *paint* and *shelf*.

(177) a. We painted the house.
       b. We [[ ]$_V$ [$_{VP}$ house [$_{V'}$ CAUSE [$_{PP}$ WITH paint]]]].
       c. We [$_{V'}$ V1 [$_{VP}$ house [$_{V'}$ V2 [$_{PP}$ P$_{with}$ paint]]]].

(178) a. We shelved the books.
       b. We [[ ]$_V$ [$_{VP}$ books [$_{V'}$ CAUSE [$_{PP}$ ON shelf]]]].
       c. We [$_{V'}$ V1 [$_{VP}$ books [$_{V'}$ V2 [$_{PP}$ P$_{on}$ shelf]]]].

The nominal root *paint* or *shelf* moves to the empty verb position V1, having combined en route with the abstract silent preposition shown here as P$_{with}$ (cp. 'provide the house with paint') or P$_{on}$ (cp. 'put books on the shelf'); and with an abstract silent verb in the position indicated by V2. Hale and Keyser propose that purely syntactic factors restrict this movement operation to targeting the object of the (abstract) preposition, and not the verb's object, thus explaining the impossibility of *house the paint and *book the shelf.

Partly echoing Clark and Clark's rejection of McCawley's analysis, Kiparsky (1997) disputes Hale and Keyser's proposal in a detailed critique. Like Clark and Clark (1979), Kiparsky sees the derivation of such verbs from nouns as conditioned by conceptual knowledge about the noun—information that is absent from the syntax-like structures posited by Hale and Keyser. Thus Hale and Keyser's proposed system fails to prevent the insertion of the noun root into the wrong structure. For example, substituting paint for books and house for shelf in (178b) yields the unwanted sentence *We housed the paint, wrongly predicted to have the meaning 'cause paint to go on the house'—i.e. 'paint the house'. Kiparsky (1997: 482) specifies a principle similar to Clark and Clark's: 'If an action is named after a thing, it involves a canonical use of the thing.' It is a canonical use of paint to put it on houses, so the action (to paint) is named after the thing (paint); but getting painted is not a canonical use of houses. This explanation crucially depends upon conceptual information that is associated with the words but absent from the syntactic or semantic form. Thus noun-to-verb conversion is a lexical and not a syntactic process.

An intermediate 'lexical syntax' view is to build the verb meanings from lexical semantic decomposition structures that include the noun meanings as components (see Section 4.4). If these semantic structures have a regular syntax, then the account is syntactic in that sense. But it only governs the formation of word meanings and is distinct from the syntax responsible for combining words into sentences. Kiparsky posits lexical decompositions in the style of Bierwisch and Schreuder (1992) and Wunderlich (1997a):

(179)   Locatum: $\lambda z \lambda y \lambda x$ [CAUSE (x, (HAVE-ON (y,z)) & SADDLE(z)]   (to saddle)
        Location: $\lambda z \lambda y \lambda x$ [CAUSE (x, (BE-IN (y,z)) & CORRAL(z)]   (to corral)

See Rappaport Hovav and Levin (1998) for a similar proposal within their templatic approach. On Kiparsky's account, the conversion from noun to verb is conditioned by the rule above: If an action is named after a thing, it involves a canonical use of the thing. That rule makes reference to 'canonical' uses (as opposed to reference to a particular token use), hence conceptual knowledge of the noun meaning is required. The need for access to conceptual information suggests a lexical process.

Meanwhile, one might wonder whether there is a need for access to facts of the syntax proper such as part of speech labels and phrasal configuration. Hale and Keyser assume so in their syntactic account of deadjectival verbs. They note that deadjectival *clear* allows the anti-causative, while the denominal *shelve* does not:

(180) a. We cleared the screen.
       b. The screen cleared.

(181) a. We shelved the books.
       b. *The books shelved.

Hale and Keyser claim that, more generally, deadjectival verbs (*clear*) allow anti-causative while denominal verbs (*shelve*) do not. For them, this follows from two main syntactic premises: (i) Predicates must have subjects, and subjects must have predicates (Principle of Full Interpretation). (ii) APs are predicates, so they project specifiers, but NPs are not predicates, so they do not project specifiers. Since NPs lack internal specifier positions for subjects, the denominal verb lacks an internal subject position (a further assumption is that the verb inherits the specification of the noun). By the Principle of Full Interpretation it must have a subject, but it lacks an internal subject position so it must have an external subject. Hence detransitivization is impossible. Conversely, incorporating an adjective (i.e. moving it to a verb position) produces a verb with an internal subject. However, the putative generalization has many exceptions in both directions: denominal verbs that allow agent-omission (*carmelize, short-circuit, carbonize, gasify*, etc.); and deadjectival verbs that disallow agent omission (*italicize, visualize, legalize*, etc.) (Kiparsky 1997). Kiparsky proposes a semantic account instead (see Section 3.4.2).

In addition to nouns and adjectives, a few English prepositions have been converted to verbs: *upping the price, outing someone, downing some pills*. This is not productive, and only works for a small subset of locative prepositions that can be used intransitively: *the price is up; he is out; the pills are down*. Some serial verb languages have very few prepositions, and instead use verbs where English might use a preposition. An example is Thai ((182a,b) are repeated from (129, 130)):

(182) a. Piti den   khâw   rooŋrian.
          Piti walk enter school
          'Piti walked into the school.'

b. Piti den   pay thửŋ   rooŋrian mửawaanníi.
   Piti walk go   arrive school   yesterday
   'Piti walked to school yesterday.'

c. Ka:nda: cháy mî:t hàn kày.
   Kanda   use   knife cut   chicken
   'Kanda cut the chicken with the knife.'

d. Ka:nda: cháy mî:t hàn kày   hâ: y nɔ̂:ŋ.
   Kanda   use   knife cut   chicken give sister

   (i) 'Kanda cut the chicken with the knife (and) gave (it) to
       her sister.' (sequential)

   (ii) 'Kanda cut(s) the chicken with the knife to give to her
       sister.' (purposive)

Examples (182a,b) are from Wechsler (2008b: exx. 1 and 2); examples
(182c,d) are from Sudmuk (2005: 49, exx. 75, 76). These sources use
different transcription systems.

Similarly, *cháy* 'use' marks instruments and *hâ: y* 'give' marks recipi-
ents, in serial VP constructions: *cháy mî:t* 'with (a) knife', *hây nɔ̂:ŋ* 'to
(my) sister'. Both the Thai verb *khâw* in (182a) and its English translation *into* indicate the transition from outside to inside, in a motion
event. In both cases the transition predicate, whether verb or preposition, is aspectually specified as telic and punctual, and in both languages that specification has been shown to control the aspect of the
clause as a whole (Wechsler 2008b). The meaning is virtually identical
but the syntax differs.

3.9 Conclusion

The syntactic argument expression of verbs is not random, but subject
to constraints. There are strong tendencies regarding the choice of a
participant as the subject of the verb. Arguments can be left unexpressed, under specific conditions that vary across languages, leading to
variable polyadicity. New participant arguments can also be added.
Often an object or subject position exhibits some flexibility as to
which participant is expressed by it, and sometimes an alternative
oblique complement is available for expressing the excluded participant. Finally, words from one part-of-speech category can be converted
into another, providing rich evidence for the lexical representation of
the source word.

4

Lexical semantic structure

4.1 Introduction

This chapter covers the lexical semantic structures that have been posited to relate syntax to word meaning and explain argument realization patterns.[1] The 'predicate argument structure' of a lexical expression consists of a semantic relation and a list of arguments (see Section 1.2). In order to explain the mapping between word meaning and syntax and to account for generalizations applying across words, the predicate argument structures must be further classified with more detailed semantic and syntactic information. That information generally takes the form of either thematic role types such as Agent, Instrument, Patient, etc., or lexical decomposition into a structure involving more basic semantic relations such as CAUSE and BECOME.

Some theories would complement or replace lexical structure with compositional semantics in the syntax, assuming that some or all apparent components of complex word meaning are actually composed within the syntax, through the semantic combination of the word with silent 'light verbs.' On radical neo-Davidsonian models these abstract light verbs replace predicate argument structure altogether. Since the point of such theories is to deny the existence of (some or all) lexical semantic structure, they are not discussed in this chapter, but rather postponed until Chapters 5 and 6 (see especially Sections 5.4 and 6.5). But it should be clear that every semantic entity discussed in this chapter could alternatively be represented in a syntactic phrase structure diagram.

---

[1] This chapter contains material from Wechsler (2005b).

4.2 Thematic roles

4.2.1 Basics of thematic roles

The verb *bake* in sentence (1a) expresses a **bake'** relation between two participants, the Baker (in this case, Jonas) and the product of the baking event or Bakee (in this case, the gingerbread). Using the standard logical notation in which $R(x_1, \ldots, x_n)$ represents an n-place relation R with arguments $x_1, \ldots, x_n$, the thematic structure of (1a) is shown in (1b):

(1) a. Jonas is baking the gingerbread.
    b. **bake'**(*Jonas, the-gingerbread*)
    c. **bake'**(Baker: *Jonas*, Bakee: *the-gingerbread*)

In an 'ordered argument system' (Dowty 1989), the arguments are distinguished from one another in order to determine which one will be subject, object, and so on. The argument positions can be given the explicit labels Baker and Bakee, as in (1c). This notation allows us to distinguish the different roles of the subjects in the intransitive (2a) and (2b):

(2) a. Jonas is baking.   **bake'**(Baker: *Jonas*)
    b. The gingerbread is baking.   **bake'**(Bakee: *the-gingerbread*)

The semantic roles played by the participants in the denoted event or state, such as Baker and Bakee, are called 'thematic roles' or 'theta-roles' (θ-roles). While (1) and (2) show the thematic structures of sentences, we may disregard the fillers of the roles and notate the thematic structure contributed by the verb *bake*: **bake'**(Baker: x, Bakee: y).

Dowty (1989) distinguished individual thematic roles from thematic role types. Baker and Bakee are individual thematic roles, since they are specific to one verb. To compare the behavior of thematic roles across many verbs, roles are assigned to more general thematic role types such as Agent and Theme. For example, the thematic roles played by the subjects of transitive *bake*, *eat*, and *sing* in (3) have in common that the individual filling the role is normally understood as purposefully causing the event to occur, hence they may be assigned the Agent thematic role type.

(3) a. Jonas is baking the gingerbread.   **bake'**(Agent: x, Theme: y)
    b. Jonas is eating the gingerbread.   **eat'**(Agent: x, Theme: y)
    c. Marie is singing.   **sing'**(Agent: x)

The role played by the objects of *bake* and *eat*, often called the Theme thematic role type, involves the participant undergoing some change in virtue of the action: the gingerbread comes into existence as a result of baking (3a) and goes out of existence as a result of eating (3b). See Section 3.2.1, (5), for a list of thematic role type definitions.

Argument structure is often conceived as a level of representation intermediate between semantics and syntax. For example, a thematic role type such as Agent has a rough semantic definition on the one hand (see Section 4.2.3, example (6a)) and a set of characteristic syntactic properties on the other (e.g. an Agent role typically gets expressed as the grammatical subject rather than the object). Because of this intermediate status, the technical terminology specialized for thematic structure has borrowed from both sides. Terms reflecting the semantic status include the terms Agent, Theme, Goal, and so on that we have already used. Terms borrowed from the side of morphological or syntactic expression include the nomenclatures of 'Deep Cases' (Fillmore 1968; see Section 4.2.3) and 'deep grammatical relations' such as 'logical subject/ object' and 'underlying subject/object.' Proposals vary, but most of them assume that this level of thematic structure has a dual status, interfacing with both semantics and syntax.

The analysis of thematic structure allows linguists to describe and explain the complex ways in which the syntax of a clause depends on the meaning of the main verb or other predicator. A related goal is to explain semantic patterns of lexicalization, i.e. to identify any universal and language-specific constraints on possible word meanings.

4.2.2 Pāṇini's kārakas

The classical Sanskrit grammar Aṣṭādhyāyī ('Eight Books'), created by the Indian grammarian Pāṇini at a time variously estimated at 600 or 300 BC (Robins 1979: 137), includes a sophisticated theory of thematic structure that remains influential to this day. (This section draws heavily from Kiparsky and Staal 1969.) Pāṇini's Sanskrit grammar is a system of rules for converting semantic representations of sentences into phonetic representations (Kiparsky and Staal 1969: 84). This derivation proceeds through two intermediate stages: the level of *kāraka* relations, which are comparable to the thematic role types described above; and the level of morphosyntax ((4), adapted from Kiparsky and Staal 1969: 84).

(4)   Semantic representations

⇓

karaka relations

⇓

Morphosyntax

⇓

Phonological representations

Grammar rules map each of the kārakas to a basic semantic relation, and a basic morphosyntactic expression. More specialized variants of both types of rule are specified as well, with the basic relation and basic expression acting as defaults whenever the conditions for the variants are not met.

For example, the kāraka called *apādāna* (Source) has as its basic semantic relation 'the fixed point from which something recedes.' But with certain verbs *apādāna* is used instead for special relations such as the source of fear, the object of hiding from, hindering, or learning from, and so on. The basic expression of *apādāna* is ablative case. The basic semantic relation of the *karman* kāraka (roughly 'Theme') is 'that which is primarily desired'; its basic expression is accusative case. The *karaṇa* kāraka (Instrument) is associated with the basic semantic relation of 'the most effective means.' While its basic expression is Instrumental case, some verbs are instead specified for the genitive case to express the *karana* (see (5)). Other kārakas include *sampradāna* (Indirect Object), *adhikaraṇa* (Locative), *kartṛ* (Agent), and *hetu* (Cause).

Alternations in the expression of arguments are handled with optional rules. For example, the kāraka *karana*, defined as the relation 'with the most effective means,' is normally expressed with instrumental case, as in (5a). But some verbs, such as *yajate* 'sacrifice,' are associated with an optional rule specifying genitive case for *karana*, as in (5b).

(5)   a. Paraśunā   vṛkṣaṃ   chinatti.
          axe.INS   tree.ACC   cuts
          'He cuts the tree with an axe.'

       b. Ghṛtasya/   Ghṛtena   yajate.
          butter.INS/   butter.GEN   sacrifice
          'He sacrifices with clarified butter.'

The more general instrumental case rule acts as a default, applying when the more specialized optional genitive rule is not selected.

Given this interplay between alternative mapping rules, the intermediate level of kārakas greatly simplifies the grammar. For example, a range of (possibly related) semantic relations map onto the *karman* kāraka. This kāraka can be expressed in a range of ways, including compounds formed with the suffix *-aN*, the Accusative case, and the 'objective' use of the Genitive case. Kiparsky and Staal (1969: 110) point out: 'If semantic representations were mapped directly into surface structures, without the mediating kārakas, the list of surface structures to which *karman* can correspond...would have to be enumerated anew for each semantic relation which can underlie a *karman* relation.' In short, the kārakas act as important equivalence classes for the statement of linguistic rules and generalizations.[2] The rules for actives and passives, for impersonal passives, for infinitive verbs and nominals, for the use of particular cases, and for the interpretation of unexpressed agents of infinitives and participles are expressed in terms of the kārakas.

4.2.3 Thematic roles in modern generative grammar

Fillmore's (1968) Case Grammar, and much subsequent work, revived Pāṇini's proposals in a modern setting. A principle objective of Case Grammar was to identify argument positions that may have different realizations in syntax, e.g. the theme of the verb *bake* that is expressed as the object of (2a) and the subject of (2b). Fillmore argued that for many grammatical processes, the reference to purely syntactic relations like subject and object is insufficient, and must be supplemented or even replaced by a reference to thematic role types, which he called 'deep cases' or simply 'cases.'

Fillmore hypothesized 'a set of universal, presumably innate, concepts which identify certain types of judgments human beings are capable of making about the events that are going on around them' (Fillmore 1968: 24). He posited the following preliminary list of cases, noting however that 'Additional cases will surely be needed' (and indeed Fillmore added more in later works):

---

[2] See Section 5.2.1 for a similar argument for grammatical relations like subject and object, from Bresnan (2001: 95).

(6) a. Agent (A), the typically animate perceived instigator of the
        action.
     b. Instrument (I), inanimate force or object causally involved in
        the action or state.
     c. Dative (D), the animate being affected by the state or action.
     d. Factitive (F), the object or being resulting from the action or
        state.
     e. Locative (L), the location or spatial orientation of the state or
        action.
     f. Objective (O), 'the semantically most neutral case . . . conceivably
        the concept should be limited to things which are affected by the
        action or state.'

Fillmore provided linguistic evidence for his deep cases, which are
called thematic roles here. He argued for example that the subjects of
(7a) and (7b) have different thematic roles, namely Agent and Instrument respectively, on the basis of the facts in (7c–e), assuming biuni-
queness of role assignment (exactly one role per argument Noun
Phrase). The unacceptable (7d) represents a failed attempt to assign
both Agent and Instrument roles to the bracketed conjoined subject,
while in (7e) the Instrument role is assigned to two different
dependents.

(7) a. John broke the window.
     b. A hammer broke the window.
     c. John broke the window (with a hammer).
     d. *[John and a hammer] broke the window.
     e. *A hammer broke the window with a chisel.
     f. The window broke.

For the mapping from deep cases to surface syntactic structure, Fillmore introduced the influential idea of a hierarchy of preference for
subject selection. The Agent, Instrument, and Objective roles form a
hierarchy for expression as the subject versus object of the verb: 'If there
is an A, it becomes the subject; otherwise if there is an I, it becomes the
subject; otherwise the subject is O' (Fillmore 1968: 33). This rule
accounts for the alternations in (7), assuming that the verb *break*
obligatorily selects O and optionally selects A and/or I.

This notion of a universal 'thematic hierarchy' relevant to linking has
since reappeared in many variants (e.g. Jackendoff 1972; Foley and Van
Valin 1984; Bresnan and Kanerva 1989). A relative (often partial)

ordering is imposed on thematic role types and on grammatical relations, as in this simplified system (repeated from Section 3.2.1):

(8)   a. agent > beneficiary > recipient/experiencer > instrument >
         theme > location
      b. Subject > Object

Linking between these two hierarchies must respect both orders, so
that, for example, in a transitive Agent/Theme verb, the Agent must
link to Subject and Theme to Object, and not the other way around (i.e.
the linked structure is an order isomorphism). This idea has been
influential in several different syntactic frameworks. Wechsler (1995)
developed this variety of hierarchical linking scheme within the framework of Head-Driven Phrase Structure Grammar (Section 5.2.2). Lexical Mapping Theory uses both absolute constraints ('Agents cannot
map to objects') and relativistic ones based on a thematic hierarchy
(Section 5.2.1).

   As for why subject selection across languages seems to be governed
by a thematic hierarchy, there are two main classes of explanations
(Bresnan and Kanerva 1989: 23–4; Levin and Rappaport Hovav 2005:
170–75). The first view focuses on the function of the subject as the
default bearer of the *topic* discourse function, hence expressing the
participant that is already familiar in the discourse. The hierarchy has
been seen as a relative ranking of topic-worthiness of different semantic
roles. Narrative discourse tends to portray the successive actions of an
agent, so agentive roles are the best candidates for topical arguments.
More generally, one tends to track human participants across a discourse more often than inanimate objects, so primarily human roles
like beneficiary, recipient, and experiencer are also high on the list for
topic-worthiness.

   The other view is that the hierarchy reflects lexico-semantic constituent structure. Kiparsky (1987) represents the thematic hierarchy
not in terms of relative prominence but in terms of semantic constituency, where the lower roles are semantically closer to the verb:

(9)   ⟨ Agent ⟨ Instrument ⟨ Recipient/Experiencer ⟨ Theme ⟨ Location
      verb ⟩⟩⟩⟩⟩

The proposal is that there is a tendency for 'lexico-semantic constituents' to be lexicalized. This tendency can be seen in patterns of noun
incorporation in those languages allowing it. Lower roles tend to
incorporate more freely, leaving higher roles to be expressed in the

usual analytic manner, while the converse is dispreferred (Mithun 1984). Similarly, idioms show a preference for including lower roles while leaving a higher role as the free position in the idiom (Kiparsky 1987). Kiparsky observed that Verb+Locative idioms are very common (*throw X to the wolves, bring X to light*), as are Verb+Theme idioms (*give X a hand, show X the door*), and even V+Theme+Locative idioms (*bring home the bacon, let the cat out of the bag*) but V+Theme+Recipient idioms are rare (*give the devil his due*) and other combinations involving higher roles (*Verb+Recipient, Verb+Agent, Verb+Goal+Agent*, etc.) are more scarce when the free position is lower on the hierarchy. (However, this characterization of idiom formation patterns was challenged by Nunberg et al. 1994.) In some lexical decomposition theories the linking to arguments is directly based on depth of embedding in the decomposition structure (this view is described in Section 4.4.4.1). On that view, the thematic roles can be seen as notations for positions in such a structure (see Gruber 1976; Foley and Van Valin 1984; Levin and Rappaport Hovav 2005: 165–70). Finally, Bresnan and Kanerva (1989: 24) pointed out that the topic-worthiness and semantic structure hypotheses can be unified, assuming that the least topical argument types are most easily lexicalized with a verb.

Pāṇini's theory of kārakas, Fillmore's Case Grammar, and other theories of thematic role types have been criticized (Dowty 1989; 1991; Levin and Rappaport Hovav 2005). One problem is the difficulty of finding reliable diagnostics or definitions for the role types. Semantic criteria tend to lead to fragmentation into finer and finer subtypes. Another problem is that a single event participant often seems to play more than one role: *John* in *John ran to the store* is arguably both the Agent (since John volitionally carries out the action) and the Theme (since he undergoes a change of location). In the event described by *Beth bought the car from Ann for $500*, Beth has three roles: she is simultaneously the Agent, the Recipient (of the car), and the Source (of the money) (Jackendoff 1990: 59). This last problem does not afflict decomposition theories, described in Section 4.4.

4.3 Proto-roles

Dowty (1991) proposed a theory of linking based on 'prototype theory' (see Section 2.4.4). The idea behind his 'proto-role' approach is that there are really only two thematic-role-like concepts involved in argument selection, and these are 'cluster concepts,' not discretely defined ones. He calls them the Agent Proto-Role and Patient Proto-Role.[3] These are to be the (only) thematic categories on which linking principles are stated. These are the specific properties Dowty (1991: 572) gives:

(10) Contributing properties for the Agent Proto-Role
     a. volitional involvement in the event or state
     b. sentience (and/or perception)
     c. causing an event or change of state in another participant
     d. movement (relative to the position of another participant)
     (e. exists independently of the event named by the verb)

(11) Contributing properties for the Patient Proto-Role
     a. undergoes change of state
     b. incremental theme
     c. causally affected by another participant
     d. stationary relative to movement of another participant
     (e. does not exist independently of the event, or at all)

The properties are 'prototypical': no single property is essential for either role. Instead, Dowty gives the following procedure:

(12) Argument selection principle: In predicates with grammatical subject and object, the argument for which the predicate entails the greatest number of Proto-Agent properties will be lexicalized as the subject of the predicate; the argument having the greatest number of Proto-Patient entailments will be lexicalized as the direct object.   (Dowty 1991: 576)

Notice that there is no attempt to find a unifying semantics behind the lists of properties in (10) and (11). Proto-Agent and Proto-Patient are 'cluster concepts' or 'higher-order generalizations about meanings' that need not even be considered as part of the competence grammar.

---

[3] Prefiguring Dowty's proto-roles is the related proposal for two 'macro-roles' (Foley and Van Valin 1984). Foley and Van Valin's Actor and Undergoer macro-roles are similar to proto-roles in that there are only two of them and they govern linking. But on Foley and Van Valin's system they are not ontological primitives, but are determined by linking to a richer underlying semantic decomposition. For that reason discussion of them is postponed until Section 4.4.4.2. See Van Valin (1999) for an overview of proposals for generalized roles and a critical comparison between Dowty's (1991) proto-roles and Role and Reference Grammar macro-roles.

Instead, Dowty suggests that the argument selection principle (12) acts as a default in the acquisition of lexical items.

A number of linguists borrowed aspects of the proto-role idea into their models of competence grammar (among others Ackerman and Moore 2001; Davis 2001). Davis's (2001) theory of linking between word meaning and syntax uses proto-role properties in a multiple inheritance type hierarchy in the Head-Driven Phrase Structure Grammar framework. Each proto-role property is encoded in the lexicon as a type within a rich hierarchy of types and subtypes. Davis assumes two 'macro-roles' called Actor and Undergoer (following the terminology of Foley and Van Valin 1984), which are, for Davis, reified versions of Dowty's (1991) Proto-Agent and Proto-Patient cluster concepts. For example, corresponding to (10c) ('causing an event or change of state in another participant') and (11c) ('causally affected by another participant') is an abstract 'affect' relation with two arguments, Actor and Undergoer. This semantic relation takes its place within a hierarchy of relations of increasing specificity. Particular verbs inherit semantic information from those types, and thereby also inherit the classification of roles into the two macro-roles, which determines the linking to the syntax. (See Section 5.2.2.3.)

4.4 Decomposition approaches

In 'lexical decomposition,' word meaning is decomposed into a structure built from more basic semantic relations such as CAUSE, BECOME, GO, STAY. Decomposition will be illustrated with an analysis of the verbs *buy* and *sell*. Those verbs can be decomposed into the following thematic structures, where GO$_{Poss}$ represents the transfer of possession (adapted from Jackendoff 1990: 191):

(13) a. *sell* ('α sold γ to β for δ')

$$\text{CAUSE}\ (\alpha, \left[\begin{array}{l} \text{GO}_{Poss}(\gamma, [\text{FROM}(\alpha)\ \text{TO}(\beta)]) \\ \text{GO}_{Poss}(\delta, [\text{FROM}(\beta)\ \text{TO}(\alpha)]) \end{array} \right])$$

b. *buy* ('β bought γ from α for δ')

$$\text{CAUSE}\ (\beta, \left[\begin{array}{l} \text{GO}_{Poss}(\gamma, [\text{FROM}(\alpha)\ \text{TO}(\beta)]) \\ \text{GO}_{Poss}(\delta, [\text{FROM}(\beta)\ \text{TO}(\alpha)]) \end{array} \right])$$

Variables index the argument positions, allowing a single participant to play multiple roles. The same entity α is both the source of the possession transfer and the causer of the event, in (13a). These sentences illustrate:

(14) a. Ann sold the car to Beth for $500.
$$\text{CAUSE (Ann,} \begin{bmatrix} \text{GO}_{\text{Poss}}(\text{car, [FROM(Ann) TO(Beth)]}) \\ \text{GO}_{\text{Poss}}(\$500, \text{[FROM(Beth) TO(Ann)]}) \end{bmatrix})$$

   b. Beth bought the car from Ann for $500.
$$\text{CAUSE (Beth,} \begin{bmatrix} \text{GO}_{\text{Poss}}(\text{car, [FROM(Ann) TO(Beth)]}) \\ \text{GO}_{\text{Poss}}(\$500, \text{[FROM(Beth) TO(Ann)]}) \end{bmatrix})$$

On this analysis of *buy* and *sell*, their structures are the same except for the identity of the first argument of CAUSE. This reflects the intuition that (14a,b) are paraphrases or very nearly so, differing only with respect to the primary instigator of the event (Jackendoff 1990: 191). That difference can be sharpened by adverbial modifiers of the causation. Parsons (1990: 84) notes that while (14a,b) seem to entail one another, it could still be true that *Ann quietly sold the car to Beth for $500* while false that *Beth quietly bought the car from Ann $500*.

   However, Wechsler (2005a: sect. 5) observes that the subject of *sell* need not be the previous owner (the 'Source') but can be a salesperson; and similarly, the subject of *buy* need not be the new owner (the 'Goal') but can be a purchasing agent acting on the new owner's behalf. Moreover, the subject of *sell* can be an instrument under the control of the Source, as in *Clever advertising sold this car*; similarly, the subject of *buy* can be an instrument under control of the Goal, as in *Five hundred dollars bought this car*. Hence Wechsler's (2005a: sect. 5) decompositions of *sell* and *buy* include a **control** relation connecting the subject-denoted participant to the Source and Goal, respectively. Van Valin (1999: 14) notes that languages tend to treat the verb meaning 'buy' as basic and derive 'sell' from it, citing German *kaufen* 'buy' → *verkaufen* 'sell', Lakhota *ophéthų* 'buy' → *iyópheya* 'sell', and Tagalog *bili* 'buy' → *mag-bili* 'sell'. Often 'sell' is 'cause to buy', as shown by the causative morphemes Lakhota *-ya* and Tagalog *mag-*. This suggests a different decomposition, perhaps one where the structure for 'buy' is embedded within that of 'sell' as the second argument of the CAUSE relation.

   The various decomposition analyses differ, but all of them make crucial use of the fact that decomposition allows a single participant to play multiple roles in different relations.

The existence of lexical decomposition has been questioned (Fodor 1998; Fodor and Lepore 1998), and its status within grammatical theory is controversial. That fundamental theoretical debate is postponed until Section 4.4.5, after we have considered some specific theories of decomposition.

4.4.1 Ontology of meaning units

The first requirement for any theory of decomposition is to establish the ontology of primitive meaningful units. Here we focus on verb meaning (see Levin and Rappaport Hovav 2005: sects. 4.1, 4.2 for an overview). The 'localist' and 'aspectual' approaches are the two most influential ones. Other theories of event structure and argument mapping, including mereological and scalar models of telicity and recent theories of affectedness, are not strictly decompositional in the sense of involving primitive sublexical formatives, so they are postponed until Section 4.5.

In localist approaches physical location and motion are taken as semantically fundamental and various abstract relations such as possession are analyzed as metaphorical extensions of locative relations (J. S. Gruber 1965; Jackendoff 1972). The structures in (13) and (14) illustrate a localist analysis of possession relations. In Jackendoff's (1983: 192) formulation, '"*y has/possesses x*" is the conceptual parallel to spatial "*x is at y*".' Change of possession is the conceptual parallel to motion. Basic relations like GO apply across different semantic fields, the most fundamental field being spatial location and movement, where GO encodes literal motion in space. Within the field of possession relations, GO_{Poss} indicates transfer of possession, where the semantic field is indicated by the subscript. Similar conceptual parallels in the temporal field are shown by the use of spatial prepositions for times: *at 5 p.m., on June 10th; from 2 p.m. to 4 p.m.* Also some very basic verbs of motion such as *go* and *move* can apply to times: *The meeting goes from 2 to 4; We moved the meeting from Tuesday to Thursday.* (Jackendoff 1983: 190–92)

The causal relation (CAUSE), which clearly applies across semantic fields, was also an element of Jackendoff's ontology. An example is seen in *buy* and *sell* in (13) and (14) . Many verb pairs are distinguished by the presence of CAUSE (see Sections 3.4 and 4.4.3). For example, transitive *move*, mentioned in the previous paragraph, is 'CAUSE to GO.' The verb *keep* entails 'CAUSE to *stay*,' patterning across semantic fields: *I kept it in the closet* entails *It stayed in the closet; We kept Mary happy* entails *Mary stayed happy;* and so on (example from Levin and Rappaport Hovav 2005: 82). As Levin and Rappaport Hovav point out, causation is not a locative relation. A CAUSE relation is found in other ontologies such as the aspectual systems based on Dowty (1979) and described in Section 4.4.3.

Gruber (1965) hypothesized that all semantic relations are generalizations of spatial and motional relations. In his earlier work, Jackendoff (1983: 188) adopted that view. His Thematic Relations Hypothesis stated that the analysis of any eventuality uses the same functions used for the analysis of spatial motion and location. According to Jackendoff's hypothesis, semantic fields are distinguished only by: (a) what sort of entities may appear as the theme; (b) what sort of entities may appear as the reference objects (for defining locations); and (c) what kind of relation assumes the role played by location in the field of spatial expressions. For example, for the possession field the answers are: (a) things; (b) things; and (c) alienable possession.

In later work Jackendoff (1990: 125ff.) abandoned this reduction of all events and states to cognitive parallels of spatial relations. He supplemented the localist structure with other relations such as AFF(ect), a two-place relation between an Actor (the one that affects) and Patient (the one that is affected). Inspired by autosegmental phonology, Jackendoff represented relations on two autonomous tiers, the 'thematic tier' for local relations and their derivatives, and the 'action tier' for the roles Actor and Patient. In another tier-based proposal, Grimshaw (1990) posited a thematic tier that contains thematic roles like Agent, Experiencer, Goal-Source-Location, and Theme, and an aspectual tier that expresses causation and change of state. (Aspectual decomposition is discussed in Section 4.4.3.)

Levin and Rappaport Hovav (2005: 83) point out that the localist approach lacks any natural analysis of the many activity verbs such as *chew, cry, knead, juggle, play.* We can understand why a localist approach works better for some verbs than others by recalling the distinction between manner and result verbs (Section 3.7.2). On Rappaport Hovav and Levin's (2010) formulation, result roots specify scalar changes while manner roots specify complex changes. A scalar change is a directed change in the value of a single attribute (see Section 4.5). Motion through space is a paradigmatic example of a simple scalar change. So the means for expressing motion and location are naturally used for expressing other scalar changes. This includes locative prepositions (*at, on, in,* etc.) as well as simple verbs of motion (*go, put, move, enter*) and location (*stay, remain, contain*), as long as they lack a manner component. In contrast, the nonscalar change specified by a 'manner' root is typically a complex combination of different types of change, with no privileged scale measuring a single change. Spatial and motion relations are inappropriate for modeling such changes.

With regard to the problem of argument realization, the cognitive parallels of local relations across semantic fields are mainly supported by the patterning of oblique markers such as prepositions, and not by subject and object selection. Local relations do not seem to play an important role in the mapping of semantic arguments to subject and object—another shortcoming of the theory that was noted by Levin and Rappaport Hovav (2005: 83). Causation plays a role, according to Levin and Rappaport Hovav, but as noted above, causation is not a local relation. Causing a physical object to undergo motion through space is just the application of causation within the domain of spatial relations. Again, we can understand why localist theories are primarily motivated by preposition selection, since the various aspects of the scalar path are typically specified by means of prepositional phrases: the source (*from Austin*), the goal (*to Houston*), and so on.

While verbal semantics cannot be completely reduced to localist relations, localist theories continue to play a role in lexical semantic analysis. There are clearly broad parallels between the expression of spatial relations and other sorts of relation. The question is how to explain those parallels. On some cognitive semantic theories, spatial relations are the vehicle for metaphorical extensions. In an illustration of cognitive semantics and embodiment, Geeraerts (2009: 207) writes: 'Metaphoric uses of the containment image schema occur when someone *enters a depression*, to take an example: the abstract emotional condition is seen as a container restricting the person's behavior.' Alternatively, it could be that the use of *enter* in *enter a depression* represents not metaphorical extension but simple semantic generalization. The semantic restriction to the physical domain is lost and so the verb can be used for emotional states as well.

If such extensions can be said to involve a 'metaphor,' then that metaphor must be strictly grammaticalized (conventionalized). This conventionalization can be observed in English nominals for mental, emotional, and medical states. Such terms are typically lexicalized as either 'locations' or 'possessions' (Grône 2011; Wechsler 2011). The semantic category varies from noun to noun:

(15)   Inherent possessions: *the flu, a cold, cancer, the blues,...*
    a. She has the flu/cancer/the blues.
    b. She got the flu/cancer/the blues.
    c. I wonder what gave her the flu/cancer/the blues.
    d. I don't want the flu/cancer/the blues.

(16)   Inherent locations: *a coma, a (good) mood, a funk, a depression, ...*
    a. She is in a good mood/a coma/a funk.
    b. Wait for him to get out of that bad mood/coma/funk.
    c. That drink should put him into a better mood/a coma/a funk.

The nominals are strictly categorized and cannot reverse their contexts:

(17)   a. ?*I have/got/want a good mood.
    b. ?*Formal semantics gives me a bad mood.
    c. *She is in the flu.
    d. *Wait for her to get out of the flu.

Constructions with *enter* like *entered a depression*, which is cited as an example of metaphorical extension in the quote from Geerarts (2009: 207), are possible with some of the 'location' type nouns (perhaps the negative ones), but none of the 'possession' type: *She entered the blues*; *She entered a bad mood*. Grône (2011) also observed the 'possession' type nouns such as *flu* appears as the direct object (NP1) in constructions like *verb NP1 out of NP2*, while the 'location' type nouns like *coma* appear as the prepositional object (NP2) in constructions like *verb NP1 into NP2*. Grône's (2011) corpus study turned up examples like those in (18a,b) and (19a,b), but none of the type shown in (18c) or (19c).

(18)   a. The fever is trying to burn the flu out of him.
    b. His mother's homemade medicine knocked the flu out of him.
    c. no strings like: *him out of the flu, *him into the flu*, etc.

(19)   a. I petted her into a coma. (picture of a very relaxed cat)
    b. Father-of-two punches woman into a coma after flying into a rage over a parking space
    c. no strings like: *a coma out of him, *a coma into him*, etc.

The bifurcation of such medical and mood nominals shows two things. First, the categorization is clearly lexicalized. Metaphor may play a role in the lexicalization process, but general (extralinguistic) cognitive processes of metaphor alone cannot be responsible for such expressions, since that would leave the lexical constraints as utterly mysterious. Second, given the very broad patterning of the two categories across different preposition and verb contexts, the categories reflect semantic and not syntactic (formal, morphological) subcategorization.

In conclusion, localist theories appear to have little direct bearing on predicting subject and object selection. But they may have an important role to play in explaining other aspects of argument realization, including preposition selection.

4.4.2 Situation aspect (Aktionsart classes)

Vendler (1957) analyzed linguistic depictions of situations (states and events) into four categories that he called 'states,' 'activities,' 'accomplishments,' and 'achievements.' This level of analysis, usually called either 'lexical aspect,' 'situation aspect' (C. S. Smith 1997), or 'Aktionsart,' will be reviewed here because it is the basis for the theories of lexical decomposition described in Section 4.4.3, which in turn are the basis for the theories of argument linking described in Section 4.4.4.

Vendler (1957) provided linguistic evidence from English for his categories, which has since been supplemented by further diagnostics (see e.g. Dowty 1979; C. S. Smith 1997). Some key properties are summarized here. States (*know, love, be happy*) do not involve change, in contrast to the three dynamic categories, which do. In the present tense, English verbs appear in the simple present for states but in the progressive for non-states:

(20)   What are you doing?
      a. I am smoking a pipe.   (*smoke a pipe*: activity)
      b. *I am knowing the answer. (*know the answer*: state)

Non-stative verbs allow the simple present only for habitual or iterative interpretations:

(21)   a. (*)Santa smokes a pipe. (habitual/iterative only)
      b. I know the answer.

Sentence (21a) can only refer to a pattern of habitual or repeated pipe-smoking, not to a single episode of smoking a pipe.

'Activity' predicates (*run, push a cart*) denote indefinite change of state, while the remaining non-stative classes denote definite changes with an inherent endpoint. 'Accomplishments' (*paint a picture, make a chair*) are complex and extended in time (i.e. 'durative'), while 'achievements' (*spot, find, die*) are simple and occur at a point in time (i.e. 'punctual'). Taking first the two durative categories, activities can be distinguished from accomplishments by a number of tests. With activities, but not accomplishments, the past progressive entails the simple past:

(22) a. He was pushing a cart.   (*push a cart*: activity)
          entails: He pushed a cart.

      b. He was running a mile.   (*run a mile*: accomplishment)
          does not entail: He ran a mile.

The intuitive reason for this difference in entailment is that activities are descriptions of events as homogeneous, without the specification of an inherent endpoint. Every part of an event described as 'pushing a cart' can also be described as 'pushing a cart.' Accomplishments, in contrast, are heterogeneous: they contain an inherent endpoint (i.e. they are 'telic'). If he was running a mile but collapsed after a half mile, then he did not run a mile. Accomplishments 'proceed toward a terminus which is logically necessary to their being what they are. Somehow this climax casts its shadow backward, giving a new color to all that went before' (Vendler 1957: 103–4). Also the temporal modifiers differ for the two classes. Activities are normally modified by durative adverbials (*for*-PPs), while accomplishments are modified by interval adverbials (*in*-PPs):

(23) a. He pushed a cart for 20 minutes/*in 20 minutes.
      b. He ran a mile in 20 minutes/*for 20 minutes.

Activities and accomplishments are durative: they last more than a moment. In contrast, achievements like *reach the top* and *find it* are punctual: they take place at a moment in time. Thus modifiers like *at that moment* are appropriate for achievements (24).

(24) He reached the top at that moment/*for 10 minutes.

Achievements reject *for*-PPs; and *in*-PPs are acceptable, but they are interpreted differently when modifying achievements than modifying accomplishments

(25) a. He wrote the letter in 10 minutes. (*write the letter*:
                                            accomplishment)
          entails: He was writing the letter during every period in that
          10 minute interval.

b. He noticed it in 10 minutes.   (*notice it*: achievement)
   does not entail: He was noticing it during every period in that
   10 minute interval.

With the accomplishment *write the letter*, the *in*-PP measures the
letter-writing interval. But with the achievement *notice it*, the *in*-PP
has an ingressive interpretation: it locates the punctual event 10 minutes past the reference time.

   Smith (1997: 46–7) distinguished between two subtypes of punctual
events. Achievements like *reach the top*, *notice it*, and *win the race* are
telic: they indicate a change of state. In contrast, 'semelfactives' like *tap
her shoulder* are atelic: they do not entail any particular change but
merely refer to an event of momentary duration. Achievements tend to
encompass a preparatory phase, the process resulting in the change of
state; but this is not so for semelfactives (26). Also achievements, being
telic, have an inherent result state, which becomes available for modification with a durative adverbial. So *borrow the book* in (27a) is an achievement with the result state that she has the book; the *for*-PP measures that
result state. But *tap her shoulder* in (27b) is semelfactive: without any result
state to modify, the only possible interpretation is an iterative one with
multiple shoulder-tapping events over the course of an hour.

(26)   a. He was winning the race.
       b. He was tapping her shoulder.

(27)   a. She borrowed the book for an hour.
       b. She tapped his shoulder for an hour.

Smith (1997) describes her system with three binary features, dyna-
mism ([±static]), duration ([±durative]), and telicity ([±telic]).

(28)   Categories of situation aspect (C. S. Smith 1997)

Situations	Static	Durative	Telic
State	+	+	−
Activity	−	+	−
Accomplishment	−	+	+
Semelfactive	−	−	−
Achievement	−	−	+

Stative predicates are inherently durative and atelic, while non-stative
predicates are cross-classified by those two features.

4.4.3 Aspectual–causal decomposition

An influential decomposition approach to verb meaning is presented in Dowty (1979). Dowty combined insights developed in Generative Semantics with the intensional logic system in the tradition of Richard Montague. He focused on deriving the aspectual classes of verbs due to Vendler (1957), described in Section 4.4.2. Dowty (1979) hypothesized that 'the different aspectual properties of the various kinds of verbs can be explained by postulating a single homogeneous class of predicates—stative predicates—plus three or four sentential operators and connectives' (Dowty 1979: 71) The operators and connectives are treated as logical constants with standard model-theoretic interpretations. Three important operators are BECOME, CAUSE, and DO.

The BECOME operator takes a single state as its scope, its interpretation fixed so that BECOME(p) is true at time t if $\neg p$ is true just prior to t and p is true just after t.

(29)

$$\frac{\neg \text{open(d)} \quad | \quad \text{open(d)}}{i" \qquad t \qquad i'}$$

For many verb–adjective cognate pairs, if predicating the adjective of an individual yields p then the cognate verb denotes BECOME(p): if *The door opened* at time t then *The door is open* is true at and after time t but *The door is not open* is true just prior to t.

Accomplishments are defined in terms of the operator CAUSE, which is meant to capture the notion of causation. Dowty (1979: 108–9) defined CAUSE as a relation between two propositions. His starting point was Lewis's (1973) analysis of causation as a counterfactual relation: 'ψ *depends causally on* ϕ' means that ψ and ϕ are true and ψ would not have been true if ϕ had not been true.[4] Dowty argues that this is too broad to characterize causation, at least in so far as that notion can be equated with the meaning of the English verb *cause*. Given a sequence of sentences such that each one causally depends on the previous one in the sequence (cf. Croft's (1998) 'causal chain'), Dowty defines the 'causal factors' for ψ as the sentences preceding ψ in that sequence. The problem is that for any proposition there are many

---

[4] Dowty (1979: 108) gave the definition as: ϕ *depends causally on* ψ if and only if ϕ, ψ and $\neg\phi \, \square\!\!\rightarrow \neg\psi$ are all true. I assume this is an error and that he meant: ψ *depends causally on* ϕ if and only if ϕ, ψ and $\neg\phi \, \square\!\!\rightarrow \neg\psi$ are all true.

causal factors but not all of them are normally seen as causes. One might agree that *If I had not lit John's cigarette, he would not have smoked it*, while disputing the claim that *My lighting John's cigarette caused him to smoke it* (Dowty 1979: 106). Dowty's solution is to define the cause of an event as the causal factor 'whose deletion from the actual course of events would result in the least departure from the actual world' (p. 107):

(30)   [ϕ CAUSE ψ] is true if and only if (i) ϕ is a causal factor for ψ, and (ii) for all other ϕ' such that ϕ' is also a causal factor for ψ, some $\neg\phi$-world is more similar to the actual world than any $\neg\phi'$-world is.

Propositions further back in the causal chain relative to the proposition ψ have more effects on the world, so they are disfavored as intuitive 'causes' of ψ. Intuitively, the cause is a factor that 'could have been otherwise'—or, to put it differently, the possible worlds in which it was otherwise are not so different from the actual one that we disregard them. In addition to BECOME and CAUSE, Dowty posits a third operator, DO, to relate volitional agents to the actions they undertake.

Dowty illustrated his system with detailed analyses, including a treatment of the systematic semantic relation between adjectives such as *cool* or *open*, and their cognate inchoative and transitive verbs. For example, the property **cool'** is the stative predicate expressed by the adjective *cool* (31a). (The logical expressions in (31) are adapted in simplified extensional form from Dowty 1979: 206–7.) The inchoative verb *cool*, as in *The soup cooled*, is translated using **cool'** in combination with the BECOME operator in (31b). This sentence can be roughly paraphrased as 'The soup became cool.' Dowty's translation of the causative verb *cool*, as in *John cooled the soup*, is an expression of the form ϕ CAUSE ψ, where ϕ and ψ are propositions (31c). The causing proposition ϕ involves the agent argument (*John*, in example (32c)) in some way, and the resulting proposition ψ is BECOME(**cool'**(the-soup)).

(31)   a. adjective *cool*: $\lambda y \, [\mathbf{cool'}(y)]$
       b. intransitive verb *cool*: $\lambda y \, [\text{BECOME}[\mathbf{cool'}(y)]]$
       c. transitive verb *cool*: $\lambda y \lambda x \exists P[\, P(x) \text{ CAUSE } [\text{BECOME} \, [\mathbf{cool'}(y)]] \,]$

(32)   a. The soup is cool: $\mathbf{cool'}(\textit{the.soup})$
       b. The soup cooled: $\text{BECOME}[\mathbf{cool'}(\textit{the.soup})]$
       c. John cooled the soup: $\exists P[\, P(\textit{John}) \text{ CAUSE } [\text{BECOME} \, [\mathbf{cool'}(\textit{the.soup})]] \,]$

The property P in (31c) and (32c) is an unspecified action undertaken by the subject argument, that causes the soup to become cool. The sentence is silent on the question of whether John blew on the soup, iced it, put it in the refrigerator, or did something else to it. So-called 'result verbs' typically specify the result but not the manner of causation (see Section 4.4.4). In a resultative construction the verb specifies the manner while the secondary predicate gives the result (Dowty (1979: 219–24) called these 'factitive constructions'):

(33)   Mary shakes John awake.
       [shake'(m, j) CAUSE [BECOME[awake'(j)]]]

The causing action is specified by the verb and the result state comes from the adjective.

Dowty posited lexical rules to capture the relation between adjective-inchoative-causative cognates like *cool* in (31) and (32). A complex predicate formation semantically composes the verb and adjective in a resultative like (33). A rule derives the inchoatives from the adjectives: if there is an adjective with form a and translation $\lambda y[a'(y)]$, then there is an intransitive verb with form *a-en* (if a ends in a non-nasal obstruent, e.g. *red~redden, black~blacken, short~shorten*) or a (elsewhere, e.g. *cool~cool, open~open, empty~empty*); and that intransitive verb has the translation $\lambda y[\text{BECOME } a'(y)]$. Another lexical rule derives the causative from the inchoative. Dowty proposed to treat many other verbs this way, even non-alternating ones, and 'suppletive' sets like *dead~die~kill*. Nearly all accomplishment predicates have the CAUSE-BECOME structure. Dowty (1979: 219–20) analyzed the English resultative construction with a lexical rule that composes a verb (e.g. *shake*) with an adjective (e.g. *awake*) to produce a complex predicate (*shake-awake*). This is described in Section 7.2.2.

Dowty (1979: ch. 6) did not see his lexical rules as part of 'the grammar proper', but rather as a means of changing the grammar of a language by enlarging its stock of basic expressions. The rules are an aid to acquisition, and are not directly responsible for the actual usage. Knowledge of a rule 'makes it possible for the speaker to know at least the *approximate* meaning of a new derived word upon first hearing it, or to make up a new word which his audience will understand approximately, but the rules do not prevent him from later deciding that the word has a more specialized meaning than that specified by a general rule' (Dowty 1979: 296–7). So possible derived words are distinguished from actual ones. Lexical rules generate the set of possible derived words, only some of which are the basis, via 'lexical extension', for actual words of the language. The lexical rule that licenses *beautify* also gives us **uglify*, which is easily understood to mean 'make ugly', but has not entered common usage. Similarly, there are no causative transitives corresponding to inchoatives *fall* or *disappear*: **Mary fell the vase*; **The magician disappeared the rabbit*. But these are 'possible words', licensed by the lexical rules.

The decompositions give only the approximate meaning. This assumption is necessary since verb meanings, like word meanings more generally, typically have extra increments of meaning, beyond what the decomposition captures. The relation in meaning between the cognate forms (and between other forms that are related by semantic rules, like *die~kill*) is not entirely transparent but instead 'translucent.' For example, transitive *x grows y* entails that *y grows*, but intransitive *grow* can involve any increase in size or extent, while the transitive relation is more specific to cultivating crops for harvest.

(34) a. The tomatoes grew.   ('increased in size, extent, etc.')
      b. The farmer grew tomatoes.   ('cultivated for harvest')
      c. The chickens/The child/The linguistics department/Mary's concerns grew.
      d. *John grew the chickens/the linguistics department/Mary's concerns.

Word meanings typically become either more general or more specialized over time, leading to autohyponomy if old meanings persist, so that old and new meanings coexist.

Following earlier work in Generative Semantics, Dowty motivated his system with a rich array of linguistic evidence. The existence of the result state expression **cool'**(y) in the structure in (31b) and (31c) is shown by the ambiguity of *John cooled the soup again*: the sentence presupposes either (i) that John cooled the soup at least once before, or (ii) that the soup was cool before.

(35)   John cooled the soup again.
       (i) 'It again happened that John cooled the soup.'
            again$([[(\text{CAUSE}(j, \text{BECOME}(\text{cool'}(s))))])$
       (ii) 'John made it be the case that the soup became again cool.'
            $([[(\text{CAUSE}(j, \text{BECOME } \textbf{again}(\text{cool'}(s))))])$

(36)   John opened the door again.
   a. 'It again happened that John opened the door.'
      again([[(CAUSE(john, BECOME(open(door)))]])
   b. 'John made it be the case that the door became again opened.'
      [CAUSE (john, BECOME(**again**(open(door))))]

The inner scope reading shown on the (b) lines is further illustrated by the familiar rhyme, *All the king's horses and all the king's men/Couldn't put Humpty Dumpty together again*. Dowty (1979: 252) notes that this 'is obviously not intended to entail that anyone had put Humpty Dumpty together on an earlier occasion, but merely that Humpty Dumpty had been "together" once before.'

  This ambiguity follows if the operator introduced by the adverb *again*, which contributes the presupposition that the situation in its scope obtained previously, can take a scope that is either wider or narrower than that of the BECOME operator. The prefix *re-* has a similar scope ambiguity: *The satellite reentered the atmosphere* minimally presupposes that the satellite was previously within the atmosphere. On this 'restitutive' or 'restorative' interpretation, the operator takes narrow scope over just the result state of the entering event (Dowty 1979; Wechsler 1989).

4.4.4 Argument mapping based on aspectual–causal decomposition

Dowty did not apply his 1979 theory to explaining regularities in the linking between lexical semantics and syntax, such as subject selection. Some regularities follow from his lexical rules. The causative rule takes an intransitive verb like *cool* (*The soup cooled*) and produces the transitive variant (*John cooled the soup*). The formulation of the rule guarantees that the added causer argument is the subject rather than object of the transitive, correctly ruling out **The soup cooled John*. So that rule captures the linking regularity for the many alternating verbs. But the regularities in the argument realization of non-alternating verbs like *John ate the soup* were not directly addressed: Dowty did not posit rules of the form 'a variable contained within the first argument of CAUSE must be linked to the subject.'[5] But other researchers have

---

[5] It is not clear that such rules would even make sense, under Dowty's assumptions. The expressions of intensional logic do not constitute a linguistic level of representation, since various parts of them can effectively be traded in for meaning postulates without affecting the resulting interpretation. Dowty's main hypothesis—that all verb meanings can be reduced to states together with a small set of primitive semantic operations—does not

adopted a reified version of Dowty's logical expressions as a basis for linking theories.

4.4.4.1 Role and Reference Grammar A detailed, typologically oriented theory of argument linking based on causal-aspectual lexical decomposition is found in Role and Reference Grammar (RRG; Foley and Van Valin 1984; Van Valin 1993; 2005). RRG uses logical structures that are based on Dowty's (1979) system, but enriched with some additional aspectual operators, often resulting in more elaborate decompositions. A hierarchy of variable positions in logical structure determines a mapping onto the two 'Macro-Roles' Actor and Undergoer (see Section 4.3), and these in turn are mapped onto the morphosyntax of the sentence.

The logical forms for the different Aktionsart classes are shown in (37). Van Valin (2005) follows Smith (1997) in including semelfactives in the aspectual taxonomy (see Section 4.4.2). He bifurcates accomplishments into two subtypes. Some accomplishments, which he calls 'active accomplishments,' comprise a separable activity followed by an endpoint: in *Carl ate the pizza*, the activity is Carl's eating and the endpoint is a state in which the pizza is consumed. But *The butter melted* is fully described by the coming-about of the endpoint (namely, melted butter), and gives no specific indication of the nature of the activity that led to the melting. The different classes are represented by logical structures built from aspectual operators similar to Dowty's CAUSE, BECOME, and DO. All activity representations contain the predicate **do'** (Van Valin 2005: 42). In addition to the predicates in boldface, there is a small set of operators shown in captal letters. Volitionality of the agent is indicated by DO (Van Valin 2005: 56, citing Ross 1973). Achievements are represented with the INGR ('ingressive') operator, which takes a state or activity and returns a predicate describing the onset of that state or activity. For example, the achievement *The vase shattered* indicates the vase's change to a shattered state, hence it is represented as INGR(**shattered'**(the-vase)). Dowty had used BECOME for this purpose but Van Valin's BECOME is reserved for accomplishments, hence *The butter melted* is represented as BECOME(**melted'**(butter)). Active accomplishments are decomposed into a formula for the activity segment followed by an ingressive formula

require that there be a unique translation of each linguistic expression into intensional logic, but only that there be at least one translation (Dowty 1979: 199).

representing the terminus. The symbol '&' in the Active Accomplishment logical form in (37), which connects the two formulae, represents temporal ordering, paraphrasable as 'and then' (Van Valin 2005: 44). The SEML ('semelfactive') operator is used to represent punctual events.

(37)   Lexical representations for Aktionsart classes (Van Valin 2005: 45, table 2.3)

Aktionsart class	Logical structure
STATE	**predicate'**(x) or (x, y)
ACTIVITY	**do'**(x, [**predicate'**(x) or (x, y)])
ACHIEVEMENT	INGR **predicate'**(x) or (x, y) INGR **do'** (x, [**predicate'**(x) or (x, y)])
SEMELFACTIVE	SEML **predicate'**(x) or (x, y) SEML **do'** (x, [**predicate'**(x) or (x, y)])
ACCOMPLISHMENT	BECOME **predicate'**(x) or (x, y) BECOME **do'** (x, [**predicate'**(x) or (x, y)])
ACTIVE ACCOMPLISHMENT	**do'**(x, [**predicate'**(x) or (x, y)]) & INGR **do'** (x, [**predicate'**(x) or (x, y)])
CAUSATIVE	α CAUSE β, where α, β are logical structures of any type

Examples of logical forms of some English sentences appear in (38).

(38)   Examples of RRG logical forms (Van Valin 2005: 46–7)
   a. States
       The cup is shattered.   **shattered'**(cup)
       Dana saw the picture.   **see'**(Dana, picture)
   b. Activities
       The children cried   **do'**(children[**cry'**(children)])
       Carl ate pizza.   **do'**(Carl [**eat'**(Carl, pizza)])
   c. Achievements
       The balloon popped.   INGR **popped'**(balloon)
   d. Semelfactives
       Mary coughed.   SEML **do'**(Mary [**cough'**(Mary)])

e. Accomplishments

The snow melted.   BECOME **melted'**(snow)

f. Active accomplishments

Jo ran to the park.   **do'**(Jo, [**run'**(Jo)]) & INGR **be-at'**(park, Jo)

Mo ate the pizza.

        do'(Mo [**eat'**(Mo, pizza)]) & INGR **consumed'**(pizza)

g. Causatives

Max melted the ice.   **do'**(Max, Ø) CAUSE [BECOME **melted'**(ice)]

The different positions in logical forms are the basis for determining the mapping to the two macro-roles, Actor and Undergoer, according to a preference hierarchy (39). The Actor is the highest (leftmost) on this hierarchy. The Undergoer is normally the lowest on the hierarchy. The DO operator is for lexicalized agency, so its argument is a volitional agent. The first argument of **do'** is an 'effector' in the activity. Taken together, the first two columns of (39) are for 'participants which do something' (Van Valin 2005: 57). While agents and effectors gravitate towards the high end of the hierarchy, affectedness goes with the low end. At the lowest (rightmost) end of the hierarchy is a column for the single participant in a state, which 'includes participants which are crushed, killed, smashed, shattered, broken, destroyed, etc.' When the result state involves a single argument, that participant is more highly affected by the event. The column to its left is for the second argument of a two-place predicate, hence 'includes those participants which are placed, moved, thrown, given, possessed, transferred, seen, heard, loved, etc.' The change involves a relation between two participants, and so it is not as deeply affected as the single participant relations.

(39)   Actor-Undergoer hierarchy (Van Valin 2005: 61, fig. 2.4, and 126, fig. 4.4)

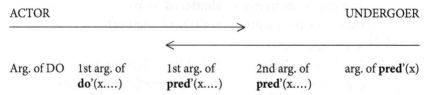

ACTOR				UNDERGOER
Arg. of DO	1st arg. of **do'**(x....)	1st arg. of **pred'**(x....)	2nd arg. of **pred'**(x....)	arg. of **pred'**(x)

The macro-role status of an argument directly affects its case and agreement properties. In an accusative system, the highest macro-role gets nominative case and the other macro-role, if any, gets accusative case. In an ergative system the lowest gets absolutive, and if there is another it gets ergative case (Van Valin 2005: 108). (On ergative case systems see Section 3.6.3.) It has been observed that selection of the subject for the purpose of construal properties such as control (called the 'privileged syntactic argument' in RRG) depends on whether the language allows subjects in oblique case: e.g. Icelandic does, but German does not (Cole et al. 1980; Zaenen et al. 1985). In RRG terms, the distinction turns on whether the 'privileged syntactic argument' is restricted to being a macro-role in a given language (Van Valin 2005: 100). Modulo such a restriction, the subject ('privileged syntactic argument') is selected according to the same hierarchy used for macro-role assignment, in (39): in an accusative construction (by far the most common cross-linguistically), the highest-ranking direct core argument is selected. In an ergative construction it is the lowest. Summarizing, macro-role status is derived from the logical forms, and case marking and 'privileged syntactic argument' (subjecthood) are each derived independently from macro-role status.

4.4.4.2 Systems based on depth of embedding

Some approaches derive linking patterns from the depth of embedding in the logical form (Bierwisch and Schreuder 1992; Wunderlich 1997a). Bierwisch and Wunderlich represent grammatically relevant aspects of lexical decomposition in a 'semantic form,' as they call it, built from universal operators such as CAUSE and BECOME. The arguments of a verb are ranked according to their relative level of embeddedness in the semantic form. Wunderlich (1997a) refers to the ranked set of arguments, elaborated with some non-semantic information, as the 'thematic structure.' For example, in a semantic form similar to (31c), the variable x would outrank y, since y is the more deeply embedded (this is a simplification; see Wunderlich 1997a for details). This ranking determines the mapping to grammatical relations like subject and object, much as the thematic hierarchy does in the systems presented in Section 4.2; but it is unnecessary to stipulate a hierarchy, since the ranking is derived from the semantic form.

4.4.4.3 A templatic approach

Rappaport Hovav and Levin (1998) use aspectual templates to divide verb meanings into a lexically 'idiosyncratic' component and a 'structural' component given by the aspectual decomposition. Their mapping theory is based on the hypothesis that the structural aspect must be given syntactic expression. The structural aspect is given in form of 'lexical semantic templates,' another near-synonym for logical forms and semantic forms:

(40)   Event structure templates
    a. [x ACT$_{\langle MANNER \rangle}$]   (activity)
    b. [x $\langle$STATE$\rangle$]   (state)
    c. [BECOME [x $\langle$STATE$\rangle$]]   (achievement)
    d. [[x ACT$_{\langle MANNER \rangle}$] CAUSE [BECOME
      [y $\langle$STATE$\rangle$]]]   (accomplishment 1)
    e. [x CAUSE [BECOME [y $\langle$STATE$\rangle$]]] (accomplishment 2)

Notice that 'states' are part of the description of achievements and accomplishments, and 'activities' are part of the description of 'accomplishment 1.'

The idiosyncratic aspect consists in filling out the positions given in angular brackets by non-logical 'constants.' Constants can be modifiers of predicates (e.g. manner, state), or they may fill particular argument slots. Some examples of verbs (from Rappaport Hovav and Levin 1998: 109):

(41)   a. Activities: [x ACT$_{\langle MANNER \rangle}$]
      MANNER specified: e.g. *jog, run, creak, whistle* . . .

    b. Activities: [x ACT$_{\langle INSTRUMENT \rangle}$]
      INSTRUMENT specified: e.g. *brush, hammer, saw, shovel*

    c. Accomplishments: [[x CAUSE [BECOME [y WITH $\langle$THING$\rangle$]]]
      PLACEABLE OBJECT specified: e.g. *butter, oil, paper, tile, wax*
      (locatum verbs)

    d. Accomplishments: [x CAUSE [BECOME [y $\langle$PLACE$\rangle$]]]
      PLACE specified: e.g. *bag, box, cage, crate, garage, pocket*
      (location verbs)

    e. Internally caused state: [x $\langle$STATE$\rangle$]
      STATE specified: e.g. *bloom, blossom, decay, rot, rust, sprout*

    f. Externally caused state: [[x ACT] CAUSE [BECOME [y $\langle$STATE$\rangle$]]]
      STATE specified: e.g. *break, dry, harden, melt, open*

Change of state verbs that alternate with causatives, such as *break, dry,* and *open*, are assumed to encode 'externally caused change of state' even when used in the inchoative form. Rappaport Hovav and Levin assume that such verbs have an implicit agent, hence the [x ACT] in the decompositions in (41f). In their analysis of the causative alternation, the Agent argument is present in both causative and inchoative. In inchoative it is realized by an abstract 'reflexive morpheme.' Thus an inchoative like *The branch broke* contains an implicit external cause. In contrast, verbs indicating an internally caused change of state, such as *bloom* and *decay*, have the simpler structure in (41e). *The flower opened* has an external cause while *bloomed* is either stative (cp. *The flower bloomed for a day*) or, when the template is augmented with BECOME, it is a change-of-state predicate (cp. *The flower bloomed in a day*). On template augmentation see below.

Certain productive alternations are captured by assuming that the templates can be augmented. The syntactic realization of such augmented templates is subject to the condition in (42):

(42) Subevent identification condition: Each subevent in the event structure must be identified by a lexical head (a V, A or P) in syntax (where "event" refers to both states and actions).

(Rappaport Hovav and Levin 1998: 112)

The condition set out in (43) governs the appearance of structure participants, i.e. participants licensed by the structure (as opposed to the constants):

(43) Argument realization condition. (Rappaport Hovav and Levin 1998: 113)
    a. There must be an argument XP in the syntax for each structure participant in the event structure.
    b. Each argument XP in the syntax must be associated with an identified subevent in the event structure.

The system captures certain patterns of argument omissibility, as illustrated with the distinct behavior of manner versus result verbs (see Section 3.7.2). Manner verbs like *sweep* and *run* lexicalize a particular type of activity that may or may not lead to a result: *John swept the floor, but it is still dirty*. Result verbs (e.g. *break*, *open*) lexicalize a particular result (e.g. *Mary broke the egg, *but it is still intact*). Result verbs leave the manner open (e.g. *Mary broke the egg by striking it with a knife/by dropping it on the floor*). Result verbs have a more complex aspectual structure, including the BECOME operator for the result state:

(44) a. Manner verbs:
       examples: *nibble, rub, scribble, sweep, flutter, laugh, run, swim, ...*
       decomposition: *sweep*: $[x \text{ ACT}_{\langle SWEEP \rangle} y]$

    b. Result verbs:
       examples: *clean, cover, empty, fill, freeze, kill, melt, open, arrive, die, enter*
       decomposition: *break*: $[x \text{ ACT}_{\langle MANNER \rangle}]$ CAUSE $[\text{BECOME } [y \langle BROKEN \rangle]]]$

The underlined y argument of (44a) corresponds to the object (the location argument) of *sweep* in *John swept the floor*. This argument is assumed to be contributed by the verb. It is not a 'structure participant' so it is not subject to the *Argument realization condition* (43). This means that it can be omitted. Rappaport Hovav and Levin use this difference in structure to explain why manner verbs allow omission of the object while result verbs do not (45a): omitting the object of the result verb means eliminating the NP that would otherwise identify the result subevent [BECOME [y ⟨BROKEN⟩]]. This would violate (43).

(45)   a. Leslie swept.
          *Kelly broke.
       b. Cinderalla scrubbed her fingers to the bone.
          *The clumsy child broke his knuckles to the bone.
       c. Leslie swept the leaves from the sidewalk/into the ditch/into a pile.
          *Kelly broke the dishes off the table/into the garbage can/into a pile.
          [but: Kelly broke/cracked the eggs into a bowl.]

Also, result verbs lexically specify a result and so they are incompatible with syntactic constructions that express another result (45b,c). This captures the long-noted prohibition against two result phrases, or two expressions that delimit an event (Tenny 1987; 1994).

Template augmentation involves the insertion of one template into another, as in the derivation of a resultative or caused motion construction:

(46)   a. *sweep:* [[x ACT⟨SWEEP⟩ y] CAUSE [BECOME [y ⟨CLEAN⟩]]]
       b. Phil swept the floor clean.

The resultative (46b) abides by the Subevent identification condition because the second subevent (the state) is specified by a lexical head, *clean*. As *the floor* now is an argument of a subevent, it is a structure participant so it becomes obligatory: *Phil swept clean*. In this case the x argument and the y argument are the main arguments of their respective subevents, and so they have to be realized.

Summarizing, the main idea of Rappaport Hovav and Levin (1998) is that words of natural language allow only certain maximal lexical aspectual structures. Subevents within aspectual structures must be supported by verbal material, including both a head predicate word, such as a verb or adjective, and the overt expression of any structural participants.

4.4.5 The lexical decomposition controversy

The notion of lexical decomposition, or complex lexical representations, remains controversial in linguistics and the philosophy of language. Two varieties of motivation for complex lexical representations have been offered. First, they are argued to allow us to capture relations between words in the lexicon (paradigmatic relations). Second, they are said to be needed in order to state rules of semantic combination and syntactic distribution (syntagmatic relations). In what follows, lexical decomposition is first contrasted with the alternative of using meaning postulates to capturing paradigmatic relations. Then we look at the case against decomposition (Quine 1951; Fodor and Lepore 1998; Fodor 1998), and refute that argument on the basis of syntagmatic motivations for decomposition. Fodor and Lepore's (1998) proposed alternative account of the syntagmatic facts that they address turns out to be a variant of the constructional view to be discussed in more detail in Chapter 6.

'Meaning postulates' capture relations between words indirectly, by placing constraints on allowable models of denotations (Carnap 1952). We can specify that in all models anything that is a poodle is also a dog; that y is the husband of x if and only if x is the wife of y; and that x buys y from z if and only if z sells y to x:

(47) a. $\Box \forall x[\mathbf{poodle}(x) \; \rightarrow \; \mathbf{dog}(x)]$
      b. $\Box \forall x \forall y[\mathbf{husband}(y)(x) \; \leftrightarrow \; \mathbf{wife}(x)(y)]$
      c. $\Box \forall x \forall y \forall z[\mathbf{buy}(x, y, z) \; \leftrightarrow \; \mathbf{sell}(z, y, x)]$

Meaning postulates allow one to relate two words together without decomposing meaning into components, or specifying a common core of meaning, or treating one as more basic than the other.

Consider those paradigmatic relations between words that appear to motivate a complex representation of one word meaning that embeds the other word meaning. For example, many English inchoative verbs (*open, redden,* etc.) are systematically related to cognate adjectives (*open, red,* etc.). The translations of the cognate adjective and inchoative verb can be related to each other by the rule in (48b).

(48)   Relation between cognate English adjectives and inchoative verbs
    a. phonological form: The form of the adjective is α and the form of the verb is α+en (if α ends in a non-nasal obstruent) or α (elsewhere).
    b. meaning: The denotation of the adjective $\lambda x[\alpha'(x)])$ and the denotation of the verb is $\lambda y[\text{BECOME } \alpha'(y)]$
    c. example: *red*, $\lambda x[\textbf{red}'(x)]$ ~ *redden*, $\lambda y[\text{BECOME } \textbf{red}'(y)]$

The lexical rule specifies the meaning of the verb by embedding within it the meaning of the adjective from which it derives.

Alternatively, a meaning postulate could indicate the same regular relation without retaining the additional structure in the lexical representation of the verb. The meaning postulate in (49a) gives the relation between *red* and *redden*. A general schema for meaning postulates of that sort is given in (49b):

(49)   a. $\Box\forall y[\textbf{redden}'(y) \leftrightarrow \text{BECOME}(\textbf{red}'(y))]$
    b. $\Box\forall y[\alpha_{\text{intr}}'(y) \leftrightarrow \text{BECOME}(\alpha_{\text{adj}}'(y))]$

On this view there is no decomposition of the verb *redden*. Its translation is simply the relation **redden'**, and the meaning postulate ensures that *y reddens* if and only if *y becomes red*.

Meaning postulates can do things decomposition cannot do: only meaning postulates that are biconditional can be translated into lexical rules involving decomposition (see Chierchia and McConnell-Ginet 2000: 448–55). Hence meaning postulates are more flexible (less constrained). For example, recall from (34) that while intransitive *grow* can be used for any increase (*Her love grew*), transitive *grow* is restricted to growing crops for harvest (**His displays of affection grew her love*). So the entailment is valid in one direction but not the other: *x grew y* entails, but is not entailed by, *x caused y to grow*. For that reason the meaning of the transitive verb cannot be entirely reduced to a decomposition containing the intransitive verb relation and the CAUSE relation. Dowty (1979) interpreted the lexical rules as acquisition defaults, and allowed for adjustment to actual word meanings (see Section 4.4.3). But suppose instead that we replace the Inchoative-to-Causative lexical rule with the rule in (50a). The translations of the intransitive and transitive verbs α_i and α_t, namely α_t' and α_i', are related to each other using the monoconditional meaning postulate in (50b):

(50)   a. If a_i is in V_i, then a_t is in V_t.
       b. $\Box\forall x\forall y[a_t'(x, y) \rightarrow CAUSE(x, a_i'(y))]$

This rule is plausibly valid for English, even for verbs like *grow*: if Farmer Brown grows tomatoes, then he causes tomatoes to grow. But reversing the arrow would not produce a valid postulate: if John causes my doubts to grow, he does not *grow my doubts*. As Chierchia and McConnell-Ginet (2000: 450–51) put it, 'Meaning postulates are well-suited for handling meaning relations that are neither completely transparent nor opaque but semantically "translucent".'

As a basis for rules that relate one word to another, meaning postulates can do anything that decomposition can do, and more. So if we focus narrowly on a single language, it is unlikely that any paradigmatic phenomena could be found to weigh decisively in favor of decomposition: the anti-decompositionalist can always point to an alternative account that does without it (that is what Fodor and Lepore (1998) do, as described below).

Fodor and Lepore argue against the notion that words have internal semantic structure, focusing their arguments on a critique of Pustejovsky (1995). Fodor and Lepore's main argument addresses the paradigmatic motivation. Pustejovsky had argued that complex lexical representations allow us to explain relations between words in a lexicon, such as synonymy, antonymy, hyponymy, meronymy, entailment and presupposition (see Chapter 2). Fodor and Lepore's counterargument is based on Quine's (1951) attack on analytic inference more generally. Kant distinguished 'analytic' and 'synthetic' knowledge (Kant 1781). Analytic knowledge concerns propositions that are 'true by virtue of meanings and independently of fact' (Quine 1951: sect. 1). In an analytic statement the predicate can be obtained by analyzing the subject. Analytic statements fall into two subtypes: (i) Logical truths like *No unmarried man is married* are true by virtue of logical connectives like *no, un-, if... then, and,* etc. (ii) Some analytic statements depend on definitions, like *Every triangle has three sides,* or *No bachelor is married,* which follow from the definitions of concepts like *triangle* or *bachelor,* together with logical laws. In contrast, synthetic knowledge is synthesized from its parts, i.e. it is not analytic. An example is *Every creature with a heart is a creature with a kidney* (example from Fodor and Lepore 1998). Twentieth-century philosophy was marked by attempts to place science on a firm epistemological footing by dictating that all synthetic knowledge must be based on induction from direct observation, and then specifying a system of logical deduction for deriving analytic truths. But Quine argued that there is not a clean line between analytic and synthetic statements. Logical truths are not problematic, as they can be derived by a system of logic. It was the second type of analytic inference, the type that depends on definitions, that concerned Quine. He argued that there is no independent test to determine whether two expressions are synonymous, i.e. equivalent by definition, such as *bachelor* and *unmarried man*; or contingently equivalent, like *creature with a heart* and *creature with kidneys* (assuming all and only creatures with a heart have kidneys). In either case, truth is preserved in all contexts where one expression replaces the other. We lack an independent criterion for analyticity, according to Quine.

That argument against the paradigmatic motivation focuses narrowly on a single language. However, looking across languages we find some possible paradigmatic motivation for decomposition.[6] In some languages, or some parts of the lexicon of a language, relations like CAUSE and BECOME are represented by overt derivational morphemes; in other languages or parts of the lexicon, the same relation between words is not marked by morphology. The English example in (48) illustrates this distinction: some inchoative verbs related to adjectives are suffixed with *-en* (*red~redden*) while others are not (*open$_A$~open$_V$*). Cross-linguistic studies reveal that roughly the same set of semantic relations marked by morphology in some instances, also characterize relations between words of the same form or suppletive pairs in others. For example, in many languages causativization is marked with a causative affix (see Section 3.4.2), while other cases involve the same form (*break* (intrans.) ~ *break* (trans.)) or suppletive pairs (*die* ~ *kill*). Assuming semantic compositionality, then the morphologically marked cases should have complex semantic representations. A general theory of word meaning explains those cross-linguistic patterns by assimilating the unmarked type to the morphologically complex type. As a result the unmarked type, while morphologically simple, would have a complex semantic representation.

Moreover, it is the syntagmatic motivation for decomposition that is more relevant for us here. A central assumption underlying much of the theorizing described in this book is that complex lexical representations are needed to explain correlations between a word's meaning and its syntactic distribution. A lexicon that represents only denotation

---

[6] The argument in this paragraph was pointed out to me by Robert Van Valin (p.c.).

would seem to miss important linguistic generalizations. In response, Fodor and Lepore (1998: 275) express skepticism that 'syntactic distribution is somehow determined or explained by, or is anyhow predictable from, meaning.' They feel the case has not been made strongly enough. They suggest: 'A priori, it seems as reasonable that syntax should be driven by what people know about what a word denotes as that it should be driven by what they know about what the word means' (p. 277). Let us consider this last claim a bit more closely.

In Fodor's view word meaning is atomistic: the lexical entry for *dog* indicates only that it denotes 'dogs' (Fodor 1998). Inferences such as 'all dogs are animals' take place in the realm of denotations, dependent not upon knowledge of the words *dog* and *animal* but rather on knowledge of dogs and animals. According to Fodor and Lepore, whenever syntactic distribution seems to be affected by word meaning, the rules of such distribution could (and should) involve the denotations rather than the words (Fodor and Lepore 1998: 277).

However, contrary to Fodor and Lepore's atomist view, it seems clear that words belong to semantic categories that affect their syntactic distribution but cannot be assigned by inspecting their denotations. Consider the distinction between count and mass nouns. Count nouns such as *suggestion* are distinguished from mass nouns such as *advice*, with respect to whether they allow plurals (*suggestions*; **advices*), indefinite articles (*a suggestion*; **an advice*), quantification by *too much* (**too much suggestion*; *too much advice*), and *one*-anaphora (*John gave me (some) suggestions and Mary gave me one too*; **John gave me (some) advice and Mary gave me one too*). Count/mass assignment is clearly semantically based but notoriously subject to lexical idiosyncrasy. English *fruit* is a mass noun while French *fruit* is a count noun (*Prenez un fruit* '(lit.) Take a fruit'). Interestingly, nouns preserve their count/mass-dependent distribution even when they denote kinds (Krifka 1995):

(51)   What do you value most in life?
        a. Flattery./Advice./Evidence./Fruit.
        b. *Compliment./*Suggestion/*Clue./*Vegetable.
                        (example (39) from Wechsler 2008a: 17)

In this example the NPs refer to the kinds or concepts themselves, not to particular specimens. It is difficult to see how a consideration of the denotations 'flattery', 'compliment', and so on, could be the basis for this assignment to count or mass types. Instead it seems clear that speakers learn these assignments to the count and mass semantic categories of nouns from the nouns' distribution in the language they hear.

To take a second example, recall from Section 4.4.1 that English nominals for mental, emotion, and medical states typically lexicalized as either 'locations' or 'possessions' (Grône 2011; Wechsler 2011). The semantic category varies from noun to noun:

(52)   Inherent possessions: *the flu, a cold, cancer, the blues,* ...
    a. She has the flu/cancer/the blues.
    b. She got the flu/cancer/the blues.
    c. I wonder what gave her the flu/cancer/the blues.
    d. I don't want the flu/cancer/the blues.

(53)   Inherent locations: *a coma, a (good) mood, a funk, a depression,* ...
    a. She is in a good mood/a coma/a funk.
    b. Wait for him to get out of that bad mood/coma/funk.
    c. That drink should put him into a better mood/a coma/a funk.

The nouns bifurcate into 'possessions' and 'locations' systematically across various verb contexts (*have, get, give,* etc.) and preposition contexts (*in, into, out of,* etc.). Hence the categories reflect semantic and not syntactic (formal, morphological) subcategorization. But it is quite implausible that speakers could formulate a rule to correlate the denotations 'the blues' and 'a funk' with the different syntactic distributions. Instead they presumably learn the respective *semantic* categories by observing their respective *syntactic* distributions.

Dowty (1979: 267–9) put forth another syntagmatic argument in favor of decomposition. He showed that decomposition is crucial for explaining certain types of semantic composition. The argument is based on demonstrating that mono-conditional meaning postulates are inadequate, and that we need decomposition in order to explain the adverbial scope facts discussed earlier (see (36)). The adverbial *for the first time* can scope over either the whole sentence (54a) or just the result state (54b):

(54)   Dr Jones hospitalized Sam for the first time.
    a. 'It happened for the first time that Dr Jones hospitalized Sam.'
       for-the-first-time([CAUSE(jones, BECOME(in-hospital(sam)))])
    b. 'Dr Jones made it be the case that for the first time Sam stayed in a hospital.' (entails that Sam never stayed in a hospital before)
       CAUSE(jones, BECOME(**for-the-first-time**(in-hospital(sam))))

With lexical decomposition the two interpretations are derived as shown, just as for *again* in (36).

Dowty argues that it is not possible to capture the internal scope reading (54b) using meaning postulates and without lexical decomposition. Let us try to do just that. The S-modifying adverbial *for the first time*, as in (54a), will be called **for-the-first-time₁**:

(55) **for-the-first-time₁**(S) is true at an instant i iff S was false at all times before i.

This gives the external scope reading in (54a). Now we want to derive the internal scope reading shown in (54b). This requires a rule to derive a new adverbial, called **for-the-first-time₂**, that scopes over the result state. The question is how to get at the result state. On the lexical decomposition account, the result state is part of the semantic representation of the unmodified sentence. But on the meaning postulate account, internal scope for the modifier must be made available by the fact that *Jones hospitalized Sam* entails that 'Sam stayed in the hospital.' Then our rule would say that when **for-the-first-time₂** modifies a VP predicate of a sentence with subject denoting x that necessarily entails an expression of the form $[CAUSE(x, BECOME(p))]$, then the resulting sentence entails that p was previously true, that is, that **for-the-first-time₁**(p).

(56) Meaningpostulate relating **for-the-first-time₂** to **for-the-first-time₁**:
$$\forall x \forall p \forall P \,\square\,[[\textbf{for-the-first-time}_2(P)(x) \wedge \square[P(x) \rightarrow CAUSE(x, BECOME(p))] \rightarrow [CAUSE(x, BECOME(\textbf{for-the-first-time}_1(p)))]]$$

This postulate effectively inspects a sentence for some necessary result state p. If it finds such a state then the adverbial is taken to scope over p. Applied to example (54):

(57) Dr Jones hospitalized Sam again.

translation: **for-the-first-time₂**(hospitalize-Sam)(Jones)

necessary result:

$\square[$hospitalize-Sam(Jones) $\rightarrow$ CAUSE(Jones, BECOME(Sam-stays-in-hospital))$)]$

Postulate (56) allows us to infer:

CAUSE(Jones, BECOME(**for-the-first-time₂**(Sam-stays-in-hospital)))

This gives the right result, but there is a problem. The problem is that *Dr Jones hospitalized Sam* has many other logical entailments besides 'Sam stays in a hospital.' Since all hospitals are buildings, *Dr Jones hospitalized Sam* also logically entails that Dr Jones caused Sam to be in a building:

(58)   [CAUSE(jones, BECOME(**in-a-building**(sam))))]

This wrongly predicts that (54) on the inner scope reading should entail that:

(59)   Sam stayed in a building for the first time.

But of course it does not. Similarly, (60) works as usual with decomposition:

(60)   John drew a square around the picture for the first time.
      a. 'It happened for the first time that John drew a square around the picture.'
         for-the-first-time([CAUSE(john, BECOME(around(square, picture)))])
      b. 'John made it be the case that for the first time a square is around the picture.'
         CAUSE(john, BECOME(**for-the-first-time**(around(square, picture))))

But since all squares are rectangles, on the meaning postulate account, it would be wrongly predicted to entail that 'for the first time a rectangle is around the picture.'

The basis of this argument is that to get the internal scope reading of adverbials we need to get hold of the result state of the unmodified sentence. In lexical decomposition theory, the result state of the action is a component of the representation of the sentential semantics, so it is available for modification. (Alternatively, in the constructional or abstract light verb accounts, the result state can be represented in the syntax but not the lexical entry of the verb.) But it is impossible to reconstruct the result state on the basis of entailments of the unmodi- fied sentence alone, because a sentence can entail other results besides than the appropriate one.

Summarizing this section, lexical decomposition has been motivated both by paradigmatic relations between words and by syntagmatic rela- tions between a word and its syntactic environment. The paradigmatic motivations are strongest when they concern typological generalizations, while they are weaker for a single language since a decomposition can be effectively replaced with a meaning postulate. But the syntagmatic motivations are even stronger.

4.5 Mereologies, scales, and affectedness

Events are inherently dynamic: all non-stative predicates describe situations as involving change or dynamicity, in some sense. But a subset of event predicates, namely 'result' predicates, are special in that they specify scalar changes, i.e. directed change in the value of a single attribute (see Section 3.7.2 for discussion of manner and result predicates) (Rappaport Hovav and Levin 1998; 2010). The scale of change can be a many-point scale (*advance, descend, fall, recede, rise, flatten, lengthen*) or a 'two-point scale' measuring only a binary change from one state to another (*crack, arrive, reach*). As the event unfolds, a particular participant in it, which may be called the 'affected theme,' undergoes a change by degrees along a scale. In the examples listed in (61), the participant undergoing the scalar change is underlined.

(61) Some verbal predicates and their scales (from Wechsler 2005c: ex. 14)

Example	Dimension of change (X = affected theme argument)
a. *drink a glass of wine*	volume of X consumed
b. *eat a sandwich*	volume of X consumed
c. *write a letter*	amount of X in existence
d. *cool the soup*	temperature of X
e. *dim the lights*	brightness of X
f. *John walked to school*	distance traversed by X
g. *Mary hiked the Ridge Trail*	distance traversed by X
h. *read a letter*	amount of X that has been read

This notion of change along a scale plays an important role in the lexicalization of events. It is also important to argument realization, as there are robust generalizations governing the syntactic expression of the affected theme.

The verbs in (61) fall into three main categories with regard to the nature of the scale (Hay et al. 1999):

(i) With verbs of consumption like *eat* and *drink*, and verbs of creation like *write*, the scale derives from the relative physical quantity of the affected theme participant that has gone out of or come into existence as the event progresses: how much food or drink has been consumed, how much of the letter has been created (61a–c).

(ii) Verbal 'degree achievement' predicates like *cool the soup* and *dim the lights* (61d,e) involve change by degrees along a scale of temperature or brightness, not a change in the quantity of soup or lights.

(iii) With predicates of motion like *walk* and *hike* (61f,g), the scale for change is the distance traveled.

The last example, *Mary read a letter*, does not fit perfectly into any of the categories: nothing comes into or goes out of existence, and no property of Mary or the letter changes by degrees. Reading is similar to motion in that 'the text being read acts as a path along which the reader moves, while the text itself is not affected by the reading process' (Wechsler 1995: 54), but there are also differences: one can jump around to different parts of the text, while telekinesis is not possible in true physical motion.

Theories of event structure can be roughly divided into three groups according to which of these three verb types is taken as fundamental. First, mereological theories are based on extending the theory of nominal quantification to events, so they fit naturally with verbs of consumption and creation. Second, degree achievement verbs involve change in properties often denoted by adjectives (*bright*, *dim*, *cold*, *hot*), inspiring the extention of scalar adjective semantics to verbs. Third, in the localist theories discussed in Section 4.4.1, movement relations are the metaphorical basis for all predicates of change. In what follows, the mereological, scalar, and localist approaches are reviewed, followed by a broader discussion of affectedness.

The earlier formal models started from a focus on parallels between quantification in the domains of objects and events (Krifka 1987; 1992; 1998).[7] Krifka addressed the classic observation by H. J. Verkuyl that the telicity of a verbal predicate can be influenced by the nature of the quantification of its object. When the object is of indefinite extent (*wine*

---

[7] This discussion borrows from Wechsler (1995: 47ff., sect. 2.1).

in 62a) then the sentence is atelic, but when it has a definite quantity (*a liter of wine* in 62b) the sentence is telic.

(62)   a. John drank wine (for an hour/*in an hour).
       b. John drank a liter of wine (*for an hour/in an hour).

Krifka approached this phenomenon by investigating the mereological (part-related) properties of the nominal predicates describing the entity being consumed (*wine*, *a liter of wine*), and the mereological properties of the clauses describing the events (sentences like 62a,b). He observed that the 'drinkee' semantic role has the property that every part of a wine-drinking event corresponds to a part of the volume of wine. Because of this homomorphism between wine and wine drinking, quantification is transferred from the nominal to the verbal domain. When the nominal describing the volume of wine is a 'quantized' predicate, i.e. when the predicate describes it as having a definite amount, such as *a liter of wine*, the event description similarly becomes quantized, hence telic. When the predicate on the volume of wine is cumulative, or indefinite, then the event description is atelic.

To make this idea precise, Krifka (1987) built upon Link's (1983) theory of quantification in the domain of objects and extended it to model quantification in the domain of events. Objects and events, as characterized respectively by nominal and verbal predicates, have a mereological structure that can be modeled with an algebra. In Link's (1983) theory the realm of physical objects, including quantities of matter, can be characterized by a predicate whose extension has the algebraic structure of a join semi-lattice, where the primitive 'Part' relation relates objects or quantities of matter. Krifka applied this analysis of quantity to both object and event predicates, and then classified semantic roles of verbs according to the systematic relations between these two algebraic structures, namely the structure of the event denoted by the clause and the structure of the entity denoted by the nominal filling the role.

Take for example the wine contained in a bottle, as in (62). Call this mass of wine x_1. Any quantity of wine x_n that one might pour out of the bottle is a Part of x_1. That quantity x_n in turn has further subparts, and so on down to the minimal units, if any. Similarly, given an event e_1 of drinking the wine in the bottle, various wine-drinking (sub)events can be recognized as *Part* of e_1; these subevents of drinking wine could in turn have a further subparts, and so on. Thus the 'part structure' (mereology) of the quantity of wine can be modeled as a lattice of objects, and the part structure of the event can be modeled as a lattice of events. Specific algebraic relations can be observed to hold between the two lattices, which becomes the basis for a theory of thematic role types. With verbs of creation and consumption, among others, the thematic role of the item being created or consumed is characterized by a homomorphism between the algebraically structured object and event. Every part of the wine-drinking event correspond to a part of the volume of consumed wine, and vice versa. Krifka referred to the two directions of this relation as the 'mapping to subevents' property and the 'mapping to subobjects' property (63) (Krifka 1998):

(63)   a.   Mapping to subevents (MSE)
             $MSE(\theta)$ iff $\forall x,y,e$ $[\theta(x, e) \wedge y <_P x \rightarrow \exists e'[e' <_E e \wedge \theta(y, e')]]$
       b.   Mapping to subobjects (MSO)
             $MSO(\theta)$ iff $\forall x,e,e'$ $[\theta(x, e) \wedge e' <_E e \rightarrow \exists y[y <_P x \wedge \theta(y, e')]]$

In prose, if a thematic role $\theta(x, e)$ has the MSE property then for every y that is a proper part of x, there is an event e' that is a part of e, and $\theta(y, e')$. If $\theta(x, e)$ has the MSO property then for every e' that is a proper part of e, there is an entity y that is a part of x, and $\theta(y, e')$. Applied to our example, if the drinkee relation holds between a glass of wine x and an event e of drinking x, then the drinkee relation also holds between subparts of x and subparts of e. Roles with this property were dubbed 'incremental themes' by Dowty (1991). Only some thematic roles are incremental themes. The direct object of *push a cart* does not express an incremental theme role: it is clearly not the case that for every subevent of the *push a cart* event, only a proper part of the cart was pushed during that subevent.

     Turning to Verkuyl's telicity puzzle in (62), the question is why a clause with an incremental theme argument becomes telic when the phrase filling that role denotes a definite quantity, like the noun phrase *a liter of wine*. Predicates with that property are said to be *quantized*, defined as follows (Krifka 1998: 200):

(64)   A predicate P is *quantized* if and only if no entity that is P can be a subpart of another entity that is P.

A subpart of a liter of wine is not a liter of wine so the predicate *a liter of wine* has quantized reference. In contrast, the phrase *wine* is not quantized: subparts of wine are also wine. Telicity is defined as follows (Krifka 1998: 207):

(65)   An event description *R* is *telic* if and only if it applies to events
       e such that all parts of *e* that fall under *R* are initial and final
       parts of *e*.

Under this definition of telicity, a verbal predicate with a quantized
incremental theme is predicted to be telic. Since the predicate *a liter of*
wine is quantized, the verbal predicate *drink a liter of wine* holds only of
events whose endpoints coincide with the time at which the last drop of
a liter of wine has been consumed. Since the predicate *wine* is not
quantized, the predicate *drink wine* is true of any event of wine
drinking, regardless of endpoint. It is not restricted to those ending
with an empty bottle, so this verbal predicate is not telic.

Because Krifka approached this problem by extending accounts of
nominal quantification into the verbal domain, his mereological
approach is particularly well suited to verbs of creation and consumption. But as shown, the phenomenon is more general and the mereological approach may be applied to certain other types of verbs that do
not involve nominal quantification (see Wechsler 1995: 49–50). The
'scalar semantics' approaches to telicity has been argued to apply more
naturally to some verbs (Kennedy and Levin 2001; Beavers 2011).
While closely related to the mereological approach, the scalar semantic
approach takes its inspiration not from nominal quantification but
from the semantics of gradable adjectives (Kennedy 1999; 2007; Hay
et al. 1999; Kennedy and McNally 2005). (See Section 2.4.2 for background on gradable adjectives and Section 7.2.3 for further discussion.)

Gradable adjectives are interpreted relative to a standard degree on
some scale: *Michael Jordan is tall* means that Jordan's height is greater
than some contextually determined standard on a 'tallness' scale. Such
adjectives vary according to the structure of the scale (Kennedy 1999).
'Maximal endpoint closed-scale' gradable adjectives like *full, empty,*
straight, clean, and *dry* have an inherent maximum that serves as a
default standard which applies when it is not overridden by context.
'Open-scale' gradable adjectives like *tall, long, wide, short,* and *tall* lack
inherent endpoints, so they rely on context for their standards (Hay
et al. 1999; Kennedy and McNally 1999). Modifiers like *totally* or
completely place the value at the inherent maximum, hence they
sound worse with open-scale gradable than closed-scale adjectives):

(66)   a. completely full/empty/straight/dry   (closed-scale)
       b. ?? completely long/wide/short/tall   (open-scale)

In scalar semantic approaches the scale is modeled as a set of points ordered with a measure function, often assumed for simplicity to be the set of real numbers between 0 and 1. Closed scales include the maximum (namely, 1) while open scales exclude it.

When applied to the verbal domain, closed scales give rise to telic predicates. Atelic predicates arise if there is an open scale (or no scale at all). Hay et al. (1999) and Kennedy and McNally (2005) point out that degree achievement verbs derived from adjectives (*wide~widen*; *dry$_V$* *~dry$_A$*) preserve the scalar structure of the adjective from which they derive. As above, the adverb *completely* picks out the maximum on the scale:

(67)   a. The clothes dried (completely).   (Hay et al. 1999: ex. 21b)
       b. The gap between rich and poor widened (??completely).

The adjective *dry* has a closed scale, hence the verb *dry* does too; the adjective *wide* has an open scale, hence the verb *widen* does too. Similarly, the adjectives appearing in resultative constructions tend to be closed-scale adjectives, since resultatives are telic (Wechsler 2005c).[8]

We have seen that the dimension of the scale varies with the verbal predicate: for verbs of motion it is the distance traveled; for degree achievements it is the degree to which some property (such as brightness or temperature) holds; for the verbs of creation and consumption it is the quantity that is created or consumed (see (61)). Returning to our example of a verb of consumption, a quantized theme gives rise to a closed scale structure, hence a telic predicate (Kennedy and Levin 2001):

(68)   a. ??John completely drank wine.
       b. John completely drank a liter of wine.

Again, whether modifying an adjective or a verb, the adverb *completely* picks out the maximum on the scale, hence requiring a quantized theme.

So far we have seen two approaches to telicity and event structure: the mereological approach, inspired by the semantics of nominal quantification and most directly applicable to verbs of consumption and creation; and the scalar approach, inspired by the semantics of scalar adjectives and most directly applicable to degree achievement verbs.

---

[8] See Section 7.2.3.

In a third approach, motion events provide the metaphor for all types of change, as in the localist approaches described in Section 4.4.1. The term 'path' is sometimes used in the sense of 'scale', hence more broadly than just for literal physical movement through space. Actual physical movement has some unique properties that introduce special issues for analysis. With regard to applying the notion of 'incremental theme' to movement events, Dowty notes that in *drive (a car) from New York to Chicago,*

what is partially but not totally affected in this case, in a way parallel to the Themes in (20) [*build a house* and other examples involving verbs of creation—*S.W.*], is the PATH John traverses in driving from NY to Chicago: if the event is started but not completed, then part of this path has been traversed by John, not all of it, but the positions of parts of John of course remain intact with respect to each other.

(Dowty 1991: 569)

For Dowty the *path*, understood as the trajectory traversed (so far) by the theme, is 'affected': it grows incrementally as the event progresses. One might prefer to say that John is the affected one, since his location changes. On the scalar approach the path of movement provides the scale, while John is the designated participant.

Movement paths also have some special properties not shared by all scales. Krifka (1998) observes that movement events have the property of 'adjacency': whenever two subevents are temporally adjacent, then their paths are spatially adjacent, and vice versa. That is, there can be neither telekinesis (moving from A to B without ever being at points in between) nor time travel (gaps in time during travel). See also Beavers (2011) for discussion.

These different approaches to event structure are rooted in the same key insight: that events as described by predicates of natural language often derive their structure from changes of a certain lexically specified kind, observed in a designated event participant. The basic underlying hypothesis can be stated as follows:

(69) Many verbal predicates break up our experience into events on the basis of a *change*, for which the predicate specifies (i) the particular dimension along which the change takes place; and (ii) the particular event participant affected by the change (the affected theme).

Along with the mereological and scalar approaches described above are some alternative formalizations that embody very similar insights

(Tenny 1987; 1994; Jackendoff 1996). Combinations of the three theories are possible. For example, see Beavers (2011) for a theory that combines aspects of the mereological and scalar approaches.

With regard to argument mapping, the single most important and influential observation is the following:

(70)   Affected themes tend to be expressed as direct objects.

More accurately, they tend to be expressed as 'deep objects,' hence objects of transitives and subjects of passives and unaccusatives. Different scholars vary regarding the strength, explanation, and grammatical encoding (if any) that they attribute to this tendency.

Tenny (1987; 1994) adopted her version of this generalization directly as a principle of universal grammar, the Measuring-Out Constraint on Direct Internal Arguments (Tenny 1994: 11, ex. 9). She moreover hypothesized that such aspectual principles are the only general argument realization principles permitted by natural language (the Aspectual Interface Hypothesis, Tenny 1994: 2). Dowty (1991) lists incremental themehood as one contributing property of the Patient Proto-Role (see Section 4.3), which means that they tend to be objects of transitives and subjects of intransitives, but not subjects of transitives. In Role and Reference Grammar, the Actor-Undergoer hierarchy involves affectedness at the Undergoer end (see Section 4.4.4.1). Wechsler and Lee (1996: 648–51) posited that the 'event-delimiter' argument, as they called it, is associated not with objecthood per se but with accusative case marking. This allowed them to assimilate this phenomenon to the assignment of accusative case to event-delimiting adverbials in some languages (see Section 3.5.2). In Korean, for example, accusative case can appear on event delimiters such as durative (71a), multiplicative (71b), and distance (71c) adverbials:

(71)   a. Tom-i   twu sikan-tongan-**ul**   tali-ess-ta.
            Tom-NOM   two hours-period-ACC   run-PST-DEC
            Tom ran for two hours.

        b. Tom-i   mikwuk-ul   twu pen-**ul**
            Tom-NOM   America-ACC   two times-ACC
            pangmwun-hay-ss-ta.
            visit-do-PST-DEC
            Tom visited America two times.

    c. Tom-i   isip mail-ul   tali-ess-ta.
        Tom-NOM   twenty miles-ACC   run-PST-DEC
        'Tom ran twenty miles.'

                            (Wechsler and Lee 1996: exx. 4, 7)

In contrast with event delimiters, other semantic types of Korean adverbial such as manner adverbs like *coyonghi* 'silently' do not allow accusative marking. This suggests that event-delimiting semantics is associated with the assignment of Case to a local, verb-governed DP position. Syntactic approaches involving silent 'light verbs' in functional head positions (see Section 5.4) usually have a designated functional head very low in the structure that is dedicated to licensing the affected theme. For example, Wechsler and Lee's (1996) analysis of accusative adverbials was later adopted in a transformational setting by Morzycki (2005) by giving the appropriate semantic function to an accusative case assigning functional head.[9]

Beavers (2010; 2011) addresses generalization (70) within the context of a broader theory of affectness and the observed preference for direct rather than oblique expression of more affected arguments (see also Ackerman and Moore 2001). The theory is supported by a study of a number of argument alternations including locative and conative alternation (see Sections 3.5.2 and 3.3.3). For example, in the conative alternation, an argument alternates between direct object and oblique realization. Beavers observes that while the oblique variant has been observed to be less affected than the direct one, the exact nature of the semantic distinction varies depending on the verb meaning. Adding *at* to the verbs *cut, eat,* and *hit* weakens the event's entailed effect on each complement argument, but the nature of the weakening varies by verb:[10]

(72)   a. Marie ate her cake.   (all of the cake consumed)
        a'. Marie ate at her cake. (at least some of the cake consumed)
        b. Marie cut the rope.   (the rope is cut)
        b'. Marie cut at the rope. (the rope may or may not be cut)
        c. Marie hit Defarge.   (Defarge hit, not necessarily affected)
        c'. Marie hit at Defarge.   (Defarge not necessarily even hit)

                          (Beavers 2010: 830, exx. 20–22)

---

[9] Morzycki (2005) supported that idea with evidence from relative scope: the DP *an hour* in *Clyde didn't sleep an hour* takes narrow scope relative to negation, while the PP *for an hour*, in its place, allows either wide or narrow scope.

[10] Some speakers, including this author, do not accept *eat* in the conative.

For *cut* (as well as *slice, scratch, slash*), the oblique argument need not be affected at all, unlike its direct counterpart. For *eat*, the difference is whether the theme is totally affected or not. The verb *hit* does not entail a change in either case; rather, what governs the alternation is whether contact was made.

Beavers establishes a hierarchy of degrees of affectedness. The strongest type of effect is 'quantized' change, where the participant is totally affected, such as the direct object of transitive *eat* in (72a). The second strongest is 'nonquantized' change, such as the object of *cut* in (72b). Weaker still is the potential for change, such as the object of *hit* in (72c). Beavers formally defines the types on the hierarchy to obtain the predication that a sentence entailing some type of effect on the hierarchy also entails all weaker effects on the hierarchy. As a result, changing an argument from direct to oblique realization has the effect of weakening truth conditions. Beavers proposes this as a principle of grammar:

(73) Morphosyntactic Alignment Principle (MAP): In direct/oblique alternations the direct realization of an alternating participant has as strong or monotonically stronger truth conditions associated with it than its corresponding oblique realization.

(Beavers 2010: 831, ex. 27)

(In a refinement of this principle, Beavers asserts that a change from direct to oblique weakens the degree of affectedness by only a minimal step along the hierarchy: Beavers 2010: 848, ex. 69.) This view of (relative) affectedness in terms of the (relative) set of semantic entailments associated with a participant opens the way to a functional, markedness-based explanation for the association of affectedness with direct arguments (Beavers 2010: 858). Direct arguments have the unmarked encoding, so when expressed as a direct object the theme simply conforms to the semantics of the predicate, with all of its lexical entailments. Oblique marking signals some deviance from that semantics, which is to say that some entailment is disregarded.

4.6 Conclusion: the problems of polysemy and vagueness

In this chapter we have seen a range of models for aspects of word meaning, involving the use of thematic role types, proto-roles, aspectual (Vendlerian) analysis, aspectual and causal decomposition, mereologies,

scales, and notions of affectedness. Most word forms are both polysemous and vague, as we saw in Chapter 2. How are these models of word
meaning to cope with lexical polysemy and vagueness?

Consider first polysemy. Suppose we associate some syntactic feature
such as a complement pattern with a property of the verb's meaning.
Must that property be found in all uses of the verb? Or do we restrict
attention to certain 'prototypical' senses? In other words, how do the
theories of systematic polysemy and argument mapping interact? For
example, consider the stative and non-stative uses of the verbs *follow*
and *surround*:

(74) a. The spy is following us.   (agentive; non-stative)
      a'. What the spy did was follow us.
      b. The vowel follows a voiced consonant.   (non-agentive; stative)
      b'. #What the vowel did was follow a voiced consonant.

(75) a. The police are surrounding the building. (agentive; non-stative)
      a'. What the police did was surround the building.
      b. Tall grass surrounded the building.   (non-agentive; stative)
      b'. #What the grass did was surround the building.

In the (a) examples we might reasonably classify the subject thematic
role as agentive, since the follower or surrounder performs the action
intentionally. Our theory tells us that agents tend to map to subjects, so
this verb fits into that generalization. But the (b) examples are stative, as
shown by the simple present aspect and infelicity with *do* in pseudo-
clefts. In these uses *follow* indicates relative location and seems to lack
any sense of agency. If we divorce the agentive and stative uses of verbs
like *follow*, applying our theory of linking to each sense independently
of the other, then the theory which worked so well for the agentive
sense has nothing to say about the stative sense. That would leave it
unexplained that the mapping of subject and object, respectively, to the
participants coming 'before' and 'after' in the sequence is constant across
the agentive and stative senses. So this misses an important source of
explanation, with broad consequences, given that agency is optional with
so many verbs (Wechsler 2005a; Van Valin and Wilkins 1996).

Alternatively, we could take the agentive sense of *follow* as basic. This
triggers the agent-as-subject linking rule. The sense is extended to the
stative use through the application of a rule of systematic polysemy that
bleaches out agency. The linking pattern observed for the agentive
sense is preserved.

Yet another view takes the stative meaning as basic, and treats agency as a supralexical property that gets added to basic verb meanings. Semantic agency could be added through a systematic polysemy rule, or else, on the constructional or 'silent light verb' approach, agency would be directly associated with the (deep) subject function (see Chapter 6). Of course this forfeits any ability to derive the mapping of the arguments. Also, the agentive sense is diachronically prior. The *Oxford English Dictionary* (online version) lists this definition for *follow:* 'To go or come after (a person or other object in motion); to move behind in the same direction.' This sense is attested starting *c.*1000. But the stative reading, 'To come after in sequence or series, in order of time, etc.; to succeed,' is first attested later, *c.*1300. Also the putative agentivizing rule does not apply to all verbs but is lexically conditioned. The verb *precede* differs from *follow* in being more biased towards stativity:

(76) a. (#)We are preceding the spy.   (#agentive; non-stative)
      a'. #What we did was precede the spy.
      b. The vowel precedes a voiced consonant. (non-agentive; stative)
      b'. #What the vowel did was precede a voiced consonant.

A clause headed by *precede*, where the subject participant is earlier in the sequence than the object participant, lacks an agentive interpretation, as shown by (76a'). It can be agentivized only by expressing the 'earlier in the sequence' participant as an oblique *with*-PP or *by*-PP, not a subject:

(77) Each winery would precede a tasting with a long series of toasts.
      (1992 *Wine Spectator*, 31 May 65/1; cited in *Oxford English Dictionary*)

In this example, each winery brings about a situation described by the stative clause 'A long series of toasts precedes a tasting.'

One might take the mapping rules to apply to a prototypical sense, as in Clark and Clark's (1979) account of innovative denominal verbs, where the 'predominant features' of the noun affect its conversion to a verb (see Section 3.8.2). For innovative uses the features must be predominant so that the speaker can rationally expect the listener to readily compute the intended meaning on the basis of their mutual knowledge. Then, as a word becomes conventionalized, whether specialized, generalized, or both, the predominant features may change while the argument mapping is retained. The predominant features are then grammaticalized, converted to features of the computational system of grammar.

However we solve the problem, it is clear that a successful approach to relating word meaning to syntax must involve carefully addressing the question of where to place the borders between one word sense and the next, and how the mapping rules interact with systematic polysemy rules.

Vagueness poses a different set of issues (see Section 2.4). Inquiry-resistant vagueness of word meaning is a source of difficulty for any semantic model. How can we expect to have a theory of the relation between word meaning and syntax, if the boundaries of word meaning are fuzzy? Some problems can be overcome by taking an implicitly supervaluationist approach to vagueness. For example, there is no sharp line between *walking* and *crawling*: someone upright on their knees and moving might be described either way, and no amount of further inquiry would settle the issue. Yet we feel confident in asserting that (78a) entails (78b):

(78) a. Mary walked to the door.
      b. Mary walked.

In order for such an entailment to hold, we must assume that whatever standard applies to *walk* (versus *crawl*) in (78a) also applies in (78b). Then the entailment is 'supertrue,' that is, true for every possible way that the vague term can be made precise by stipulating a standard (i.e. every 'precisification' of the vague term; see Section 2.4.3). Much of the research in this area seems to rely on this implicit assumption.

More problematic is vagueness with regard to whether a word satisfies a semantic category or not. We let speaker intuitions determine whether a category such as 'agent' or 'cause' is appropriate for a given verb. But are those intuitions consistent? For example, Levin and Rappaport Hovav (2005: 38) criticize the use of semantic role classifications because of the lack of clear criteria for them:

The use of semantic roles has been criticized because it is difficult to find reliable diagnostics for isolating precisely those arguments bearing a particular role. There do not seem to be diagnostic tests which can be consistently applies to an argument with relatively uncontroversial results to determine whether that argument bears a particular role in the way there are tests for, say, lexical and syntactic categories.

While this critique is valid, making the semantic representation more precise will not necessarily solve this problem. Even if we can decide with confidence whether a particular real situation involves a semantic notion such as 'causation,' we may lack clear judgments of whether a sentence is true or false in the situation, due to the vagueness of the predicate itself.

There are a few avenues for addressing this problem. Dowty (1979) provides a theory of 'approximate' word meanings. As discussed in Section 4.4.3, Dowty's lexical rules generate the set of possible derived words, only some of which are the basis, via 'lexical extension', for actual words of the language. Alternatively, on a prototype based theory of word meaning, one may consider important or 'typical' semantic features of a word, as in Clark and Clark's (1979) approach to the denominal verbs (Section 3.8.2). Finally, probabilistic approaches to word meaning would leave room for indeterminacy, opening the way to a theory of vagueness. All of these approaches have an important commonality: the word itself has a semantic representation that transcends any particular instantiation or use of the word. That representation arises from generalization across different uses of the word.

5

Argument mapping approaches

5.1 Introduction: lexical and phrasal approaches to argument realization

This chapter surveys some of the main theoretical frameworks charged with mapping the arguments of a verb or other predicate to the syntax. In lexical (or lexicalist) approaches, words are phonological forms paired with 'valence structures,' also called 'predicate argument structures.' Two lexical mapping frameworks are described in this chapter, respectively formalized within Lexical-Functional Grammar (Section 5.2.1) and Head-Driven Phrase Structure Grammar (Section 5.2.2). In phrasal (or constructional) approaches, different morphological cognates and diathesis alternants are captured by plugging a single word or root into different constructions. The construction carries a meaning that combines with the word's meaning. The meaning of the construction is modeled either by positing specific meaningful phrasal or argument structures (Section 5.3) or by positing silent 'light verbs' that occupy functional head positions in a standard endocentric structure (Section 5.4).

5.2 Lexical approaches to mapping

5.2.1 The LFG lexicon

5.2.1.1 Predicate argument structure In Lexical-Functional Grammar (Bresnan 2001; Dalrymple 2001; Bresnan et al., in preparation), the predicate argument structure of a lexical item is a mapping between the grammatical functions governed by the predicate and thematic roles assigned by the predicate. This is the structure for the transitive verb *discuss*, as in *Mary discussed the proposal*:

(1)   An LFG predicate argument structure

$$
\begin{array}{cc}
(\uparrow\text{SUBJ}) & (\uparrow\text{OBJ}) \\
| & |
\end{array}
$$

discuss   'discuss < ____   ____ >'

agent   patient

The grammatical functions (SUBJ, OBJ, OBL, XCOMP, COMP, etc.) are interpreted by rules of syntax for a given language. Each function is expressed by a case, a phrase structure position, a verbal inflection (incorporated pronouns or agreement markers), or some combination of those. The expression structure of the language, including phrasal and morphemic structure, is called 'c-structure,' for 'categorial' or 'constituent' structure. The grammatical functions mediate the mapping between semantic argument structure and c-structure, where each grammatical function represents a class of equivalently mapped c-structure expressions.

Removing that mediating level of grammatical functions, the f-structure, would result in a loss of generalization. (This discussion closely follows that of Bresnan 2001: 94–6 and Bresnan et al., in preparation.) For example, suppose the SUBJ is expressed by a certain combination of nominative case, verbal agreement, and a phrasal position (such as the daughter of IP and left-sister of VP). That combination is represented in (2) as 'NOM/agr/position.' Then the same combination applies to the agentive subject of a transitive as in (2a), the subject of a theme-only ('unaccusative'; 2b) or agent-only intransitive ('unergative'; 2c), or the subject of a passive (2d).

(2)   a. transitive   b. unaccusative   c. unergative   d. passive

tickle   fall   speak   (be) eaten

< agt , th >   < th >   < agt >   < ~~agt~~ , th >
    | | | |
NOM/agr/position NOM/agr/position NOM/agr/position   NOM/agr/position

To state the same combination of case, agreement, and position for every argument structure variant obviously loses a generalization. Instead, the SUBJ abstraction captures the equivalence across different argument structures and c-structures:

(3)   a. transitive   b. unaccusative   c. unergative   d. passive

    tickle   *fall*   *speak*   *(be) eaten*

    < agt , th >   < th >   < agt >   < ~~agt~~ , th >
       | | | |
    SUBJ   SUBJ   SUBJ   SUBJ

In this way grammatical functions act as equivalence classes across mappings between semantics and morphosyntax.

5.2.1.2 Early LFG valence-changing rules   In early LFG, valence-changing rules such as passive were formulated as procedures or transformations operating on an input predicate argument structure by systematically modifying it. For example, the passive rule replaces the OBJ function by SUBJ, and either suppresses the SUBJ or replaces it with a designated oblique (in English it is OBL$_{by}$, the grammatical function expressed with a *by*-PP).

(4)   Early LFG passive lexical rule (Bresnan 1982b; Kaplan and Bresnan 1982)

Morphological change: V $\Rightarrow$ V$_{past.part}$

OBJ $\Rightarrow$ SUBJ

SUBJ $\Rightarrow$ {Ø/OBL$_{by}$}

This rule takes the structure in (5a) and returns this passive verb *discussed* in (5b):

(5)   a. *discuss*   'discuss $\langle$ ($\uparrow$SUBJ)   ($\uparrow$OBJ) $\rangle$'
                          agent   patient

    b. *discussed*   'discuss $\langle$ {($\uparrow$OBL$_{by}$)/Ø}   ($\uparrow$SUBJ) $\rangle$'
                          agent   patient

Similar functional replacement rules were posited for alternations such as the dative alternation:

(6)   An early LFG dative rule (Bresnan 1982b; Kaplan and Bresnan 1982)

OBJ $\Rightarrow$ OBJ2

OBL$_{to}$ $\Rightarrow$ OBJ

This rule converts the prepositional-object variant of the verb *hand* (*A girl handed a toy to the baby*) to the double-object variant (*A girl handed the baby a toy*):

(7)   a. '*hand* ⟨ (↑SUBJ) (↑OBL$_{to}$) (↑OBJ) ⟩'

  b. '*hand* ⟨ (↑SUBJ) (↑OBJ) (↑OBJ2) ⟩'

However compelling the theoretical argumentation for capturing alternations like passive and dative within the lexicon (see Section 5.4), there were shortcomings to formulating them as functional replacement rules. The theory of possible lexical rules was arguably weaker than the then-current transformational theory of NP-movement (A-movement) in Goverment and Binding theory (Chomsky 1981). At the same time, the functional replacement rules were basically transformations applying within the lexicon, and hence conflicted with LFG's more general embrace of declarative over procedural grammatical formalisms.

5.2.1.3 Lexical Mapping Theory   Beginning in the late 1980s, Lexical Mapping Theory (LMT) was developed to remedy those problems in the context of a theory of argument mapping. Instead of functional replacement rules, LMT assumes that a basic argument structure of a verb does not yet specify its grammatical functions. For a given verb, a single underspecified argument structure underlies both the active and passive forms, and also underlies the various diathesis alternates of a verb, for at least some alternations. After the application of any morpholexical processes such as passive formation, defaults apply to derive the grammatical functions.

The basic 'argument structure' (a-structure) consists of the set of argument slots classified into thematic role types, and ordered according to the thematic hierarchy:

(8)   agent > benefactive > experiencer/goal > instrument > patient/theme > locative

Roles also have a primitive syntactic 'intrinsic classification' with the two Boolean features *thematically restricted* ([+r] vs. [−r]) and *objective* ([+o] vs. [−o]). Transitive *cook* has this argument structure:

(9)   *cook*   < ag   pt >
               [−o] [−r]

Those intrinsic classifications of arguments condition the possible grammatical functions associated with them. The features cross-classify the four nominal functions:

(10)

	$[-o]$	$[+o]$
$[-r]$	SUBJ	OBJ
$[+r]$	OBL_θ	OBJ_θ

Thus the agent of *cook* in (9) must be expressed as a subject or oblique, but not an object, while the patient can alternate between object (of an active transitive) or subject (of a passive or unaccusative). Here OBL_θ is a cover term for a set of more specific oblique functions, where θ can be either a thematic role type (OBL_{exp}, OBL_{instr}, etc.) or a governed oblique case or adposition (OBL_{dative}, OBL_{with}, etc.). The special restricted object function OBJ_θ is realized in English, for example, by the position of the second of two NP objects of a ditransitive, which is restricted to the theme role, hence OBJ_{theme}.[1]

Intrinsic classifications are constrained by the argument structure by rules like the following (this version is from Bresnan and Zaenen 1990):

(11) Intrinsic classification

Patient-like roles: θ
$[-r]$ ($[-r]$: passivizable and unaccusative objects)

Secondary patient-like roles: θ
$[+o]$ ($[+o]$: unpassivizable objects)

Other roles: θ
$[-o]$ ($[-o]$: 'external arguments')

The patient argument of *cook* is a 'patient-like role', hence it is $[-r]$. As noted above, this captures a patient role's alternation between object realization (for transitives) and subject realization (for passives and unaccusatives). The agent argument of *cook* is not 'patient-like' so its

---

[1] Restricted objects are similar to the Goverment/Binding notion of inherent Case, a Case associated with a θ-role at d-structure. Unrestricted objects are analogous to structural Case. See Chomsky (1981: 170–71) for a proposal that the second of two objects receives inherent case.

intrinsic classification is [−o], alternating between subject realization (for actives) and oblique realization (for the *by*-phrase of a passive).

The features left unspecified in the intrinsic classification are filled in by a Subject mapping principle, and a Default mapping for the remaining roles. The symbol $\hat{\theta}$ represents the role in the a-structure that is higher on the thematic hierarchy than any coarguments. Roles are ordered from left (most prominent) to right (least prominent), so this $\hat{\theta}$ role is shown as the leftmost one. If the highest role has an intrinsic classification of [−o], then it maps to the SUBJ (see 12a.i); if not then a [−r] role maps to the SUBJ. This captures one version of the subject selection preference hierarchy (see Sections 3.2.1 and 4.2.1). Remaining roles map to the most marked compatible grammatical function, where positive values are more marked than negative ones: OBJ_θ is the most marked function, SUBJ is the least, and the others are in between. This means that any unspecified features for the remaining roles are filled in with positive values by default.

(12)   a. Subject mapping. Assign SUBJ

        (i) to $\hat{\theta}$ (when initial in a-structure), otherwise:
              [−o]
        (ii) to θ
             [−r]

     b. Default mapping. Map other roles to the lowest (most marked) compatible function in the partial ordering: SUBJ>{OBJ, OBL_θ}>OBJ_θ

The grammatical functions for the strict transitive *cook* are derived from the Intrinsic Classifications (I.C.) of the roles by applying the Subject mapping (Subj.) and Default mapping (Def.):

(13)   Mary cooked the turkey.

     cook <   ag   pt   >

     I.C.   [−o]   [−r]

     Subj.   [−r]

     Def.   _____[+o]_____

              S   O

The mapping regime allows for diathesis alternations under certain conditions. First of all, multiple function mappings can result if the word allows for multiple alternative intrinsic classifications in the first place. Such analyses are usually supported with evidence for verb polysemy. For a second source of alternations, suppose the second subject mapping rule (12a.ii) applies, because the word lacks a [−o] $\hat{\theta}$, hence fails to satisfy the conditions for the first subject mapping rule. Then if two different roles have the intrinsic classification [−r], either one of those two roles can map to the SUBJ function, predicting an alternation between two different argument realizations.

The first condition, where a verb has multiple alternative intrinsic classifications, has been exploited to account for diathesis alternations like the dative alternation. Suppose that a verb like *send* is polysemous: the recipient argument may or may not be conceived as 'affected' by action, hence 'patient-like,' since it comes into possession of the theme. (See Section 7.1 for discussion of the view that diathesis alternations depend on verb polysemy.) If the recipient is classified as 'patient-like', then it is intrinsically classified [−r]. The theme becomes a 'secondary patient-like role,' hence [+o]. The result is a ditransitive:

(14)   John sent Mary the books.

send	<	ag	rec	th	>
I.C.		[−o]	[−r]	[+o]	
Subj.		[−r]			
Def.			[+o]	[+r]	
		S	O	O$_{pt}$	

Now suppose instead that the recipient is not conceived as 'patient-like.' Then it falls into the 'other roles' group and receives a [−o] classification. But then the theme is not a *secondary* patient but rather simply 'patient-like,' hence it is [−r]. The result is the prepositional variant:

(15)   John sent the books to Mary.

send	<	ag	rec	pt	>
I.C.		[−o]	[−o]	[−r]	
Subj.		[r]			
Def.			[+r]	[+o]	
		S	OBL$_{rec}$	O	

Notice that the role with the [−r] intrinsic classification surfaces as the object in both variants. A [−r] intrinsic classification represents a role type that can in principle alternate between object and subject, under the appropriate conditions. The default mapping principle adds the [+o] feature and the result is OBJ. But if the highest role is not [−o], then the first Subject mapping condition is not met and so the [−r] becomes the subject. This latter situation arises in the passive, to which we turn next.

Morpholexical operations like passivization apply to the initial argument structure (which includes the intrinsic classification), but before the subject mapping and other mapping defaults apply. The passive morpheme indicates that the highest role in an a-structure is suppressed, indicated by the null sign Ø. (Following Grimshaw (1990) and others, Bresnan and Zaenen (1990) and Bresnan (2001) treat passive *by*-phrases as adjuncts.) Applied to the two different variants of *send* shown above, passivization yields the two derivations in (16):

(16)   a. Mary was sent the books.

send$_{pass}$	<	ag	go	pt	>
I.C.		[−o]	[−r]	[+o]	
passive		Ø			
Subj.			[−o]		
Def.				[+r]	
		Ø	S	O$_{pt}$	

b. The books were sent to Mary.

send$_{pass}$	<	ag	go	pt	>
I.C.		[−o]	[−o]	[−r]	
passive		Ø			
Subj.				[−o]	
Def.			[+r]		
		Ø	OBL$_{rec}$	S	

Having been suppressed, the highest role is no longer available to be subject, leaving the [−r] role as the subject.

In principle, a verb with two [–r] intrinsically classified roles allows for two alternative mappings, since the Subject Mapping rule (12a.ii) could apply to either one of them. Example (17) shows derivations of hypothetical three-argument verbs where the highest role is suppressed through passivization, and the remaining two roles are both classified [–r].

(17)　a.

		<	ag	go	pt	>
	I.C.		[–o]	[–r]	[–r]	
	passive		Ø			
	Subj.			[–o]		
	Def.				[+o]	
			Ø	S	O	

　　b.

		<	ag	go	pt	>
	I.C.		[–o]	[–r]	[–r]	
	passive		Ø			
	Subj.				[–o]	
	Def.			[+o]		
			Ø	O	S	

Bresnan and Moshi (1990) analyze Bantu 'symmetrical-object' languages as languages allowing more than one [–r] classification in a single lexical argument structure. Their Asymmetrical Object Parameter divides languages into those prohibiting and allowing multiple [–r] classification. Some Bantu languages allow 'symmetrical objects,' where either of two roles can have a range of direct-object type properties such as the ability to become the subject of the corresponding passive as in the hypothetical derivation in (17). Other languages have 'asymmetrical objects.' Among Bantu languages, the Symmetrical Object type includes Kichaga, Kinyarwanda, Kihaya, Kimeru, Mashi, and Luyia; while the Asymmetrical Object type includes Chichewa, Kiswahili, Bokamba, Chimwi:ni, and Hibena. For example, when a Kichaga applied verb is passivized, either the original object ('food' in the example (18)) or the applied object ('wife') can become the subject, as shown in (18):

(18) a. N-a-i-lyi-i-a   m-ka   k-elya.
         FOC-1Sb-PRS-eat-APPL-FV   1-wife   7-food
         'He is eating food for/on his wife.'
         (i.e. He is eating food for the benefit or to the detriment of his
         wife)

      b. M-ka   n-a-i-lyi-i-o   k-elya.
         1-wife   FOC-1Sb-PRS-eat-APPL-PASS   7-food
         'The wife is benefiting/adversely affected by someone eating
         food.'

      c. K-elya   k-i-lyi-i-o   m-ka.
         7-food   7Sb-PRS-eat-APPL-PASS   1-wife
         'The food is being eaten for/on the wife.'

An asymmetrical language like Chichewa allows the equivalents of
(18a) and (18b), but unlike Kichaga, Chichewa does not allow the
equivalent of (18c). A host of other 'primary object' properties similarly
can go with either object in Kichaga, while only going with one of the
objects (the applied one, in an applicative) in Chichewa. According to
Bresnan and Moshi's analysis, this split reflects two different settings of
the Asymmetrical Object Parameter: Kichaga, but not Chichewa, allows
multiple [−r] intrinsic classifications for coarguments of a verb.

5.2.1.4 Syntacticized argument structure   Syntactic ergativity is a
relatively rare phenomenon in which the subject and object roles are
reversed from the usual mapping (Dixon 1979; 1994). For example,
Balinese (Austronesian) verbs can have two main voices, Objective
Voice (OV) and Agentive Voice (AV) (Wechsler and Arka 1998;
Wechsler 1999):

(19) Bawi-ne punika tumbas   tiang   (high register)
      pig-DEF that   OV.buy   1.pro
      SUBJ   OBJ
      'I bought the pig.'

(20) Tiang   n-umbas   bawi-ne punika
      1.pro   AV-buy   pig-DEF that
      SUBJ   OBJ
      'I bought the pig.'

Irrespective of the verb's voice, the preverbal NP is the subject and the
postverbal NP is the object, as shown by a battery of tests involving
raising, binding, intransitives, quantifier float, relativization, and other

phenomena (Wechsler and Arka 1998). So the OV and AV reverse their subject and object roles relative to one another.

This phenomenon is a challenge for LMT, as shown below. Manning (1994), Manning and Sag (1995), and Wechsler and Arka (1998) propose an alternative to LMT that works for syntactically ergative languages as well as other languages. The 'syntacticized argument structure' level called ARG-ST mixes properties of LFG's a-structure and f-structure. The ARG-ST is a list consisting of first all the direct roles (terms), ordered by thematic prominence, then all oblique roles, ordered by thematic prominence.

(21)   ARG-ST $\langle$ term$_1$, term$_2$, ...$\rangle \oplus \langle$ obl$_1$, obl$_2$, ...$\rangle$

Comparing to LFG, the obliques correspond to OBL, and terms subsume SUBJ, OBJ, and OBJ$_\theta$. The linking rules for Balinese state that for an AV verb, the highest (leftmost) term is selected as the subject; for an OV verb, some term other than the highest is selected as the subject. Any remaining terms are objects. Subject selection for 'buy' in (19) and (20) is shown here:

(22)   AV.buy:

$$
\begin{array}{c}
\text{SUBJ} \\
| \\
\text{ARG-ST} \quad \langle \quad \text{ag} \quad\quad \text{pt} \quad \rangle \oplus \langle \ \rangle
\end{array}
$$

(23)   OV.buy:

$$
\begin{array}{c}
\text{SUBJ} \\
| \\
\text{ARG-ST} \quad \langle \quad \text{ag} \quad \text{pt} \quad \rangle \oplus \langle \ \rangle
\end{array}
$$

The remaining term is an object. In a ditransitive, the subject of the AV verb must be the agent, while the subject of an OV verb can be either of the non-agent terms:

(24)   a. Ia   ngedengin   I Wayan   potlot-e ento
           3.pro   AV-show   I Wayan   pencil-DEF that

       b. Potlote ento   edengin=a   I Wayan.
           pencil-DEF that   OV.show=3.pro   I Wayan

       c. I Wayan   edengin=a   potlote ento.
           I Wayan   OV.show=3.pro   pencil-DEF that
           'He/She showed I Wayan the pencil.'

These three sentences all have the same propositional content, differing only in discourse prominence. Linking for the ditransitive is shown here:

(25) AV.show:

$$\text{SUBJ}$$
$$|$$
$$\text{ARG-ST} \ \langle \quad \text{ag} \quad \text{rec} \quad \text{pt} \ \rangle \oplus \langle \ \rangle$$

(26) OV.show:

$$\text{SUBJ}$$
$$|$$
$$\text{ARG-ST} \ \langle \quad \text{ag} \quad \text{rec} \quad \text{pt} \ \rangle \oplus \langle \ \rangle$$

or:

$$\text{SUBJ}$$
$$|$$
$$\text{ARG-ST} \ \langle \quad \text{ag} \quad \text{rec} \quad \text{pt} \ \rangle \oplus \langle \ \rangle$$

Again, the remaining terms map to objects.

Balinese also has a true passive, where the agent is suppressed or else expressed as an oblique PP.

(27) a. OV-verb:

[Anake cenik ento]$_i$ edengin=a$_j$ awakne$_{i/j}$
person small that   OV.show=3.pro self
di kaca-ne
at mirror-DEF
'He$_j$ showed the child$_i$ himself$_{i/j}$ in the mirror.'

b. Passive (high register):

Anake alit punika$_i$ ka-edengin ragane$_{i/*j}$ ring kaca-ne
person small that   PASS-show self   at mirror-DEF
antuk ida$_j$
by   3
'The child$_i$ was shown himself$_{i/*j}$ in the mirror by him$_j$.'

Passivization causes a reordering of the agent, since it is relegated to the oblique part of the list.

(28) PASS.show:

$$\text{SUBJ} \quad \text{OBJ} \qquad \text{OBL}$$
$$| \qquad\quad | \qquad\qquad |$$
$$\text{ARG-ST} \ \langle \quad \text{rec} \quad\quad \text{pt} \ \rangle \oplus \langle \ \text{ag} \ \rangle$$

Interestingly, an agent antecedent can bind a patient reflexive if the verb is in AV or OV (for OV see (27a)); but in a passive clause the oblique agent cannot bind a reflexive (see (27b)). This follows in a straightforward manner if binding (like raising and control) is defined on the ARG-ST list: a less oblique item can bind a more oblique reflexive, i.e. in the relative order on the ARG-ST list, the binder must precede the reflexive that it binds. In LMT neither the a-structure nor the f-structure would give us the right structure for binding. OV clauses contradict the view that (at f-structure) subjects asymmetrically bind objects; passive clauses contradict the view that (at a-structure) higher arguments asymmetrically bind lower ones. The more general problem is that in syntactically ergative clauses (such as a Balinese OV) the agent remains a term but maps to the object instead of subject. This class of problems is addressed in a similar way for a number of languages by Manning (1994).

5.2.2 The HPSG lexicon

5.2.2.1 Basics of the formalism   From its inception, Head-Driven Phrase Structure Grammar has featured a rich and detailed theory of the lexicon (Pollard and Sag 1987; Flickinger 1987). An HPSG lexicon is not a collection of separate lexical entries but rather a single complex data structure in which any information common to multiple words can be factored out and presented only once for the whole lexicon. This data structure is modeled by a multiple-inheritance type hierarchy (with defaults, on some versions), a formal mechanism that continues to play an important role in the theory. In addition to the type hierarchy, HPSG uses lexical rules to capture derivational and inflectional relations between word forms, as well as some diathesis alternations, on some analyses. In this section we first describe the functioning of lexical inheritance hierarchies, and focus in particular on how they have been applied to argument structure. Then we turn to the various formulations of lexical rules.

HPSG employs a system of 'feature descriptions' to model the grammar. These descriptions constrain the set of 'feature structures' that represent real linguistic entities. A feature is a pairing of an 'attribute' that is conventionally shown in capital letters and a 'value.' In the feature shown in (29), HEAD is the attribute; *verb* is the value:

(29)   [HEAD *verb*]

The HEAD feature indicates part-of-speech category and other information shared between a phrase and its head. A feature description is defined as a set of features, usually represented as a two-column matrix called an 'attribute-value matrix' or AVM:

(30) Attribute-value matrix

$$
\begin{bmatrix}
\text{HEAD} & \textit{verb} \\
\text{TENSE} & \textit{present}
\end{bmatrix}
$$

Feature descriptions can be recursive. In addition to atomic values (*verb*, *present*, etc.), values may be non-atomic descriptions, such as the value of SPR here:

(31) AVM with complex values

$$
\begin{bmatrix}
\text{HEAD} & \textit{verb} \\
\text{SPR} & \left\langle \begin{bmatrix} \text{HEAD} & \textit{noun} \\ \text{SPR} & \langle\,\rangle \\ \text{COMPS} & \langle\,\rangle \end{bmatrix} \right\rangle \\
\text{COMPS} & \langle\,\rangle
\end{bmatrix}
$$

The valence features SPR ('specifier') and COMPS ('complements') are used to indicate the phrasal types that an element must combine with (see Section 5.2.2.2). Their values are lists of feature descriptions: in (31) the values of SPR and COMPS at the top level are lists of length one and zero, respectively.

HPSG has a system of types that is not shared by LFG. In HPSG, every AVM description and every value (atomic or otherwise) is assigned to a type. The type name appears in italics, usually written inside the top left-hand corner of the AVM, as in this AVM of type *word*:

(32) Typed AVM with complex values

$$
\begin{bmatrix}
\textit{word} \\
\text{HEAD} & \textit{verb} \\
\text{SPR} & \left\langle \begin{bmatrix} \text{HEAD} & \textit{noun} \\ \text{SPR} & \langle\,\rangle \\ \text{COMPS} & \langle\,\rangle \end{bmatrix} \right\rangle \\
\text{COMPS} & \langle\,\rangle
\end{bmatrix}
$$

Constraints called 'type declarations' (collectively referred to as the 'signature') effectively interpret each type by specifying the features required by AVMs of a given type. For example, the following constraint requires any structure of type *verb-lxm* ('verb lexeme') to contain a feature with the attribute SPR and value a list with one item satisfying the description abbreviated as 'NP':

(33) *verb-lxm*: [SPR ⟨ NP ⟩] 'verb lexeme'

The condition that every verb must have a subject (i.e. a specifier list with one item) can be encoded by assigning descriptions of verbs to the type *verb-lxm*.

Types are organized into a hierarchy of supertypes and subtypes. An AVM belonging to a type T is subject to the feature declarations for T and all of T's supertypes. For those who adopt default inheritance, the values specified by those constraints can be either hard values or defeasible ones, as explained below. Type declarations play the important roles of stating what features are appropriate for what categories and stating grammatical generalizations.

Type declarations can specify either hard (indefeasible) values or soft (default) values for its features. When default values for a supertype and subtype come into conflict, the subtype wins: the default value specified for the supertype is overridden by a contrasting value specified by a subtype. This mechanism of default inheritance is motivated by the ubiquitous phenomenon of generalizations with exceptions. For example: in English, most nouns in English are not marked for CASE, but pronouns are; most verbs only distinguish two agreement categories (3sg and non-3sg), but the verb *be* distinguishes more; most prepositions in English are transitive, but *here* and *there* are intransitive; most proper nouns are singular, but some are plural, such as *the Sierras*; and so on. Default inheritance allows for generalizations and exceptions of any size.[2]

To illustrate, consider the type hierarchy in (34) and the type declarations in (35). Default values appear to the right of a rightward slash.

(34) Example type hierarchy

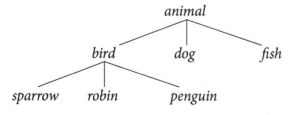

---

[2] Default inheritance has been proposed for LFG as well (Asudeh et al. 2008).

(35) Type declarations

$$\textit{animal:} \quad \begin{bmatrix} \text{MOTION} & \textit{motion} \\ \text{HABITAT} & \textit{earth} \end{bmatrix}$$

$$\textit{bird:} \quad \begin{bmatrix} \text{MOTION} & [\text{FLY} & / +] \end{bmatrix}$$

$$\textit{penguin:} \quad \begin{bmatrix} \text{MOTION} & [\text{FLY} & / -] \end{bmatrix}$$

$$\textit{motion :} \quad \begin{bmatrix} \text{FLY} & \textit{Boolean} \\ \text{WALK} & \textit{Boolean} \\ \text{SWIM} & \textit{Boolean} \end{bmatrix}$$

The Boolean type has two subtypes, + and –. Thus the feature FLY allows two values, + for creatures that fly and – for creatures that do not fly. The type declaration for *bird* states that birds generally do fly (we know it is a default since the + value appears to the right of the slash). The type declaration for *penguins* states that penguins generally do not fly. However, a special flying penguin, analogous to an idiosyncratic lexical entry, could be specified for the [FLY +] feature, hence preempting the default value declared for its type *penguin*. This system captures generalizations, exceptions to those generalizations, exceptions to the exceptions, and so on.

HPSG default inheritance is applied not only to the analysis of words, but also increasingly to phrases. Default inheritance is used in the analysis of semantically compositional constructions such as relative clauses, which are subject to syntactic idiosyncrasies (Sag 1997), as well as idioms and other multi-word expressions ranging from fixed expressions to those exhibiting various degrees of flexibility (Sag 2012). This answers the complaint occasionally levelled against theories that supposedly allow only a dichotomy of two levels, the 'productive' and the 'idiosyncratic,' for example with productive rules versus words that are learned by rote (Pinker 1991; 1999), or 'core' versus 'periphery' (Chomsky 1980). For example, Tomasello (2003: 101–2) sees this dichotomization as a problematic aspect of 'algebraic approaches such as generative grammar,' observing that linguistic competence 'involves the mastery of all kinds of routine formulas, fixed and semi-fixed expressions, idioms, and frozen collocations.' He cites both fixed idioms like *kick the bucket* and *spill the beans* and more flexible constructions like 'X let alone Y' as in *I wouldn't live in New York, let alone Boston.* Clearly Tomasello's (2003: 102) complaint there is 'no provision for in-between cases' does not apply to theories like HPSG.

5.2.2.2 Valence and argument structure   In early HPSG, as represented in work stretching from Pollard and Sag (1987) through the first eight chapters of Pollard and Sag (1994), subcategorization by a head verb or other predicator was specified in a feature called SUBCAT. The SUBCAT value is a 'list' (an ordered set), where each item in the list describes a dependent of the word, including the subject and any complements. The SUBCAT list items are effectively 'cancelled' from the SUBCAT list, in order from one end of the list to the other, as phrases are joined with the head. The SUBCAT feature is embedded in the syntax (SYN) value.

The semantic content of a verb or other predicator, encoded as the value of the feature SEM, is a structure representing a relation and its arguments, as in (36). The mapping between syntactic dependents and semantic roles is shown by structure-sharing *tags*, the boxed numbers [1] and [2] . The subscripts [1] and [2] on the NPs are abbreviations for referential indices within the SEM field of the NP. As a result, when the verb *likes* combines with its subject and object NPs, the referential indices of those NPs are identified with the relata of the verb-denoted relation. The boxed numbers behave essentially as variables, indicating token identity in a directed graph.

(36)   Early HPSG entry for the transitive verb *like*

$$
\begin{bmatrix}
\text{SYN} & \begin{bmatrix} \text{HEAD} & verb \\ \text{SUBCAT} & \langle \text{NP}_{[1]}, \text{NP}_{[2]} \rangle \end{bmatrix} \\[2ex]
\text{SEM} & \begin{bmatrix} \text{RELN} & like \\ \text{LIKER} & [1] \\ \text{LIKED} & [2] \end{bmatrix}
\end{bmatrix}
$$

The relative order of items on the SUBCAT list, called 'relative obliqueness,' is a primitive relation, and forms the foundation for the asymmetries observed in anaphoric binding and various other grammatical processes (Pollard and Sag 1987; 1992; 1994). Grammatical relations could be defined on this obliqueness ordering. The 'subject' of a verb was defined as the least oblique item on the verb's SUBCAT list; the 'objects' are other NPs on the list. Thus in that earlier version of HPSG, the notions 'subject' and 'object' were not part of the grammatical description itself but rather meta-level notions. However, Borsley (1987) and Pollard and Sag (1994: ch. 9) argued for an explicit distinction between the subject and complements within the valence specifications of verbs and other predicators. Among other problems noted by Borsley, defining the subject as the least oblique argument gives the wrong result for a non-predicative preposition, whose least oblique argument is its object, not its subject. Also in German the subject is the first direct argument in the list, so a German clause with only obliques lacks a subject. Hence the old SUBCAT list was bifurcated into a COMPS list for complements, and a list for the subject called either SUBJ (Pollard and Sag 1994: ch. 9) or SPR ('specifier'; Sag et al. 2003).[3] The latter list, which we call SPR following the more recent convention, is often assumed to contain at most one element (but see Müller and Ørsnes, 2013, for a proposal with multiple specifiers). The SPR and COMPS lists replace the old SUBCAT list as the representation regulating the syntactic combination of the head with its phrasal dependents. But recall that the SUBCAT list also served to represent systematic grammatical asymmetries needed for anaphoric binding and certain other processes. For such functions a single list corresponding to the old SUBCAT was retained and renamed ARG-ST or ARG-S ('argument structure'). In most cases the ARG-ST list consists of the SPR and COMPS lists appended together, as in (37).

(37) The verb *like*, with distinct specifier (SPR) and complements (COMPS) lists

$$
\begin{bmatrix}
\text{SYN} & \begin{bmatrix} \text{HEAD} & verb \\ \text{SPR} & \langle [3] \rangle \\ \text{COMPS} & \langle [4] \rangle \\ \text{ARG -ST} & \langle [3]\text{NP}_{[1]}, [4]\text{NP}_{[2]} \rangle \end{bmatrix} \\
\text{SEM} & \begin{bmatrix} \text{REL} & like \\ \text{LIKER} & [1] \\ \text{LIKED} & [2] \end{bmatrix}
\end{bmatrix}
$$

The SPR feature indicates VP-external arguments and COMPS indicates VP-internal ones.

---

[3] Pollard and Sag (1994: ch. 9) actually argued that both SUBJ and SPR are needed, on the basis of predicate nominals where the specifier and subject are distinct. In the sentence *John is an idiot*, the word *idiot* has both a SUBJ *John* and a SPR *an*.

5.2.2.3 Passive and lexical rules in HPSG   The passive voice changes the ARG-ST list but leaves the verb's semantics unchanged. The first item on the ARG-ST list disappears and its referential index appears on an optional *by*-PP, appended to the end of the list:

(38)   a. Kim likes Sandy.
        like (active):   ARG-ST $\langle$ NP$_{[1]}$, NP$_{[2]}$ $\rangle$
    b. Sandy is liked (by Kim).
        liked (passive):   ARG-ST $\langle$ NP$_{[2]}$ (, PP[by]$_{[1]}$) $\rangle$

HPSG analyses of passive generally work by altering the valence (or ARG-ST) list of the verb. The passive verb *liked* expresses the same semantic relation as its active counterpart but the ARG-ST list differs, and as a consequence the valence lists SPR and COMPS also differ:

(39)   The passive verb *liked*, as in *Sandy is liked (by Kim)*.

$$
\begin{bmatrix}
\text{SYN} & \begin{bmatrix}
\text{HEAD} & verb \\
\text{SPR} & \langle [3] \rangle \\
\text{COMPS} & \langle [4] \rangle \\
\text{ARG-ST} & \langle [3]\text{NP}_{[2]}(,\ [4]\text{PP}_{[1]}) \rangle
\end{bmatrix} \\
\text{SEM} & \begin{bmatrix}
\text{REL} & like \\
\text{LIKER} & [1] \\
\text{LIKED} & [2]
\end{bmatrix}
\end{bmatrix}
$$

There are two main ways that lexical rules can fit into the architecture of the grammar, as 'meta-level' rules or 'description level' rules (Meurers 2001). The distinction is important to understanding the theoretical status of the passive and similar alternations as seen from a lexicalist perspective.

The meta-level approach is sketched in (40a), where L$_1$ and L$_2$ are descriptions of lexical items (Calcagno 1995; Calcagno and Pollard 1995).

(40)   Meta-level lexical rule
    a. L$_1$ → L$_2$
    b. $\begin{bmatrix} lr\text{–}type \\ \text{INPUT} & \text{L}_1 \\ \text{OUTPUT} & \text{L}_2 \end{bmatrix}$

The rule states that if the language contains a lexical object satisfying L_1 then it also contains another lexical object satisfying L_2. In (40b) the lexical rule is represented as a type *lr-type* ('lexical rule type') declaring two features, representing the input and output descriptions. The rule is not itself a description of the language but a 'meta-description' connecting two descriptions of the language.

On the description level approach, the lexical rule is (or is replaced by) a lexical object description into which the 'input' description is embedded (Copestake 1992b; Riehemann 1993; 1998; Briscoe and Copestake 1999; Meurers 2001):

(41)　Description-level lexical rule

$$\begin{bmatrix} word\text{–}type \\ L_2 \\ \text{ATTRIBUTE} \quad L_1 \end{bmatrix}$$

The 'rule' in (41), shown as the type *word-type*, represents a description of language that can be used directly in further analyses since it basically has the properties of L_2. Let us compare meta-level and description-level approaches to the passive.

The meta-level passive lexical rule in (42), taken from Sag et al. (2003) states that for every lexeme satisfying the description in the value of INPUT, there is another lexeme satisfying the value of OUTPUT.

(42)　Passive lexical rule (from Sag et al. 2003)

$$\begin{bmatrix} d\text{-}rule \\ \text{INPUT} \quad \left\langle \boxed{1}, \begin{bmatrix} tv\text{–}lxm \\ \text{ARG–ST} \quad \langle\, [\text{INDEX } i] \,\rangle \quad \oplus \quad \boxed{A} \end{bmatrix} \right\rangle \\ \\ \text{OUPUT} \quad \left\langle F_{PSP}(\boxed{1}), \begin{bmatrix} part\text{–}lxm \\ \text{SYN} \quad [\text{HEAD} \quad [\text{FORM} \quad \text{pass}]] \\ \text{ARG–ST} \quad \boxed{A} \quad \oplus \quad \left\langle \begin{bmatrix} PP \\ \text{FORM} \quad \text{by} \\ \text{INDEX} \quad i \end{bmatrix} \right\rangle \end{bmatrix} \right\rangle \end{bmatrix}$$

In the Sag et al. (2003) system, a word or lexeme is an ordered pair whose first element represents the phonological form. The function F_{psp}

produces the past participle form from the stem's phonological form. For example, F_{psp}(/eat/) = /eaten/. Sag et al. (2003) analyze passive as a derivational (lexeme-to-lexeme) rule, rather than as an inflectional (lexeme-to-word) rule. One reason for this is that it maintains the generalization that inflectional rules for English, such as rules for deriving different tense and agreement forms of verbs, do not alter the ARG-ST. Also, in some languages, further inflections can be added to passive verb forms.

In a morphological approach to the passive, description-level accounts may take the embedded 'input' to correspond to the verb *stem*. The passive verb form (in English, the passive participle) includes a feature for its stem. The verb stem as listed in the lexicon has the basic active verb's ARG-ST list. The STEM attribute, the realization of ATTRIBUTE in (41), embeds the 'input' description. A constraint on the passive participle type specifies its ARG-ST as a function of its stem's ARG-ST, as shown in (43).

(43)   English passivization as a type constraint on passive participles

pass-part:
$$
\begin{bmatrix}
\text{PHON } F_{psp}(\boxed{1}) \\[2ex]
\text{SYNSEM} \begin{bmatrix} \text{SYN} \begin{bmatrix} \text{ARG–ST} & [a] \ (\oplus \ \langle PP[by]_i \rangle) \end{bmatrix} \\[1ex] \text{SEM} \quad \boxed{2} \end{bmatrix} \\[4ex]
\text{STEM} \quad \text{SYNSEM} \begin{bmatrix} \text{PHON} \ \boxed{1} \\[1ex] \text{SYN} \begin{bmatrix} \text{ARG–ST} \ \langle NP_i \rangle \oplus [a] \end{bmatrix} \\[1ex] \text{SEM} \quad \boxed{2} \end{bmatrix}
\end{bmatrix}
$$

The tag [a] represents a list of all ARG-ST items except the subject of the active voice verb. This morphological approach to passive is a description-level approach. It posits a constraint on the description of possible passive verb forms.

The morphological and lexical rule approaches differ in whether the underlying 'active' argument structure is part of the grammatical representation of a passive verb. Consider LFG's Lexical Mapping Theory (LMT) by way of comparison. In LMT, the a-structure represents the relative thematic prominence of the semantic arguments. The first (leftmost) position in the a-structure is reserved for the thematically most prominent role in the a-structure, sometimes called the 'a-subject' or 'logical subject.' But HPSG's ARG-ST list represents the relative syntactic obliqueness of the grammatical relations, not thematic prominence per se. The treatment of the agent of the passive illustrates that difference. In the HPSG analyses described above, the demoted agent is moved from the beginning to the end of the ARG-ST list, but in LFG it remains at the beginning. On the HPSG morphological account, what corresponds to LFG's a-subject is the argument expressed by the initial ARG-ST item in the STEM feature (see 43). In contrast, on the meta-level account only the output ARG-ST ordering is retained.

Grammatical construal phenomena in some languages have been argued to target the so-called 'logical subject' (a-subject) of a verb, irrespective of the voice of the verb form. Anaphoric binding in some languages is sensitive to this notion, for example in the binding of Marathi *aapan* 'self' (Joshi 1989), as well as reflexives in other languages (Bresnan 1995; 1998). The controller of purposive adjuncts must be the a-subject in some languages, such as French (Ruwet 1972). Some HPSG proposals, such as Wechsler (1991; 1995) and Davis and Koenig (2000), use a list in which passivization leaves the agent at the front of the list. For Wechsler (1991; 1995) the subject linking rule dictates that the subject expresses the highest 'available' role in the list (following Kiparsky 1987). Passivization designates the highest role for suppression, so it is unavailable to be subject. The preposition *by* is grammatically specified for marking the 'sublimation' of an otherwise suppressed role. Davis and Koenig (2000) specify different mappings for active and passive: for an active verb the first item in ARG-ST list maps to the subject and any others are complements, while for a passive verb the first item in ARG-ST list is suppressed, the second item maps to the subject, and any others are complements.

5.2.2.4 Lexical rules in Sign-Based Construction Grammar   Sign-Based Construction Grammar (SBCG) is a variant of HPSG that incorporates ideas from Berkeley Construction Grammar (Fillmore 1982; Fillmore et al. 1988). See the papers on SBCG collected in Boas and Sag (2012), especially Sag (2012). Like the Berkeley school, SBCG pays special attention to multi-word expressions.

An interesting aspect of SBCG is the modeling of lexical rules as unary branching structures. Such structures are intended as description-level representations, as in the morphological approach, but the daughter–

mother relation mimics the input/output structure of meta-level lexical rules. The passive construction (*passive-cxt*) type constraint in (44) licenses a unary structure where the sole daughter node (the single item in the DTRS list) represents a transitive verb lexeme and the mother node (MTR) is the corresponding passive lexeme.

(44) Passive lexical rule as a unary branching construction (from course slides by Ivan Sag for the Sign-Based Construction Grammar course, LSA Linguistic Institute 2011, Boulder, Colorado)

$$
passive\text{-}cxt \Rightarrow
\begin{bmatrix}
\text{MTR} & \begin{bmatrix} der\text{-}intr\text{-}v\text{-}lxm \\ \text{FORM} \quad \langle F_{pastp}\,(Y) \rangle \\ \text{SYN} \quad X\,{:}[\text{CAT}\,[\text{VF}\;pas]] \\ \text{ARG-ST} \quad L \oplus \langle (\text{PP}[by]_i) \rangle \end{bmatrix} \\[4em]
\text{DTRS} \quad \left\langle \begin{bmatrix} trans\text{-}v\text{-}lxm \\ \text{FORM} \quad {<}Y{>} \\ \text{SYN} \quad X \\ \text{ARG-ST} \quad {<}NP_i{>} \oplus L \end{bmatrix} \right\rangle
\end{bmatrix}
$$

For example, this rule licenses a local subtree in which the daughter is the verb lexeme BREAK and its mother is the passive lexeme BROKEN, as seen in the derivation tree for the sentence *Toys were broken* in (45). In that diagram each node label abbreviates a sign, which is a feature structure that includes phonology, syntax, and semantic features. Lexemes are notated with full capitals (TOY, BE, BREAK), while words and phrases are notated with lower-case mnemonics for the FORM (phonology) values. Notice that the phonology of the sentence is not read off of the terminal string but rather the root node.

(45) Schematic SBCG derivation tree for *Toys were broken*.

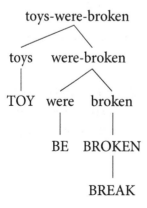

Like the derivational rule deriving the passive verb lexeme, the inflectional rules that derive words (*toys, were, broken*) from lexemes (TOY, BE, BROKEN) are also modeled as unary branching constructions.

The unary branching construction model for lexical rules has an interesting theoretical status. First note that this is a decidedly lexicalist theory. Passivization is a lexical process, not a syntactic one, in the following sense. The valence properties of the passive verb *broken*—the fact that the breaker argument is suppressed and the breakee is expressed by the subject—are directly represented in a feature structure that is associated with the phonology of only that verb, not with some larger syntactic structure including more of the sentence. This fulfills the desiderata arising from the important evidence for the lexical treatment of passive (see Chapter 6.6). It is local to the verb, so it is consistent with evidence from locality; and the mother–daughter relation is recursive, so the output of passive can feed further derivational processes such as adjectivalization, thus satisfying another set of arguments for the lexical treatment of passive (Bresnan 1982b).

At the same time, the items inserted into the syntactic derivation are not fully inflected words but rather lexemes. Thus morphological processes are assimilated to syntax in a move reminiscent of Distributed Morphology. However, an important difference is that in SBCG the tree diagram for a full sentence is not a description of the sentence; it is not part of the language model. In Sag's conception, the grammar provides 'constructions' which function as descriptions. The items in the language model that satisfy those descriptions are called 'constructs.' For example, the model for the English sentence *Toys were broken* includes a construct for the verb *broken* consisting of a mother node representing the passive verb lexeme (BROKEN) and the daughter representing the underlying root lexeme (BREAK). But the tree diagram for the sentence as a whole represents neither the grammar nor the language model. It is instead a proof-theoretic object indicating a possible derivation of a sentence. The model for that sentence could not include the phrase structure of the sentence, as that would violate the strict locality conditions that Sag assumes for syntax (Sag 2008). In that deeper sense, SBCG differs markedly from Distributed Morphology, for example.

5.2.2.5 Word meaning and argument linking in HPSG   HPSG does not have a single 'standard' theory of argument structure comparable to LFG's Lexical Mapping Theory, but a number of detailed proposals have been made.

Wechsler's (1991; 1995) theory works by placing meta-level lexico-semantic constraints on the possible argument list orderings for a verb. If the verb denotation has certain lexical entailments, then the relative ordering of two coarguments is constrained. In this way, verbs are intrinsically classified and the classification is not arbitrary but governed by the verb's meaning.

Wechsler (1991; 1995) posits three main rules. (i) Covering the usual ground for 'experiencers' and some 'agents', the Notion Rule states that if the verb entails that participant x mentally conceives of participant y, then x must outrank y in the ARG-ST ordering (called the ROLES list in those works). This covers transitive verbs expressing mental states (x *wants/likes/fears/expects y*), perception (x *sees/hears/tastes/smells y*), and volitional action (x *murders/chases/flees y*). (ii) A second rule covers the ground of 'affected themes' and related thematic role types. A 'nuclear role' is defined as a role for which a change of state in the participant filling the role lends the denoted event its temporal constitution. These include incremental themes (see Krifka 1987; 1992; 1998; Dowty 1991) and holistic themes (see Dowty 1991) as well as certain path participants that are not actually affected by the action but still determine its endpoint, such as the object of *read the article*. The Nuclear Role Rule states that if y is nuclear and x is not, then x outranks y. Hence affected themes and other participants that determine the aspectual properties of the event tend to be objects, not subjects. (iii) A third rule called the Part Rule states that in a part–whole relation, if y is the part and x is the whole, then x outranks y. Examples include *This toothpaste contains sugar* and *The book includes an appendix* (Wechsler 1995: 58). There are no thematic role types or other semantic diacritics on this theory, nor does decomposition play any part in determining argument linking. The grammatical description is hardly enhanced beyond the basic obliqueness hierarchy needed for complementation, binding theory, and other basic functions of the syntactic system. (The one *syntactic* enhancement is a feature [±r] for distinguishing 'obliques' from 'terms.') The rules operate as meta-level constraints on possible argument list orders, given the verb's meaning.

The HPSG-based theories of argument linking due to Anthony Davis and Jean-Pierre Koenig are similar to Wechsler's, but they are richer and more elaborate (Davis and Koenig 1999; 2000; Davis 2001; Koenig and Davis 2001). Linking regularities are based on a semantically defined classification of verbs. In addition the *roles* of verbs are semantically classified, as in many other theories. Davis and Koenig (1999;

2000) posit a small set of 'proto-roles,' the main ones being Actor and Undergoer, corresponding to Dowty's (1991) proto-agent and proto-patient, respectively. Each proto-role is associated with a set of characteristic entailments. Arguments of verbs are designated with proto-role attributes (ACT, UND, etc.) under the condition that at least one proto-role entailment must follow from the relation for the argument (see 46).

(46)   Lexical semantic relations with proto-roles (from Davis and Koenig 2000: 72)

Relation	Semantic role attributes	Characteristic entailment
act-rel	ACT	Causally affects/influences other participant(s) or event(s)
		Volitionally involved in event
		Has a notion or perception of other participant(s)
		Posesses an entity
und-rel	UND	Causally affected/influenced by another participant
		Undergoes a change of state
		Is an incremental theme
		Possessed by entity
soa-rel	SOA	Resulting state of affairs
		Perceived or conceived of by another participant
		A circumstance aspectually or temporally delimited by the relation
fig-grnd-rel	FIG	Entity located w.r.t. another participant.
		Moves w.r.t. another participant
		Contains or constitutes another participant
	GRND	Entity with respect to which another entity is located
		Trajectory along which another participant moves
		Is contained by or part of another participant
property-rel	P-BEARER	Entity-bearing property

For example, the eater participant of the verb *eat* causally affects another participant, and this is a proto-role entailment associated with ACT participants. So the eater can be the ACT role. The eaten role is causally affected by another participant, which is the proto-role entailment associated with UND. So the eaten can be the UND role. ACT and UND are specified as role attributes for the general relations *act-rel* and *und-rel*, which are both supertypes of the *eat-rel* relation denoted by *eat*, in an HPSG multiple type inheritance hierarchy. Hence the *eat-rel* inherits its ACT and UND designations for its roles. Notice that it is not necessary for an argument to have *all* of the characteristic entailments associated with its proto-role; one entailment suffices. The linking rules (for accusative languages like English) state that the ACTor maps to the first item in ARG-ST list and the UNDergoer maps to the last NP in ARG-ST list.

Davis and Koenig also employ a limited amount of lexical decomposition, for example decomposing causative type verbs that appear to have two actors:

(47) a. Chris jumped the horse over the gate.

   b. Bart fed the cat a dead bird.

Davis (1996; 2001) analyzes the verb *feed* as a causative with an embedded *eat-rel* relation, as in (48):

(48) *feed*:

$$
\begin{bmatrix}
\textit{cause-und-rel} \\
\text{ACT} \quad \textit{causer} \\
\text{UND} \quad \boxed{1}\textit{causee} \\
\text{SOA} \quad \begin{bmatrix} \textit{eat-rel} \\ \text{ACT} \quad \boxed{1}\textit{eater} \\ \text{UND} \quad \textit{eaten} \end{bmatrix}
\end{bmatrix}
$$

A flat, unembedded structure would require multiple actors and undergoers for one relation. Davis argues that introducing more attribute types, such as CAUSER in addition to ACTOR, would not be an adequate general solution, since some languages with morphological causatives such as Turkish allow recursive causativization through multiple application of causative morphemes.

Like LFG's Lexical Mapping Theory, both of these are lexicalist theories. The grammatical information determining a verb's argument linking is intrinsic to the verb, and constrained by the meaning of the verb. Wechsler's theory directly stipulates the argument realization possibilities for each verb in its lexical entry, crucially governed by a set of lexicosemantic conditions. LMT and the Davis–Koenig theory lexically stipulate a quasi-semantic (or perhaps syntactico-semantic) representation for each verb, again governed by a set of lexico-semantic conditions. In LMT, that representation consists of thematic role labels (ag, rec, pt, and so on) and intrinsic classifications ([±r], [±o]). In the Davis–Koenig theory it consists of attribute names like ACT and UND, plus some further structure.

5.2.2.6 Diathesis alternations in HPSG and SBCG

HPSG and SBCG accounts of diathesis alternations like the dative and locative alternations usually work by assuming a subtle polysemy in the verb. Each verb sense allows for a different mapping in accordance with the mapping rules of the language. This is broadly similar to the LFG Lexical Mapping Theory analysis of dative alternation described in Section 7.1, where alternations arise when a verb allows multiple alternative intrinsic classifications. Davis and Koenig (2000: 84) follow Green (1974) and Pinker (1989) in assuming that alternating ditransitive verbs are ambiguous between a 'caused ballistic motion' and 'caused possession' meaning (see Section 7.1). This makes them eligible for either of two verb classes, 'strict transitive PP verbs' (*str-trans-pp-vb*) or 'ditransitive verb' (*ditrans-vb*):

(49)   a. The strict transitive PP verb class (from Davis and Koenig 2000: 84)

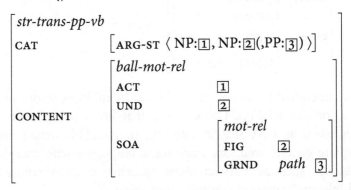

b. The ditransitive verb class

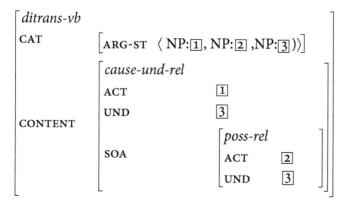

Davis and Koenig distinguish 'ballistic motion' (*ball-mot-rel* in the CONTENT of 49a) like throwing or kicking, where force is applied only at the beginning of the trajectory, from 'entrained motion' like pulling or dragging, where force is applied throughout (see Section 7.1).

(50)   Ballistic versus entrained motion (from Davis and Koenig 2000: 84)

   a. Pat threw/tossed/kicked/rolled the groceries to me.
   b. Pat threw/tossed/kicked/rolled me the groceries.
   c. Pat pulled/dragged/lifted/hauled the groceries to me.
   d. *Pat pulled/dragged/lifted/hauled me the groceries.

Following Pinker (1989), Davis and Koenig (2000: 84) assume a systematic polysemy rule. Koenig (1999) also assumes polysemy but avoids the use of a lexical rule, instead incorporating the systematic polysemy into a type hierarchy for lexemes. The diathesis alternation follows from the systematic polysemy. Like Koenig's (1999) analysis, Sag's (2012) SBCG account does not appeal to lexical rules. Following Rappaport Hovav and Levin (2008), Sag assumes that some alternating verbs such as *throw* are ambiguous, while others, such as *give*, unambiguously denote change of possession on both alternants. For the latter *give*-type, Sag (2012: 136–7) simply assumes two different lexeme classes with the same 'caused possession' semantics but with different valence features.

   Productive processes that seem to add an argument, such as resultative or causative formation, cannot plausibly be treated as cases of polysemy. The usual lexicalist approach is to posit a lexical rule that adds arguments and alters the semantics appropriately. Müller (2002; 2006) analyzes German resultative constructions in this way (see Section 7.2.2). German allows the addition of AP and PP resultative secondary predicates with intransitive verbs.[4] The process of resultativization adds a new object of the verb which serves as subject for the resultative predicate:

(51) a. Die Jogger liefen den Rasen platt.
          the joggers ran   the lawn   flat

    b. Es regnete die Stühle naß.
          it rained   the chairs wet

The resultative rule transitivizes an intransitive verb. Müller formulates the following lexical redundancy rule, stating that for every word stem satisfying the description to the left of the arrow, there is another one satisfying the description to the right of the arrow (this slightly simplified version is from Müller 2006).

(52) German resultative lexical rule (Müller 2006: 873)

$$
\begin{bmatrix}
\text{CAT} & \begin{bmatrix} \text{HEAD} & \textit{verb} \\ \text{SUBCAT} & \boxed{1}\ \langle \text{NP}[\textit{str}]\,\rangle \end{bmatrix} \\
\text{CONT}\ \boxed{2} \\
\textit{stem}
\end{bmatrix}
\longrightarrow
$$

$$
\begin{bmatrix}
\text{CAT} & \begin{bmatrix} \text{SUBCAT}\ \boxed{1} \oplus \boxed{3} \oplus \left\langle \begin{bmatrix} \text{CAT} & \begin{bmatrix} \text{HEAD} & \textit{adj-or-prep} \\ \text{SUBCAT} & \boxed{3}\ \langle \text{NP}_{\textit{ref}} \rangle \end{bmatrix} \\ \text{CONT}\ \boxed{4} \end{bmatrix} \right\rangle \end{bmatrix} \\
\text{CONT} & \begin{bmatrix} \text{ARG1}\ \boxed{2} \\ \text{ARG2} \begin{bmatrix} \text{ARG1} & \boxed{4} \\ \textit{become} \end{bmatrix} \\ \textit{cause} \end{bmatrix} \\
\textit{stem}
\end{bmatrix}
$$

The rule adds both an NP object (the single element of the list shown as $\boxed{3}$) and an AP or PP secondary predicate whose subject is the NP

---

[4] German permits resultative with transitive verbs like *streichen* 'paint' and *schneiden* 'cut,' but these verbs can also be used intransitively. Müller argues that all of these German resultatives are based on intransitive verbs. See Sect. 7.2.2.

object. The semantic content of the output consists of a causal relation whose 'causer' argument is filled by the semantics of the input verb (shown as ②) and whose 'result' argument is the coming into being of the AP-denoted state.

The key to lexical analyses like Müller's is that the verb's valence structure is augmented while its meaning is embedded within a larger constructional meaning. A similar analysis has been proposed for English resultatives (Wechsler 1997b; Wechsler and Noh 2001). The analysis is lexicalist, since the effects of the resultative rule, namely the introduction of the causal relation and the extra phrases, are not associated with the syntactic structure but only with the verb itself. It is not the actual syntactic structure of the sentence that is affected by the result rule, but only the potential for syntactic combination encoded in the valence features of the verb.

An important consequence of that view is that the resultativized verb, with its augmented argument structure, can serve as input to further derivational processes. One example is the formation of passivize participles (*plattgefahrene Reifen* 'flat-driven tires,' from Müller 2002: 218). Resultativization also feeds deverbal nominalization to form nominals like *Leerfischung* 'empty-fishing':

(53)   a. jemand   die Nordsee   leer   fischt
          somebody the North.Sea.ACC empty   fishes
          'Somebody is fishing the North Sea empty.'

       b. wegen   der Leerfischung der   Nordsee
          through the empty.fishing of.the North.Sea.GEN
          (taz, 6/20/1996, p. 6)
          'because of the fishing-empty of the North Sea'

                                                    (Müller 2002: 219)

On this basis, among others, Müller argues for a lexicalist analysis of resultatives, and against a constructional analysis.

To conclude this section, lexicalist theories treat most diathesis alternations as side-effects of the more general constraints on argument expression. The grammar links certain types of valence structure with certain types of verb meaning. A diathesis alternation can result if the verb is polysemous, and the linking rules assign each sense to a different syntactic valence structure. Or the verb could be monosemous, but the grammar provides two different options for expressing the single sense (as in the dative alternation of *give*, on some analyses). For productive processes that add meaning or dependents to the verb, a polysemy analysis is not plausible. Instead, such processes are usually analyzed as lexical rules. Those rules have been formalized in a variety of ways.

5.3 Constructional approaches

5.3.1 Introduction

An alternative to lexical rules that appeared in the 1990s, constructional approaches capture morphological cognates and diathesis alternants for a single word (or root) by plugging the word into different autonomous grammatical entities called constructions. The construction itself carries a meaning that combines with the word's meaning. The ditransitive construction means 'X caused Y to receive Z' and can combine with either a three-argument verb like *fax* (*Pat faxed Bill the letter*) or a two-argument verb like *bake* (*Pat baked Bill a cake*). In the latter case the verb contributes the agent and theme arguments while the construction contributes the recipient argument. The constructional approaches to argument realization that interest us here are those that would adopt constructions as an alternative to lexical rules. Instead of rules that relate one word with another, or relate one subcategorization frame of a word to another variant of the same word, the word is plugged into different constructions. Somewhat confusingly, the label 'construction grammar' is also applied more generally to certain theories that place an emphasis on the representation of specific phrasal constructions. For example, Sign-Based Construction Grammar (Sag 2012) is an explicitly lexicalist theory that includes lexical rules, but also emphasizes phrasal constructions that carry meaning (see Section 5.2.2.4). What concerns us here are approaches to argument realization that eschew lexical rules in favor of constructions.

Approaches to argument structure differ as to whether the constructions are phrasal structures or argument structures.

In the first version constructions are phrase structure-like objects, i.e. a certain configuration with part of speech and phrasal constituent information is paired with a certain meaning (Alsina 1996; Goldberg and Jackendoff 2004; Bergen and Chang 2005; Culicover and Jackendoff 2005; Asudeh et al. 2008; Jackendoff 2011). On this view, the ditransitive construction meaning 'X caused Y to receive Z' would be something like *[NP verb NP NP]*. However, such phrasal structures are too rigid to serve as the basis for an adequate theory of syntax, unless the theory also includes transformations or lexical rules (or both). Ditransitive verbs like *give* certainly have the 'X caused Y to receive Z' meaning in stuctures like [NP verb NP NP]: *Mary gave John the books* means that Mary caused John to receive the books. But the verb retains that meaning in many other phrasal structures, arising through an interaction with passive (*John was given the books*), raising (*Mary tends to give John the books*), fronting (*The books, Mary gave John*), and so on. In the absence of lexical rules, phrasal constructions are therefore most naturally paired with transformational approaches (see Section 5.4). In the transformation based theories the meaningful structures are usually indicated by silent 'light verbs' with meanings like CAUSE (such as *v*), which occupy functional head positions in endocentric phrase structures (Marantz 1997; Borer 2005a; Ramchand 2008).

Taking a non-transformational approach, Goldberg (1995; 2006) assumes a notion of a construction not as a phrasal object but as a valence frame containing grammatical functions, which is called an 'argument structure construction' (ASC). ASCs contain grammatical relation names like SUBJ, OBJ, and OBL (Goldberg 1995: 3). An ASC closely resembles an LFG f-structure 'nucleus,' defined as a PRED feature and all the functions determined by it—only without a particular verb specified. Goldberg (2013) gives the ditransitive construction as [Subj, V, Obj, Obj2]. This grammatical function structure allows for greater flexibility in the surface realization of the arguments. The idea is that a sentence inherits information from the verb, the ditransitive construction, and also other constructions such as passive, raising, and so on (see Section 5.4).[5]

5.3.2 Lexical mapping with argument structure constructions

Goldberg (1995; 2006) describes constructions like the ones in (54). When a particular verb is inserted into a frame, the verb meaning and the frame meaning are combined. A given verb can appear in multiple frames, thus allowing for diathesis alternations and thereby apparently obviating the need for lexical rules or other devices.

---

[5] Argument structure constructions specify grammatical functions that have to be realized together with the head but are underspecified with regard to linear order (Goldberg 1995; 2006). This proposal has not been worked out explicitly.

(54)   Constructions (Goldberg 1995: 3–4, 117–19)

Name	Meaning	Syntactic form and example
Ditransitive	X causes Y to receive Z	Subj V Obj Obj2 *Pat faxed Bill the letter.*
Caused motion	X causes Y to move Z (place)	Subj V Obj Obl *Pat sneezed the napkin off the table.*
Resultative	X causes Y to become Z	Subj V Obj XCompl *She kissed him unconscious.*
Intransitive motion	X move Y (place)	Subj V Obl *The fly buzzed into the room.*
Conative	X directs action at Y	Subj V Obl$_{at}$ *Pat kicked at Bill.*
Transitive	X acts on Y	Subj V Obj *Pat cubed the meat.*

Each verb is specified for a set of 'participant roles,' such as ⟨thief, target, goods⟩ for the verbs *rob* or *steal*. In (55a) and (56a), the three entities playing these participant roles are *Jesse, the rich*, and *the money*, respectively. (The more common term 'argument role' is reserved for the positions in the semantic structure portion of the *construction*, not the roles assigned by the verb.)

(55)   a. Jesse robbed the rich (of all their money).
      b. *Jesse robbed a million dollars (from the rich).

(56)   a. Jesse stole money (from the rich).
      b. *Jesse stole the rich (of money).

Certain participant roles are specified as 'profiled roles,' indicated by boldface. A profiled role must be realized as a direct grammatical function, as distinct from obliques (Goldberg 1995: 45). Goldberg gives the verbs *rob* and *steal* the lexical specifications in (57):

(57)   rob ⟨ **thief target** goods ⟩
      steal ⟨ **thief** target **goods** ⟩

The 'profiled' arguments are realized as direct grammatical functions (i.e. terms). Profiled participants are subject to the Correspondence Principle:

(58)   The Correspondence Principle
        Each participant that is lexically profiled and expressed must be
        fused with a profiled argument role of the construction. If a verb
        has three profiled participant roles, then one of them may be
        fused with a nonprofiled argument role of a construction.

                                                    (Goldberg 1995: 50)

(Presumably the second sentence specifies exceptions to the first.) The
term 'profiled argument role' in (58) refers to an argument role that
the construction maps to a direct grammatical function, i.e. one of the
functions SUBJ, OBJ, or OBJ2. However, a verb with three such roles
need only realize at least two of them as direct grammatical functions.
(Non-profiled roles are not constrained in this regard.) Profiling is
an intrinsic classification of roles for the term-oblique distinction,
roughly as in LMT, and more specifically as in the 'syntacticized
argument structure' view, in which arguments are sorted into terms
and obliques (Section 5.2.1.4). Profiling is 'lexically determined and
highly conventionalized—it cannot be altered by context' (Goldberg
1995: 46).

Profiled participant roles must be expressed, apart from certain
exceptional cases where profiled roles may remain unexpressed: argument suppression in the passive (*The sushi was eaten*); agent omission
in the middle construction (*She annoys easily*); and definite object
omission (*Jo won*) (Goldberg 1995: 45, 49, 56). As noted by Fillmore
(1986), the possibility of definite object omission is a lexical fact that
varies from verb to verb (see Section 3.3.1). A second diacritic notated
with square brackets around the role name, like [**theme**] for theme role
of *win*, indicates it can undergo definite object omission. Indefinite
object omission (e.g. *Pat ate*), on the other hand, arises because the
omitted theme argument of verbs like *eat* is not lexically profiled.

Summarizing so far, the lexical entry indicates a set of participant
roles, each classified for whether or not it is profiled, and whether it is a
potential target for definite object omission. A lexical entry has additional information. A verb is 'conventionally associated with a construction' and the verb–construction pairs are stored in memory
(Goldberg 1995: 50). This important aspect of the theory is apparently
not always fully appreciated. The theory is sometimes promoted on the
basis of the incorrect assumption that verbs and constructions can
combine freely (see Section 6.3.3).

However, further constraints on allowable verb–construction pairings are stipulated. The verb meaning and construction meaning must be properly related in order for the combination to succeed, where the possibilities for being properly related are grammatically specified. A common option is for the verb meaning to entail the constructional meaning: *She handed him the ball* entails that she caused him to receive the ball. Many lexical theories are based on entailments. The theory allows for this option (see 59a), but allows for other possibilities as well (from Goldberg 1995):

(59) Let e_c be the event type designated by the construction and e_v the event type designated by the verb.
a. e_v may be a subtype of e_c
b. e_v may designate the **means** of e_c
c. e_v may designate the **result** of e_c
d. e_v may designate a precondition of e_c
e. To a very limited extent, e_v may designate the manner of e_c, the means of identifying e_c, or the intended result of e_c

An example of (59b), *kicking* is a means by which the transfer is effected, so *kick* can fuse with the ditransitive construction as well. For (59c) we have certain sound emission verbs in the intransitive motion construction, as in *The wooden-legged man clumped into the room* (Goldberg 1995: 62, ex. 69a). The idea is that the clumping sound is the result of the motion into the room.[6] In a conative like *Ethel struck at Fred*, the verb meaning (striking Fred) is the 'intended result' (see 59e) of the constructional meaning (directing action at Fred) (Goldberg 1995: 63, ex. 74a).

Goldberg illustrates the need for such constraints on verb–construction combinations with this unacceptable example:

(60) *Joe angered Bob the pink slip.
('Joe gave Bob a pink slip, causing Bob to become angry.')
(Goldberg 1995: 60, ex. 61)

Combining the verb *anger* with the ditransitive construction, which means 'X CAUSES Y to RECEIVE Z,' would yield something akin to the interpretation shown, which is impossible. But it is not clear what prevents (60) from being generated as an instance of (59c), where e_v

---

[6] Goldberg (1995: 62, ex. 69c) cites *The fly buzzed out of the window*. The fly's motion does not cause the buzzing sound, so it is not clear how this one works.

('Joe angered Bob') is the *result* of e_c ('Joe causes Bob to receive a pink slip'). Apparently fitting one of these relations is a necessary but not sufficient condition for a verb and construction to combine. In any case, the main idea is that there is a finite set of possible relations between the meaning of a verb and the meaning of the construction it appears in.

When a verb is composed with a construction, their semantic contents are pooled and the verb's and the construction's respective roles are fused, subject to the condition that they be 'semantically compatible', meaning that one of them 'may be construed as an instance' of the other (the Semantic Coherence Principle). The kicker participant of the *kick* frame may be fused with the agent role of the ditransitive construction because the kicker role can be construed as an instance of the agent role.

An interesting aspect of the theory is that the construction can contribute roles of its own that do not fuse with a verb role. This feature has applications in a few English constructions. The ditransitive construction has three arguments, and means 'X caused Y to receive Z.' When it combines with a two-argument verb like *bake* (*Pat baked Bill a cake*), the verb contributes the agent and theme arguments while the construction contributes the recipient argument (see Section 7.1). To take another example, in certain resultatives an object appears that is not selected by the verb. Hence in *We ran the soles off our shoes*, the semantic role for 'the soles' would be contributed by the resultative construction (see Section 7.2).

5.4 Abstract light verbs in the syntax

Complementing the theories of lexical decomposition is the idea that the apparent internal structure of word meanings is actually composed within the combinatorial syntax itself. This recurring theme has resurfaced in generative syntax under different guises.

An early version of this theme appeared in the 1960s under the rubric of Generative Semantics (Lakoff 1965; McCawley 1968). Semantically contentful primes such as CAUSE and BECOME were directly inserted into syntactic deep structure representations of the sentence meaning. For example, the systematic relation between adjectival, intransitive, and transitive forms like *cool* was derived by positing distinct though related deep structures for the sentences. Those deep structures resembled the later aspectual–causal lexical decompositions (see Section 4.4.3).

Although Generative Semantics itself died out, vestiges of the syntactic composition approach to word meaning survived, and that approach later returned in full force. It is noteworthy that even Chomsky's (1970) influential article 'Remarks on nominalization,' which persuasively argued against syntactic accounts of the relation between derivational cognates such as *destroy/destruction*, still posited an abstract CAUSE node in syntax for the derivation of causative variants of verbs, as noted by Marantz (1997). That analysis is discussed in Sections 6.5.3 and 6.7.

In later variants of transformational grammar such as Government/Binding Theory, Deep Structure (or 'D-structure,' as it came to be called) lost its status as a true semantic representation, but remained a representation of thematic structure (Chomsky 1981: ch. 2, sect. 2.2). The idea was that a particular thematic role of a lexeme must be consistently assigned to the same position in phrase structure. One formulation of this conception was Baker's (1988) Uniformity of Theta Assignment Hypothesis (UTAH):

(61)   Identical thematic relationships between items are represented by identical structural relationships between those items at the level of D-structure. (Baker 1988: 46)

Baker illustrated with the causative alternation:

(62)   a. Julia melted the ice cream into mush.

      b. The ice cream melted into mush.

Since the thematic relationship between *melted* and *the ice cream* is the same in (62a) and (62b), it follows from UTAH that they must be in the same relative positions at D-structure. Specifically, the NP *the ice cream* is the (D-structure) object of the verb in both sentences. Baker posits the following D-structures for (63a) and (63b) respectively:

(63)   a. [$_S$ Julia [$_{VP}$ melted [the ice cream] into mush]].

      b. [$_S$ e [$_{VP}$ melted [the ice cream] into mush]].

To derive sentence (63b), a transformation moves the NP *the ice cream* into the subject position, where it replaces the empty element marked by *e*. In Government/Binding theory, D-structure functioned as a kind of thematic structure for the sentence.

The Generative Semantics idea of building complex word meaning by combining simpler semantic elements within the syntax was revived in the 1990s. Kratzer (1996) hypothesized that the 'external arguments' (Williams 1981)—i.e. arguments realized outside the VP, hence roughly those with Agent thematic roles—are not selected by the verb at all. For Kratzer (1996) the lexical entry for the verb *buy* lacks any mention of a buyer argument, so in the sentence *Sue bought the doll*, the subject *Sue* is not an argument of the verb *buy*. Instead the agent role is assigned in the syntax by what is sometimes characterized as an abstract 'light verb' or secondary predicate.

In an actual light verb construction like *John did the laundry*, most of the semantic content describing the laundering event is carried by the noun *laundry*, while the light verb *do* merely serves to introduce the subject (*John*) which expresses the agent of that event. Notating the abstract light verb with lower-case *v* (Chomsky 1995: 315), the underlying syntactic structure of *Sue bought the doll* is shown in (64a). This structure is intuitively analogous to the (somewhat awkward) sentence (64b), provided here for illustrative purposes.

(64)   a. [Sue [*v* [bought the doll]]]

     b. [Sue [did [the buying of the doll]]]

     c. $\exists e[\text{buy(the-doll, e)} \wedge \text{Agent(Sue, e)}]$

Kratzer hypothesized that in composing the semantic form in (64c) from the sentence structure in (64a), the expression **buy**(the-doll, e) comes from the verb *bought* (and its argument, the NP *the doll*), while the expression **Agent**(Sue, e) is provided by *v* (and its argument, the NP *Sue*). This use of the abstract light verb is similar to the use of semantic primes such as CAUSE in the theories that compose word meaning in the syntax. One innovation has been the attempt to assimilate the abstract semantic primes into the system of functional heads in extended X-bar theory, so that *v* projects a *v*P shell over the VP or other phrasal projection of a lexical item. This theory is critiqued in Section 6.5.

Borer (2005a; 2005b), Ramchand (2008), and others extended this analysis from the agent to all other arguments of the verb as well. Borer's (2005a; 2005b) system distinguishes two types of formative, 'listemes' and 'f-morphs.' Listemes are content words such as nouns, verbs, and adjectives. Borer puts forth the radical hypothesis that listemes have only an agrammatical conceptual representation but no grammatical features such as subcategorization frames, argument structure, lambda abstracts, part-of-speech categories like N and V, or minor category features such as count versus mass noun. Like Fodor (1998) and Fodor and Lepore (1998), Borer views word meaning as grammatically atomistic, so the distribution of the word *dog* is determined by knowledge of the denotation 'dogs' and not by knowledge of the word itself. Borer explains that, in her system,

> there is no direct interface between the conceptual system and the grammar, in that properties of concepts do not feed directly into any determination of grammatical properties. A substantive listeme is a unit of the conceptual system, however organized and conceived, and its meaning, part of an intricate web of layers, never directly interfaces with the computational system.   (Borer 2005a: 11)

For Borer, the grammar (or 'computation') deals in rigid, categorical values, while the conceptual system is highly malleable and subject to contextual factors. The meanings of listemes are highly malleable, fluid, context-sensitive, while the meanings of f-morphs are fairly rigid.

In keeping with the atomist credo, Borer's verb lacks a grammatical argument structure entirely. Semantic role assignment is understood as an interaction between agrammatical listemes and the properly grammatical formatives, the latter consisting of functional heads and f-morphs. Words lack arguments or category specification. Sound–meaning pairs called 'encyclopedic items' lack any formal grammatical information concerning category, argument structure, or word formation. To generate a sentence, we start with an unordered set of encyclopedic items , e.g. *sink*, *boat*, and *dog*. The functional lexicon includes features like Past <pst> and grammatical formatives like *the* and *will*. The set of selected encyclopedic items is embedded under some functional projection such as TP (Tense Phrase).

(65)   a. $[_T$ <pst> $[_{L-D}$ *sink, boat, dog*]]

       b. $[_T$ <pst>+*sink* $[_{L-D}$ ~~*sink*~~, *boat, dog*]]

A word moves into T, thereby becoming effectively a verb. A 'post-derivational phonological storage area' spells out these features: <pst> +*sink* $\Rightarrow$/sank/, for example. The other words move into positions determining their argument status, and 'argument structure, an event complex, emerges through functional syntactic structure' (Borer 2003: 7). Whatever moves into the specifier of EP (Event Phrase) is interpreted as the 'originator' (roughly Agent) of the event. Whatever moves into the specifier of ASP_QP (Aspect Phrase) is interpreted as the 'subject-of-quantity,' which is 'an interpretation associated with undergoing a structured change,' roughly an Affected Theme or Incremental Theme. Various other functional morphemes are introduced to encode different thematic role types (Borer 2005a: ex. 37). See Section 6.5 for further discussion of such theories.

5.5 Conclusion

Theoretical frameworks for mapping lexical arguments to the syntax fall into two main categories, lexical and phrasal approaches. Lexical frameworks treat argument alternations within the lexicon, based on two different strategies. Lexical Mapping Theory is an example of the underspecification strategy, in which the alternatives share a common underspecified lexical argument structure, and the variants result from different ways to specify the remaining unspecified features. HPSG is an example of a transformation-like strategy, in which a valence list is subject to an operation that derives a new list, albeit an operation formalized in declarative terms. In phrasal approaches, different morphological cognates and diathesis alternants are captured by plugging a single word or root into different meaningful constructions. In some versions those constructions are represented by silent pseudolexical 'light verbs' that occupy functional head positions in a standard endocentric phrasal structure. The next chapter addresses whether the available linguistic evidence favors the lexical approach, the phrasal approach, or some combination of the two.

6

The lexical–constructional debate

Stefan Müller and Stephen Wechsler

6.1 Introduction

The previous chapter introduced two general categories of approaches
to argument realization, lexical and phrasal approaches. This chapter
examines the theoretical debate between these two sides.[1]

In lexical (or lexicalist) approaches, words are phonological forms
paired with predicate argument structures. A word's predicate argument structure contains descriptions of the argument phrases the word
combines with, and specifies the meaning of the combination as a
function of the meanings of the parts. Lexical rules grammatically
encode the systematic relations between cognate forms and diathesis
alternations. Syntactic rules combine the words into sentences.

In contrast, phrasal (or 'constructional,' but see the end of this
subsection for an important caution regarding the use of this term)
approaches avoid the use of lexical rules. Instead, different morphological cognates and diathesis alternants are captured by plugging
a single word or root into different constructions. The construction
carries a meaning that combines with the word's meaning. In some
versions the constructions are phrasal structures, while in others they
are non-phrasal grammatical constructs called 'argument structure
constructions' that resemble the lexicalist's predicate argument structure, minus the specific verb or other predicator (Goldberg 1995: 3).

For many research questions the choice between these approaches
is not terribly important. As noted by Levin and Rappaport Hovav
(2005), one may seek to determine the identity and character of the
basic semantic relations, such as causation and possession, that are

---

[1] For further discussion of this issue see Van Valin (2013).

involved in the syntax–lexicon interface, without caring whether those relations are part of a lexical decomposition or part of a constructional meaning. In fact, lexical decomposition is actually consistent with either a lexical or constructional theory. A great deal of research formulated in one framework can be translated into another.

At the same time, the lexical and phrasal approaches differ in important ways. The lexicalist's predicate argument structure abstracts away from the phrasal context. This allows the lexical predicate argument structure to feed lexical rules such as passivization and conversion to other part of speech categories. It also allows for some arguments to be expressed in the local syntactic structure while saving others for expression elsewhere (as in partial fronting). And it allows for coordination of two or more verbs with matching argument structures.

The phrasal approach seeks to avoid lexical rules. A phrasal construction or argument structure construction is tied to a particular phrasal syntactic structure that results from combining the verb with its dependents. Such a construction is 'grounded' in actual sentences. Also, as noted, the construction carries a meaning, and some of the phrasal approaches would even replace standard phrase structure rules or syntactic valence frames with meaningful constructions. For both of these reasons, constructional approaches are often affiliated with usage-based theories of human language that deny the existence, or downplay the importance, of 'meaningless' algebraic syntactic rules such as phrase structure rules defined purely on syntactic categories like V and NP. On the usage-based view, the progressive generalization over input patterns that explains language acquisition and use is incapable of abstraction to the point of removing communicative content entirely (Tomasello 2003). So the resolution of the lexical–constructional debate could have profound theoretical consequences.

This chapter examines the arguments, ultimately deciding in favor of lexical approaches. As noted, lexical approaches include lexical rules to relate lexical items (i.e. roots, stems, and words) to each other. We show that the attempts to eliminate lexical rules have been unsuccessful. Section 6.2 provides a brief historical overview of certain relevant developments in theoretical linguistics of the last century. The development has progressed in waves oscillating between phrasal and lexical approaches. We discuss the reasons for changes and thereby point to problems that still exist in current approaches, or have been reintroduced into them.

As it turns out, considerations of usage-based grammar and coercion have little bearing on the lexical versus phrasal issue, despite claims to the contrary (Sections 6.3.1 and 6.3.2). The misperception that constructions are simpler than lexical rules is dispelled in Section 6.3.3. Section 6.4 examines challenges to lexicalism involving acquisition (Tomasello 2003; Goldberg et al. 2004). Neo-Davidsonian and 'exoskeletal' approaches, in which some or all thematic roles are assigned by silent light verbs, are critiqued in Section 6.5. Section 6.6 presents evidence for lexical valence structure from verb coordination and derivational morphology. We conclude in favor of the lexical approach.

The term 'construction grammar' is sometimes used for what we are calling the 'phrasal view,' and the title of this chapter reflects that common usage. However, the terms are not used consistently, and to avoid confusion we use the term 'phrasal view.' The term 'construction grammar' is also used for grammars that include meaningful phrasal constructions, or place a special emphasis on them. This chapter presents arguments favoring the claim that the grammars of natural languages include lexical rules operating on lexical valence structures, and that valence alternations and cognate relations involve the application of such rules. Our name for that claim is the 'lexical (or lexicalist)' view. Our name for the opposing view—that grammars of natural language do *not* include lexical rules—is the 'phrasal view.' We are not arguing against the existence or importance of meaningful phrasal constructions. A lexicalist grammatical framework can also include meaningful phrasal constructions, and indeed they typically do. An example of such a framework is Sign-Based Construction Grammar, which is described in Section 5.2.2.4. Despite its name, Sign-Based Construction Grammar is an explicitly lexical (or lexicalist) theory of exactly the type we favor, and which we counterpose to the phrasal view.

6.2 The pendulum of lexical and phrasal approaches

The following section discusses various frameworks that were suggested in the past 75 years of theoretical linguistics. Many assumptions of these frameworks play a role in current theories. We will zoom in on one clearly phrasal approach (GPSG) and discuss its problems in further subsections.

6.2.1 GPSG as construction grammar

A phrasal approach was proposed in the 1980s in the form of Generalized Phrase Structure Grammar (GPSG; Gazdar et al. 1985). It is instructive to consider the problems that it faced and why it was abandoned, since those critiques also apply to current approaches. We begin with a brief look at the theoretical landscape prior to GPSG.

Categorial Grammar (CG) is the prototype for a lexical model: every word (every functor) comes with descriptions of its arguments and the rules that combine functors with their arguments are very general and few in number (Ajdukiewicz 1935; Steedman 2000). An English transitive verb like *devour* is assigned the lexical entry (s\np)/np. This means that *devour* takes an NP to its right and an NP to its left. The rules for combination do not contain any part of speech information. For instance the rule that combines a verb like *devour* with its object has the form X/Y * Y = X. Such general combinatory rules have a component for semantic combination (e.g. functional application or composition).

Another branch of theoretical linguistics assumed phrase structure rules as a base component that generates structures to which transformations apply (Chomsky 1957). While the rules of CG are restricted to binary branching, the phrase structure rules of early Transformational Grammar were not. There were rules for VPs with ditransitive verbs that had three daughters (for examples see Chomsky 1965: 72, 96, 107). This rich, flexible system allowed for the representation of syntactic constructions at any level of specificity. On some analyses, phrase structure rules introduced rich semantic features directly into the phrase structure, such as CAUSE for causation (Chomsky 1970: 192), an approach greatly expanded in the Generative Semantics school (Lakoff 1969). In the more current parlance, it can be said that such analyses involved positing constructional meaning.

There were different views of how to integrate semantics into generative grammar. Transformational Grammar originally assigned semantics on the level of Deep Structure, but problems quickly became apparent, which led to modifications of the framework and to interpretation rules that took into account Surface Structure as well (see Bach 1976 for an overview). An alternative to the prevalent view in Transformational Grammar was proposed by Montague (1974), who assumed that interpretation accompanies the rules of syntactic combination. Bach (1976: 184) called this the 'rule-to-rule' assumption.

Also in the 1970s other non-transformational theories like TAG (Joshi et al. 1975), LFG (Bresnan and Kaplan 1982), and GPSG (Gazdar et al. 1985) were developed and some of them came with detailed semantic representations. For instance, Gazdar (1982) and Gazdar et al. (1985: ch. 10) are very explicit about the semantic representations and the combination rules for GPSG. They allow for rule-specific semantic interpretation. That is, they share the rule-to-rule assumption.

While Montague's proposal was in the spirit of Categorial Grammar and assumed binary branching structures, GPSG was not. The authors of GPSG assume classical context-free phrase structure rules, including for example a VP rule with a verb and two objects on the right-hand side.

The GPSG of the 1980s resembled some current versions of Construction Grammar in its adoption of what may be called a plugging proposal: a verb that is semantically compatible with a certain phrasal construction is plugged into this construction. Valence information is not represented as part of lexical items in GPSG. Instead, lexical items had a number assigned to them and could be inserted into phrasal rules that had the same number. It is only in interaction between rules and these numbers that lexical items are paired with certain arguments. For instance *laugh* is of category 2, so it can form a VP if used with rule (1a); and *devour*, of category 3, can form a VP with rule (1b).

(1)   a. VP → H[2]
       b. VP → H[3], NP

The H stands for head, hence in (1) H is the verb. On this model the verb has no valence feature to which lexical rules could apply. Alternations like the passive, for example, were captured entirely within the phrase structure component, through 'meta-rules' that systematically expanded the stock of phrase structure rules.

To sum up, GPSG resembles recent constructional approaches in several respects. It allows for rich, direct representation of the phrasal patterns found in natural language. It adopts the rule-to-rule assumption, so that meaning is built up in tandem with syntactic combination. And it rejects lexical rules in favor of rules relating constructions to one another. While practitioners of GPSG did not use the formalism in the same ways that construction grammar (Goldberg 1995; 2006) has been used—the GPSG rule for ditransitive VPs did not specify a meaning like 'x causes y to receive z'—the architecture of the two theories is nonetheless similar, allowing us to understand the pitfalls of that architecture by examining its history.

The next subsections look at some of the problems that this proposal faced, in order to understand why it was finally given up and replaced by theories that assume a lexical representation of valence information. We will look at two phenomena here: morphological derivation, and partial frontings.

6.2.2 Problem 1: morphological derivation

The first problem with the GPSG model is that there are morphological processes that are sensitive to lexical valence (Müller 2010: 129). Verb-to-adjective conversion with English *-able* or German *-bar* is productive with transitive verbs only. To the right of each German adjective is the root verb and the set of cases it assigns:

(2) Adjective   Gloss   Verb and cases

a. *lösbar*   'solvable'   *lösen* (nominative, accusative)
b. *vergleichbar* 'comparable' *vergleichen* (nominative, accusative, PP[*mit*])
c. **schlafbar*   'sleepable'   *schlafen* (nominative)
d. **helfbar*   'helpable'   *helfen* (nominative, dative)

In order to serve as a base for a *-bar* adjective, the verb must have at least a nominative and an accusative argument, as the examples in (2) show. So intransitive verbs like *schlafen* 'sleep' and *helfen* 'help' do not allow for the *-bar* derivation.

Moreover, it will not work to say that *-bar* derivation applies only to verbs with certain category numbers (recall (1)). For example, *lösen* ('solve') and *vergleichen* ('compare') have different valence frames, hence different numbers. This means that a GPSG rule for *-bar* derivation would have to mention several numbers that correspond to different valence frames that allow for *-bar* derivation. Since the numbers by themselves do not contain any information about the presence of a direct object, such a formulation of the *-bar* derivation rule would amount to stipulating a seemingly arbitrary set of numbers, and thereby miss an important generalization.

This should be contrasted with models that assume a lexical representation of valence: the *-bar* suffix can be specified to attach to verbs whose valence list starts with a nominative and an accusative. The generalization is captured easily in such models.

6.2.3 Problem 2: partial fronting

Another reason for needing valence information is to allow for variation in where in the sentence structure the arguments are discharged. For example, German allows for partial frontings like (3):

(3) a. [Erzählen]   wird   er   seiner Tochter   ein
         tell   will   he.NOM   his daughter.DAT   a
         Märchen   können.
         fairy.tale.ACC   can
         'He will be able to tell his daughter a fairy tale.'

     b. [Ein   Märchen   erzählen] wird   er   seiner
         a   fairy.tale.ACC   tell   will   he   his
         Tochter   können.
         daughter.DAT   can

     c. [Seiner Tochter   ein   Märchen   erzählen] wird
         his daughter.DAT   a   fairy.tale.ACC   tell   will
         er   können.
         he.NOM   can

The non-finite verb *erzählen* 'tell' may be contiguous with all of its complements (3c) or with a proper subset of its complements (3a,b), in the so-called 'prefield' to the left of the finite verb (subjects can also be fronted with non-finite verbs, but this is rather restricted). The problem for GPSG-like approaches is that the arguments are licensed by a certain phrase structure rule. Such an approach requires phrase structure rules that license the verb without any argument (for (3a)) and with a single argument (for (3b)). Moreover, it has to be ensured that the arguments that are missing in the prefield are realized in the remainder of the clause. One cannot omit obligatory arguments or realize arguments with other properties like a different case, as the examples in (4) show:

(4) a. Verschlungen   hat   er   es   nicht.
         devoured   has   he   it.ACC   not
         'He did not devour it.'

     b. *Verschlungen   hat   er   nicht.
          devoured   has   he   not

     c. *Verschlungen   hat   er   ihm   nicht.
          devoured   has   he   pro.M.DAT   not

The obvious generalization is that the fronted and unfronted arguments must add up to the total set belonging to the verb. This shows
that the verb has a lexical valence structure, unless some other explanation can be found.

There have been various attempts to solve the partial fronting problem within GPSG. A review of those attempts reveals that the only
successful one crucially adopted aspects of the lexical approach.
Nerbonne (1986) and Johnson (1986) suggest GPSG analyses that can
deal with the data. However, they assume a valence representation with
binary features like ±NPacc and ±NPdat to represent the fact that the
accusative or dative object is realized in the prefield in (4b) and may not
be realized in the remainder of the clause (in the so-called middle field).
As both Nerbonne and Johnson state clearly, this incorporates ideas
from Categorial Grammar into GPSG. Theories like HPSG (Pollard
and Sag 1987; 1994), developed after GPSG, explicitly borrow from CG
(see e.g. Nerbonne 1994; Pollard 1996; Meurers 2000; Müller 1996;
2002; Kathol 2001; Hinrichs and Nakazawa 1989; 1994a).

If one does not want to go with the lexical specification of valence
frames, there seem to be just two alternatives: the remnant-movement
analysis as often assumed in the transformational literature (G. Müller
1998) and linearization-based approaches that allow for discontinuous
constituents (Reape 1994). In remnant movement approaches it is
assumed that the prefield is filled by a VP. The elements that are not
realized in the prefield are moved out of the VP before the (remnant of
the) VP is fronted. (Such movement-based analyses are usually not
assumed in non-transformational frameworks, although Hinrichs and
Nakazawa (1994b) show that a remnant movement analysis is possible
even in a framework that does not make use of movement transformations to empty a VP and then move it.) But there are empirical
problems with remnant movement (Haider 1993: 281; De Kuthy 2002:
sect. 4.2.5; De Kuthy and Meurers 2001: sect. 2; Fanselow 2002).[2]

The last alternative is that the verb and all of its arguments form a
constituent, albeit a discontinuous constituent in the partial fronting
cases. On such a view, one does not generate alternative phrase structures for cases such as (3), but rather the grammar allows for discontinuous pronunciation of the VP (this is called a *linearization* account

---

[2] For instance, there are wh-indefinites that do not scramble but a remnant movement
approach has to assume that they scramble out of VP in order to front the VP remnant.

since words must be 'linearized' for pronunciation).[3] The linearization proposal by Reape (1994) was criticized by Kathol (2001: sect. 8.6), who argued on the basis of agreement, case assignment, and passive for a CG-like analysis of German verbal complexes. The problem for linearization is that the elements in the fronted position can interact with the local syntactic environment, so it is not just a matter of pronouncing words in a different position. This can be seen with raising of an argument. In his linearization account Reape assumed that a raising verb like *scheinen* 'seem' embeds a full clause and allows for a discontinuous linearization of the parts of this clause. Kathol argued that such an approach fails to capture local agreement relations between the finite verb and the subject of a clause that is embedded under a raising verb. Consider his examples in (5):

(5) a. Den Mädchen scheint/*scheinen   schlecht zu werden.
         the girls.DAT seem.3SG/seem.3PL   ill   to become
         'The girls seem to be getting sick to their stomachs.'

     b. Du   scheinst/*scheint   nicht zu verstehen.
         you seem.2SG/seem.3SG   not   to understand
         'You don't seem to understand anything.'

The verb that selects the subject (*werden, verstehen*) does not agree with that subject, since it is an infinitive with *zu*, a type which does not show agreement. Instead the subject triggers agreement with the finite verb one level up (*scheinen*). The example in (5a) shows that there does not have to be a subject at all. This is due to the fact that German allows for subjectless predicates, and that raising verbs do not care whether the downstairs predicate selects for a subject or not. An approach that assumes that *du* ('you') in (5b) is a syntactic dependent of *scheinen* ('seem') can account for the agreement relation locally.[4]

---

[3] Such a linearization account may be what Goldberg (2006: 10) has in mind when she writes that argument structure constructions are 'fused' with other constructions like a VP construction.

[4] Working in the HPSG framework, Meurers (2000) and Meurers and De Kuthy (2001) suggested an approach where dependents of a head that are not realized within the domain of this head are visible for a higher head. Similar techniques were suggested by Lichte (2013) in the TAG framework. Such mechanisms, which allow an account of the agreement facts, have not been incorporated into Construction Grammars. In order to evaluate the Construction Grammar notion of fusion (see fn. 3) and to compare it with its competitors, the respective solutions would have to be worked out in detail.

6.2.4 Problem 3: cross-linguistic comparison

Constructional approaches that assume phrase-structure representations encounter another problem, one that has been observed in different settings over the years: the constructions are necessarily language-specific and are not easily generalized across languages. For example, in terms of lexical argument structure the passive voice can be described uniformly for many different types of language, even though the phrasal expression may differ widely depending on whether grammatical functions in a given language are encoded with case, word order, or head marking. Perlmutter and Postal (1977; 1983) made this observation as part of an argument for treating grammatical relations as primitives, as in Relational Grammar, rather than defining grammatical relations in terms of phrasal configurations as advocated by Chomsky (1965). The same point has also been a part of the argumentation, beginning in the 1970s and 1980s, in favor of lexical accounts of alternations like the passive, as opposed to employing transformations that are defined over syntactic configurations (Bresnan 1982b; 2001: ch. 3). Transformational approaches addressed this problem by appealing to more abstract 'underlying' configurational representations with more elaborate operations to map those representations to the observable syntax. But phrasal construction grammar explicitly rejects such a move, leaving it open to similar criticism, which has indeed been raised against it (Van Valin 2007; Müller 2006: sect. 6.3; 2013a: sect. 1). Assuming the importance of cross-linguistic generalizations within linguistic theory, then this is a serious problem for constructional approaches.

Concluding this section, we have seen how the pendulum has swung between lexical and phrasal approaches. The arguments against the GPSG phrasal model from morphological derivation and partial fronting are still valid, and the problems are not addressed by current phrasal approaches. Of the theories on offer, the best place for that pendulum to come to rest, in our view, is at a theory in which words are equipped with valence information that is subject to the effects of lexical rules.

6.3 Arguments for constructional models

This section examines the claims to purported advantages of phrasal versions of Construction Grammar over lexical rules. Then in later sections we turn to positive arguments for lexical rules.

6.3.1 Usage-based theories of language

For many practitioners of Construction Grammar, their approach to syntax is deeply rooted in the ontological strictures of usage-based theories of language (Langacker 1987; Goldberg 1995; Croft 2001; Tomasello 2003). Usage-based theorists oppose the notion of 'linguistic rules conceived of as algebraic procedures for combining symbols that do not themselves contribute to meaning.' All linguistic entities are symbolic of things in the realm of denotations: 'all have communicative significance because they all derive directly from language use' (Tomasello 2003: 99). Although the formatives of language may be rather abstract, they can never be divorced from their functional origin as a tool of communication. The usage-based view of constructions is summed up well by Tomasello (2003: 100):

> The most important point is that constructions are nothing more or less than patterns of usage, which may therefore become relatively abstract if these patterns include many different kinds of specific linguistic symbols. But never are they empty rules devoid of semantic content or communicative function.

Thus constructions are said to differ from 'abstract' grammatical rules in two ways: they must carry meaning; and they directly reflect the actual 'patterns of usage.'

Consider first the constraint that every element of the grammar must carry meaning, which we call the 'semiotic dictum.' Do lexical or phrasal theories hew the most closely to this dictum? Categorial Grammar, the paradigm of a lexical theory (see Section 6.2), is a strong contender: it consists of meaningful words, with only a few very general combinatorial rules such as $X/Y * Y = X$. Given the rule-to-rule assumption those combinatorial rules specify the meaning of the whole as a function of the parts. Whether Tomasello, for example, would consider such a rule to be 'meaningful' in itself is not clear.

What does seem clear is that the combinatorial rules of Construction Grammar, such as Goldberg's Correspondence Principle for combining a verb with a construction, have the same status as those CG combinatorial rules (see Chapter 5, (58), repeated here):

(6)   The Correspondence Principle
       Each participant that is lexically profiled and expressed must be
       fused with a profiled argument role of the construction. If a verb
       has three profiled participant roles, then one of them may be
       fused with a non-profiled argument role of a construction.

                                                        (Goldberg 1995: 50)

Both verbs and constructions assign participant roles, some of which are profiled. Profiled argument roles of a construction are expressed as direct grammatical functions, i.e. SUBJ, OBJ, or OBJ2. By (6) the lexically profiled argument roles must be direct, unless there are three of them, in which case one may be indirect. (Recall that argument profiling for verbs is 'lexically determined and highly conventionalized': Goldberg 1995: 46.) With respect to the semiotic dictum, the Correspondence Principle has the same status as the Categorial Grammar combinatorial rule: a 'meaningless' algebraic rule that specifies the way to combine meaningful items.

Which structures have meaning is an empirical question, on the lexical view.

Lexical valence structures clearly carry meaning since they are associated with particular verbs. In an English ditransitive, the first object expresses the role of 'intended recipient' of the referent of the second object. Hence *He carved her a toy* entails that he carved a toy with the intention that she receive it. So the lexical rule that adds a benefactive recipient argument to a verb adds meaning. Alternatively, a phrasal ditransitive construction might contribute that 'recipient' meaning.

In contrast, on the usage-based view as articulated by Tomasello, meaning is assumed a priori for all constructions. But while the ditransitive construction plausibly contributes meaning, no meaning has yet been discovered for either the intransitive or monotransitive constructions. Even if we grant the meaningfulness of certain constructions such as the ditransitive, this does not constitute evidence that all phrasal constructions have meaning. So the lexical and phrasal approaches seem to come out the same, as far as the semiotic dictum is concerned.

The second usage-based dictum, that the elements of the grammar directly reflect patterns of usage, will be called the 'transparency dictum.' The Construction Grammar literature often present their constructions informally in ways that suggest that they represent surface constituent order patterns: the transitive construction is 'X VERB Y' (Tomasello 2003) or 'Subj V Obj' (Goldberg 1995; 2006); the passive construction is 'X was VERBed by Y' (Tomasello 2003: 100) or 'Subj aux Vpp (PPby)' (Goldberg 2006: 5).[5] But a theory in which constructions

---

[5] In actual passive sentences any complements of the passive verb would intervene between the participle and the by-PP (e.g. *a book* in *John was given a book by Mary*). These representations seem to ignore that.

actually consist of surface patterns was considered in detail and rejected by Müller (2006: sect. 2). In any case, that view does not accurately reflect Goldberg's theory. She assumes, not word patterns, but argument structure constructions, which are more abstract and rather like the lexicalists' grammatical elements (or an LFG f-structure nucleus): the transitive construction, for example, resembles a transitive valence structure, minus the verb itself; the passive construction resembles the passive lexical rule; and so on.

Regardless of whether one feels that the semiotic dictum and the transparency dictum are desirable, it is not at all clear that the non-lexical approaches do any better at satisfying them. With respect to fulfilling the desiderata of usage-based theorists, there does not seem to be any significant difference between the non-lexical and lexical approaches.

6.3.2 Coercion

Researchers working with plugging proposals usually take coercion (see Section 2.3.3.4) as showing the usefulness of phrasal constructions. For instance, Anatol Stefanowitsch discussed the example in (7):[6]

(7) und ihr...   träumt ihnen   ein   Tor.
    and you.PL dream   them.DAT   a.ACC   gate
    'and you dream a gate for them'

The word *träumen* 'dream' is normally intransitive, but in the fantasy context of this quote it is forced into the ditransitive construction and therefore gets a certain meaning. This forcing of a verb corresponds to overwriting the properties of the verb by the phrasal construction.

In cases in which the plugging proposals assume that information is overwritten or extended, lexical approaches assume mediating lexical rules. Briscoe and Copestake (1999: sect. 4) have worked out a lexical approach in detail. They discuss the ditransitive sentences in (8), which either correspond to the prototypical ditransitive construction (8a) or deviate from it in various ways.

---

[6] Stefanowitsch cited this example in a lecture in the series 'Algorithmen und Muster: Strukturen in der Sprache' (2009). The full quote is 'Das Tor zur Welt Hrnglb öffnete sich ohne Vorwarnung und verschlang [sie]...die Welt Hrnglb wird von Magiern erschaffen, die Träume zu Realität formen können, aber nicht in der Lage sind zu träumen. Haltet aus, Freunde. Und ihr da draußen, bitte träumt ihnen ein Tor' ('The gate to the Hrnglb world opened without warning, and swallowed them. The Hrnglb world is created by magicians that can form reality from dreams but cannot dream themselves. Hold out, friends! And you out there, please, dream a gate for them').

(8)   a. Mary gave Joe a present.
     b. Joe painted Sally a picture.
     c. Mary promised Joe a new car.
     d. He tipped Bill two pounds.
     e. The medicine brought him relief.
     f. The music lent the party a festive air.
     g. Jo gave Bob a punch.
     h. He blew his wife a kiss.
     i. She smiled herself an upgrade.

For examples like (8b,i) Briscoe and Copestake assume lexical rules that relate transitive (*paint*) and intransitive (*smile*) verbs to ditransitive ones and contribute the respective semantic information or the respective metaphorical extension. The example in (8i) is rather similar to the *träumen* example discussed above, and is also analyzed with a lexical rule (Briscoe and Copestake 1999: 509). Briscoe and Copestake note that this lexical rule is much more restricted in productivity than other lexical rules suggested by them. They take this as motivation for developing a representational format in which lexical items (including those that are derived by lexical rules) are associated with probabilities, so that differences in productivity of various patterns can be captured.

Looking narrowly at such cases, it is hard to see any rational grounds for choosing between the phrasal analysis and the lexical rule. But if we broaden our view, the lexical rule approach can be seen to have much wider application. Coercion is a very general pragmatic process, occurring in many contexts where no construction seems to be responsible (Nunberg 1995). Nunberg (p. 115) cites many cases of reference transfer, such as the restaurant waiter asking

(9)   Who is the ham sandwich?

To take another example, Copestake and Briscoe (1992: 116) discuss the conversion of animal terms to mass nouns (see also Copestake and Briscoe 1995: 36–43). Example (10) is about a substance, not an animal.

(10)   After several lorries had run over the body, there was rabbit splattered all over the road.

The authors suggest a lexical rule that maps a count noun onto a mass noun. This analysis is also assumed by Fillmore (1999: 114–15). Such coercion can occur without any syntactic context: one can answer the question *What's that stuff on the road?* or *What are you eating?* or

What are you wearing? with the one-word utterance *Rabbit*. Some coercion happens to affect the complement structure of a verb, but this is simply a special case of a more general phenomenon that has been analyzed by rules of systematic polysemy.

Nonetheless, it may seem that the phrasal account is the simpler one since it does not require a lexical rule. The ditransitive construction is independently needed, and monotransitive and intransitive verbs are independently needed. It might be suggested that in the coercion cases one simply combines the two. The simplicity claim is addressed next.

6.3.3 Simplicity and polysemy

Much of the intuitive appeal of the plugging approach stems from its apparent simplicity relative to the use of lexical rules. But the claim to greater simplicity for Construction Grammar is based on misunderstandings of both lexical rules and Construction Grammar (specifically of Goldberg's (1995; 2006) version). It draws the distinction in the wrong place and misses the real differences between these approaches. This argument from simplicity is often repeated, and so it is important to understand why it is incorrect. Tomasello (2003) presents the argument as follows. Discussing first the lexical rules approach, Tomasello (p. 160) writes that

One implication of this view is that a verb must have listed in the lexicon a different meaning for virtually every different construction in which it participates [...]. For example, while the prototypical meaning of *cough* involves only one participant, the cougher, we may say such things as *He coughed her his cold*, in which there are three core participants. In the lexical rules approach, in order to produce this utterance the child's lexicon must have as an entry a ditransitive meaning for the verb *cough*.

Similarly,

Positing additional senses for each new argument structure pattern is an ad hoc way to defend the idea that verbs determine their complement configurations. When faced with a new complement configuration, one is always free to posit an additional verb sense.   (Goldberg 2013: 443)

Tomasello (2003: 160) then contrasts the Construction Grammar approach that he favors (citing Fillmore et al. 1988; Goldberg 1995; Croft 2001). He concludes:

The main point is that if we grant that constructions may have meaning of their own, in relative independence of the lexical items involved, then we do not need to populate the lexicon with all kinds of implausible meanings for each of the verbs we use in everyday life. The construction grammar approach in which constructions have meanings is therefore both much simpler and much more plausible than the lexical rules approach.

This reflects a misunderstanding of lexical rules, as they are normally understood. There is no 'implausible sense' populating the lexicon. On the lexical rule approach there is only one listed item for the word *cough*. The lexical rule, as applied to *cough*, states that when *cough* appears with two objects as in *He coughed her his cold*, the whole complex has a certain meaning (see Müller 2006: 876).

The simplicity argument also relies on a misunderstanding of a theory Tomasello advocates, namely the theory due to Goldberg (1995; 2006). For his argument to go through, Tomasello must tacitly assume that verbs can combine freely with constructions, i.e. that the grammar does not place extrinsic constraints on such combinations. (This assumption underlies the simplicity argument sketched in the final paragraph of Section 6.3.2.) If it is necessary also to stipulate which verbs can appear in which constructions, then the claim to greater simplicity collapses: each variant lexical item with its 'implausible meaning' under the lexical rule approach corresponds to a verb-plus-construction combination under the phrasal approach.

Passages such as the following may suggest that verbs and constructions are assumed to combine freely:[7]

> Constructions are combined freely to form actual expressions as long as they can be construed as not being in conflict (invoking the notion of construal is intended to allow for processes of accommodation or coercion)....Allowing constructions to combine freely as long as there are no conflicts, allows for the infinitely creative potential of language. [...] That is, a speaker is free to creatively combine constructions as long as constructions exist in the language that can be combined suitably to categorize the target message, given that there is no conflict among the constructions.
>
> (Goldberg 2006: 22)

But despite what these passages may imply, in fact Goldberg's theory does not assume free combination. Rather, she assumes that a verb is 'conventionally associated with a construction' (Goldberg 1995: 50): verbs specify their participant roles and which of those are obligatory direct arguments ('profiled', in Goldberg's terminology; see Section 5.3.2). In fact Goldberg herself (2006: 211) argues persuasively against Borer's (2003) putative assumption of free combination, on the grounds that Borer is unable to account for the difference between *dine* (intransitive), *eat* (optionally

---

[7] The context of these quotes makes clear that the verb and the argument structure construction are considered constructions. See Goldberg (2006: 21, ex. 2).

transitive), and *devour* (obligatorily transitive).[8] Despite Tomasello's comment above, Construction Grammar is no simpler than the lexical rule approach.

The resultative construction is often used to illustrate the simplicity argument. For example, Goldberg (1995: ch. 7) assumes that the same lexical item for the verb *sneeze* is used in (11a) and (11b). It is simply inserted into different constructions:

(11)   a. He sneezed.
       b. He sneezed the napkin off the table.

The meaning of (11a) corresponds more or less to the verb meaning, since the verb is used in the Intransitive Construction. But the Caused-Motion Construction in (11b) contributes additional semantic information concerning the causation and movement: his sneezing caused the napkin to move off the table. The verb *sneeze* is plugged into the Caused Motion Construction, which licenses the subject of *sneeze* and additionally provides two slots: one for the theme (*napkin*) and one for the goal (*off the table*). But the lexical approach is essentially parallel, except that the lexical rule can feed further lexical processes like passivization (*The napkin was sneezed off the table*), and conversion to nouns or adjectives (see Section 7.2). Comparing a single pair of construction and lexical rule in isolation, there is no difference in simplicity. But when we look at interactions between constructions, a big difference emerges: the lexical rule approach is simple, while construction interaction in construction grammar has not yet been worked out successfully.

6.3.4 Retaining the input in the representation

In a nuanced comparison of the two approaches, Goldberg (1995: 139–40) considers again the added recipient argument in *Mary kicked Joe the ball*, where *kick* is lexically a 2-place verb. She notes that on the constructional view, 'the composite fused structure involving both verb and construction is stored in memory.' The verb itself retains its original meaning as a 2-place verb, so that 'we avoid implausible verb senses such as "to cause to receive by kicking".' The idea seems to be that the lexical approach, in contrast, must countenance such implausible verb senses, since a lexical rule adds a third argument.

---

[8] Goldberg's critique cites a 2001 presentation by Borer with the same title as Borer (2003). See Section 7.4 for more discussion of this issue. As far as we know, the *dine/eat/devour* minimal triplet originally came from Dowty (1989: 89–90).

But the lexical and constructional approaches are actually indistinguishable on this point. The lexical rule does not produce a verb with the 'implausible sense' in (12a). Instead it produces the sense in (12b):

(12) a. **cause-to-receive-by-kicking**(x, y, z)
 b. **cause(kick**(x, y)**,(receive**$(z, y))$**)**

The same sort of 'composite fused structure' is assumed under either view. With respect to the semantic structure, the number and plausibility of senses, and the polyadicity of the semantic relations, the two theories are identical.

6.4 Language acquisition

6.4.1 The acquisition of patterns

Tomasello (2003) argues for a surface-oriented, pattern-based view on language acquisition. According to him a child hears sentences like (13) and realizes that certain slots can be filled freely (see also Dąbrowska 2001 for analogous proposals in Cognitive Grammar).

(13) a. Do you want more juice/milk?
 b. Mommy/The juice is gone.

From such utterances, so-called 'pivot schemata' are derived. Such schemata contain open slots into which words can be inserted. Examples of schemata that are abstracted from utterances like (13) are shown in (14):

(14) a. more juice/milk $\rightarrow$ more ___
 b. mommy/juice gone $\rightarrow$ ___ gone

At this stage (22 months) children do not generalize over such schemata. The schemata are construction islands and do not have syntax (Tomasello et al. 1997). Children exposed to English acquire the capability to use novel verbs with a subject and an object in the SVO order slowly in their third or fourth year of life (Tomasello 2003: 128–9). More abstract syntactic and semantic generalizations emerge in the course of time: after a sufficient amount of encounters with the transitive construction, the child can generalize over the patterns:

(15) a. [$_S$ [$_{NP}$ The man/the woman] sees [$_{NP}$ the dog/the rabbit/it]].
 b. [$_S$ [$_{NP}$ The man/the woman] likes [$_{NP}$ the dog/the rabbit/it]].
 c. [$_S$ [$_{NP}$ The man/the woman] kicks [$_{NP}$ the dog/the rabbit/it]].

Tomasello shows that children first acquire the item-specific patterns such as (14)—those involving specific verbs are called 'verb islands'—and only later generalize to the broader transitive syntactic pattern. He sees this as evidence against the sort of abstract syntax rules assumed in almost all versions of generative syntax.

According to Tomasello (2003: 107) the abstraction of the patterns in (15) is [Sbj TrVerb Obj], the so-called 'transitive construction.' Constructions such as the transitive construction continue to carry meaning, according to Tomasello. Children never abstract away from the verbal meaning to a 'meaningless' phrase structure rule. The constructions at various levels of generality are related to one another by inheritance hierarchies (Langacker 1987; Goldberg 1995: ch. 3; Croft 2001: 26; Tomasello 2003: 106–7). In language production a number of such constructions combine to form a sentence (Goldberg 2006: 10).

From the lexicalist perspective, item-specific verb islands would seem to be perfect precursors to the acquisition of the lexicalist's valence structures. The lexicalist can assume that children simply hold onto the lexical valence structures for which the verb island stage apparently provides such striking evidence. When they notice alternative verb islands for a particular verb, they discover patterns relating those variant realizations of a given verb. In other words, they acquire lexical rules. Next we contrast the two approaches.

6.4.2 Challenges for patterns: discontinuities and unexpressed arguments

A purely pattern-based approach faces difficulties from discontinuities in the realization of a head and its arguments (Müller 2010: sect. 11.4.3). For instance, adjuncts can be serialized between the subject and the verb. Bergen and Chang (2005: 170), who implement the phrasal approach, suggest an active–ditransitive construction with the pattern in (16):

(16)   [RefExpr Verb RefExpr RefExpr]

RefExpr stands for referential expression. Bergen and Chang's formalization allows a discontinuity between the first referential expression and the verb. This makes it possible to analyze (17a,b), but excludes (17c) because the adverb intervenes between verb and the first object:

(17)   a. Mary tossed me a drink.
        b. Mary happily tossed me a drink.
        c. *Mary tossed happily me a drink.

However, by enforcing the adjacency between verb and object the analysis of coordinations like (18) becomes impossible.

(18) Mary tossed me a juice and Peter an apple.

One part of the meaning of this sentence is contributed by the ditransitive construction for *Mary tossed Peter an apple*. However, *tossed* and *Peter* are discontinuous. Similarly, one can construct examples with a discontinuity between the two objects of the ditransitive construction:

(19) He showed me and bought for Mary the book that everyone was talking about.

The noun phrases *me* and *the book that everyone was talking about* are not adjacent, although they are part of the ditransitive construction. If one does not use empty elements and dislocation, one cannot maintain the claim that the items of the ditransitive construction have to be contiguous. The point here is that it is not a certain fixed configuration that has to be acquired, but rather the fact that there is a certain dependency between material in a clause. If material is realized together in a certain syntactic environment, a certain meaning can be observed.

Note also that a purely pattern-based approach is weakened by the existence of examples like (20):

(20) a. John tried to sleep.
      b. John tried to be loved.

Although no argument of *sleep* is present in the phrase *to sleep* and neither a subject nor an object is realized in the phrase *to be loved*, the phrases are recognized as containing an intransitive and a transitive verb, respectively.

The same applies to arguments that are supposed to be introduced or licensed by a phrasal construction. In (21) the resultative construction is passivized and then embedded under a control verb, resulting in a situation in which only the result predicate and the matrix verb are realized overtly.

(21) Der kranke Mann wünschte sich, tot   geschossen zu werden.
      the sick   man wished   SELF dead shot   to be
      'The sick man wanted to be shot dead.' (Müller 2007a: ex. 18)

Passivization and control are responsible for these occurrences. The point is that arguments can remain unexpressed or implicit and nevertheless a meaning that is usually connected to some overt realization of arguments is present (Müller 2007a: sect. 4). So what must be acquired by the language learner is that when a result predicate and a main verb are realized together, they contribute the resultative meaning. An additional example that shows that the NP arguments that are usually realized in active resultative constructions may remain implicit are nominalizations like the ones in (22):

(22)   a. Dann   scheint   uns   das   Totschießen   mindestens
          then   seems   us   the   dead-shooting   at.least
          ebensoviel Spaß   zu machen[9]
          as.much fun   to make
          'The shooting to death seems to us to be as least as much fun.'

       b. Wir lassen   heut   das Totgeschieße,   Weil   man sowas
          we let   today   the shooting.dead   since one   such.thing
          heut   nicht tut.   Und wer einen Tag sich   ausruht,
          today not   does   and who a   day SELF rests
          Der schießt morgen   doppelt gut.[10]
          this shoots   tomorrow   twice   good
          'We do not shoot anybody today, since one does not do this,
          and those who rest a day shoot twice as good tomorrow.'

The argument corresponding to the patient of the verb (the one who is shot) can remain unrealized, because of the syntax of nominalizations. The resultative meaning is still understood, which shows that it does not depend upon the presence of a resultative construction involving the pattern [Subj V Obj Obl].

The upshot is that phrasal constructions are too rigid to replace lexical valence structures. In the next section we review a lexical alternative that is minimally different from the phrasal view, but has the necessary flexibility.

6.4.3 The acquisition of dependencies

Children surely acquire some fixed phrasal patterns. But as we saw in the previous section, children must develop a representation of head–argument dependencies that is more flexible than what is allowed by rigid schemata such as (16). Discontinuities between heads and their

---

[9] https://www.elitepartner.de/forum/wie-gehen-die-maenner-mit-den-veraenderten-anspruechen-der-frauen-um-26421-6.html. 26.03.0212.
[10] http://home.arcor.de/finishlast/indexset.html?dontgetmestarted/091201-1.html. 26.03.2012.

arguments have to be allowed. Lexical theories seem to provide representations at the right place on the spectrum between the rigid and the flexible.

Consider Categorial Grammar (Ajdukiewicz 1935; Steedman 2000). Tomasello's Transitive Construction [Sbj TrVerb Obj] corresponds to the following lexical item in Categorial Grammar: (s\np)/np. In the lexical entry for the transitive verb *likes* this expresses the fact that *likes* takes an np to its right (indicated by the rightward-leaning slash '/') and an np to its left (indicated by the leftward-leaning slash '\'). The lexical item licenses structures like the one that is displayed as a tree in (23). The combinations are licensed by combinatorial rules that combine a functor with an argument.

(23)   Categorial Grammar analysis of *Kim likes Sandy*

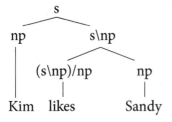

So all lexical items that are assigned to the category (s\np)/np can appear in configurations like the one shown in (23). A child who has acquired some structures of this kind is at the verb island stage discussed in section 6.4.1. As she observes unknown words in the position of the verb, she can infer that the unknown words must belong in the same lexical class as *likes*.

The child who has acquired such a verb has acquired more than just a linear concatenation of words coupled with a meaning. She also has acquired dependencies between the words that correlate with denoted relations in the world. On the other hand, if we assume that she only acquires these dependencies, without regard to ordering, then the result is too flexible. She will not learn to put the words and phrases in the right order. The CG representation seems to capture the right degree of flexibility. The structure in (23) is not the only one that is possible for items of the category (s\np)/np. For instance an adjunct of the category (s\np)/(s\np) may intervene between the subject and the combination of verb and object. This is shown in (24). The adjunct *probably* takes a VP (s\np) to its right and the result of the combination is a VP again. Similarly, lexical items like *likes* can appear in coordination structures of the kind discussed above. See Steedman (1991) for details on coordination.

(24)   Categorial Grammar analysis of *Kim probably likes Sandy*

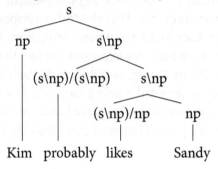

The bracketing in (s\np)/np ensures that the rightmost np in the expression is combined with the verb first and then the combination with the second np takes place. This results in the SVO order that can be observed for languages like English. For languages with a freer constituent structure Steedman and Baldridge (2006) suggest a generalized representation. The arguments are represented in a set, and for the combination of a head with an argument, one element from this set is chosen. This results in different orders. For a head-final language the lexical item of a transitive verb would be s {\np, \np}. See also Hoffman (1995: sect. 3.5) for a similar proposal for Turkish. Such a lexical item stands for trees in which the two np arguments precede their head in any order. Such an approach to constituent order was also suggested by Gunji (1986) in the framework of HPSG and by Fanselow (2001) in the framework of Minimalism.

6.5 Abstract light verbs

6.5.1 Neo-Davidsonianism

In Section 6.4 we examined proposals that assume that verbs come with certain argument roles and are inserted into prespecified 'constructions' that may contribute additional arguments. While we showed that this is not without problems, there are even more radical proposals that the construction adds all agent arguments, or even all arguments. The notion that the agent argument should be severed from its verbs is put forth by Marantz (1984; 1997), Kratzer (1996), Embick (2004), and others. Others suggest that no arguments are selected by the verb. Borer (2003) calls such proposals 'exoskeletal.' since the structure of the clause is not determined by the predicate, i.e. the verb does not project an inner 'skeleton' of the clause. Counter to such proposals are 'endo-skeletal' approaches, in which the structure of the clause is determined by the predicate, i.e. lexical proposals. The radical exoskeletal proposals are mainly proposed in Mainstream Generative Grammar (Borer 1994; 2003; 2005a; Schein 1993; Hale and Keyser 1993; Lohndal 2012) but can also be found in HPSG (Haugereid 2009). We will not discuss these proposals in detail here, but we review the main issues insofar as they relate to the question of lexical argument structure.[11] We conclude that the available empirical evidence favors the lexical argument structure approach over such alternatives.

Davidson (1967) argued for an event variable in the logical form of action sentences. The verb selects an event variable along with arguments corresponding to the participants, as in (25a). Dowty (1989) called the system in (25a) an 'ordered argument system.' Dowty (1989) coined the term 'neo-Davidsonian' for the variant in (25b), in which the verb translates to a property of events, and the subject and complement dependents are translated as arguments of secondary predicates such as **agent** and **theme**. Kratzer (1996) further noted the possibility of mixed accounts such as (25c), in which the agent (subject) argument is severed from the **kill** relation, but the theme (object) remains an argument of the **kill** relation.

(25) a. *kill:* $\lambda y \lambda x \exists e[\textbf{kill}(e, x, y)]$ (Davidsonian)
  b. *kill:* $\lambda y \lambda x \exists e[\textbf{kill}(e) \wedge \textbf{agent}(e, x) \wedge$ (neo-Davidsonian)
     $\textbf{theme}(e, y)]$
  c. *kill:* $\lambda y \lambda x \exists e[\textbf{kill}(e, y) \wedge \textbf{agent}(e, x)]$ (mixed)

Kratzer (1996) observed that a distinction between Davidsonian, neo-Davidsonian, and mixed models can be made either 'in the syntax' or 'in the conceptual structure' (Kratzer 1996: 110–11). For example, on a lexicalist approach any of the three alternatives in (25) could be posited as the semantic content of the verb *kill*. A lexical entry for *kill* on the mixed model appears in (26).

(26)
$$\begin{bmatrix} \text{PHON} & \langle \, \text{kill} \, \rangle \\ \text{ARG-ST} & \langle \, \text{NP}_x, \text{NP}_y \, \rangle \\ \text{CONTENT} & \textbf{kill}(e, y) \wedge \textbf{agent}(e, x) \end{bmatrix}$$

---

[11] See Müller (2010) for a detailed discussion of Haugereid's approach.

In other words, the lexical approach is neutral on this question of the 'conceptual structure' of eventualities, as noted already in a different connection in Section 6.3.4. For that reason, certain semantic arguments for the neo-Davidsonian approach, such as those put forth by Schein (1993: ch. 4) and Lohndal (2012), do not directly bear upon the issue of lexicalism, as far as we can tell.

But Kratzer (1996), among others, has gone further and argued for an account that is neo-Davidsonian (or rather, mixed) 'in the syntax.' Kratzer's claim is that the verb specifies only the internal argument(s), as in (27a) or (27b), while the agent (external argument) role is assigned by the phrasal structure. On the 'neo-Davidsonian in the syntax' view, the lexical representation of the verb has no arguments at all, except the event variable, as shown in (27c).

(27) a. *kill:* $\lambda y \lambda e[\text{kill}(e, y)]$ (agent is severed)
      b. *kill:* $\lambda y \lambda e[\text{kill}(e) \wedge \text{theme}(e,y)]$ (agent is severed)
      c. *kill:* $\lambda e[\text{kill}(e))]$ (all arguments severed)

On such accounts, the remaining dependents of the verb receive their semantic roles from silent secondary predicates, which are usually assumed to occupy the positions of functional heads in the phrase structure. A standard term for the agent-assigning silent predicate is 'little v.' These extralexical dependents are the analogs of those contributed by the constructions in Construction Grammar. Note that the existential quantifier that was binding the event variable in (25) has been replaced by a lambda operator in (27). This is crucial for Kratzer's account, since it allows that event variable to be unified with the event variable contributed by little v. This unifying of event variables is needed in order to account for the clear intuition that if *Mary killed a houseplant*, then the event that Mary is the agent of is the same event as the killing event. That aspect of the theory plays a key role in the critique presented in Section 6.5.2.

The following sections address arguments in favor of the 'little v' hypothesis, from idiom asymmetries (Section 6.5.2) and deverbal nominals (Section 6.5.3). We argue that the evidence actually favors the lexical view. Then we turn to problems for exoskeletal approaches, from idiosyncratic syntactic selection (Section 6.5.4). We conclude with a look at the treatment of idiosyncratic syntactic selection under Borer's exoskeletal theory (Section 6.5.5).

6.5.2 'Little v' and idiom asymmetries

Marantz (1984) and Kratzer (1996) argued for severing the agent from the argument structure as in (27a), on the basis of putative idiom asymmetries. Marantz (1984) observed that while English has many idioms and specialized meanings for verbs in which the internal argument is the fixed part of the idiom and the external argument is free, the reverse situation is considerably rarer. To put it differently, the nature of the role played by the subject argument often depends on the filler of the object position, but not vice versa. To take Kratzer's examples:

(28) a. kill a cockroach
      b. kill a conversation
      c. kill an evening watching TV
      d. kill a bottle (i.e. empty it)
      e. kill an audience (i.e. wow them)   (Kratzer 1996: 114)

On the other hand, one does not often find special meanings of a verb associated with the choice of subject, leaving the object position open (although this is only a tendency; see below):

(29) a. Harry killed NP.
      b. Everyone is always killing NP.
      c. The drunk refused to kill NP.
      d. Silence certainly can kill NP.   (Marantz 1984: 26)

Kratzer observes that a mixed representation of *kill* as in (27a) allows us to specify varying meanings that depend upon its sole NP argument.

(30) a. kill: $\lambda y \lambda e[\text{kill}(e, y)]$
      b. If a is a time interval, then kill(e, a) = truth if e is an event of wasting a
          If a is animate, then kill(e, a) = truth if e is an event in which a dies . . . etc.

On the polyadic (Davidsonian) theory, the meaning could similarly be made to depend upon the filler of the agent role. On the polyadic view, 'there is no technical obstacle' (Kratzer 1996: 116) to conditions like those in (30b), except reversed, so that it is the filler of the agent role instead of the theme role that affects the meaning. But, she writes, this could not be done if the agent is not an argument of the verb. According to Kratzer, the agent-severed representation (such as (27a)) disallows similar constraints on the meaning that depend upon the agent, thereby capturing the idiom asymmetry.

But as noted by Wechsler (2005a), 'there is no technical obstacle' to specifying agent-dependent meanings even if the Agent has been severed from the verb as Kratzer proposes. It is true that there is no variable for the agent in (27a). But there is an event variable e, and the language user must be able to identify the agent of e in order to interpret the sentence. This is why the event variable cannot be existentially bound, as discussed in the previous section. So one could replace the variable a with 'the agent of e' in the expressions in (30b), and thereby create verbs that violate the idiom asymmetry.

While this may seem to be a narrow technical or even pedantic point, it is nonetheless crucial. For Kratzer's argument to go through, it requires an additional assumption: that modulations in the meaning of a polysemous verb can only depend upon arguments of the relation denoted by that verb, and not on other participants in the event. But under that additional assumption, it makes no difference whether the agent is severed from the lexical entry or not. For example, consider (31), showing a (mixed) neo-Davidsonian representation of the semantic content in the lexical entry of *kill*:

(31)   *kill*: $\lambda y \lambda x \exists e[\mathbf{kill}(e, y) \wedge \mathbf{agent}(e, x)]$

Assuming that modulations in the sense of the verb *kill* can only be affected by arguments of the **kill** relation, we derive the idiom asymmetry. In the lexical entry for *kill* in (31), y is an argument of **kill** but x is not.

Moreover, recasting Kratzer's account in lexicalist terms allows for verbs to vary. This is an important advantage, because the putative asymmetry is only a tendency. Following are examples in which the subject is a fixed part of the idiom and there are open slots for non-subjects:

(32)   a. A little bird told X that S.
          'X heard the rumor that S'   (Nunberg et al. 1994: 526)

       b. The cat's got x's tongue.
          'X cannot speak.'   (Bresnan 1982a: 349–50)

       c. What's eating x?
          'Why is X so galled?'   (Bresnan 1982a: 349–50)

Further data and discussion of subject idioms in English and German can be found in Müller (2007b: sect. 3.2.1).

The tendency towards a subject–object asymmetry plausibly has an independent explanation. Nunberg et al. (1994) argue that the subject–object asymmetry is a side-effect of an animacy asymmetry. The open positions of idioms tend to be animate, while the fixed positions tend to be inanimate. Nunberg et al. derive these animacy generalizations from the figurative and proverbial nature of the metaphorical transfers that give rise to idioms. Whatever the explanation for this asymmetry tendency, a lexicalist grammar can encode that tendency, perhaps with a mixed neo-Davidsonian lexical decomposition, as explained above (see Wechsler 2005a for such a lexical account of the verbs *buy* and *sell*). But the 'little v' hypothesis rigidly predicts this asymmetry for all agentive verbs, and that prediction is not borne out.

6.5.3 Deverbal nominals

An influential argument against lexical argument structure involves English deverbal nominals and the causative alternation. It originates from a mention in Chomsky (1970), and is developed in detail by Marantz (1997); see also Pesetsky (1995) and Harley and Noyer (2000). The argument is often repeated, but it turns out that the empirical basis of the argument is incorrect, and the actual facts point in the opposite direction, in favor of lexical argument structure (Wechsler 2008a; 2008c).

Certain English causative alternation verbs allow optional omission of the agent argument (33), while the cognate nominal disallows expression of the agent (34):

(33)   a. that John grows tomatoes
       b. that tomatoes grow

(34)   a. * John's growth of tomatoes
       b. the tomatoes' growth, the growth of the tomatoes

In contrast, nominals derived from obligatorily transitive verbs such as *destroy* allow expression of the agent, as shown in (36a):

(35)   a. that the army destroyed the city
       b. *that the city destroyed

(36)   a. the army's destruction of the city
       b. the city's destruction

Following a suggestion by Chomsky (1970), Marantz (1997) argued on the basis of these data that the agent role is lacking from lexical entries. In verbal projections (33) and (35) the agent role is assigned in the syntax by little v. Nominal projections like (34) and (36) lack little v. Instead, pragmatics takes over to determine which agents can be expressed by the possessive phrase: the possessive can express 'the sort of agent implied by an event with an external rather than an internal cause' because only such an agent can 'easily be reconstructed' (Marantz 1997: 218). The destruction of a city has a cause external to the city, while the growth of tomatoes is internally caused by the tomatoes themselves (Smith 1970). (See Section 3.4.2.1.) Marantz points out that this explanation is unavailable if the noun is derived from a verb with an argument structure specifying its agent, since the deverbal nominal would be expected to inherit the agent of a causative alternation verb.

The empirical basis for this argument is the putative mismatch between the allowability of agent arguments, across some verb–noun cognate pairs: e.g. *grow* allows the agent but *growth* does not. But it turns out that the *grow/growth* pattern is rare. Most deverbal nominals precisely parallel the cognate verb: if the verb has an agent, so does the noun. Moreover, there is a ready explanation for the exceptional cases that exhibit the *grow/growth* pattern (Wechsler 2008a).

First consider non-alternating theme-only intransitives ('unaccusatives'), as in (37) and non-alternating transitives as in (38). The pattern is clear: if the verb is agentless, then so is the noun:

(37)   *arriv(al), disappear(ance), fall,* etc.:
       a. A letter arrived.
       b. the arrival of the letter
       c. *The mailman arrived a letter.
       d. *the mailman's arrival of the letter

(38)   *destroy/destruction, construct(ion), creat(ion), assign(ment),* etc.:
       a. The army is destroying the city.
       b. the army's destruction of the city

This parallelism favors the view that the noun inherits the lexical argument structure of the verb. For the anti-lexicalist, the unacceptability of (37c) and (37d), respectively, would have to receive independent explanations. For example, on Harley and Noyer's (2000) proposal, (37c) is disallowed because a feature of the root ARRIVE

prevents it from appearing in the context of v, while (37d) is instead
ruled out because the cause of an event of arrival cannot be easily
reconstructed from world knowledge. This exact duplication in two
separate components of the linguistic system would have to be replicated across all non-alternating intransitive and transitive verbs—a
situation that is highly implausible.

Turning to causative alternation verbs, Marantz's argument is based
on the implicit generalization that noun cognates of causative alternation verbs (typically) lack the agent argument. But apart from the one
example of *grow/growth*, there do not seem to be any clear cases of this
pattern. Besides *grow(th)*, Chomsky (1970: exx. 7c and 8c) cited two
experiencer predicates, *amuse* and *interest*:

(39)   a. John amused (interested) the children with his stories.
        b. *John's amusement (interest) of the children with his stories.

But this was later shown by Rappaport (1983) and Dowty (1989) to
have an independent aspectual explanation. Deverbal experiencer
nouns like *amusement* and *interest* typically denote a mental state,
where the corresponding verb denotes an event in which such a mental
state comes about or is caused. These result nominals lack not only the
agent but all the eventive arguments of the cognate verb, because the
nouns, unlike the verbs, do not refer to events. Moreover, the possessor
is the experiencer of the state, not the cause (cf. *John's amusement*).
Exactly to the extent that such nouns can be construed as representing
events, expression of the agent becomes acceptable; for example, some
speakers accept (39b) (with *amusement*) on an event reading.

In a response to Chomsky (1970), Carlota Smith (1972) surveyed
Webster's dictionary and found no support for Chomsky's claim that
deverbal nominals do not inherit agent arguments from causative
alternation verbs. She listed many counterexamples, including 'explode,
divide, accelerate, expand, repeat, neutralize, conclude, unify, and so on
at length' (Smith 1972: 137). Harley and Noyer (2000) also noted many
so-called 'exceptions', including *explode, accumulate, separate, unify,
disperse, transform, dissolve/dissolution, detach(ment), disengage-
(ment)*. The simple fact is that these are not exceptions because there
is no generalization to which they can be exceptions. These long lists
of verbs represent the norm, especially for suffix-derived nominals
(in *-tion*, *-ment*, etc.). Many zero-derived nominals from alternating
verbs also allow the agent, such as *change, release,* and *use*:

(40)   a. My constant change of mentors from 1992–1997.
       b. The frequent release of the prisoners by the governor.
       c. The frequent use of sharp tools by underage children.

(Borer 2003: fn. 13)

Pesetsky (1995: 79, ex. 231) assigns a star to *the thief's return of the money*, but it is acceptable to many speakers, the *Oxford English Dictionary* lists a transitive sense for the noun *return* (definition 11a), and corpus examples like *her return of the spoils* are not hard to find.

Like the experiencer nouns mentioned above, many zero-derived nominals lack event readings. Some reject all the arguments of the corresponding eventive verb, not just the agent: **the freeze of the water*, **the break of the window*. In the judgment of the author of this book, *his drop of the ball* is slightly odd, but *the drop of the ball* has exactly the same degree of oddness. The locution *a drop in temperature* matches the verbal one *The temperature dropped*, and both verbal and nominal forms disallow the agent: **The storm dropped the temperature. *the storm's drop of the temperature.* In short, the cognate nouns and verbs are parallel. The facts seem to point in exactly the opposite direction from what has been assumed in this oft-repeated argument against lexical valence. Apart from the one isolated case of *grow/growth*, event-denoting deverbal nominals match their cognate verbs in their argument patterns.

Turning to *grow/growth* itself, we find a simple explanation for its unusual behavior (Wechsler 2008c). When the noun *growth* entered the English language, causative (transitive) *grow* did not exist. The *OED* provides these dates of the earliest attestations of *grow* and *growth*:

(41)   a. intransitive *grow*:   c.725 'be verdant' ... 'increase' (intransitive)
       b. the noun *growth*:   1587 'increase' (intransitive)
       c. transitive *grow*:   1774 'cultivate (crops)'

Thus *growth* entered the English language at a time when transitive *grow* did not exist. The argument structure and meaning were inherited by the noun from its source verb, and then preserved into present-day English. This makes perfect sense if, as we claim, words have predicate argument structures. Nominalization by *-th* suffixation is not productive in English, so *growth* is listed in the lexicon. To explain why *growth* lacks the agent, we need only assume that a lexical entry's predicate argument structure dictates whether it takes an agent argument or not. So even this one word provides evidence for lexical argument structure.

6.5.4 Idiosyncratic syntactic selections

As discussed in the first chapter of this book, the assumption of lexical valence structure immediately explains why the argument realization patterns are strongly correlated with the particular lexical heads selecting those arguments. It is not sufficient to have general lexical items without valency information and let the syntax and world knowledge decide about argument realizations, because not all realizational patterns are determined by the meaning. The form of the preposition of a PP complement is sometimes loosely semantically motivated but in other cases arbitrary. For example, the valence structure of the English verb *depend* captures the fact that it selects an *on*-PP to express one of its semantic arguments:

(42)   a. John depends on Mary. (*counts, relies*, etc.)
      b. John trusts (*on) Mary.
      c. $\begin{bmatrix} \text{PHON} & \langle\,\text{depend}\,\rangle \\ \text{ARG-ST} & \langle\,\text{NP}_x\,,\,\text{PP[on]}_y\,\rangle \\ \text{CONTENT} & \textbf{depend}(x,y) \end{bmatrix}$

Such idiosyncratic lexical selection is utterly pervasive in human language. The verb or other predicator often determines the choice between direct and oblique morphology, and for obliques, it determines the choice of adposition or oblique case. In some languages such as Icelandic the subject case can also be selected by the verb (Zaenen et al. 1985). Selection is language-specific. English *wait* selects *for* or *on* while German *warten* selects *auf* ('on'), but not *für* ('for'), with an accusative object:

(43)   a. I am waiting for/on the man.
      b. Ich   warte   auf/*für   den   Mann.
        I   wait   on/for   the   man.ACC

The synonyms *treffen* and *begegnen* ('to meet') govern different cases (examples from Pollard and Sag 1987: 126):

(44)   a. Er   traf   den Mann.
        he.NOM   met   the man.ACC

      b. Er   begegnete   dem Mann.
        he.NOM   met   the man.DAT
        'He met the man.'

One has to specify the case that the respective verbs require in the lexical items of the verbs. This may be simplified, for example by marking only that *begegnen* takes a dative object and treating the accusative on the object of *treffen* as the default case for objects in German (see Haider 1985; Heinz and Matiasek 1994; Müller 2001 on structural and lexical case in German). But the difference must be lexically encoded somehow.

A radical variant of the plugging approach is suggested by Haugereid (2009). Haugereid (pp. 12–13) assumes that the syntax combines a verb with an arbitrary subset of five different argument roles. Which arguments can be combined with a verb is not restricted by the lexical item of the verb. One specific problem for such views is that the meaning of an ambiguous verb sometimes depends on which of its arguments are expressed. The German verb *borgen* has the two translations, 'borrow' and 'lend,' corresponding to whether the subject is interpreted as the source or the recipient in the transaction (see Kunze 1991; 1993 for discussion of German verbs of change of possession). Interestingly, the dative object is obligatory only with the 'lend' reading:

(45) a. Ich borge ihm   das Eichhörnchen.
         I   lend   him.DAT   the squirrel
         'I lend the squirrel to him.'

      b. Ich borge (mir)   das Eichhörnchen.
         I   borrow me.DAT   the squirrel
         'I borrow the squirrel.'

If we omit the dative argument, we get only the 'borrow' reading. So the grammar must specify for specific verbs that certain arguments are necessary for a certain verb meaning or a certain perspective on an event (see Müller 2010: 403).

Synonyms with differing valence specifications include the minimal triplet mentioned earlier: *dine* is obligatorily intransitive (or takes an *on*-PP), *devour* is transitive, and *eat* can be used either intransitively or transitively (Dowty 1989: 89–90).[12] Many other examples are given in Levin (1993) and Levin and Rappaport Hovav (2005).

In a phrasal constructionist approach one would have to assume phrasal patterns with the preposition or case, into which the verb is inserted. For (43b), the pattern includes a prepositional object with *auf* and an accusative NP, plus an entry for *warten* 'wait' specifying that it

---

[12] As the term is used here, two words qualify as synonyms if their meanings are similar. The meanings need not be identical.

can be inserted into such a structure (see Kroch and Joshi 1985: sect. 5.2) for such a proposal in the framework of TAG). There are many generalizations regarding verbs with such valence representations (see Chapter 3). If such generalizations are to be captured only with inheritance hierarchies, then two inheritance hierarchies would needed: one for lexical entries with their valency properties and another one for specific phrasal patterns that are needed for the specific constructions in which these lexical items can be used.

A final illustration of the irreducibility of valence to semantics are verbs that select for expletives and inherently reflexive verbs in German:

(46) a. weil   es   regnet
         because   it   rains
         'because it is raining'
      b. weil   (es)   mir (vor   der Prüfung) graut
         because   EXPL   me before   the exam   dreads
         'because I am terrified (before the exam)'
      c. weil   er   es   bis   zum   Professor   bringt
         because   he   EXPL until to.the professor   brings
         'because he made it to professor'
      d. weil   es   sich um   den   Montag   handelt
         because   EXPL REFL around the   Monday   trades
         'It is about Monday.'
      e. weil   ich   mich (jetzt) erhole
         because   I   myself now   relax
         'because I am relaxing'

The lexical heads need to contain information about dependents that do not fill semantic roles: expletive subjects (46a,b), expletive objects (46c), and 'inherent' reflexive pronouns (46d,e). Note that German allows for subjectless predicates and hence the presence of expletive subjects does not merely follow from general principles of German syntax. (In any case explanations referring to the obligatory presence of a subject would fail for expletive objects as in (46c).) For (46e) the **erholen'** ('relax') relation is a one-place predicate and hence *erholen* is semantically compatible with the [Sbj IntrVerb] construction, but instead this verb requires a semantically null reflexive object. Semantic compatibility or plausibility does not fully determine complement selection.

6.5.5 Is there an alternative to lexical valence structure?

The question for theories denying the existence of valence structure is what replaces it to explain idiosyncratic lexical selection. In her exoskeletal approach, Borer (2005a; 2005b) explicitly rejects lexical valence structures. But she posits post-syntactic interpretive rules that are difficult to distinguish from them. To explain the correlation of *depend* with an *on*-PP, she posits the following interpretive rule (2005b: 29):

$$(47) \quad \text{MEANING} \Leftrightarrow \pi_9 + [\langle e^{on} \rangle]$$

Borer refers to all such cases of idiosyncratic selection as 'idioms.' In rules such as this one, 'MEANING is whatever the relevant idiom means' (2005b: 27). In this rule, π_9 is the 'phonological index' of the verb *depend* and e^{on} 'corresponds to an open value that must be assigned range by the f-morph *on*' (p. 27), where f-morphs are function words or morphemes. Hence this rule brings together much the same information as the lexical valence structure in (42c). Borer notes that such 'idiom' rules could play the same role as subcategorization in other theories, including indicating the intransitivity of verbs like *arrive*, obligatory transitivity of other verbs, the obligatory locative argument of *put*, selection of sentential complements, and so on. Borer concludes that introducing them into her theory therefore 'may represent somewhat of a concession' to the lexicalist position (2005b: 354–5).

The question of which arguments must be realized in a sentence, and how those arguments are formally marked, cannot be reduced to semantics and world knowledge or to general facts about subjects. The consequence is that valence information must be connected to lexical items. One therefore must either assume a connection between a lexical item and a certain phrasal configuration, as in Croft's (2003) approach and in LTAG, or assume a lexicalist argument structure. In a Minimalist setting the right set of features must be specified lexically to ensure the presence of the right case assigning functional heads. This is basically similar to the lexical valence structures. However, there are still differences related to the problem of coordination, to be discussed next.

6.6 Evidence for lexical approaches

6.6.1 Valence and coordination

An essential difference between the lexical and contructional approaches can be illustrated with benefactive ditransitives such as (48a).

(48) a. Mary painted Lee a picture.
      b. Mary painted a picture.

The verb *paint* is lexically a 2-argument verb, as shown by its ordinary use in (48b). The question is how the benefactive 'intended recipient' argument gets added in (48a). On the lexicalist approach there are different formulations of lexical rules that add an argument (Section 5.2), and they all have in common that in the analysis of a sentence like (48a) a 3-argument valence is associated with the phonological string *paint*. For concreteness take the view of lexical rules as licensing unary branching trees. The 2-argument root PAINT^2 is inserted into the structure in (49). The lexical rule licenses a unary structure with that root as the sole daughter and a node immediately dominating it that effectively represents a 3-argument root PAINT^3. A separate rule is responsible for deriving the inflected verb, as shown in (50).

(49)   Benefactive applicative as unary branching lexical rule

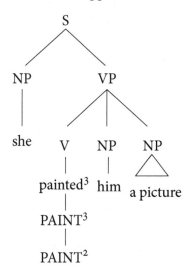

(50)

a. PAINT² =
$$\begin{bmatrix} \text{PHON} & \langle\,\text{paint}\,\rangle \\ \text{ARG-ST} & \langle\,\text{NP}_x,\,\text{NP}_y\,\rangle \\ \text{CONTENT} & \textbf{paint}(x,y) \end{bmatrix}$$

b. PAINT³ =
$$\begin{bmatrix} \text{PHON} & \langle\,\text{paint}\,\rangle \\ \text{ARG-ST} & \langle\,\text{NP}_x,\,\text{NP}_z,\,\text{NP}_y\,\rangle \\ \text{CONTENT} & \textbf{paint}(x,y) \wedge \textbf{intend}(x,\,\textbf{receive}(z,y)) \end{bmatrix}$$

So on the lexicalist view a 3-argument predicate meaning 'x painted y with the intention that z receive y' is associated with the phonological string *paint*. On the constructional view there is no such predicate seeking three arguments that dominates only the verb. Verb coordination provides evidence for the lexical account. A generalization about word coordination is that two constituents that select the same number and type of dependents can be coordinated. The result of coordination is an item that has the selectional properties of each conjunct. The German examples in (51) show that the case requirement of the involved verbs have to be observed. In (51b,c) the coordinated verbs require accusative and dative respectively and since the case requirements are incompatible with unambiguously case marked nouns both of these examples are out.

(51) a. Ich kenne und unterstütze diesen Mann.
　　　　I　　know　and　support　　　this　man.ACC

　　　b. *Ich kenne und helfe diesen Mann.
　　　　 I　　know　and　help　this　man.ACC

　　　c. *Ich kenne und helfe diesem Mann.
　　　　 I　　know　and　help　this　man.DAT

It is possible to coordinate basic ditransitive verbs with verbs that have additional arguments licensed by the lexical rule. Following are naturally occurring English (52a) and the German (52b) examples, the latter quoted from Müller (2013b: 420):

(52) a. She then [offered and made] me a wonderful espresso—nice.[13]

　　　b. ich hab ihr jetzt diese Ladung Muffins mit
　　　　 I　 have her now　this　 load　 muffins　with
　　　　 den Herzchen drauf [gebacken und gegeben].[14]
　　　　 the little.heart there.on baked and given
　　　　 'I have now baked and given her this load of muffins with the little heart on top.'

---

[13] http://www.thespinroom.com.au/?p=102 07.07.2012
[14] http://www.musiker-board.de/diverses-ot/35977-die-liebe-637-print.html. 08.06.2012

These sentences show that both verbs are 3-argument verbs at the V^0 level, since they are involved in V^0 coordination:

(53) $[_{V0}$ $[_{V0}$ offered] and $[_{V0}$ made]] $[_{NP}$ me] $[_{NP}$ a wonderful espresso]

This is expected under the lexical rule analysis but not the non-lexical constructional one.

One might wonder whether the English sentences could be instances of Right Node Raising out of coordinated VPs (Bresnan 1974; Abbott 1976):

(54) She [offered ___] and [made me ___] a wonderful espresso.

But this view is problematic. Under such an analysis the first verb has been used without a benefactive or recipient object, while *me* is interpreted as the recipient of both the offering and making. (Right node raising of two constituents is difficult.) Also Right Node Raising is not possible for the German case where the verbs follow the shared objects. Another possibility is to analyze such examples as elliptical, as proposed in the HPSG framework and applied to different sorts of coordination examples by Beavers and Sag (2004). On such an analysis, the grammatical content of the words *me a wonderful espresso* appears twice, but the phonological content appears only once, as shown schematically in (55a). However, some challenges for such an approach were noted already by Beavers and Sag (2004: sects. 5 and 8). Further problems for the ellipsis analysis were recently raised by Kubota and Levine (2013). For example, sentence (55b) naturally receives an interpretation where she offered me one thing and made me a different one, but that interpretation is absent from the putative unelided sentence in (55c).

(55) a. She offered ~~me a wonderful espresso~~ and made me a wonderful espresso.
      b. She offered and made me two different things.
      c. ≠ 'She offered me two different things and made me two different things.'

If the problems for the ellipsis or right node raising accounts can be solved, and if a successful account can be incorporated into construction grammar, then this could provide an alternative. Otherwise we must assume these are cases of V^0 coordination.

Summarizing the coordination argument: coordinated verbs generally must have compatible valence properties. This means that in (52b), for example, *gebacken* ('baked') and *gegeben* ('given') have the same valence properties. In the lexical approach the creation verb *gebacken*, together with a lexical rule, licenses a ditransitive valence structure. So it can be coordinated with *gegeben*. In the phrasal approach however, the verb *gebacken* has two argument roles and should not be compatible with the verb *gegeben*, which has three argument roles. In the phrasal model, *gebacken* can only realize three arguments when it enters the ditransitive phrasal construction or argument structure construction. But in sentences like (52b) it is not *gebacken* alone that enters the phrasal syntax, but rather the coordinated combination of *gebacken* and *gegeben*. On that view the verbs should be incompatible as far as the semantic roles are concerned.

The X^0 coordination facts illustrate a more general point. The output of a lexical rule such as the one that would apply in the analysis of *gebacken* in (52b) is just a word (an X^0), so it has the same syntactic distribution as an underived word with the same category and valence feature. This important generalization follows from the lexical account while on the phrasal view it is at best mysterious. The point can be shown with any of the lexical rules that the anti-lexicalists are so keen to eliminate in favor of phrasal constructions. For example, the active and passive verbs can be coordinated, as long as they have the same valence properties:

(56)   She requested and was granted two different things.

The passive of the ditransitive verb *grant* retains one object, so it is effectively transitive and can be coordinated with the active transitive *request*.

Moreover, the English passive verb form, being a participle, can feed a second lexical rule deriving adjectives from verbs. All categories of English participles can be converted to adjectives (Bresnan 1982b; 2001: ch. 3):

(57)   a. active present participles (cf. The leaf is falling): the *falling* leaf
       b. active past participles (cf. The leaf has fallen): the *fallen* leaf
       c. passive participles (cf. The toy is being broken.): the *broken* toy

That the derived forms are adjectives, not verbs, is shown by a host of properties, including negative *un-* prefixation: *unbroken* means 'not broken', just as *unkind* means 'not kind,' while the *un-* appearing on verbs indicates, not negation, but action reversal, as in *untie* (Bresnan 1982b: 21; 2001: ch. 3). Predicate adjectives preserve the subject of predication of the verb and for prenominal (attributive) adjectives the rule is simply that the role that would be assigned to the subject goes to the modified noun instead (*The toy remained (un-)broken.; the (un-) broken toy*). Being an A^0, such a form can be coordinated with another A^0, as in the following:

(58)   a. The suspect should be considered [armed and dangerous].
       b. any [old, rotting, or broken] toys

In (58b), three adjectives are coordinated, one underived (*old*), one derived from a present participle (*rotting*), and one from a passive participle (*broken*). Such coordination is completely mundane on a lexical theory. Each A^0 conjunct has an argument selection feature: in HPSG it would be the SPR valence feature for predicate adjectives or the MOD feature for the prenominal modifiers. But the point of the phrasal (or ASC) theory is to deny that words have such valence features.

The claim that lexical derivation of valence structure is distinct from phrasal combination is further supported with evidence from deverbal nominalization (Wechsler 2008c). To derive English nouns from verbs, *-ing* suffixation productively applies to all declinable verbs (*the shooting of the prisoner*), while morphological productivity is severely limited for various other suffixes such as *-(a)tion* (**the shootation of the prisoner*). So forms such as *destruction* and *distribution* must be retrieved from memory while *-ing* nouns such as *looting* or *growing* could be (and in the case of rare verbs or neologisms, must be) derived from the verb or the root through the application of a rule of *-ing* suffixation (Zucchi 1993). This difference explains why *ing*-nominals always retain the argument structure of the cognate verb, while other forms show some variation. A famous example, discussed in Section 6.5.3, is the lack of the agent argument for the noun *growth* versus its retention by the noun *growing*: **John's growth of tomatoes* versus *John's growing of tomatoes* (Chomsky 1970).

But what sort of rule derives the *-ing* nouns, a lexical rule or a phrasal one? On Marantz's (1997) phrasal analysis, a phrasal construction (notated as *v*P) is responsible for assigning the agent role of *-ing* nouns such as *growing*. For him, none of the words directly selects an agent via its argument structure. The *-ing* forms are permitted to appear in the vP construction, which licenses the possessive agent. Non-*ing* nouns such as *destruction* and *growth* do not appear in vP. According to Marantz (1997), whether those non-*ing* nouns allow expression of the agent depends on semantic and pragmatic properties of the word: *destruction* involves external causation so it does allow an agent, while *growth* involves internal causation so it does not allow an agent.

However, a problem for Marantz's 'little v' analysis is that these two types of nouns can coordinate and share dependents (example 59a is from Wechsler 2008c: sect. 7):

(59)   a. With nothing left after the soldier's [destruction and looting] of their home, they reboarded their coach and set out for the port of Calais.[15]

b. The [cultivation, growing or distribution] of medical marijuana within the County shall at all times occur within a secure, locked, and fully enclosed structure, including a ceiling, roof or top, and shall meet the following requirements.[16]

On the phrasal analysis, the nouns *looting* and *growing* occur in one type of syntactic environment (heading a phrase with the *vP* shell over it), while forms *destruction, cultivation,* and *distribution* occur in a different syntactic environment (heading a phrase lacking the *vP* shell). This places contradictory demands on the structure of sentences like those in (59).

A last example involves an influential phrasal analysis. Hale and Keyser (1993) derived denominal verbs like *to saddle* through noun incorporation out of a structure akin to [PUT a saddle ON x] (see Section 3.8.2). Again, verbs with this putative derivation routinely coordinate and share dependents with verbs of other types:

(60)   Realizing the dire results of such a capture and that he was the only one to prevent it, he quickly [saddled and mounted] his trusted horse and with a grim determination began a journey that would become legendary.[17]

---

[15] http://www.amazon.com/review/R3IG4M3Q6YYNFT, 21.07.2012.
[16] http://www.scribd.com/doc/64013640/Tulare-County-medical-cannabis-cultivation-ordinance#page=1, 22.10.2012.
[17] http://www.jouetthouse.org/index.php?option=com_content&view=article&id=56&Itemid=63, 21.07.2012.

(61) Derivation of *saddled (his trusted) horse* (based on Hale and Keyser 1993)

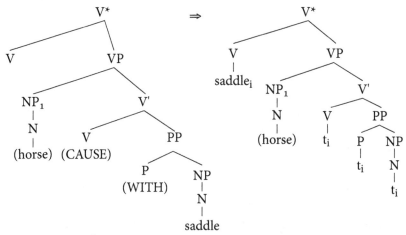

As in the other X^0 coordination cases, under the phrasal analysis the two verbs place contradictory demands on a single phrase structure. The verb *saddled* occurs in the structure shown in (61), while the verb *mounted* is not a locatum verb so it requires a different structure.

A lexical valence structure is an abstraction or generalization over various occurrences of the verb in syntactic contexts. To be sure, one key use of that valence structure is simply to indicate what sort of phrases the verb must (or can) combine with, and the result of semantic composition; if that were the whole story, then the phrasal theory would be viable. But it is not. As it turns out, this lexical valence structure, once abstracted, can alternatively be used in other ways: among other possibilities, the verb (crucially including its valence structure) can be coordinated with other verbs that have a similar valence structure; or it can serve as the input to lexical rules specifying a new word bearing a systematic relation to the input word. The coordination and lexical derivation facts follow from the lexical view, while the phrasal theory at best leaves these facts as mysterious and at worst leads to irreconcilable contradictions for the phrase structure.

6.6.2 Valence and derivational morphology

Goldberg and Jackendoff (2004) and Alsina (1996) suggest analyzing resultative constructions and/or caused motion constructions as phrasal constructions. Stefan Müller (2006) argued that this is incompatible with the assumption of Lexical Integrity, i.e. that word formation happens before syntax (Bresnan and Mchombo 1995). Let us consider a concrete example, such as (62):

(62) a. Er tanzt   die Schuhe blutig/ in   Stücke.
         he dances the shoes   bloody/into   pieces
      b. die blutig/ in   Stücke getanzten Schuhe
         the bloody/into pieces   danced   shoes
      c. *die getanzten Schuhe
         the danced   shoes

The shoes are not a semantic argument of the verb *tanzt*. Nevertheless the argument that is realized as accusative NP in (62a) is the element the adjectival participle in (62b) predicates over. An adjectival participle like the one in (62b) is derived from a passive participle of a verb that governs an accusative object. On the lexical account, a lexical rule gives the verb that object-governing specification. But if instead the accusative object is licensed phrasally by configurations like the one in (62a), then the formation of the participle *getanzte* becomes mysterious. In other words, it is the potential for combination with an accusative object, and not actual combination with an object, that makes the verb an appropriate base for adjective formation. See Müller (2006: sect. 5) for further examples of the interaction of resultatives and morphology.

The conclusion, which was drawn in the late 1970s and early 1980s by Dowty (1978: 412) and Bresnan (1982b: 21), is that phenomena that feed morphological processes should be treated lexically. The natural analysis in non-transformational frameworks is therefore one that assumes a lexical rule for the licensing of resultative constructions. See Verspoor (1997), Wechsler (1997b; 2005c; 2012), Wechsler and Noh (2001), Wunderlich (1997b: 120–26), Müller (2002: ch. 5), Kay (2005), and Simpson (1983) for lexical analyses of resultatives in some of these frameworks.

This argument is similar to the one that was discussed in connection with the GPSG representation of valence in Section 6.2.2: a morphological process must be able to see the valence of the stem it applies to. This is not possible if arguments are introduced by phrasal configurations after the morphology level.

6.7 Arguments based on (the lack of) interactions with syntax

6.7.1 Introduction

An important theoretical question about the lexicon–syntax interface is whether there is true lexical decomposition, i.e. sublexical semantic structure. The alternative is that apparent sublexical semantic structure is actually built within the syntax, by the combination of verb roots with abstract (silent) light verbs (see Section 5.4). In this section we review some key arguments in the history of that debate.

In the classic paper 'Remarks on nominalization', Chomsky (1970) argued that derived nominals (such as 63c) are not syntactically related to clauses (such as 63a) via transformations (see also Section 3.8.1). Instead Chomsky argued for the lexicalist hypothesis, according to which the verb *construct* and the noun *construction* are related within the lexicon.

(63) a. John constructed a house.
      b. John's constructing a house   (gerundive nominal)
      c. John's construction of a house (derived nominal)

One influential argument took a form that that has been updated and repeated many times in different theoretical and empirical contexts. Chomsky noted that certain clausal constructions such as the *tough-*movement construction in (64a) lack a corresponding derived nominal:

(64) a. John is easy to please.
      b. John's being easy to please   (gerundive nominal)
      c. *John's easiness to please   (derived nominal)

Chomsky used the lexicalist hypothesis to explain such gaps. Within the framework of the time, the construction in (64a) was derived through application of two transformations (Chomsky 1970: 23):

(65) a. [to please John]$_S$ is easy   =extraposition$\Rightarrow$
      b. it is easy [to please John]$_S$ =raising$\Rightarrow$
      c. John is easy [to please]$_S$

(The raising transformation is a case of *tough-*movement.) In this derivation the adjective *easy* lexically selects a clausal subject as shown in (65a). As long as the extraposition and raising transformations apply in the clausal domain but not the nominal domain, then there is no way to derive the unacceptable nominal in (64c). But if derived nominals were generated transformationally from structures like (64a), then there would be no principled way to block the derivation of (64c). The essence of Chomsky's argument is that the systematic relationship between the syntactic properties of cognate forms such as *easy* and *easiness* should not be directly captured in the syntax, because that relationship, if formulated as a syntactic rule, would then need to be blocked from interacting with known syntactic processes. Capturing that relationship within the lexicon explains the lack of interaction with syntactic processes.

Arguments taking the same general form have been put forth for the view that apparent sublexical semantic structure really is sublexical, just as it appears, and not assembled in the syntax—even though some syntactic processes are sensitive to that structure (e.g. Aissen 1974; Dowty 1979; Wechsler 2008a). This reasoning informed the early discussion between the Generative Semantics camp (Lakoff 1965), other transformationalists (Newmeyer 1976), and proponents of the lexical decomposition alternative (Dowty 1979). In Generative Semantics the semantic primes are assembled to compose words by predicate raising transformations. For example, predicate raising moves CAUSE, BECOME, and *dead* together, in order to license the insertion of *kill*. But Newmeyer (1976) argued that the putative 'predicate raising' transformations do not interact with any other syntactic processes. For example,

(66) a. John CAUSE [a furor to exist]   =Predicate Raising⇒
      b. John CAUSE-exist furor   =lexical insertion⇒
      c. John created a furor.

A transformation of 'there insertion' derived the existential construction *There is a furor* from a structure like *A furor exists*. If applied within the complement clause of CAUSE, the result is a deviant derivation:

(67) a. John CAUSE [a furor exists]   =*there*-insertion⇒
      b. John CAUSE [there be a furor]   =Predicate Raising⇒
      c. John CAUSE-be [there __ a furor]   =lexical insertion ⇒
      d. *John created there a furor.

Significantly, no transformations feed the putative operation of predicate raising. This led Newmeyer to classify predicate raising as a 'pre-cyclic' transformation, meaning that it applies before others. Similar proposals to place sublexical semantic structure within the 'syntax' while insulating it from syntactic processes have recurred in many forms. A recent one is 'first phase syntax', which Ramchand (2008: 16) describes as the 'event-building portion of a proposition' which she assumes to be 'prior to case marking/checking, agreement, tense and modification.'

Such proposals involve a special component of 'syntax' that must be blocked from interaction with the rest of the syntax. On the lexicalist view, the lack of interaction is simply a consequence of the fact that the information in question is not part of the combinatorial syntax: in the competence grammar, such information is associated with lexemes, in the form of lexical valence structures and some lexico-semantic decomposition, and not with sentences.

Like some of the other earlier arguments, the specific argument in 'Remarks on nominalization' cannot be directly applied within the context of contemporary lexicalist theories that reject the transformations Chomsky assumed.[18] But the form of the argument continues to have relevance. The next two sections look at further arguments of the same form.

6.7.2 want + HAVE and other verbs of possession

The debate over lexical versus syntactic decomposition has been revived and repeated, often involving some of the same phenomena as the earlier debate. In this section we review some arguments on the two sides of this debate, as they apply to certain verbs that incorporate the notion of possession (e.g. McCawley 1974; Ross 1976; Dowty 1979; Fodor and Lepore 1998; Harley 2004; Beavers et al. 2008; Wechsler 2008a).

Verbs like *get*, *give*, and transitive *want* incorporate a possession component:

(68) a. John wants the car.   ↔ John wants to have the car.
      b. John got the car.   ↔ John came to have the car.
      c. Mary gave John the car. ↔ Mary caused John to have the car.

Durative adverbials can modify the implicit 'have' state (McCawley 1974; Ross 1976; Dowty 1979):

(69) a. John wanted the car (for two days). (*want* or *have* for two days)
      b. John got the car (for two days).   (*have* for two days)
      c. John gave me the car (for two days). (*have* for two days)

---

[18] E.g. HPSG analyses of 'tough movement' cases like (64c) generally involve positing a lexical variant of the adjective *easy* that selects an infinitival VP with a 'gap', i.e. an item removed from the valence list of some predicator in the infinitive. The subject and gap share a referential index (the index i in (ii)).

(i) John is easy [to please]
(ii) *easy*: [ARG-ST ⟨ NP$_i$, VP[*inf*; SLASH {NP$_i$}] ⟩]

The question returns of why this 'tough movement' version of *easy* cannot feed a nominalization rule to produce (64c), *John's easiness to please. Rappaport's (1983) answer to that question is discussed in Section 3.8.1.

This suggests these sentences have an underlying semantic 'have' formative. If so, then the question is how this formative enters the semantic representation of the sentence.

On the lexical view 'have' is in the lexical decomposition of the verb, as in (70b) for *want* (a simplified version of the analysis in Dowty 1979). The verb *want$_1$* in (70a) takes a clausal (or controlled) complement, as in *John wants very much [for it to rain]*. The verb *want$_2$* in (70b) is the transitive variant in (68a). Using an underspecification semantics such as Minimal Recursion Semantics (Copestake et al. 2005), we need do little more than merely introduce the 'have' state as an elementary predication, as in (70c). This alone makes it available for durative adverbials to scope over.

(70)   a. $want_1 = \lambda P \lambda x[\text{want}'(x,P)]$
        b. $want_2 = \lambda y \lambda x[\text{want}'(x, \text{have}'(x, y))]$
        c. $want_2 = \begin{bmatrix} \text{SUBJ} & \langle \text{DP}_i \rangle \\ \text{COMPS} & \langle \text{DP}_j \rangle \\ \text{CONTENT} & s_1: \{\textbf{want}(s_1, i, s_2) \wedge \textbf{have}(s_2, i, j))\} \end{bmatrix}$

See Egg (1999) and Beavers et al. (2008) for detailed formal accounts of sublexical scope within underspecification semantics.

The syntactic approach posits a silent syntactic formative meaning 'have' (McCawley 1974). In the version of the analysis by Harley (2004) the possessive formative is a preposition:

(71)

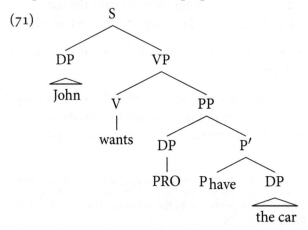

Durative adverbials can adjoin to the putative PP, thus explaining the scope facts. Harley (2004) motivated the PP on the basis of controlled PP complements of *want*:

(72)   John wants [PRO off the team].

Harley argued that since *want* allows this type of complement anyway, we need only posit the silent preposition P_{HAVE}.

   Different phrase structures are posited under the lexicalist analysis (73a) and the syntactic analysis (73b):

(73)   a. Lexicalist analysis: John wants [DP a lollipop].
       b. Syntactic analysis: John wants [PP PRO P_{HAVE} a lollipop].

Syntactic analyses posit a phrasal shell around the DP. The details vary across different versions; (73b) presents Harley's (2004) version in which the shell is of category PP (see (71) and (72)). Wechsler (2008a) argues for the lexicalist structure. For example, in contrast to a PP complement (74a), a direct object resists separation from its governing verb by an adverb (74b). A complement of *want* that sounds like a DP also behaves like a DP, and not like a PP (74c,d):

(74)   a. He nibbled quietly [on the carrot].
       b. He nibbled (??quietly) [the carrot].
       c. He wants desperately [out of his job].
       d. He wants (??desperately) [a better job].

On the syntactic view, the bracketed constituents in both (74c) and (74d) are PPs, making this contrast mysterious. Wechsler (2008a) gives further evidence of this kind from coordination, passivization, relativization, and various other syntactic phenomena. All of the evidence supports the view that the complement of *want* is simply a nominal and not some larger structure such as a PP.

   The historical development of complementation options could provide evidence for one or the other view. In contemporary English the verb *want* allows DP, infinitival, and PP complements. On the lexicalist view, this is a fact about the lexical entry for the verb and not a consquence of a general syntactic rule or structure such as (73b). The history of *want* is interesting in this regard. The earliest attestations of *want* took a DP object, with the meaning to 'not have,' i.e. to 'lack' (*c*.1200). From 'lack' it subjectivized, drifting to a meaning of 'desire.' It also started taking infinitive complements (1706), and eventually also motion PPs and particles, as in the (1836) *OED* example *I want in, I want in*. On the lexical view, these represent innovations in the complement structure of a particular verb. If a change in the syntax is responsible instead, then we would expect to find that all verbs with the same relevant grammatical features would simultaneously undergo the same changes.

Idioms and contextual polysemy (sense modulation conditioned by the local syntactic environment of a word) have been cited as evidence on both sides of the debate between lexical and syntactic analyses. McCawley (1974), Richards (2001), and Harley (2004) argued that the 'have' formative is syntactic. They note the parallel verb+DP idioms across *have*, *want*, *get*, and *give*, such as *give/get the creeps* and *give/take/get flak*:

(75)   a. John gave everyone flak.
        b. You get flak (when you take a stand)

They explain the parallelism by positing a single underlying idiom, *HAVE flak*, which then combines with causal or inchoative semantic formatives:

(76)   a. John CAUSE everyone [HAVE flak].
        b. You BECOME [HAVE flak].

According to their account, the verb *have* is the spell-out of BE+HAVE, *get* is BECOME+HAVE, and *give* is CAUSE+HAVE. So the idiom parallels are argued to follow from the syntactic approach to sub-lexical scope.

McCawley (1974) made the same argument regarding *want+DP*, an argument later revived by Harley (2004: 258–9): 'significantly, the various "readings" that any *have DP* expression can have are all available with a *want DP* expression.' The idea was that on the lexical decomposition view, the 'have' formative is embedded in a lexical decomposition and hence unavailable to form idioms. So the idiomatic interpretations would have to be stipulated separately for each *have DP* and *want DP*.

On the other hand, the lexicalist need not assume different *haves*. When *have* is followed by a relational DP like *a sister*, the main predicate comes from the noun, not the verb. Simplifying somewhat, analyses along the following lines have long been proposed (Partee 2008, citing a 1987 Landman and Partee unpublished abstract; Tham 2006; Wechsler 2008a; Beavers et al. 2008):

(77)   a. *have* = $\lambda P \lambda x \exists y [P(x, y)]$
        b. *a sister* = sister$'$
        c. *a headache* = headache$'$
        d. *John has a sister* = $\exists y [\text{sister}'(\text{John}, y)]$
        e. *John has a headache* = $\exists y [\text{headache}'(\text{John}, y)]$

On this analysis the same verb *have* appears with all relational nouns, whether *sister*, *headache*, etc. The verb *have* does not denote a two-place relation between John and his sister. Rather, the noun *sister* denotes a two-place relation; in this example the two relata are John and an existentially bound variable. This analysis is extended to the other verbs in (78):

(78)   a.   *want* = $\lambda P \; \lambda x[\text{want}'(x, \exists y[P(x, y)])]$
     b.   *get* = $\lambda P \lambda x[\text{BECOME}(\exists y[P(x,y)])]$
     c.   *give* = $\lambda y \lambda P \lambda x[\text{CAUSE}(x,\text{BECOME}(\exists y[P(x,y))]$
     d.   *John wants a sister* = $\text{want}'(\text{John}, \exists y[\text{sister}'(\text{John}, y)])$
     e.   *Eliza got a headache* = $\text{BECOME}(\exists y[\text{headache}'(\text{Eliza},y)])$
     f.   *The music gave me a headache* =
        $\text{CAUSE}(\text{music},\text{BECOME}(\exists y[\text{headache}'(\text{me},y)]))$

On this view there is just one of each support verb, for use with all relational nouns: one *have*, one *want*, one *get*, and so on.[19] Collocations like *get flak*, *give flak*, and *take flak* are not really idioms. They are compositional phrases involving a figurative word sense. The word *flak* refers to 'a barrage of abuse or adverse criticism' (*OED*), and frequently appears without any of the support verbs *get*, *take*, or *give* ((79a–c) are cited in the *OED*; (79d,e) are from the British National Corpus):

(79)   a.   In spite of the current flak between Mayor Lindsay and...
       the...administrator of Boston and New Haven..., the potential for the city is unlimited. (1968 *N.Y. Times 20 May*, 46.)
     b.   Well, all right. So why all the flak? (1969 A. LURIE *Real People*, 163.)
     c.   Isn't that going to cause rather a lot of flak in the...P.L.P.? (1976 T. STOPPARD *Dirty Linen*, 25.)
     d.   Just imagine the flak flying about if we have bad results.
     e.   I expect the flak. If we get beat, it's my fault.

---

[19] Beavers et al. (2008) further propose a unified analysis of relational DP complements with true possessional uses. They cite non-zeugmatic coordination (on zeugma tests see Sect. 2.2.2):

(i) John has a nice car and an even nicer sister who bought it for him.

(ii) I would rather have a bottle in front of me than a frontal lobotomy.

Both variants are treated as the light verb *have*, roughly (77a). In *John has a nice car*, the possession relation comes from *car*. This extends Barker's analysis of genitives like *John's car*, in which the noun *car* is type-shifted to select a possessor argument.

As long as the relational noun belongs to the right semantic type, it can combine with a range of support verbs. This accounts for the patterns observed above, without assuming a syntactic HAVE formative.

Some idiomatic collocations behave differently. The collocation *have X* can have the special sense of 'give birth to X,' but this special meaning does not transfer to the other verbs, as shown in (80) (from Wechsler 2008a).

(80)   a. Natalie doesn't want to have a baby, so she's going to adopt one.
    b. #Natalie doesn't want a baby, so she's going to adopt one.

The phrase *have a baby* is ambiguous, so it is possible to negate it on just the 'birth' sense, as in (80a). But the phrase *want a baby* is general, and not ambiguous between 'want to give birth to a baby' and other possibilities such as adoption. So negating it as in (80b) negates all those possibilities.

Both the lexical and syntactic analyses of possession verbs allow for an account of both the *give/get flak* type and the *have a baby* type, so these idiom facts do not force a choice between theories. The lexical theory does make some predictions that are not made by the syntactic theory. On the lexical theory, parallellism across support verbs is expected only for *relational* DPs, including event nominals (*flak, criticism, a kiss, a headache*) and other relational nominals (*a sister, a black eye*). Parallellism is not expected for entity-denoting DPs like *a baby* or other objects of *have* when the verb is used in the 'give birth' sense. Similarly, parallellism is unexpected for expressions that lack such DPs, like *have it out with* or *have at it*, and this seems to be a correct prediction:

(81)   a. I had it out with Fred.   ('argued angrily')   (McCawley 1974)
       *I want it out with Fred.
    b. The okra is ready. Go ahead, have at it! ('do something heartily')
       *But I don't want at it! Yuck!

A more systematic study would be needed to see whether this prediction is borne out.

In conclusion, the facts of contextual polysemy do not weigh heavily in favor of either the lexical or syntactic account. However, earlier we saw evidence against any syntactic analysis of *want a car* that depends on assigning a special phrasal category to *a car*, reflecting the meaning 'have a car,' that differs from the category *a car* otherwise has (such as DP).

6.8 Conclusion

The essence of the lexical view is that a verb is stored with a valence structure indicating how it combines semantically and syntactically with its dependents. Crucially, that structure is abstracted from the actual syntactic contexts of past tokens of the verb. Once abstracted, that valence structure can meet other fates besides licensing the phrasal structure that it most directly encodes: it can undergo lexical rules that manipulate that structure in systematic ways (voice, applicativization, category conversion); it can be composed with the valence structure of another predicate (complex predicate formation); it can be coordinated with similar verbs; and so on. Such an abstraction allows for simple explanations of a wide range of robust, complex linguistic phenomena. We have surveyed the arguments against the lexical valence approach, and in favor of a phrasal representation instead. We find the case for a phrasal representation of argument structure to be unconvincing: there are no compelling arguments in favor of such approaches, and they introduce a number of problems. Assuming a lexical valence structure allows us to solve all the problems that arise for phrasal approaches.

7

Some battlegrounds in the theory wars

This chapter presents a number of specific phenomena that have drawn attention from scholars from a wide range of theoretical perspectives.

7.1 The dative and benefactive alternations

In the English dative alternation, the arguments of a ditransitive or double object verb can alternatively be expressed with a single object followed by a prepositional phrase headed by *to*:

(1) a. Ann sold Beth the car.   (Double Object (DO) frame)
     b. Ann sold the car to Beth.   (Prepositional Object (PO) frame)

The dative alternation is highly productive. In fact, almost all verbs that permit the DO frame also allow the PO frame. New verbs such as verbs of communication reflecting changing technology seem to instantly and effortlessly take on the two alternants:

(2) *text, fax, email,...*
     a. Ann texted Beth the news.
     b. Ann texted the news to Beth.

The converse is not true, however. Latinate verbs, which are mainly borrowings from French, strongly favor the PO frame, rejecting the DO frame. The same set of verbs also tend to resist verb–particle constructions (DiSciullo and Williams 1987):

(3) *donate, contribute, distribute, ...*
     a. Ann donated the books to the library.
     b. *Ann donated the library the books.

(4) *donate, contribute, distribute,...*
     a. Ann gave out free tickets.
     b. *Ann distributed out free tickets.

The Latinate restriction does not appear to be a semantic restriction, but rather a morphological one. It is historically rooted in the fact that French does not allow ditransitives. Apparently many verbs retained those subcategorization restrictions when borrowed into English. Given the productivity of the dative alternation, whatever rule or other grammatical process is responsible for that productivity must be prevented from applying to this category of verbs. This suggests that such a category of 'Latinate vocabulary' is discerned within the synchronic grammar of English (Oehrle 1976).

Early transformational analyses involved a dative transformation to relate one syntactic structure to the other. Larson's (1988) influential Government/Binding analysis addressed binding and scope problems by introducing a functional projection within the VP. But these syntactic approaches did not address the question of what semantic factors, if any, drive the alternation.

Dowty (2001) has suggested in connection with the *swarm* alternation that diathesis alternations generally exist in order to convey different meanings. Do the two alternative dative expressions differ in meaning? Pinker (1989) noted the following semantic factors affecting relative acceptability of the two frames.[1] First, in the DO form the sentence entails that NP_1 comes to possess NP_2, while this entailment need not follow from sentences in the PO form.

(5) a. Ann drove the car to Beth.
     b. *Ann drove Beth the car.

This extends to possession of information:

(6) a. Ann showed the car to Beth.
     b. Ann showed Beth the car.

Second, in the PO form, the theme undergoes 'movement.' The notion of movement includes not only literal motion through space but also abstract movement of the theme into the recipient's 'possession space.'

---

[1] Corpus studies have turned up exceptions to all of these purported factors (Bresnan and Nikitina 2003; Bresnan, Cueni, et al. 2005); see examples in (21). See also Rappaport-Hovav and Levin (2008).

The motivation for this claim is that figurative uses lacking movement, like *give NP a headache* do not alternate, allowing only the DO form:

(7)   a. The music gave Ann a headache.
      b. *The music gave a headache to Ann.

To account for these two semantic restrictions, Pinker (1989) proposed two distinct semantic representations, related to each other by a lexical rule. Each links to a different syntactic frame:

(8) NP_0 CAUSE NP_1 to HAVE NP_2 $\Leftrightarrow$ NP_0 CAUSE NP_2 to GO TO NP_1

$$\Downarrow \qquad\qquad\qquad\qquad\qquad \Downarrow$$

NP_0 V NP_1 NP_2 $\Leftrightarrow$ NP_0 V NP_2 *to* NP_1

Goldberg (1995) adopts a similar account in a construction grammar setting, positing the Ditransitive and Caused Motion constructions with the meanings of Pinker's two structures (see Section 5.3.2, (54)). Goldberg (1995) further posits that the DO (Ditransitive) construction is polysemous and lists six different senses.

(9)   a. Central sense: Agent successfully causes recipient to receive patient (*give, pass, hand, serve, feed, throw, toss, slap, kick, poke, fling, shoot, bring, take,...*)
      b. Conditions of satisfaction imply that agent causes recipient to receive patient (*guarantee, promise, owe,...*)
      c. Agent causes receipient not to receive patient (*refuse, deny*)
      d. Agent acts to cause recipient to receive patient at some future point in time (*leave, bequeath, allocate, reserve, grant*)
      e. Agent enables recipient to receive patient (*permit, allow*)
      f. Agent intends to cause recipient to receive patient (*bake, make, build, cook, sew, knit, get, grab, win, earn,...*)
                                                  (Goldberg 1995: 38)

However, a problem with assuming this proliferation of constructional senses is that it compounds the constructionist's problem of overgeneration (see Section 6.3.1). Each verbal lexeme is predicted to allow multiple meanings depending on which construction meaning it combines with, unless it is prevented from doing so somehow. The alternative is that the verbs simply have a variety of meanings, almost all consistent with the caused possession sense posited by Pinker.

Under the 'modal transparency' hypothesis later proposed by Anthony Davis and Jean-Pierre Koenig (Davis and Koenig 1999; Koenig and

Davis 2001; 2003), linking rules disregard modal operators such as negation, intention, enablement, and so on. This is hypothesized to be a general principle of linking. This allows for most of the categories in (10). The fact that those meanings cluster together into subgroups does not need not be represented in the grammar as in Goldberg's 'polysemous construction.' It could simply result from the tendency for new words to be patterned on existing ones (recall (2)).

Pinker's two structures account for the two generalizations above. But as pointed out by Krifka (1999; 2004), two further conditions noted by Pinker were not explained by these structures. The third is that the DO form disallows verbs expressing continuous imparting of force, like *pull*:

(10) a. Beth kicked the ball to Ann.   (*hit, throw, fling,...*)
      b. Beth kicked Ann the ball.

(11) a. Beth pulled the box to Ann.   (*push, lower, haul, drag,...*)
      b. *Beth pulled Ann the box.

Verbs like *pull* that involve application of continuous force to an object generally resist the ditransitive frame, while verbs like *kick* allow it. To capture this fact, Pinker stipulated that if the causing event and motion event are simultaneous, DO is not an option. Pinker's fourth generalization is that the DO form disallows manner of speaking verbs like *shout*:

(12) a. Ann told the news to Beth.
      b. Ann told Beth the news.

(13) a. Ann shouted the news to Beth.   (*whisper, yell,...*)
      b. *Ann shouted Beth the news.

If the speech act verb has a manner component, DO is not an option.

Krifka (1999) proposed a unified account of Pinker's four semantic factors. Like Goldberg, Krifka posits that the frame itself contributes some meaning. Krifka spells out the meanings of the verbs and frames formally so as to account for which combinations are possible. The PO frame (14a) encodes a relation between two events, the causing event (e) and the motion event (e'). The DO frame (14b) contributes a relation between a causing event (e) and a state of possession.

(14)   a. PO frame: Ann . . . the box to Beth.
          $\exists e \exists e'$[AGENT(e, Ann) $\land$ THEME(e, box) $\land$ CAUSE(e, e')
             $\land$ MOVE(e') $\land$ THEME(e', box) $\land$ GOAL(e', Beth)]
       b. DO frame: Ann . . . Beth the box.
          $\exists e \exists s$[AGENT(e, Ann) $\land$ THEME(e, box) $\land$ CAUSE(e, s) $\land$
             s: HAVE(Beth, box)]

The verb contributes 'manner' to the semantics of the sentence. If that
manner characterizes the causing event (e) alone, then the verb is
compatible with both frames. The verb *throw* characterizes the causing
event as 'an event in which an agent accelerates and then releases an
object.' This throwing manner MANNER(*throw*)(e) is conjoined with
the other relations in the PO or DO frame. In contrast, *pull* specifies a
relation between the causing (e) and motion (e') events, namely a
homomorphism between them: 'each part of e corresponds to a part
of e' and vice versa.'

(15)   MANNER(*pull*)(e, e'):
       e: the causing event (application of continuous force to an
            object, directed towards the causer)
       e': the movement of the object, caused by e
       Condition: Each part of e corresponds to a part of e' and vice
       versa.

Krifka noted that this account is possible only if those semantic conditions, and hence the causing event itself, are specified in the lexical
entry of the verb. So this provides further indirect evidence against the
neo-Davidsonian treatment of the agent (see Section 6.5.1).
   Given the meaning of *pull* in (15), it can combine with the PO frame
but not the DO frame. The verb expresses a homomorphism between
the causing and motion events, but the DO frame does not provide any
motion event.

(16)   a. Ann pulled the box to Beth.
          $\exists e \exists e'$[AGENT(e, Ann) $\land$ **MANNER(*pull*)(e, e')** $\land$ THEME
             (e, box) $\land$ CAUSE(e, e') $\land$ MOVE(e') $\land$ THEME
             (e', box) $\land$ GOAL(e', Beth)]
       b. *Ann pulled Beth the box.
          $\exists e \exists s$[AGENT(e, Ann) $\land$ **MANNER(*pull*)(e, e')** $\land$ THEME
             (e, box) $\land$ CAUSE(e, s) $\land$ s: HAVE(Beth, box)]

In (16b), **MANNER(*pull*)** cannot be expressed because there is no motion event supplied by the construction. Technically, the problem is that the variable e' is not bound.[2]

Krifka applies this same reasoning to manner of speaking verbs in (13). Such verbs specify the manner of the causing event, i.e. the creation of sound. The verb *whisper* specifies that the causing event is quiet and the vocal cords do not vibrate. Krifka crucially posits that such verbs impose a homomorphism between the causing event (creation of sound) and resulting event (imparting of information). He illustrates with the following scenario. Suppose that Ann uttering *That's a good one* to Beth is understood as a signal to leave. Then we cannot report this scenario with the manner of speaking verb *whisper*, as in *Ann whispered to Beth that they should leave*, because it is not the case that all parts of the sound creation correspond to information being conveyed. Meanwhile, it is fine to say *Ann told Beth that they should leave*. So manner speaking verbs like *whisper*, much like *pull*, are incompatible with the DO frame.

Pinker, Goldberg, and Krifka all assume that the *to*-PP expresses 'motion' into the recipient's 'possession space.' Wechsler (1991; 1995) and Rappaport Hovav and Levin (2008) challenged that assumption. Unlike a locative goal, the dative argument of verbs like *give* and *hand* cannot be questioned with *where*:

(17)   a. *Where did you give the ball?
       b. Where did you kick/throw the ball? To third base.
       c. Where did you send the bicycle? To Rome.
          (Rappaport Hovav and Levin 2008: 137, ex. 14)

The suggests that verbs like *give* and *hand* have only the 'caused possession' meaning, regardless of whether the recipient is expressed as a *to*-PP or the first of two NPs. But *kick* and *throw* express caused motion, plus caused possession if there is a recipient of the *kick* or the *throw*. The English preposition *to* ambiguously marks either a locative goal or a recipient of a possession, while the first of two NPs expresses

---

[2] A possible problem for Krifka's analysis is the well-formedness of:

(i)   Ann dragged the box.

If *Ann dragged Beth the box* is ruled out because the DO frame lacks the motion event, then how is a simple transitive like (i) possible? While the verb *drag* as in (i) entails that the box moved, the same problem arises with *pull*, *push*, etc., which lack that entailment, since the non-motion variant of the verb should be acceptable in DO frame.

only the latter meaning. Wechsler (1995; 1991) came to a similar (though not identical) conclusion on the basis of the benefactive alternation illustrated in (18).

(18)   a. Ann baked/got a cake for Beth.
       b. Ann baked/got Beth a cake.

Benefactive ditransitives can be built on two-argument verbs such as verbs of creation (*bake, carve, make,...*) and verbs involving obtaining something (*get, buy,...*). Assuming that such verbs are lexically two-place, the benefactive constructions allow one to tease apart the respective semantic constributions of the verb and the construction. Recall that Pinker, Goldberg, and Krifka all assumed that the DO construction involves *causation*: 'X causes Y to receive Z' (see (54) in Chapter 5, and (8) and (14) in this chapter). But (18a) or (18b) does not entail that the baking or getting *caused* Beth to receive a cake, nor does it even entail that Beth received a cake. Rather, Ann baked or got a cake with the intention that Beth receive it. Causation varies with the verb: in *Sue gave Mary a cake*, the giving causes the receiving, while in *Sue baked Mary a cake*, the baking does not cause the receiving. Wechsler analyzed the DO construction and 'recipient *for*' as synonymous, meaning 'x performs an action on z with the intention that y receive z.' The 'recipient *to*' encodes causation within the agent's intention: 'x performs an action with the intention that the action cause y to receive z.' Thus (19a) means 'John mailed a cake with the intention that mailing the cake *cause* Mary to receive it.' And (19b) is odd because baking a cake cannot *cause* Mary to receive it.

(19)   a. John mailed a cake to Mary.
       b. *John baked a cake to Mary.

Wechsler (1991; 1995) addressed the question of how the recipient argument gets added, and how to unify benefactive and dative ditransitives. The analysis draws on Kiparsky's (1987; 1989) notion of a 'thematically restricted positional linker' semantically analogous to adpositions and oblique case. The 'inner object' phrase structure position, i.e. the first of two objects, grammatically expresses the recipient role semantics. A phrase slotted into that position is automatically interpreted as the intended recipient. This prefigures the later constructional accounts.

   All of the above authors assume that a semantic distinction between the frames, in combination with the lexical semantics of the verbs, drives the dative alternation. That assumption has been challenged from the perspective of radical stochastic theories (Bresnan and Nikitina 2003; Bresnan et al. 2005). Instead of looking at verb meaning, Bresnan et al. (2007) focused on the verb *give* and investigated properties of the NP complements that have been claimed to affect the choice of frame, such as weight and discourse status. They examined a number of such factors in 2,360 dative constructions culled from the Switchboard Corpus, seeking factors affecting the choice of DO versus PO. The factors are stated in terms of relative linear position. For example, 'discourse given > nongiven' in (20a) means that an NP referring to something already mentioned in previous discourse tends to precede an NP that refers to something newly introduced into the discourse. The examples illustrate data that would support each hypothesis, where the checkmarked form is favored over the form in parentheses: if John has been mentioned recently, then the hypothesis favors *give John a book* over *give a book to John*. The last hypothesis, (20e), predicts that a shorter argument precedes a longer one.

(20)   Causal factors driving the dative alternation (Bresnan, Cueni et al. 2005)

   a. **discourse given** > *nongiven*
      ...John...   ✓give John a book   (give a book to John)
      ...the book...✓give the book to John (give John the book)

   b. **pronoun** > *nonpronoun*
      ✓give **it** to *John*, ✓give **him** *books* (give John it, give books to him)

   c. **animate** > *inanimate*
      ✓give John the book   (give the book to John)
      ✓give the man a book   (give a book to the man)

   d. **definite** > *indefinite*
      ✓give the book to a man   (give a man the book)

   e. **shorter constituent** > *longer constituent*
      ✓give John the book we talked about (give the book we talked about to John)
      ✓give the book to the guy we talked about (give the guy we talked about the book)

Bresnan and colleagues used logistic regression to control simultaneously for multiple variables related to a binary response. They found that each of these is an independent, statistically significant causal factor.

Bresnan and Nikitina (2009) directly challenged the four semantic generalizations observed by Pinker and Krifka (see above). Bresnan and Nikitina (2009) reject Krifka's semantic account, and indeed all polysemy accounts. First, the Switchboard Corpus contained exceptions to each generalization. Examples (21a) and (21b) are exceptions to the claim that the PO involves change of possession (recall (7)). Examples (21c) and (21d) contain a verb of continuous imparting of force and a manner-of-speaking verb, respectively, both of which use the ditransitive frame that they are reputed to disallow.

(21)   Exceptions from Switchboard Corpus:
      a. A stench or smell is diffused over the ship that would give a headache to the most athletic constitution.
      b. It would cost nothing to the government.
      c. He pulled himself a steaming piece of the pie.
      d. You just mumble him an answer.

Bresnan and Nikitina hypothesize that both DO and PO syntax can be used to express transfer of possession, but there is a strong skewing toward the DO construction for transfer of possession. Fully 78.6% of the alternating dative constructions appeared in DO. The one verb *give*, which accounted for 51% of the total dative dataset, took the DO form 84.6% of the time.

Bresnan and Nikitina doubt that the grammar is responsible for this skewing. Rather, grammaticality judgments are biased by the probability of similar descriptions of the event types depicted by the examples (Bresnan and Nikitina 2009: 169) As for why DO is disfavored by verbs expressing continuous imparting of force, they claim that transfers of possession are more likely to be described in the discourse of sports with its motional verbs of instantaneous imparting of force (*throw, toss, kick, flip, slap, fling*, etc.). Meanwhile, possession transfers are less likely in discourse about dragging, lowering, pushing, pulling, and even carrying, because in present-day American life, if a person accompanies and holds, clings to, or otherwise stays in contact with a possession, it is less likely that a transfer of possession is going on. They observe that prior to the advent of automobiles, the ditransitive was used with the verb *carry*:

(22)   I went back to Mrs. Kate's to carry her some mustard salad.

As for why DO is disfavored by manner of speaking verbs, Bresnan and Nikitina contrast means-of-communication verbs such as *cabling*, *emailing, faxing, phoning, telegraphing*, etc. with manner-of-speaking verbs: *whispering, yelling, mumbling, barking, muttering*. The former almost always involve communication (i.e. transfers of the possession of information), while the latter are more often non-communicative, as illustrated here:

(23) He whispered/yelled/mumbled/barked/muttered (but he wasn't saying anything).
      He whispered/yelled/mumbled/barked/muttered at us/in our direction.

Bresnan and Nikitina conclude that the grammaticality judgments reflect biases in the data, not structural differences in the grammatical representation of meaning. Krifka (2004) responded to the discovery of exceptions in the corpus data by maintaining the ambiguity hypothesis, but allowing that the preferred representations can be cancelled in case of stronger requirements by information structure.

7.2 Resultatives

7.2.1 Explananda

Resultative constructions express an action together with the result of that action. In many languages including English, resultative secondary predicates indicate the result of the action described by the primary predicate. The predicate *flat* in sentence (24) is a resultative because the sentence entails that the metal became flat as a result of the hammering (the secondary predicate is in italics and its predication subject is underlined).

(24) Resultative:
      John hammered the metal *flat*.
      ⇒'John hammered the metal; as a result, the metal became flat.'

Halliday (1967: 62–7) distinguished 'resultative' from 'depictive' secondary predicates. The latter do not entail a result:

(25) Depictive:
      The chairman came to the meeting *drunk*.
      ⇒ 'The chairman was drunk when he came to the meeting.'

Resultatives present several syntactic and semantic explananda.

The first question is the origin of the causal semantics. The verb *hammer* alone does not entail that the hammering causes anything, and the adjective *flat* alone entails neither causation nor an inchoative sense of 'flattening.' But the combination of the two somehow introduces the notion that the hammering *caused* the flattening.

A second issue, which is familiar from many phenomena involving word meaning, is that the resultative construction is semi-productive. The relative acceptability of the construction depends on the particular words appearing in it ((26a) is from Green 1972: exx. 6b and 7b):

(26) a. He wiped it clean/dry/smooth/*damp/*dirty/*stained/*wet.
      b. He hammered <u>the metal</u> *flat/smooth/into the ground/*beautiful/*safe/ *tubular.*
      c. <u>The puddle</u> froze *solid/*slippery/*dangerous.*

The meanings of the starred examples are clear and paraphrasable as we did above: 'Mary wiped the table; as a result the table became wet' makes perfect sense, but it is nonetheless odd to say *Mary wiped the table wet.*

A third property of resultatives is that the addition of the resultative predicate often renders the sentence telic. Sentence (27a) is atelic while (27b) is telic, according to the standard tests such as the imperfective entailment (27a,b) and the durative versus interval time adverbials (27c,d).

(27) a. John is hammering the metal.
        ⇒ John has hammered the metal. (atelic)
      b. John is hammering the metal flat.
        ⇏ John has hammered the metal flat. (telic)
      c. John hammered the metal (for an hour/*in an hour).
      d. John hammered the metal flat (*for an hour/in an hour).

(With the addition of certain operators such as comparatives, resultatives become atelic, as in *For hours, Bill hammered the metal ever flatter* (Goldberg and Jackendoff 2004: 543, ex. 23b).)

A final observation is that English resultatives fall into two classes. In one type, the predication subject for the secondary predicate is a semantic argument of the verb, while in the other it is not (Dowty 1979; Carrier and Randall 1992; Simpson 1983).

(28) a. Control resultative: resultative phrase whose predication sub-
          ject is a semantic argument of the matrix verb.

          He wiped the table *clean.*   ⇒ He wiped the table.
          The water froze *solid.*   ⇒ The water froze.

     b. ECM ('exceptional case-marking') resultative: resultative
        phrase whose predication subject is NOT a semantic argu-
        ment of the matrix verb.

        We drank the pub dry.   ↛ *We drank the pub.
        The dog barked itself *hoarse.*   ↛ *The dog barked itself.
        Mary ran the soles *off her shoes.* ↛ *Mary ran the soles.

One question is how the extra object gets added to the sentence in the
ECM type resultative, given that the verb does not normally select one.
In his study of German resultatives, Müller (2002: ch. 5) argues that all
German resultatives are of the ECM variety (see below).

   The many analyses of resultatives can be grouped into two broad
categories. In 'complex predicate' theories, the verb and the resultative
adjective form a complex predicate such as 'hammer-flat.' (The complex predicate theories can be further subdivided according whether the
semantics of the resultative complex involves a result state or a closed
scale. See Section 7.2.3.) In 'light verb-based' theories, the resultative
construction is patterned on sentences with a light causative verb like
make, as in *She made the metal flat.* The main verb (the verb *hammer* in
our example) replaces and/or semantically combines with *make*. In
some versions an abstract light verb *v* is analogous to *make*.

7.2.2 Complex predicate accounts

Dowty (1979: 219–20) analyzed the English resultative construction
with a lexical rule that composes a transitive verb (e.g. *hammer*) with an
adjective (e.g. *flat*) to produce a complex predicate (*hammer-flat*).
Where δ is the transitive verb and α is the adjective, the derived
predicate is a transitive verb ($\delta\alpha$) that translates as (29a). The symbol
α' represents the semantic translation of α. In the derivation of sentence
(27b), the variables x and y are replaced by the semantic translations of
John and *the metal*, respectively, yielding (29b):

(29) a. $\lambda y \lambda x[\delta'(x, y)$ CAUSE [BECOME [$\alpha'(y)$]]]
      b. **hammer**'(john,metal) CAUSE [BECOME [**flat**'(metal)]]]

Dowty's rule introduces causation into the semantics of the resultative. He also analyzes ECM resultatives like the following (examples from Dowty 1979: 221):

(30) a. John drank himself silly.
      b. John slept himself sober.

The rule for combining verb δ and adjective α here is technically a little different because the verb is intransitive (again, δ' and α' are the translations of the verb and adjective, respectively). In the derivation of (30a), the variables x and y are replaced by the semantic translations of *John* and *himself*, respectively, yielding (31b):

(31) a. $\lambda y \lambda x [\delta'(x)$ CAUSE [BECOME [α'(y)]]]
      b. **sleep'**(john) CAUSE [BECOME [**sober'**(himself)]]]

Dowty (1979: 223) notes similar locutions involving a resultative PP instead of AP, such as *He drank the officers under the table.*

Dowty's lexical rules directly account for three of the four explananda listed above. The causal semantics is added by the rule. On Dowty's (1979) theory of aspect, the resultative is predicted to be telic since it contains the result state operator BECOME. The ECM resultative contains an added object because, while *sleep* is intransitive, the output of the rule ('*sleep-sober*') is transitive. As for the lexical variation (recall (26)), Dowty (1979: 303) suggested that the verb–adjective pairs in the resultative construction are conventionalized (see Section 7.2.3 for discussion).

Rappaport Hovav and Levin (1998) built on Dowty's theory (see Section 4.4.4). They reified the semantic structures and stated conditions on how those structures can map to the syntax, in order to explain patterns of optionality. Verb meanings are divided into an 'idiosyncratic aspect' (cf. 'manner') and a 'structural aspect,' where the elements of the structural aspect must be given syntactic expression. The structural aspect is given in form of lexical semantic templates that are built on Dowty's (1979) decompositional approach. They illustrate resultative formation with the verb *sweep*. The manner verb *sweep* is an activity:

(32) a. *sweep*: [x ACT$_{\langle SWEEP \rangle}$ y]
      b. Phil swept the floor.
      c. Phil swept.

The object (*the floor*) is optionally selected by the verb; it is called a 'constant participant.' (Other participants, called 'structure participants,' are licensed by the templatic structure. Those are obligatory; see Section 4.4.4.3.) Templates can be augmented by inserting one template into another:

(33) a. *sweep:* [[x ACT$_{\langle SWEEP \rangle}$ y] CAUSE [BECOME [y $\langle$STATE$\rangle$]]]
     b. Phil swept the floor clean.

According to the 'Subevent identification condition,' each subevent in the event structure must be identified by a lexical head (a V, A or P) in the syntax. In (33) the second subevent (the state) is specified by a lexical head, *clean*. According to the 'Argument realization condition,' there must be an argument XP in the syntax for each structure participant in the event structure. As *the floor* is a structure participant, and is the argument of a subevent, it cannot be omitted (**Phil swept clean*). The state may also be specified as a place:

(34) a. *sweep:* [[x ACT$_{\langle SWEEP \rangle}$ y] CAUSE [BECOME [z $\langle$PLACE$\rangle$]]]
     b. Phil swept the crumbs onto the floor.   (y = the floor)
     b'. Phil swept the crumbs into the dustbin.
                        (y = the floor(etc.), PLACE = in the dustbin)
     c. *Phil swept the crumbs.
     d. *Phil swept onto the floor.

In this case the *x* argument and the *z* argument are the main arguments of their respective events, and so they have to be realized. The *y* argument (e.g. the table in *Phil swept the table*) 'need not be expressed since it is a constant participant.' (34c) is impossible because the *z* argument is licensed only by the state subevent, and (34d) is impossible because *z* is a main argument.

   Like Dowty (1979), Rappaport Hovav and Levin (1998) combine the verb and resultative predicate prior to mapping to the surface syntax. A third example of this approach is found in Van Valin's (2005: 239) Role and Reference Grammar analysis. The combination of predicates in this way is called a 'complex predicate.'

   Müller (2002, Chapter 5; 2006) analyzes the syntax and semantics of German resultatives as complex predicates. Müller argues that all German resultatives are of the 'ECM' type, where the resultative rule transitivizes a normally intransitive verb. Some clearly involve non-selected accusatives. These sentences become unacceptable if the resultative adjective is omitted (Müller 2002: exx. 485, 490):

(35) a. Die Jogger liefen den Rasen platt.
          the   joggers ran   the   lawn   flat

      b. Es   regnete die Stühle nass.
          it   rained   the chairs wet

      c. Er läuft sich müde.
          he runs   self tired
          'He runs himself tired.'

Others appear to contain lexically transitive verbs (Müller 2002: exx.
481, 493):

(36) a. Sie streicht die Tür   schwarz.
          she paints   the door black

      b. Er schneidet die Wurst in Scheiben.
          he cuts   the sausage in pieces

      c. Er fuhr das Auto kaputt.
          he drove the car   broken

But Müller argues that the sentences in (36) are made not from
transitives but from intransitive *streichen* 'paint,' *schneiden* 'cut,' and
fahren 'drive.' The object need not be an argument of the verb. For
example, (36c) could mean he drove the car, or that he rode a bicycle
and crashed into a car (Müller 2002: 214). The examples in (35) and
(36) can be paraphrased with intransitives as follows:

(37) a. 'The joggers ran; as a result, the lawn became flat.'
      b. 'It rained; as a result, the chairs became wet.'
      c. 'He ran; as a result, he was tired.'
      c. 'She painted; as a result, the door became black.'
      d. 'He cut; as a result, the sausage was in slices.'
      e. 'He drove; as a result the car was broken.'

Also, inherent reflexives, which are transitive, disallow resultatives.
Although it does not receive a theta role from the verb, the accusative
nominal behaves syntactically like an object. For example, it can be
passivized.

   Müller posits a lexical rule applying to the verb, which adds a
predicate AP or PP, and the NP subject of that predicate, to the
verb's valence feature (this is the slightly simplified version from
Müller 2006: 873):

(38) Lexical rule for resultatives (Müller 2006: 873)

$$
\begin{bmatrix}
\text{CAT} & \begin{bmatrix} \text{HEAD} & verb \\ \text{SUBCAT} & \boxed{1}\,\langle \text{NP}[str]\,\rangle \end{bmatrix} \\
\\
\text{CONT}\,\boxed{2} \\
stem
\end{bmatrix} \rightarrow
$$

$$
\begin{bmatrix}
\text{CAT} & \begin{bmatrix} \text{SUBCAT}\,\boxed{1}\oplus\boxed{3}\oplus\left\langle \begin{bmatrix} \text{CAT} & \begin{bmatrix} \text{HEAD} & adj\text{-}or\text{-}prep \\ \text{SUBCAT} & \boxed{3}\,\langle\,\text{NP}_{ref}\rangle \end{bmatrix} \\ \text{CONT}\,\boxed{4} \end{bmatrix} \right\rangle \end{bmatrix} \\
\\
\text{CONT} & \begin{bmatrix} \text{ARG1}\,\boxed{2} \\ \text{ARG2} & \begin{bmatrix} \text{ARG1} & \boxed{4} \\ become \end{bmatrix} \\ cause \end{bmatrix} \\
stem
\end{bmatrix}
$$

Applied to intransitive *fischen* 'to fish,' this produces a new valence frame with an added object NP and predicative AP:

(39) Resultative rule applied to *fischen*

$$
\begin{bmatrix} \text{SUBCAT} & \langle \text{NP}_i \rangle \\ \text{CONTENT} & \textbf{fish}(i) \end{bmatrix} \Rightarrow
$$

$$
\begin{bmatrix} \text{SUBCAT} & \langle \text{NP}_i,\ [1]\text{NP},\ \text{AP}[\text{SUBCAT}\,\langle[1]\rangle]:s \rangle \\ \text{CONTENT} & \textbf{cause}(\textbf{fish}(i),\ \textbf{become}(s)) \end{bmatrix}
$$

The output of this rule combines with *leer* 'empty' to produce the following:

(40) $\begin{bmatrix} \text{SUBCAT} & \langle \text{NP}_i,\ [1]\text{NP}_j,\ \text{AP}[\text{SUBCAT}\,\langle[1]\rangle]:\textbf{empty}\,(j)\rangle \\ \text{CONTENT} & \textbf{cause}(\textbf{fish}(i),\ \textbf{become}(\textbf{empty}(j))) \end{bmatrix}$

Important evidence that this is a lexical process comes from the fact that it feeds deverbal nominalization (Müller 2006: ex. 37):

(41) a. jemand die Nordsee leer fischt
        somebody the North.Sea empty fishes

    b. wegen der Leerfischung der Nordsee
        because.of the empty.fishing of.the North.Sea

Dowty (1979), Rappaport Hovav and Levin (1998), and Müller (2002; 2006) are all very similar accounts. They differ mainly in what aspects they emphasize.

7.2.3 Complex predicates with scalar semantics

Neither Dowty nor Rappaport Hovav and Levin offer an explanation for the effects of word choice illustrated by the following (repeated from (26a)):

(42)   He wiped it clean/dry/smooth/*damp/*dirty/*stained/*wet.

Dowty (1979: 303) saw such variation as unpredictable, and suggested that the verb–adjective combination was a discontinuous 'lexicalized compound verb.'

A general account was offered by Wechsler (2001; 2005c; 2012). The account relies on a different semantic analysis, involving scalar semantics. The proposal is based on semantic subcategories of scalar adjectives as defined by the structure of the scale (Kennedy 1999; Rotstein and Winter 2004; Kennedy and McNally 2005). Gradable adjectives can be modeled with scales, i.e. ordered sets with a measure function (Section 2.4.2). The adjective is interpreted relative to a standard degree on that scale: *Michael Jordan is tall* means that Jordan's height is greater than some contextually determined standard of tallness (Kennedy 1999).

Gradable adjectives are classified according to the structure of the scale. 'Maximal endpoint closed-scale' (MaxEndPt) gradable adjectives like *full*, *empty*, *straight*, *clean*, and *dry* have an inherent maximum that serves as a default standard which applies when it is not overridden by context (Kennedy 1999). 'Minimal endpoint closed-scale' (MinEndPt) gradable adjectives like *wet* and *dirty* have an inherent standard at the minimal end of the scale. The inherent standard for the MaxEndPt adjective (e.g. *clean*) is always at the minimal point of the scale associated with the antonymous MinEndPt adjective (e.g. *dirty*), but not vice versa. So on the dirtiness scale, *clean* means roughly 'no degree of dirtiness,' while *dirty* means 'some degree of dirtiness.' But on the cleanliness scale, *dirty* does not mean 'no degree of cleanliness,' nor does *clean* mean 'some degree of cleanliness.'

Turning to a third type, 'open-scale' gradable adjectives like *tall*, *long*, *wide*, *short*, and *tall* lack inherent endpoints altogether. They must rely on context for their standards (Hay et al. 1999; Kennedy and McNally 1999). Modifiers like *totally* or *completely* sound worse with open-scale gradable than closed-scale adjectives:

(43) a. completely full/empty/straight/dry (closed-scale)
      b. ?? completely long/wide/short/tall (open-scale)

Kennedy and McNally (1999: fn. 1) note that the *completely*-test is complicated by the fact that *completely* sometimes means not 'maximal on the scale' but rather 'very,' and in that latter meaning it appears with open-scale adjectives. (Similarly, Sapir (1944: 114) commented that the use of the superlative in locutions like *a most pleasing personality* is 'logically unreasonable but psychologically somehow inevitable.') Kennedy and McNally (1999) tease these apart by their different entailments, which make (44a) but not (44b) contradictory:

(44) a. #The line is completely straight, but it could be straighter.
      b. I'm completely uninterested in finances, but Bob is even less interested.

As a second test, MaxEndPt adjectives systematically differ from both other types in the acceptability and interpretation of modifiers like *almost* (Rotstein and Winter 2004):

(45) a. It is almost dry. (total)
      b. #It is almost wet. (partial)
      c. #It is almost long. (open-scale)

In certain rich contexts, MinEndPt and open-scale adjectives also allow modification by *almost*, but the interpretation differs systematically from total adjectives: *almost wet*, if acceptable, entails 'not dry,' while *almost dry* does not entail 'not wet' (Rotstein and Winter 2004: 267). Hence (46a) is coherent but (46b) is not:

(46) a. The towel is wet but it is almost dry.
      b. #The towel is dry but it is almost wet.

Other phenomena that have been claimed to distinguish these adjective types include the (a)telicity of cognate 'degree achievement' verbs like *straighten, flatten,* and *cool$_V$* (Hay, Kennedy, and Levin 1999) and differences involving plurals and 'donkey anaphora' (Yoon 1996).

    When the verb in a resultative construction is durative, a 'maximal endpoint closed-scale gradable adjective' (i.e. a total adjective) is strongly preferred. Referring to example (42), the acceptable adjectives *clean, dry,* and *smooth* are all 'maximal endpoint adjectives' (MaxEndpt), while the unacceptable *damp, dirty, stained,* and *wet* are 'minimal end-point adjectives' (MinEndpt). The generalization that maximal endpoint adjectives are favored for the English resultative construction is supported by corpus data (Wechsler 2005c; 2012). Boas's (2000) exhaustive study of a 100-million-word corpus, primarily from the British National Corpus, turned up 958 control resultative constructions containing the following MaxEndpt adjectives: *awake, clean, dry, empty, flat, full, open, red, shut, smooth, solid, sober, unconscious*. Meanwhile, the same sample turned up no resultatives with the MinEndpt adjectives *dirty* and *wet*, and only 20 tokens containing any of the following open-scale adjectives: *crooked, famous, fat, ill, sleepy, sore, tired, insane, safe, mad, hoarse, sick, soft, stupid, tender*, and *thin*. The data are summarized in (47). The 'All' column shows the total number of tokens of this adjective in the corpus. The 'Resultatives' column shows how many of those tokens occur in resultative constructions where the adjective heads the resultative secondary predicate. The correlation is highly significant statistically ($p < .0001$).

(47)   Frequency of adjective by type in control resultative versus other functions (Wechsler 2012)

	All	Resultative	Non-resultative	% resultative
MaxEndpt:	97,985	938	97,047	0.957
Non-MaxEndpt:	53,905	20	53,885	0.037

(Analysis: The chi-square value (Yates chi-square, corrected for continuity) for these data is $\chi^2 = 468.34$ (df = 1); $p < .0001$.)

The corpus data also included counts of adjectives in analytic causative constructions with causative verbs like *make, get, render, drive*, and *send*:

(48)   a. Mary got her hair dry.
      b. Evaporation will have made the drop even flatter.
      c. They also render life experiences flat.
      d. The music drove them insane.

These examples allow one to compare frequency of resultatives with a given adjective to the overall frequency of sentences expressing the causation of the adjective-denoted state. Such sentences include both resultatives like *Mary wiped the table dry* and analytic causatives like *Mary got her hair dry*. The table in (49) compares MaxEndpt adjectives with other adjectives, across these two construction types.

(49)   Frequency of MaxEndpt and non-MaxEndpt adjectives in resultatives versus lexical causatives (Wechsler 2012)

	All eventive	Resultative	*Make* (etc.) causatives	% resultative
MaxEndpt:	976	938	38	96.1
Non-MaxEndpt:	625	20	605	3.2

The percentages in the rightmost column show that for MaxEndpt adjectives X, resultatives make up a very large percentage (96.1%) of the total number of expressions of 'causing to become X,' while for non-MaxEndpt adjectives, resultatives make up a very small percentage (3.2%). Again, this correlation is highly significant. (Analysis: The chi-square value (Yates chi-square, corrected for continuity) for these data is $\chi^2 = 1364.61$ (df = 1); p < .0001.) This suggests that when a speaker of English chooses to express the notion 'cause to become X,' they are much more likely to use a resultative to do so if the adjective X is a MaxEndpt adjective than if it is not.

The fact that resultatives favor MaxEndPt adjectives so strongly suggests a different compositional semantics for combining the verb and adjective meanings. When those meanings are combined, the adjective's scale fuses with the verb's aspectual structure. The result is a homomorphic mapping between the adjective's property scale and the temporal structure of the verb-denoted event. Assuming the event-argument homomorphism theory of telicity (Krifka 1998; Jackendoff 1996), we predict that resultatives, being telic, would favor adjectives with scales bounded by an inherent maximum, hence MaxEndpt adjectives. The paraphrase given by the older result state theory assumed by Dowty (1979), Rappaport Hovav and Levin (1998), and others is given informally in (50i). The paraphrase given by the scalar semantic theory appears in (50ii):

(50)   Mary wiped the table dry.
    (i) Result state theory: 'Mary wiped the table, causing the table to become dry.'
    (ii) Scalar semantics theory: 'As Mary wiped the table, the table became drier and drier, until it was dry.'

The adjective *dry* has an inherent maximum, which the table reaches when it contains no water. But *wet* is a minimal endpoint adjective:

(51)   ??Mary wiped the table wet.
     #As Mary wiped the table, the table became wetter and wetter,
     until it was wet.'

Since *wet* has a minimal endpoint, the table becomes wet at the very
beginning of the process. As a consequence, the last part of the paraphrase in (51), 'until it was wet,' does not make sense.

Larson (2014) adopts the scalar semantics for resultatives in an
analysis designed to remove the stipulation that resultative constructions are telic. Larson's proposal is based on the supposition that the
grammar must allow the scalar adjective some means for fixing its
standard. Recall that the degree standard for an attributive or primary
predicate scalar adjective can normally come from the context, and for
an open-scale adjective it must come from context: *Michael Jordan is
tall* means that Jordan's height exceeds some standard of tallness
defined by the context, perhaps relative to other basketball players, or
to people in general. But in a resultative construction, the adjective and
verb compose semantically so that the scalar structure of the adjective
fuses with the temporal structure of the verb. Assuming that this fusion
renders the verb–adjective semantic complex opaque to contextual
valuation of the scalar standard, then the context is not available to
set the standard. Instead, an inherent standard must be exploited. Thus,
only those adjectives with an inherent standard, i.e. only maximal
endpoint closed-scale adjectives, are possible.

7.2.4 Light verbs and small clauses

Assuming the earlier 'Result State' semantics of resultatives, the resultative rule or template augmentation adds a CAUSE predicate to the
semantic structure (see (29), (33), and (38)). Within constructional
approaches to the Result State semantic analysis, it is natural to associate the added CAUSE predicate with a syntactic formative of some
sort. That formative can be either an actual causative light verb such as
make or *get*, or an abstract light verb such as 'little v.'

As background to the light verb analysis, let us first review the small
clause analysis of Hoekstra (1988) and many others. Hoekstra started
from a consideration of ECM resultatives, in which the verb does
not appear to assign a semantic role to its object (Hoekstra 1988: 116,
exx. 35, 36):

(52)   a. He washed [the soap out of his eyes]_{SC}.
       b. The sopranos sang [us sleepy]_{SC}.

       c. Zij   at   [zich   moddervet]_{SC}.   (Dutch)
          she   ate   herself very.fat

       d. Hij   kocht   [de   winkel   leeg]_{SC}.   (Dutch)
          he   bought the   shop   empty

Hoekstra posited a small clause (SC) as complement to the verb, as shown by the bracketing. This is very plausible for ECM resultatives, given the theory Hoekstra assumed, in which thematic structure is reflected directly in the phrase structure. More controversial was his further claim that such structures also characterized control resultatives (Hoekstra 1988: 117, exx. 37, 38):

(53)   a. They painted [the door green]_{SC}.
       b. They cooked [the chicken dry]_{SC}.
       c. They wiped [the table clean]_{SC}.

       d. Hij   reed   [zijn   auto   in de prak]_{SC}.
          he   drove   his   car   to pieces

       e. Zij   kookten   [de   aardappels   kapot]_{SC}.
          they   cooked   the   potatoes   falling.apart

This analysis was criticized for failing to capture the thematic role assigned by the verb to the nominal following it. Hoekstra argued that no thematic role is assigned (recall Müller's arguments regarding German resultatives like (31)–(36)). While this may be viable for Dutch, it is hard to square with English verbs with strongly obligatory patient roles, such as *crack*:

(54)   a. She cracked the eggs open.
       b. (*)She cracked.
       c. The container cracked open.

Example (54b) has only the inchoative interpretation in which she ends up cracked.

Folli and Harley (2004; see also Embick 2004) posited a sort of small-clause complement selected by a causal abstract light verb *v*. The light verb can verbalize a resultative denoting root, leading to a lexical causative as in (55a). Merging an activity-encoding root such as *wipe* with the *v* yields a resultative as in (55b).

(55)   a. [John [clean$_i$+v [the floor t$_i$]]]
       b. [John [wipe+v [the floor clean]]]

Beavers (2012: 929, fn. 16) raises the same criticism as the one leveled against Hoekstra, namely that the analysis does not capture the thematic relationship between the verb and its object in control resultatives. Beavers notes, however, that Ramchand (2008: 121–31) solves this problem with a more complex structure and movement operations to model argument sharing.

Goldberg and Jackendoff's (2004) constructional account of English resultatives involves a similar thematic structure, but they draw a direct connection to actual causative light verbs. Illustrating with the example in (56a), they render the semantics in two parts as shown in (56b) (Goldberg and Jackendoff 2004: 538, ex. 13):

(56)   a. Willy watered the plants flat.
       b. Semantics: WILLY CAUSE [PLANTS BECOME FLAT]
                       MEANS: WILLY WATER PLANTS

Goldberg and Jackendoff (2004: 538, ex. 14) specify the semantic contribution of the construction itself as the first line of the semantics shown here:

(57)   Causative property resultative
       Syntax: NP_1 V NP_2 AP_3
       Semantics: X_1 CAUSE [Y_2 BECOME Z_3]
                    MEANS: [*VERBAL SUBEVENT*]

On their construction grammar theory, the construction itself is a grammatical formative with argument structure properties similar to words (see Section 5.3). The idea behind this analysis is that the resultative construction derives from the syntax of the light verbs. They reason that causal light verbs like *make* and *get*, as in *Willy made/got the plants flat*, have the same meaning, 'X cause Y to become Z,' and the same distribution of arguments in syntax, as the construction they posit. So the same rules that map the causal light verbs to their syntactic argument structure can also be used to map the construction to its syntactic argument structure (Goldberg and Jackendoff 2004: 538). They speculate more generally that 'productive constructions likely arise from speakers generalizing over verbs that lexically specify the corresponding forms and meanings' (p. 539).

Goldberg and Jackendoff's construction is a small-clause-type structure, where the bracketed [Y_2 BECOME Z_3] is the small clause. As in the earlier small-clause analyses, the causee Y_2 is not an argument of the CAUSE relation. But Goldberg and Jackendoff encode the semantic relation between the verb and its object separately in the argument structure of the verb, represented by 'VERBAL SUBEVENT' in (57). This mismatch between the thematic structures of the verb and the construction is possible on their theory because they do not assume the Projection Principle. Instead they stipulate the linking between the arguments of the verb (the VERBAL SUBEVENT) and the arguments of the construction. This corresponds to Ramchand's (2008: 121–31) movement operations to model argument sharing, which are also stipulated.

A problem with applying small-clause and light-verb-related analyses to control resultatives is that they fail to address the lexical variation facts discussed in Section 7.2.3. The abstract light verb (little v), or the construction that derives from actual light verb constructions, adds the CAUSE predicate. As a consequence, such analyses must assume the Result State semantic theory, rather than Scalar Semantics. Such analyses fail to place intrinsic constraints on the scalar structure of the adjective that could explain why maximal endpoint closed-scale adjectives are so heavily favored.

As such, the light-verb analysis may be more appropriate for ECM resultatives, for which there does not appear to be any homomorphism condition. The corpus study described in Section 7.2.3 turned up examples of ECM resultatives with both Maximal Endpoint and open-scale adjectives. In fact, in contrast to control resulatives, the ECM resultatives were more likely to use open-scale than closed-scale adjectives, as shown in (58).

(58)   Frequency of adjective by type in resultative versus other functions

	All	Control resultative	ECM resultative	Non-resultative	% resultative
MaxEndpt	97,985	938	6	97,047	0.957
Non-MaxEndpt	53,905	20	26	53,885	0.037

ECM resultatives like (30) and (52) closely match the causal light verb constructions both semantically and syntactically. Every ECM resultative can be paired with a causal light-verb construction that it parallels and entails:

(59)
a. John slept himself sober.   ⇒ John made himself sober.
b. The sopranos sang us sleepy.   ⇒ The sopranos made us sleepy.
c. We laughed them off the stage. ⇒ We forced them off the stage.

Suppose that ECM resultatives are licensed by causal light verbs, perhaps because the light-verb construction gave rise to a construction with which the verb combines, as Goldberg and Jackendoff suggest. But we need not follow Goldberg and Jackendoff in extending this analysis to control resultatives, which have a different thematic structure since the verb theta-marks its object. Instead suppose the control resultatives are complex predicates with the scalar semantics described above in Section 7.2.3. This allows us to explain the inability to omit so-called 'fake reflexives' from ECM constructions (e.g. Simpson 1983; Bresnan and Zaenen 1990):

(60)   a. We danced ourselves tired. ⇒ We made ourselves tired.
        b. *We danced tired.   *We made tired.
                                        (*tired* is open-scale)

The (60b) example lacks any causative model (cp. *We made tired*), and the adjective *tired* lack the proper scalar structure to form a resultative through complex predicate formation (Section 7.2.3). But when the adjective is a Maximal Endpoint closed-scale adjective like *free*, then both options are possible (for corpus examples of this kind, see Rappaport Hovav and Levin 2001: 774, ex. 23):

(61)   a. She wriggled herself free.   ⇒ She made herself free.
        b. She wriggled free.   *free* is MaxEndpt

In contrast to ECM resultatives, control resultatives never match the thematic structure of a light verb construction, as explained already. In transitive control resultatives the verb theta-marks its object. The putative parallel between *hammer the metal flat* and *make the metal flat* is illusory, since *the metal* is an argument of *hammer* but not *make*. This illusion becomes apparent when we turn to intransitive control resultatives, whether 'unaccusatives' (theme-only verbs, as in (62a)) or 'unergatives' (agent-only verbs, as in (62b)). Then the illusion of a parallel disappears:

(62)   a. The water froze solid.   ⇔ *The water made solid.
        b. He jumped clear of the fire. ⇔ *He made clear of the fire.

This avoids the stipulation of argument sharing noted above in connection with small clause analyses of control resultatives.

7.3 German applicatives

The German verbal prefix *be-* has the effect of promoting or adding a locative argument to expression as the direct object (these two examples from Wunderlich 1997a and Brinkmann 1997 respectively):

(63) a. Sie   sprühte   Farbe   an   die   Wand.
         She   sprayed   paint   on   the   wall
         'She sprayed paint on the wall.'

      b. Sie   besprühte   die Wand   (mit Farbe).
         she   be-sprayed   the wall   (with paint)
         lit. 'She be-sprayed the wall with paint.'

(64) a. Bernd   steigt   auf die Mauer.
         Bernd   climbs   on the wall
         'Bernd is climbing onto the wall.'

      b. Bernd   besteigt   die Mauer.
         Bernd   be-climbs   the wall
         lit. 'Bernd is be-climbing the wall.'

Michaelis and Ruppenhofer (2001; M&R) adopt a constructional model, and argue in some detail that it is superior to the earlier decomposition analyses by Wunderlich (1997a) and Brinkmann (1997). Let us briefly review the two proposals, beginning with the Wunderlich–Brinkmann approach, and then compare them.

The preposition *be-* is historically derived from an earlier preposition *bi* meaning 'around' (Stiebels 1991). Hence Wunderlich referred to the modern prefix as a preposition, so that *be-*prefixation is treated as 'preposition incorporation' that takes place in the morphology. The predicates denoted by the prefix *be-* and the verb are combined through function composition, yielding a complex predicate (Brinkmann 1997: 86–7). The verb and the preposition are combined to form a complex predicate that now expresses jointly all the arguments of the two previously independent predicates. Brinkmann notes that the complex predicate may be acquired as part of the input language or it may arise through on-line application of the rule as a speaker invents a new word (Brinkmann 1997: 86–7).

The analysis is formalized within Wunderlich's Lexical Decomposition Grammar (LDG) briefly described in Section 4.4.3. First consider the decomposition of the non-*be*-prefixed verb taking a locative PP complement such as *sprühen* 'spray' seen in (63a) (Brinkmann 1997):

(65) *sprühen* 'spray'

$\lambda P \quad \lambda y \quad \lambda x \quad$ (SPRAY (x, y) & $P(y)$)

[+DIR] | |

acc   nom

The three lambda operators are discharged by the three arguments of the verb: λP is for the PP, e.g. *an die Wand* 'on the wall' in (63a), with the feature [+DIR] restricting this argument to directional elements; λy and λx are for the object (in accusative case) and subject (in nominative case), respectively. As explained in Section 4.4.3, the positions of the subject ('nom') and object ('acc') annotations are not stipulated but derived within the LDG system from the depth of embedding of the variables within the decomposition structure: the object variable is less embedded than subject variable. The two-place relation SPRAY hold between the agent (*sie* 'she') and theme (*Farbe* 'paint'). In (65) the property P corresponds to the whole directional PP, e.g. *an die Wand* 'on the wall' in (63a). This is predicated of the y variable, hence after lambda conversion $P(y)$ is roughly 'paint is on the wall.' Taken together with SPRAY(x,y), we get 'she sprayed paint; paint is on the wall.'

The ampersand connective '&' is called 'SF conjunction' and has a special status in this theory. It is non-commutative and is interpreted according to two principles attributed by Wunderlich (1997a: 36, 42) to Kaufmann (1995a; 1995b):

(66) a. Coherence: A lexical SF conjunction is contemporaneously or causally interpreted.

b. Connexion: The second member in a lexical SF representation specifies inferences about the first member.

These are general constraints on possible word meanings. Coherence specifies that the pieces of the word meaning must be related by referring to situations that either take place at the same time or are causally related. In the case of the *be*-construction, the interpretation is usually that of causation. Wunderlich illustrates Connexion with the *be*-construction, among others, noting that from the sentence *Sie besprühte die Wand* 'She sprayed the wall,' 'one can infer that it is the sprayed substance that covers the wall.'

The preposition *an* 'onto' is a two-place predicate. Its internal argument, the relatum or reference object is filled by its object NP, 'the wall' in our example (Brinkmann 1997: 95):

(67) *an* [+DIR] 'onto'

    λz λu [BECOME (LOC $(u, AT^*(z))$)]

    |

    acc

In deriving the PP 'onto the wall' the predicate *an* applies to its internal argument but has one argument remaining, hence the PP is the one-place predicate ($Q(y)$) sought by the verb *sprühen*. Turning now to the prefix *be-*, it has essentially the same semantics except that it is a bound morpheme, notated by the feature [+BOUND]:

(68) *be* [+DIR, +BOUND]
    $\lambda z \lambda u$ [BECOME (LOC $(u, AT^*(z))$)]

Crucially, when this 'preposition' combines with the verb, it has not discharged its internal argument yet. Function composition produces the following representation:

(69) *besprühen* 'be-spray'
    $\lambda z \lambda y \lambda x \lambda s$ [SPRAY (x, y) & BECOME (LOC $(y, AT^*(z))$)]

That undischarged internal argument of the preposition is now the most embedded variable (z) so it will become the new applied locative object of the *be*-prefixed verb, according to the LDG linking principles. In this way the Wunderlich–Brinkmann analysis cleverly captures a noted cross-linguistic generalization about preposition incorporation: the object of the derived preposition–verb complex expresses the argument corresponding to the object of the analytic preposition—not the object of the analytic verb (Craig and Hale 1988). For example, in Swedish the argument expressed as the object of the preposition *från* 'from' becomes the object of the preposition–verb complex *från-taga* 'from-take' or 'deprive' (example from Wechsler 1995: 96):

(70) a. De   tog   chefskap-et   från   honom.
          they   took   headship-DEF   from   him
          'They took the headship from him.'

      b. De   från-tog   honom   chefskapet.
          they   from-took   him   headship-DEF
          'They deprived him of the headship.'

      c. Han   fråntogs   chefskapet.
          he   from-took-PASS   headship-DEF
          'He was deprived of the headship.'

Example (70c) provides evidence that the added argument (*honom* 'him') is a true object, since it passivizes. A similar generalization characterizes applicativization in languages with highly productive applicative processes, such as Bantu languages. The applied argument is typically treated as the primary object, rather than a secondary one. This observation, due to Marantz (1984), was dubbed 'Marantz's Generalization' by Baker (1988).

The least embedded variable (*x*, the agent of SPRAY) becomes the subject. As for the middle variable (*y*, the theme), Wunderlich's theory allows for such middle arguments to be expressed as dative NPs under certain conditions.[3] In any case, those conditions are not met here, forcing that argument to remain unexpressed (existentially quantified) or expressed in an appropriate oblique, here a *with*-phrase (*mit Farbe* 'with paint').

Brinkmann discusses three special semantic properties of the German *be-* applicatives that are not necessarily found in the corresponding PP construction. First, the applied locative argument is understood as wholly affected or involved in the event, a property often referred to as 'holism.' Thus (71b) suggests that the speaker traveled all over China, while (71a) would be true if she had merely passed through it; sentence (72b), but not sentence (72a), suggests that the whole plot is covered with houses (Wechsler and Lee 1996); and in (73) (from Brinkmann 1997: 71) the sugar is understood as distributed across the whole of the cake's exterior:

(71)   a. Ich reiste in China.
           'I traveled in China.'
       b. Ich bereiste China.
           'I be-traveled China.'

(72)   a. Die Firma baute neue Häuser auf das Grundstück.
           'The company built new houses on(to) the plot of land.'
       b. Die Firma bebaute das Grundstück (mit neuen Häusern).
           'The company be-built the plot of land with new houses.'

(73)   Donna bestreut den Kuchen mit Zucker.
       'Donna be-sprinkles the cake with sugar.'

---

[3] A structurally linked argument must L-command the lowest argument (Wunderlich 1997a; Brinkmann 1997: 97).

Similar semantic 'holism' effects have long been noted for direct arguments that alternate with obliques (see Section 4.5). For that reason Wunderlich and Brinkmann attribute this semantic property not to the *be*-prefix construction per se, but rather to a side-effect of the direct argument status of the locative. Specifically, they build on Löbner's Presupposition of Indivisibility hypothesis: 'Whenever a predicate is applied to one of its arguments, it is true or false of the argument as a whole' (Löbner 2000). This presupposition applies only to direct predication, hence to a direct object but not an oblique.

Another special property of the *be*-construction is that it resists interpretations in which the event denotes movement into the interior of an object (Brinkmann 1997):

(74) a. Ted bewirft   die Wand/*den Abfluß (mit Dreck).
          Ted be-throws   the wall/*the   outlet   (with dirt).
          lit. 'Ted throws the wall with dirt.'

      b. Sue begießt   den Braten/*das Glas (mit Wasser).
          Sue be-pours   the roast/*the   glass (with water).'
          lit. 'Sue pours the roast with water.'

Wunderlich and Brinkmann attribute this 'exteriority constraint' directly to the semantics of the *be*-morpheme. Following Wunderlich, Brinkmann (1997) assumes that the prefix *be-* derives from the Old High German preposition *bi* 'around something, with respect to something.' Modern German has lost the independent preposition *bi*, and *be*-verbs correspond closely to verbs that take prepositional complements headed by *an* 'at' or *auf* 'on' (Brinkmann 1997: 79). The prepositions *an* and *auf* denote contact between a theme and the outer surface of a reference object, paralleling the exteriority constraint on the applicative (Brinkmann 1997: 80; Michaelis and Ruppenhofer 2001: 32). Noting the resemblence to *an* and *auf*, Brinkmann (1997: 81–2) comments:

The restriction also shows that *be-* is more than a simple marker on the verb to indicate a certain argument structure—it is closely associated with specific independent prepositions. This supports an analysis according to which *be*-verbs are derived by incorporating a preposition…*be-* has a rather specific meaning and so introduces language-specific restrictions on the locative alternation.

Summarizing the Wunderlich–Brinkmann LDG analysis: the prefix *be-* and the verb each denote predicates, which are composed into a single complex predicate according to general principles of predicate composition. The resulting complex predicate expresses its arguments in the usual way for a verbal predicate. The semantic properties of the construction are attributed to various sources. The causal relation derives from the Coherence principle (66). The holistic effect on the applied locative object follows from general principles of predication: direct arguments tend to have this property. The exteriority constraint derives from the semantics of the *be-* morpheme.

Now let us turn to the critique of Brinkmann by Michaelis and Ruppenhofer (2001) and their alternative constructional approach. Using the unification based formalism of Berkeley Construction Grammar (see Section 5.2.2.4), M&R propose the following bivalent and trivalent constructions, respectively for the two-argument type in (71b) and the three-argument type in the other examples such as (72) and (73):

(75)   German Applicative Constructions (Michaelis and Ruppenhofer 2001)

   a.   The bivalent Applicative Construction

$$
\left[
\begin{array}{ll}
\text{syn} & \left[\begin{array}{ll} \text{cat} & \text{V} \\ \text{form} & \text{Be - prefix} \end{array}\right] \\
\text{sem} & [\text{COVER} \langle \text{THEME, LOCATION} \rangle] \\
\text{PRED} & \langle\ \rangle \\
\text{val} & \left\{[\text{role theme}], \left[\begin{array}{ll} \text{sem} & \text{planar region} \\ \text{role} & \left[\begin{array}{ll} \text{gf} & \text{obl-} \\ \theta & \text{location} \end{array}\right] \end{array}\right]\right\}
\end{array}
\right]
$$

   b.   The trivalent Applicative Construction

$$
\left[
\begin{array}{ll}
\text{syn} & \left[\begin{array}{ll} \text{cat} & \text{V} \\ \text{form} & \text{Be - prefix} \end{array}\right] \\
\text{sem} & [\text{CAUSE - COVER} \langle \text{AGENT, THEME, LOCATION} \rangle] \\
\text{PRED} & \langle\ \rangle \\
\text{val} & \left\{[\text{role agent}],[\text{role theme}], \left[\begin{array}{ll} \text{sem} & \text{planar region} \\ \text{role} & \left[\begin{array}{ll} \text{gf} & \text{obl-} \\ \theta & \text{location} \end{array}\right] \end{array}\right]\right\}
\end{array}
\right]
$$

To derive a clause headed by a *be*-prefixed verb, the construction unifies with the structure for the verb. They do not spell out the how this works technically for the relations specified in the sem(antics) field (actually they do not provide an AVM for a verb at all). The idea is that the two relations combine: for example, in the derivation of (73) the relation denoted by the (unprefixed) verb stem *streuen*, call it SPRINKLE, combines with CAUSE-COVER. That combination might be something like conjunction, so that the meaning is predicted to be 'Donna sprinkled sugar on the cake, and she caused sugar to cover the cake.'

Comparing the two accounts, it is clear that M&R's '*be*-construction' (75) corresponds to Brinkmann and Wunderlich's '*be*-morpheme' (68). A reified lambda abstract, as in Wunderlich's theory, is roughly equivalent to a construction. Necessarily, every instance of the *be*-construction contains a *be*-morpheme, and every instance of the *be*- morpheme appears in a *be*-construction. M&R's composing of the verb meaning with the constructional meaning corresponds to Brinkmann and Wunderlich's predicate composition. The differences between the two analyses do not seem to depend in any essential way on differences between the two models of grammar, *pace* M&R. Michaelis and Ruppenhofer's critique includes the puzzling claim that 'For Brinkmann, the applicative pattern has no inherent semantics, polysemous or otherwise.' (p. 95) M&R argue that their constructional model is superior because it allows for different degrees of fit between the semantics of the verb, as represented in a predicate argument structure, and the construction.

But this critique of Brinkmann is inaccurate. For Wunderlich and Brinkmann, the applicative pattern has inherent semantics. In fact, it will be recalled that Brinkmann argues for the analysis of *be*- as an incorporated preposition precisely from the fact that it has rich, word-like meaning. M&R also see it as problematic for B&W's account that the *be*- morpheme sometimes adds a new argument that is not normally selected by the base verb (e.g. (71) and (72)). But again there seems to be no reason why the incorporated preposition could not add an argument in Brinkmann and Wunderlich's system.

The two semantic analyses differ in many details. Where Brinkmann and Wunderlich tease apart three different sources for the semantics of the *be*-applicative, M&R attribute everything to the construction. Causation is also built into the meaning of the construction, in contrast to the Brinkmann and Wunderlich analysis, where causation follows from the general Coherence principle of word meaning. M&R collapse the holism and exteriority properties into a single semantic property they call *coverage*. In (73) the sugar *covers* the cake, perhaps with gaps between the grains of sugar but distributed over the whole of the cake. M&R attribute this 'coverage' meaning directly to the *be*-construction, taking it to be the prototypical meaning (see the sem features in (75)). The source of this meaning, according to M&R, is one sense of the historical preposition *bi*. Grimm (1854) translated that sense with the Latin *circum* 'around, (entire or partial) encompassing and surrounding of an object,' and exemplified it with *sehen* 'see' versus *besehen* 'look at from all sides,' the latter a metaphorical 'coverage' of an object with one's gaze (Lewis and Short 1879).

However, Loos (2012) points out that Grimm's dictionary also gives a second usage of the prefix *be-* as expressing what Loos translates as 'the consummate impact on an object' (Grimm 1854, vol. I, ll. 1202–6). Loos (2012: 15) concludes: 'Affectedness and coverage readings thus coexist since at least the 19th century, making both plausible candidates for a prototypical scenario associated with German applicatives.' Loos notes that many modern German examples suggest affectedness rather than coverage. For example, *befummeln* ('feel up') 'can describe a scenario where only specific parts of a person's body are touched, hence full coverage is not necessarily implied—but, crucially, this person's privacy is invaded, affecting them physically and mentally.' In keeping with the style of much of construction grammar, M&R's construction is semantically rather rich, polysemous, and subject to metaphorical extension, with putative senses and extensions involving not only coverage but event iteration, transfer of a theme onto a surface, and so on. Loos points out exceptions, and argues instead that the various putative senses can be subsumed under the single notion of affectedness.

In conclusion, we can see a number of differences between the Brinkmann–Wunderlich and M&R analyses. They differ in the division of labor between the components of the grammar. As already noted, causation and holism come into the picture via general principles of word meaning on one view, but are specific to the construction on the other. All the cited studies contain interesting observations on the richness of meaning of the morpheme or construction, including various metaphorical and inferential extentions. But descriptions within the two frameworks are intertranslatable.

8

Postscript

The research discussed in this book is directed at a complex question: what is the relation between the meaning of a word and its syntactic behavior? We have focused especially on argument-taking words like verbs. The question seems to presuppose an answer to a more fundamental, and more ancient question: What is a word meaning? That more basic question, which we will look at directly below, has received many different answers, so it should not surprise us that there are many different views of how best to look at it. Let us consider some tentative conclusions about where this quest for understanding might be leading.

First let us consider normative aspects of word meaning, by returning to the question 'What is the meaning of a word?' Wittgenstein observed that when we ask that question, 'We are up against one of the great sources of philosophical bewilderment: we try to find a substance for a substantive' (1934: 1). He famously answered that one should look at how a word is *used*. A 'word meaning' does not correspond to a 'substance' so much as a rich pattern of use. We know that people modulate their interpretations of words based on recent exposure to particular interlocutors (Section 2.4.5). My interpretation of the verb *cherish* in the context of a speech act cannot be reduced to something associated with that sound that I retrieve from my own repertoire of concepts. It is also influenced by my estimation of my interlocutor's intention. I don't just consult my own repertoire of concepts for my concept of 'cherish'; I also ask myself, 'What does *she* mean by that?' This means that word meanings cannot be equated with extralinguistic 'concepts.' They cannot be divorced from the language itself.

One issue of controversy is whether words are equipped with semantic structure, or lexicosemantic decomposition. It seems quite clear that they are (Section 4.4.5). A word is often accompanied by instructions on what the word can combine with and what the combination means. Speakers of English, if they are lucky, know about happiness and about ecstasy. But they also have semantic knowledge about the words *happiness* and *ecstasy* that is unlikely to be derived from knowing about actual happiness or ecstasy. For example, we know that certain things can *give us great happiness* and that when that happens, we *have great happiness*. But we cannot **be given ecstasy*, nor can we **have ecstasy*. Conversely, we know that we can be *in ecstasy*—but we cannot be **in happiness*. The words belong to categories that are not formal but rather semantic: happiness is a possession, ecstasy is a location. Many other words for moods, diseases, and so on, similarly bifurcate into those two semantic classes. It is implausible that we learn the semantic categories of those words through exposure to the denotations, such as actual experiences of happiness and ecstasy. Instead we learn them from exposure to the words *happiness* and *ecstasy*, in the context of sentences containing those words. This and many other facts show clearly that words have semantic decompositions.

When we turn to argument-taking predicates like verbs, again we find certain semantic components regularly recurring across many different verbs. Since a verb selects arguments, it is natural to see those semantic components as forming a structure *around* the verb, an 'event structure' that is built on top of the root meaning of the verb (Section 4.4.4.3). Specifically, the two most robust generalizations to have emerged are these: (i) For verbs expressing causation, the first argument of the CAUSE relation is regularly expressed as the subject (of an active verb, in an accusative language). (ii) For transitive verbs expressing some change of state, the participant that undergoes the change is regularly expressed as the object. The event structure has a 'syntax' in the sense that there are rules to generate it, but whether it is part of the syntax of word combination is another question. This event structure does not seem to interact with the syntax of word combination in any way beyond what is summarized in a simple predicate argument structure (Section 1.2). Moreover, while the symbols representing these pieces of the semantic structure (such as causation and effect) can annotate the syntactic 'addresses' of arguments such as subject and object positions in a phrase structure, in the vast majority of cases these arguments of the event structure still must maintain an explicit link to the arguments of the verb root. Understanding Mary's role in *Mary bought a bike from Sam* involves more than knowing that Mary 'caused' the transaction. After all, Sam was equally involved in causing it. It also involves knowing that Mary is the buyer (Wechsler 2005a). That 'buyer' role is associated with the root *buy*.

Although I have argued for a lexicalist position, the constructionists have provided important insights. Some aspects of the event predicate seem to transcend the particular verb heading the clause, and may be seen as arising from an argument structure construction. For example, the highest argument of a clause can quite often be optionally interpreted as an agent, typically a volitional agent responsible for causing the event. In *John moved the cat over (in order to see the newspaper)*, John is the agent of the moving; the cat undergoes motion. In *The cat moved over (in order to see better)*, the cat still undergoes motion but now it is also agentive. Agency seems to be optionally layered on the highest role of a verb (blocked by some verbs, however). Similarly, the direct object often can get a holistic or affected interpretation irrespective of which participant is realized as object, as shown by the locative alternation (Sections 3.5.2 and 4.5). These semantic components (agency, affectedness) are connected to grammatical relations or positions in a general argument structure schema, and transcend the particulars of the relations denoted by the verb root. Agency or affectedness is layered on a semantic role that is already lexically assigned by the verb root. In other words, this represents a *fusion* of the constructional and lexical roles, as in some versions of construction grammar (Section 5.3), and not the *licensing* of an agent role that the verb does not otherwise select, as in the 'neo-Davidsonian in the syntax' abstract light verb theories (Section 5.4).

On the lexicalist view, verbs are stored with predicate argument structures. Let us now address a question that has rarely been asked. Assuming the lexicalist view is correct, what causes language to work this way? Why *must* the lexicalist view be right? I will look at the related issues of vagueness, prototypes, and polysemy, and show how they might be the basis of an explanation.

There is considerable psychological evidence that we represent the centers of conceptual categories rather than the full sets out to the boundaries (Section 2.4.4). When we apply a word to something, we express the thing's similarity to the best cases, perhaps in the form of a prototype. There are clear cases near the center and a probability distribution at the edges, grading off to zero. So the meaning of a word can be modeled as a probability distribution as a function of similarity to the prototype. The lines between related senses of a word are often blurred (Section 2.4.6).

When the word in question is a verb, then what happens to the mapping of arguments from the verb meaning to the subject and object functions, as we look across different senses of the verb? Almost invariably that mapping is preserved across senses. Consider different senses of the verb *follow*. In this example, *follow* and *precede* have the same meaning (i.e. (1a) and (1b) have the same truth-conditions) but the verbs show opposite mappings to subject and object:

(1) a. E follows D in the alphabet.
     b. D precedes E in the alphabet.

Both verbs have an 'earlier in the sequence' argument and a 'later in the sequence' argument, but those arguments map to the subject and object in opposite ways.

The verb *follow* in (1a) exemplifies the meaning 'To come after in sequence or series, in order of time, etc.; to succeed' (this and subsequent definitions are from the *Oxford English Dictionary*). Another example of that sense appears in (2a).[1] We also find agentive uses of the word like (2b), illustrating the sense 'To go or come after (a person or other object in motion); to move behind in the same direction'.[2] Example (2c) could be either one of those two senses; it illustrates the fuzzy border between them. A final sense, 'To come after or succeed as a consequence or effect; to result from,' is illustrated by (2d).[3]

(2) a. Transverse ridges which follow each other in succession.
     b. He follows me about like a dog.
     c. A red car is following the blue car.
     d. Form follows function.

Looking at a range of uses of the verb *follow*, all of them show the same mapping of the 'earlier' and 'later' arguments to object and subject, respectively. None exhibits the reverse mapping found for *precede*.

This means the mapping is associated with the lexeme (the 'root') and not the particular senses. For that reason, in our attempt to find the rules for how word meaning influences syntactic expression, it is not an adequate method to look solely at particular uses of verbs in context. One must also look at the range of other uses of the same verb. To be sure, the syntactic expression of arguments can be influenced by sense

---

[1] (2a) is from John Tyndall 1860, *The Glaciers of the Alps*, i. vii, p. 51; cited in *Oxford English Dictionary*.

[2] (2b) is from Effie Maria Albanesi 1910, *For love of Anne Lambert*, p. 59; cited in *Oxford English Dictionary*.

[3] (2d) is quoted from the architect Louis Sullivan 1896, 'The tall office building artistically considered'. It was adopted as a credo of functionalism in architecture.

modulation: for example, the sense affects omissibility of arguments and oblique versus direct expression of arguments (Sections 3.3 and 3.4.2.1). But as the sense of a verb is extended, either through bleaching out of meaning components, generalization, or specialization, the basic mapping is typically preserved. The verb root is subject to a strong conservative pressure to preserve its argument mapping in the face of sense modulation. The lexical predicate argument structure is the grammatical representation of that strong conservative pressure.

References

Aarts, Bas (2004). Modelling linguistic gradience. *Studies in Language* 28(1): 1–49.

Abbott, Barbara (1976). Right node raising as a test for constituenthood. *Linguistic Inquiry* 7(4): 639–42.

Abney, Stephen (1987). The English noun phrase in its sentential aspect. PhD dissertation, MIT.

Ackema, Peter, and Maaike Schoorlemmer (2005). Middles. In Martin Everaert and Henk van Riemsdijk (eds), *The Blackwell Companion to Syntax*, vol. 3, 131–203. Oxford: Blackwell.

Ackerman, Farrell, and John Moore (2001). *Proto-Properties and Grammatical Encoding*. Stanford, Calif.: CSLI.

Aissen, Judith (1974). Verb raising. *Linguistic Inquiry* 5(3): 325–66.

Aissen, Judith, and Jorge Hankamer (1980). Lexical extension and grammatical transformations. *Proceedings of the 6th Annual Meeting of the Berkeley Linguistics Society* 6: 238–49.

Ajdukiewicz, Kasimir (1935). Die syntaktische Konnexität. *Studia Philosophica* 1: 1–27.

Alexiadou, Artemis (2001). *Functional Structure in Nominals: Nominalization and Ergativity*. Amsterdam: Benjamins.

Alexiadou, Artemis (2009). On the role of syntactic locality in morphological processes: the case of (Greek) derived nominals. In Anastasia Giannakidou and Monika Rathert (eds), *Quantification, Definiteness and Nominalization*, 253–80. Oxford: Oxford University Press.

Alexiadou, Artemis (2014). Nominal derivation. In Rochelle Lieber and Pavol Štekauer (eds), *Oxford Handbook of Derivational Morphology*. Oxford: Oxford University Press.

Alexiadou, Artemis, Elena Anagnostopoulou, and Martin Everaert (2004). Introduction. In *The Unaccusativity Puzzle: Explorations of the Syntax–Lexicon Interface*, 1–13. Oxford: Oxford University Press.

Alexiadou, Artemis, Liliane Haegeman, and Melita Stavrou (2007). *Noun Phrase in the Generative Perspective*. Berlin: Mouton de Gruyter.

Alsina, Alex (1992). On the argument structure of causatives. *Linguistic Inquiry* 23(4): 517–55.

Alsina, Alex (1996). Resultatives: a joint operation of semantic and syntactic structures. In *Proceedings of the Lexical-Functional Grammar 1996 Conference*. Stanford, Calif.: CSLI Online. http://web.stanford.edu/group/cslipublications/cslipublications/LFG/.

Anderson, Stephen (1971). On the role of deep structure in semantic interpretation. *Foundations of Language* 7(3): 387–96.

Anderson, Stephen (1977). On mechanisms by which languages become
ergative. In Charles Li (ed.), *Mechanisms of Syntactic Change*, vol. 2,
317–64. Cambridge: Cambridge University Press.

Anderson, Stephen (1988). Morphological change. In Frederick Newmeyer
(ed.), *Linguistics: The Cambridge Survey*, 324–62. Cambridge: Cambridge
University Press.

Apresjan, J. D. (1974). Regular polysemy. *Linguistics* 142: 5–32.

Armstrong, Sharon Lee, Lila R. Gleitman, and Henry Gleitman (1983). What
some concepts might not be. *Cognition* 13(3): 263–308.

Asher, Nicholas (2011). *Lexical Meaning in Context: A Web of Words.*
Cambridge: Cambridge University Press.

Asudeh, Ash, Mary Dalrymple, and Ida Toivonen (2008). Constructions with
lexical integrity: templates as the lexicon–syntax interface. In Miriam Butt
and Tracy H. King (eds), *Proceedings of the Lexical-Functional Grammar
2008*, 66–88. Stanford, Calif.: CSLI. http:/web.stanford.edu/group/
cslipublications/cslipublications/LFG/.

Austin, Peter, and Joan Bresnan (1996). Non-configurationality in Australian
Aboriginal languages. *Natural Language & Linguistic Theory* 14(2): 215–68.

Bach, Emmon (1976). An extension of classical Transformation Grammar.
In *Problems in Linguistic Metatheory: Proceedings of the 1976 Conference
at the Michigan State University*, 183–224. Lansing: Michigan State
University.

Bach, Emmon (1979). Control in Montague Grammar. *Linguistic Inquiry*
10(4): 515–31.

Baker, Mark C. (1988). *Incorporation: A Theory of Grammatical Function
Changing*. Chicago: University of Chicago Press.

Barker, Chris (2002). The Dynamics of Vagueness. *Linguistics and Philosophy*
25: 1–36.

Bartlett, Frederic (1932). *Remembering: A Study in Experimental and Social
Psychology*. Cambridge: Cambridge University Press.

Beavers, John (2006). Argument/oblique alternations and the structure of
lexical meaning. PhD dissertation, Stanford University.

Beavers, John (2010). The structure of lexical meaning: why semantics really
matters. *Language* 86(4): 821–64.

Beavers, John (2011). On affectedness. *Natural Language & Linguistic Theory*
29(2): 335–70.

Beavers, John (2012). Resultative constructions. In Robert I. Binnick (ed.),
Oxford Handbook on Tense and Aspect, 908–34. Oxford: Oxford University
Press.

Beavers, John, and Andrew Koontz-Garboden (2012). Manner and result in
the roots of verbal meaning. *Linguistic Inquiry* 43(3): 331–69.

Beavers, John, Beth Levin, and Shiao Wei Tham (2010). The typology of motion expressions revisited. *Journal of Linguistics* 46(2): 1–47.

Beavers, John, Elias Ponvert, and Stephen Wechsler (2008). Possession of a controlled substantive: light *have* and verbs of possession. In T. Friedman and S. Ito (eds), *Proceedings of Semantics and Linguistic Theory (SALT)*. *XVIII*, 108–25. Ithaca, NY: Cornell University.

Beavers, John, and Ivan A. Sag (2004). Coordinate ellipsis and apparent non-constituent coordination. In *Proceedings of the 11th International Conference on Head-Driven Phrase Structure Grammar*, 48–69. Stanford, Calif.: CSLI Online. http://web.stanford.edu/group/cslipublications/cslipublications/HPSG.

Bergen, Benjamin K., and Nancy Chang (2005). Embodied Construction Grammar in simulation-based language understanding. In Jan-Ola Östman and Mirjam Fried (eds), *Construction Grammars: Cognitive Grounding and Theoretical Extensions*, 147–90. Amsterdam: Benjamins.

Bierwisch, Manfred, and Robert Schreuder (1992). From concepts to lexical items. *Cognition* 42(1–3): 23.

Bisetto, Antonietta, and Chiara Melloni (2005). Result nominals: a lexical-semantic investigation. In *On-Line Proceedings of the Fifth Mediterranean Morphology Meeting (MMM5)*, 15–18. Università degli Studi di Bologna. http://mmm.lingue.unibo.it/proc-mmm5.php.

Boas, Hans (2000). Resultative constructions in English and German. PhD dissertation, University of North Carolina.

Boas, Hans, and Ivan Sag (eds) (2012). *Sign-Based Construction Grammar*. Stanford, Calif.: CSLI.

Bobzien, Susanne (2002). XII: Chrysippus and the epistemic theory of vagueness. *Proceedings of the Aristotelian Society* 102(1): 217–38.

Borer, Hagit (1994). The projection of arguments. In E. Benedicto and J. Runner (eds), *Functional Projections*, 19–47. Amherst, Mass.: University of Massachusetts Graduate Linguistic Student Association.

Borer, Hagit (2003). Exo-skeletal vs. endo-skeletal explanations: syntactic projections and the lexicon. In John Moore and Maria Polinsky (eds), *The Nature of Explanation in Linguistic Theory*. Stanford, Calif./Chicago: CSLI/University of Chicago Press.

Borer, Hagit (2005a). *Structuring Sense*, vol. 1: *In Name Only*. Oxford: Oxford University Press.

Borer, Hagit (2005b). *Structuring Sense*, vol. 2: *The Normal Course of Events*. Oxford: Oxford University Press.

Borsley, Robert D. (1987). Subjects and complements in HPSG. Stanford, Calif.: CSLI.

Brennan, S. E., and Herbert H. Clark (1996). Conceptual pacts and lexical choice in conversation. *Journal of Experimental Psychology: Learning, Memory, and Cognition* 22(6): 1482–93.

Bresnan, Joan (1974). The position of certain clause-particles in phrase structure. *Linguistic Inquiry* 5(4): 614–19.

Bresnan, Joan (1982a). Control and complementation. *Linguistic Inquiry* 13(3): 343–434.

Bresnan, Joan (1982b). The passive in lexical theory. In Joan Bresnan (ed.), *The Mental Representation of Grammatical Relations*, 3–86. Cambridge, Mass.: MIT Press.

Bresnan, Joan (1995). Linear order, syntactic rank, and empty categories: on weak crossover. In M. Dalrymple, R. M. Kaplan, J. T. Maxwell III, and A. Zaenen (eds), *Formal Issues in Lexical-Functional Grammar*, 241–78. Stanford, Calif.: CSLI.

Bresnan, Joan (1997). Mixed categories as head sharing constructions. In Miriam Butt and Tracy H. King (eds), *Proceedings of the Lexical-Functional Grammar 1997 Conference*. San Diego, Calif.: CSLI Online. http://web.stanford.edu/group/cslipublications/cslipublications/LFG/.

Bresnan, Joan (1998). Morphology competes with syntax: explaining typological variation in weak crossover effects. In Pilar Barbosa, Danny Fox, Paul Hagstrom, Martha McGinnis, and David Pesetsky (eds), *Is the Best Good Enough? Optimality and Competition in Syntax*, 59–92. Cambridge, Mass.: MIT Press.

Bresnan, Joan (2001). *Lexical-Functional Syntax*. Oxford: Blackwell.

Bresnan, Joan, Ash Asudeh, Ida Toivonen, and Stephen Wechsler (in preparation). *Lexical-Functional Syntax*, 2nd edn. Oxford: Blackwell.

Bresnan, Joan, Anna Cueni, Tatiana Nikitina, and R. Harald Baayen (2007). Predicting the dative alternation. In G. Bouma, I. Kraemer, and J. Zwarts (eds), *Cognitive Foundations of Interpretation*, 69–94. Amsterdam: Royal Netherlands Academy of Science.

Bresnan, Joan, and Jonni Kanerva (1989). Locative inversion in Chichewa: a case study of factorization in grammar. *Linguistics Inquiry* 20: 1–50.

Bresnan, Joan, and Ronald Kaplan (1982). *The Mental Representation of Grammatical Relations*. Cambridge, Mass.: MIT Press.

Bresnan, Joan, and Sam A. Mchombo (1987). Topic, pronoun, and agreement in Chichewa. *Language* 63(4): 741–82.

Bresnan, Joan, and Sam A. Mchombo (1995). The lexical integrity principle: evidence from Bantu. *Natural Language & Linguistic Theory* 13(2): 181–254.

Bresnan, Joan, and Lioba Moshi (1990). Object asymmetries in comparative Bantu syntax. *Linguistic Inquiry* 21(2): 147–85.

Bresnan, Joan, and Tatiana Nikitina (2009). The gradience of the dative alternation. In Linda Uyechi and Lian Hee Wee (eds), *Reality Exploration and Discovery: Pattern Interaction in Language and Life*, 161–84. Stanford, Calif.: CSLI.

Bresnan, Joan, and Annie Zaenen (1990). Deep unaccusativity in LFG. In Katarzyna Dziwirek, Patrick Farrell, and Errapel Mejías-Bikandi (eds), *Grammatical Relations: A Cross-Theoretical Perspective*, 45–57. Stanford, Calif.: Stanford Linguistics Association and CSLI.

Brewer, William F. (1999). Schemata. In Robert A. Wilson and Frank C. Keil (eds), *Massachusetts Institute of Technology Encyclopedia of the Cognitive Sciences*. Cambridge, Mass.: MIT Press.

Brinkmann, Ursula (1997). *The Locative Alternation in German: Its Structure and Acquisition*. Amsterdam: Benjamins.

Briscoe, Ted, and Ann Copestake (1999). Lexical rules in constraint-based grammars. *Computational Linguistics* 25(4): 487–526.

Brown, Susan (2008). Polysemy in the mental lexicon. *Colorado Research in Linguistics* 21. http://www.colorado.edu/ling/CRIL/Volume21_Issue1/index.htm.

Burzio, Luigi (1986). *Italian Syntax: A Government-Binding Approach*. Dordrecht: Reidel.

Butt, Miriam (2001). A reexamination of the accusative to ergative shift in Indo-Aryan. In Miriam Butt and Tracy King (eds), *Time Over Matter: Diachronic Perspectives on Morphosyntax*, 105–41. Stanford, Calif.: CSLI.

Bybee, Joan, Revere Perkins, and William Pagliuca (1994). *The Evolution of Grammar: Tense, Aspect, and Modality in the Languages of the World*. Chicago: University of Chicago Press.

Calcagno, Mike (1995). Interpreting lexical rules. In Glyn Morrill and Richard Oehrle (eds), *Proceedings of the Formal Grammar Conference*, 33–45. Barcelona: Universidad Politecnica de Catalunya.

Calcagno, Mike, and Carl J. Pollard (1995). Lexical rules in HPSG: what are they? MS, Dept of Linguistics, Ohio State University, Columbus.

Carlson, Gregory N. (1977). Reference to kinds in English. PhD dissertation, University of Massachusetts at Amherst.

Carnap, Rudolf (1952). Meaning postulates. *Philosophical Studies* 3(5): 65–73.

Carrier, Jill, and Janet Randall (1992). The argument structure and syntactic structure of resultatives. *Linguistic Inquiry* 23(2): 173–234.

Cedergren, Henrietta J., and David Sankoff (1974). Variable rules: performance as a statistical reflection of competence. *Language* 50(2): 333–55.

Chierchia, Gennaro, and Sally McConnell-Ginet (2000). *Meaning and Grammar: An Introduction to Semantics*. Cambridge, Mass.: MIT Press.

Choi, Soonja, and Melissa Bowerman (1991). Learning to express motion events in English and Korean: the influence of language-specific lexicalization patterns. *Cognition* 41(1–3): 83–121.

Chomsky, Noam (1957). *Syntactic Structures*. The Hague: Mouton.

Chomsky, Noam (1964). *Current Issues in Linguistic Theory*. The Hague: Mouton.

Chomsky, Noam (1965). *Aspects of the Theory of Syntax*. Cambridge, Mass.: MIT Press.

Chomsky, Noam (1970). Remarks on nominalization. In Roderick A. Jacobs and Peter S. Rosenbaum (eds), *Readings in English Transformational Grammar*, 184–221. Waltham, Mass.: Ginn.

Chomsky, Noam (1980). Rules and representations. *Behavioral and Brain Sciences* 3: 1–61.

Chomsky, Noam (1981). *Lectures on Government and Binding*. Dordrecht: Foris.

Chomsky, Noam (1995). *The Minimalist Program*. Cambridge, Mass.: MIT Press.

Cinque, Guglielmo (1988). On *si* constructions and the theory of Arb. *Linguistic Inquiry* 19(4): 521–81.

Clark, Eve V., and Herbert H. Clark (1979). When nouns surface as verbs. *Language* 55(4): 767–811.

Clark, Herbert H. (1996). *Using Language*. Cambridge: Cambridge University Press.

Cole, Peter, Wayne Harbert, Gabriella Hermon, and S. N. Sridhar (1980). The acquisition of subjecthood. *Language* 56: 719–43.

Condoravdi, Cleo (1989). The middle: where semantics and morphology meet. *MIT Working Papers in Linguistics* 11: 16–30.

Copestake, Ann (1992a). The representation of lexical semantic information. PhD dissertation, University of Sussex.

Copestake, Ann (1992b). The representation of lexical semantic information. Cognitive Science Research Paper 280. University of Sussex.

Copestake, Ann (1995). The representation of group denoting nouns in a lexical knowledge base. In P. Saint-Dizier and E. Viegas (eds), *Computational Lexical Semantics*, 207–31. Cambridge: Cambridge University Press.

Copestake, Ann, and Ted Briscoe (1992). Lexical operations in a unification based framework. In James Pustejovsky and Sabine Bergler (eds), *Lexical Semantics and Knowledge Representation*, 101–19. Berlin: Springer. http://www.cl.cam.ac.uk/Research/NL/acquilex/papers.html.

Copestake, Ann, and Ted Briscoe (1995). Semi-productive polysemy and sense extension. *Journal of Semantics* 12(1): 15–67.

Copestake, Ann, Daniel P. Flickinger, Carl J. Pollard, and Ivan A. Sag (2005). Minimal recursion semantics: an introduction. *Research on Language and Computation* 4(3): 281–332.

Croft, William (1991). *Syntactic Categories and Grammatical Relations: The Cognitive Organization of Information*. Chicago: University of Chicago Press.

Croft, William (1998). Event structure in argument linking. In Miriam Butt and Wilhelm Geuder (eds), *The Projection of Arguments: Lexical and Compositional Factors*, 21–64. Stanford, Calif.: CSLI.

Croft, William (2001). *Radical Construction Grammar: Syntactic Theory in Typological Perspective*. Oxford: Oxford University Press.

Croft, William (2003). Lexical rules vs. constructions: a false dichotomy. In Hubert Cuyckens, Thomas Berg, René Dirven, and Klaus-Uwe Panther (eds), *Motivation in Language: Studies in Honour of Günter Radden*, 49–68. Amsterdam: Benjamins.

Cruse, D. A. (1986). *Lexical Semantics*. Cambridge: Cambridge University Press.

Cruse, D. A. (1995). Polysemy and related phenomena from a cognitive linguistic viewpoint. In P. Saint-Dizier and E. Viegas (eds), *Computational Lexical Semantics*, 33–49. Cambridge: Cambridge University Press.

Culicover, Peter W., and Ray S. Jackendoff (2005). *Simpler Syntax*. Oxford: Oxford University Press.

Dąbrowska, Ewa (2001). From formula to schema: the acquisition of English questions. *Cognitive Linguistics* 11(1–2): 83–102.

Dalrymple, Mary (2001). *Lexical Functional Grammar*. New York: Academic Press.

Davidson, Donald (1967). The logical form of action sentences. In Nicholas Rescher (ed.), *The Logic of Decision and Action*, 81–95. Pittsburgh, Penn.: Pittsburgh University Press.

Davis, Anthony (1996). Linking and the hierarchical lexicon. PhD dissertation, Stanford University.

Davis, Anthony (2001). *Linking by Types in the Hierarchical Lexicon*. Stanford, Calif.: CSLI.

Davis, Anthony, and Jean-Pierre Koenig (1999). Sublexical modality and Linking Theory. *West Coast Conference on Formal Linguistics* 17: 162–74.

Davis, Anthony, and Jean-Pierre Koenig (2000). Linking as constraints on word classes in a hierarchical lexicon. *Language* 76(1): 56–91.

De Kuthy, Kordula (2002). *Discontinuous NPs in German*. Stanford, Calif.: CSLI.

De Kuthy, Kordula, and Walt Detmar Meurers (2001). On partial constituent fronting in German. *Journal of Comparative Germanic Linguistics* 3(3): 143–205.

DiSciullo, Anna-Maria, and Edwin Williams (1987). *On the Definition of Word*. Cambridge, Mass.: MIT Press.

Dixon, R. M. W. (1979). Ergativity. *Language* 55: 59–138.

Dixon, R. M. W. (1982). *Where Have All the Adjectives Gone? And Other Essays in Semantics and Syntax*. The Hague: Mouton de Gruyter.

Dixon, R. M. W. (1994). *Ergativity*. Cambridge: Cambridge University Press.

Dowty, David (1978). Governed transformations as lexical rules in a Montague Grammar. *Linguistic Inquiry* 9(3): 393–426.

Dowty, David (1979). *Word Meaning and Montague Grammar: The Semantics of Verbs and Times in Generative Semantics and in Montague's PTQ.* Dordrecht: Reidel.

Dowty, David (1989). On the semantic content of the notion of 'thematic role'. In Gennaro Chierchia, Barbara H. Partee, and Raymond Turner (eds), *Properties, Types and Meaning*, vol. 2: *Semantic Issues*, 69–129. Dordrecht: Kluwer.

Dowty, David (1991). Thematic proto-roles and argument selection. *Language* 67(3): 547–619.

Dowty, David (2000). 'The garden swarms with bees' and the fallacy of 'argument alternation'. In Yael Ravin and Claudia Leacock (eds), *Polysemy: Theoretical and Computational Approaches*, 111–28. Oxford: Oxford University Press.

Dowty, David (2001). The semantic asymmetry of 'argument alternations' (and why it matters). *Groninger Arbeiten zur germanistischen Linguistik* 44: 171–86.

Egg, Markus (1999). Derivation and resolution of ambiguities in *wieder*-sentences. In Paul J. E. Dekker (ed.), *Proceedings of the 12th Amsterdam Colloquium*, 109–14. Amsterdam: ILLC.

Embick, David (2004). On the structure of resultative participles in English. *Linguistic Inquiry* 35(3): 355–92.

England, N. C. (1983). Ergativity in Mamean (Mayan) languages. *International Journal of American Linguistics* 49(1): 1–19.

Erk, Katrin, Diana McCarthy, and Nicholas Gaylord (2012). Measuring word meaning in context. *Computational Linguistics* (16 Nov.): 501–44. doi: 10.1162/COLI_a_00142

Fagan, Sarah (1992). *The Syntax and Semantics of Middle Constructions: A Study with Special Reference to German.* Cambridge: Cambridge University Press.

Fanselow, Gisbert (2001). Features, theta-roles, and free constituent order. *Linguistic Inquiry* 32(3): 405–37.

Fanselow, Gisbert (2002). Against remnant VP-movement. In Artemis Alexiadou, Elena Anagnostopoulou, Sjef Barbiers, and Hans-Martin Gärtner (eds), *Dimensions of Movement: From Features to Remnants*, 91–127. Amsterdam: Benjamins.

Fara, Delia Graff (2000). Shifting sands: an interest-relative theory of vagueness. *Philosophical Topics* 28(1): 45–81.

Fara, Delia Graff (2008). Profiling interest relativity. *Analysis* 68(4): 326–35.

Fassi-Fehri, Abdelkader (1993). *Issues in the Structure of Arabic Clauses and Words.* Dordrecht: Kluwer Academic.

Field, Hartry (2010). The magic moment. In Richard Dietz and Sebastiano Moruzzi (eds), *Cuts and Clouds: Vaguenesss, Its Nature and Its Logic*, 200–208. Oxford: Oxford University Press.

Fillmore, Charles (1968). The case for Case. In Emmon Bach and Robert T. Harms (eds), *Universals in Linguistic Theory*, 1–90. New York: Holt, Rinehart and Winston.

Fillmore, Charles (1982). Frame Semantics. In Dirk Geeraerts (ed.), *Cognitive Linguistics: Basic Readings*, 373–400. New York: Mouton de Gruyter.

Fillmore, Charles (1986). Pragmatically controlled zero anaphora. *Proceedings of the 12th Annual Meeting of the Berkeley Linguistics Society*, 95–107.

Fillmore, Charles (1999). Inversion and constructional inheritance. In Gert Webelhuth, Jean-Pierre Koenig, and Andreas Kathol (eds), *Lexical and Constructional Aspects of Linguistic Explanation*, 113–28. Stanford, Calif.: CSLI.

Fillmore, Charles, and Collin Baker (2010). A frames approach to semantic analysis. In Bernd Heine and Heiko Narrog (eds), *The Oxford Handbook of Linguistic Analysis*, 313–39. Oxford: Oxford University Press.

Fillmore, Charles, Paul Kay, and Mary Catherine O'Connor (1988). Regularity and idiomaticity in grammatical constructions: the case of 'let alone'. *Language* 64(3): 501–38.

Fine, Kit (1975). Vagueness, truth and logic. *Synthese* 30(3): 265–300.

Flickinger, Daniel (1987). Lexical rules in the hierarchical lexicon. PhD dissertation, Stanford University.

Fodor, Jerry A. (1998). *Concepts: Where Cognitive Science Went Wrong*. Oxford: Oxford University Press.

Fodor, Jerry A., and Ernie Lepore (1998). The emptiness of the lexicon: reflections on James Pustejovsky's *The Generative Lexicon*. *Linguistic Inquiry* 29(2): 269–88.

Foley, William, and Robert D. Van Valin (1984). *Functional Syntax and Universal Grammar*. Cambridge: Cambridge University Press.

Folli, Raffaella, and Heidi Harley (2004). Consuming results: flavors of little-V. In P. Kempchimsky and R. Slabakova (eds), *Aspectual Enquiries*, 1–25. Dordrecht: Kluwer.

Fong, Vivienne, and Christine Poulin (1998). Locating linguistic variation in semantic templates. In Jean-Pierre Koenig (ed.), *Discourse and Cognition: Bridging the Gap*, 29–39. Stanford, Calif.: CSLI.

Frazee, Joey, and David Beaver (2010). Vagueness is rational under uncertainty. In Maria Aloni, Harald Bastiaanse, Tikitu de Jager, and Katrin Schulz (eds), *Logic, Language and Meaning: 17th Amsterdam Colloquium*, 153–62. Berlin: Springer.

Frazier, Lyn, and Keith Rayner (1990). Taking on semantic commitments: processing multiple meanings vs. multiple senses. *Journal of Memory and Language* 29(2): 181–200.

Garrett, Andrew (1990). The origin of NP split ergativity. *Language* 66(2): 261–96.

Gaylord, Nicholas (2013). The 'resolution' of verb meaning in context. PhD dissertation, University of Texas, Austin.

Gaylord, Nicholas, Micah Goldwater, Colin Bannard, and Katrin Erk (2012). Default verb meanings and verb meaning-in-context: a speed–accuracy tradeoff study. In *Proceedings of Architectures and Mechanisms for Language Processing (AMLaP 2012)*. Riva del Garda, Italy.

Gazdar, Gerald (1982). Phrase Structure Grammar. In Pauline Jacobson and Geoffrey K. Pullum (eds), *The Nature of Syntactic Representation*, 131–86. Dordrecht: Reidel.

Gazdar, Gerald, Ewan Klein, Geoffrey Pullum, and Ivan Sag (1985). *Generalized Phrase Structure Grammar*. Oxford/Cambridge, Mass.: Blackwell/Harvard University Press.

Geeraerts, Dirk (1993). Vagueness's puzzles, polysemy's vagaries. *Cognitive Linguistics* 4(3): 223–72.

Geeraerts, Dirk (2009). *Theories of Lexical Semantics*. New York: Oxford University Press.

Givón, Talmy (1976). Topic, pronoun and grammatical agreement. In Charles N. Li (ed.), *Subject and Topic*, 149–88. New York: Academic Press.

Goldberg, Adele E. (1995). *Constructions: A Construction Grammar Approach to Argument Structure*. Chicago: University of Chicago Press.

Goldberg, Adele E. (2006). *Constructions at Work: The Nature of Generalization in Language*. Oxford: Oxford University Press.

Goldberg, Adele E. (2013). Argument structure constructions versus lexical rules or derivational verb templates. *Mind and Language* 28(4): 435–65.

Goldberg, Adele E., Devin Casenhiser, and Nitya Sethuraman (2004). Learning argument structure generalizations. *Cognitive Linguistics* 15(3): 289–316.

Goldberg, Adele E., and Ray Jackendoff (2004). The English resultative as a family of constructions. *Language* 80(3): 532–68.

Green, Georgia (1972). Some observations on the syntax and semantics of instrumental verbs. *Chicago Linguistic Society* 8: 83–97.

Green, Georgia (1974). *Semantics and Syntactic Regularity*. Bloomington: Indiana University Press.

Grice, H. Paul (1975). Logic and conversation. In Peter Cole and Jerry Morgan (eds), *Speech Acts*, 41–58. New York: Academic Press.

Grimm, Jacob, and Wilhelm Grimm (1854). *Deutsches Wörterbuch*, vol. 1, pt 1. http://dwb.uni-%20trier.de/de/das-woerterbuch/.

Grimshaw, Jane (1982). On the lexical representation of Romance reflexive clitics. In Joan Bresnan (ed.), *The Mental Representation of Grammatical Relations*, 87–148. Cambridge, Mass.: MIT Press.

Grimshaw, Jane (1990). *Argument Structure*. Cambridge, Mass.: MIT Press.

Grône, Maryse (2011). La productivité des tournures résultatives du type *He charmed the scruples out of her/I'll scare some sense into you* en anglais. Presented at 'Du discours au système : variation et changements linguistiques autour du verbe', Institut d'études anglophones de Paris 3 Sorbonne Nouvelle, 20 June.

Gruber, J. S. (1965). Studies in lexical relations. PhD dissertation, MIT.

Gruber, Jeffrey (1976). *Lexical Structures in Syntax and Semantics*. Amsterdam: North-Holland.

Guerssel, M., K. Hale, M. Laughren, B. Levin, and J. W. Eagle (1985). A cross-linguistic study of transitivity alternations. *Papers from the Parasession on Causatives and Agentivity at the Twenty-First Regional Meeting, CLS* 21: 48–63.

Gunji, Takao (1986). Subcategorization and word order. In William J. Poser (ed.), *Papers from the Second International Workshop on Japanese Syntax*, 1–21. Stanford, Calif.: CSLI.

Haider, Hubert (1985). The case of German. In Jindrich Toman (ed.), *Studies in German Grammar*, 65–102. Dordrecht: Foris.

Haider, Hubert (1993). *Deutsche Syntax—generativ: Vorstudien zur Theorie einer projektiven Grammatik*. Tübingen: Narr.

Hale, Kenneth, and Samuel Keyser (1993). On argument structure and the lexical expression of syntactic relations. In Kenneth Hale and Samuel Keyser (eds), *The View from Building 20: Essays in Linguistics in Honor of Sylvain Bromberger*, 53–109. Cambridge, Mass.: MIT Press.

Hale, Kenneth, and Samuel Jay Keyser (1997). On the complex nature of simple predicators. In Alex Alsina, Joan Bresnan, and Peter Sells (eds), *Complex Predicates*, 29–65. Stanford, Calif.: CSLI.

Halliday, Michael A. K. (1967). Notes on transitivity and theme in English (pt 1). *Journal of Linguistics* 3(1): 37–81.

Hampton, James A. (2007). Typicality, graded membership, and vagueness. *Cognitive Science* 31(3): 355–84.

Hare, Mary, Jeffrey L. Elman, Tracy Tabaczynski, and Ken McRae (2009). The wind chilled the spectators, but the wine just chilled: sense, structure, and sentence comprehension. *Cognitive Science* 33(4): 610–28.

Hare, Mary, Michael Jones, Caroline Thomson, Sarah Kelly, and Ken McRae (2009). Activating event knowledge. *Cognition* 111(2): 151–67.

Harley, Heidi (2004). Wanting, having, and getting: a note on Fodor and Lepore 1998. *Linguistic Inquiry* 35(2): 255–67.

Harley, Heidi, and Rolf Noyer (2000). Formal versus encyclopedic properties of vocabulary: evidence from nominalizations. In Bert Peeters (ed.), *The Lexicon–Encyclopedia Interface*, 349–74. Amsterdam: Elsevier.

Harris, Alice C. (1981). *Georgian Syntax: A Study in Relational Grammar*. Cambridge: Cambridge University Press.

Haspelmath, Martin (1993). More on the typology of inchoative/causative verb alternations. In Bernard Comrie and Maria Polinsky (eds), *Causatives and Transitivity*, 87–120. Amsterdam: Benjamins.

Haugereid, Petter (2009). Phrasal subconstructions: a constructionalist grammar design, exemplified with Norwegian and English. PhD dissertation, Norwegian University of Science and Technology.

Hay, Jennifer, Christopher Kennedy, and Beth Levin (1999). Scalar structure underlies telicity in 'degree achievements'. *Proceedings of Semantics and Linguistic Theory 9, 1999.*

Heinz, Wolfgang, and Johannes Matiasek (1994). Argument structure and case assignment in German. In John Nerbonne, Klaus Netter, and Carl J. Pollard (eds), *German in Head-Driven Phrase Structure Grammar*, 199–236. Stanford, Calif.: CSLI.

Hinrichs, Erhard W., and Tsuneko Nakazawa (1989). Subcategorization and VP structure in German. In *Aspects of German VP Structure*. Tübingen: Eberhard Karls Universität.

Hinrichs, Erhard W., and Tsuneko Nakazawa (1994a). Linearizing AUXs in German verbal complexes. In John Nerbonne, Klaus Netter, and Carl J. Pollard (eds), *German in HPSG*, 11–38. Stanford, Calif.: CSLI.

Hinrichs, Erhard W., and Tsuneko Nakazawa (1994b). Partial-VP and split-NP topicalization in German: an HPSG analysis. In Erhard W. Hinrichs, Walt Detmar Meurers, and Tsuneko Nakazawa (eds), *Partial-VP and Split-NP Topicalization in German: An HPSG Analysis and Its Implementation*, 1–46. Tübingen: Eberhard Karls Universität.

Hitchings, Henry (2013). Those irritating verbs-as-nouns. *New York Times* (30 Mar.), 'Opinionator' section. http://opinionator.blogs.nytimes.com/2013/03/30/those-irritating-verbs-as-nouns/.

Hoekstra, Teun (1988). Small clause results. *Lingua* 74(2–3): 101–39.

Hoffman, Beryl Ann (1995). The computational analysis of the syntax and interpretation of 'free' word order in Turkish. PhD dissertation, University of Pennsylvania, Philadelphia.

Hyde, Dominic (2011). Sorites Paradox. In Edward Zalta (ed.), *The Stanford Encyclopedia of Philosophy*. http://plato.stanford.edu/archives/win2011/entries/sorites-paradox/.

Im, Sung-Chool (2001). Typological patterns of motion verbs in Korean. PhD dissertation, State University of New York at Buffalo.

Im, Sung-Chool (2002). Characteristic lexicalization patterns of motion events in Korean. In Noriko M. Akatsuka and Susan Strauss (eds), *Japanese/Korean Linguistics*, vol. 10, 50–61. Stanford, Calif.: CSLI.

Jackendoff, Ray (1972). *Semantic Interpretation in Generative Grammar*. Cambridge, Mass.: MIT Press.

Jackendoff, Ray (1983). *Semantics and Cognition*. Cambridge, Mass.: MIT Press.

Jackendoff, Ray (1985). Multiple subcategorization and the theta-criterion: the case of *climb*. *Natural Language & Linguistic Theory* 3(3): 271–95.

Jackendoff, Ray (1990). *Semantic Structures*. Cambridge, Mass.: MIT Press.

Jackendoff, Ray (1996). The proper treatment of measuring out, telicity, and perhaps even quantification in English. *Natural Language & Linguistic Theory* 14(2): 305–54.

Jackendoff, Ray (2011). What is the human language faculty? Two views. *Language* 87(3): 586–624.

Jaswal, V. K., and E. M. Markman (2007). Looks aren't everything: 24-month-olds' willingness to accept unexpected labels. *Journal of Cognition and Development* 8(1): 93–111.

Johnson, Mark (1986). A GPSG account of VP structure in German. *Linguistics* 24(5): 871–82.

Jørgensen, Eric (1981). Gerund and *to*-infinitives after 'it is (of) no use', 'it is no good', and 'it is useless.' *English Studies* 62: 156–63.

Joshi, Aravind K., Leon S. Levy, and Masako Takahashi (1975). Tree Adjunct Grammar. *Journal of Computer and System Science* 10(2): 136–63.

Joshi, Smita (1989). Logical subject in Marathi grammar and the predicate argument structure. In *Proceedings of the Eighth West Coast Conference on Formal Linguistics*, 207–19. Stanford, Calif.: CSLI.

Kamp, Hans (1975). Two theories of adjectives. In Edward Keenan (ed.), *Formal Semantics of Natural Language*, 123–55. Cambridge: Cambridge University Press.

Kamp, Hans, and Barbara Partee (1995). Prototype theory and compositionality. *Cognition* 57: 129–91.

Kanchanawan, Nittaya (1978). Expression for time in the Thai verb and its application to Thai–English machine translation. PhD dissertation, University of Texas at Austin.

Kant, Immanuel (1781). *Critique of Pure Reason*. Translated by Paul Guyer and Allen W. Wood. Cambridge: Cambridge University Press.

Kaplan, Ronald M., and Joan Bresnan (1982). Lexical-Functional Grammar: a formal system for grammatical representation. In Joan Bresnan (ed.), *The Mental Representation of Grammatical Relations*, 173–281. Cambridge, Mass.: MIT Press.

Kathol, Andreas (2001). Positional effects in a monostratal grammar of German. *Journal of Linguistics* 37(1): 35–66.

Kaufmann, Ingrid (1995a). *Konzeptuelle Grundlagen semantischer Dekompositionsstrukturen: Die Kombinatorik lokaler Verben und prädikativer Komplemente*. Tübingen: Niemeyer.

Kaufmann, Ingrid (1995b). What is an (im-)possible verb? Restrictions on semantic form and their consequences for argument structure. *Folia Linguistica* 24: 67–103.

Kay, Paul (2005). Argument structure constructions and the argument–adjunct distinction. In Mirjam Fried and Hans C. Boas (eds), *Grammatical Constructions: Back to the Roots*, 71–98. Amsterdam: Benjamins.

Kennedy, Christopher (1999). *Projecting the Adjective: The Syntax and Semantics of Gradability and Comparison*. New York: Garland.

Kennedy, Christopher (2007). Vagueness and gradability: the semantics of relative and absolute gradable predicates. *Linguistics and Philosophy* 30(1): 1–45.

Kennedy, Christopher (2011). Ambiguity and vagueness. In Claudia Maienborn, Paul Portner, and Klaus von Heusinger (eds), *Handbook of Semantics*, 507–35. The Hague: Mouton de Gruyter.

Kennedy, Christopher, and Beth Levin (2001). Telicity corresponds to degree of change. Presented at the 75th Annual Meeting of the Linguistic Society of America, Washington, DC.

Kennedy, Christopher, and Louise McNally (1999). From event structure to scale structure: degree modification in deverbal adjectives. *Proceedings of Semantics and Linguistic Theory* 9, 163–80. Fort Washington, Penn.: CLC.

Kennedy, Christopher, and Louise McNally (2005). Scale structure, degree modification, and the semantics of gradable predicates. *Language* 81(2): 345–81.

Kiparsky, Paul (1987). *Morphology and Grammatical Relations*. MS, Stanford, Calif.

Kiparsky, Paul (1988). Agreement and Linking Theory. MS, Stanford University.

Kiparsky, Paul (1997). Remarks on denominal verbs. In Alex Alsina, Joan Bresnan, and Peter Sells (eds), *Complex Predicates*, 473–99. Stanford, Calif.: CSLI.

Kiparsky, Paul, and Johan F. Staal (1969). Syntactic and semantic relations in Pāṇini. *Foundations of Language* 5(1): 83–117.

Klein, Devorah E., and Gregory L. Murphy (2001). The representation of polysemous words. *Journal of Memory and Language* 45(2): 259–82.

Klein, Devorah E., and Gregory L. Murphy (2002). Paper has been my ruin: conceptual relations of polysemous senses. *Journal of Memory and Language* 47(4): 548–70.

Klein, Ewan (1980). A semantics for positive and comparative adjectives. *Linguistics and Philosophy* 4(1): 1–45.

Klepousniotou, Ekaterini, Debra Titone, and Carolina Romero (2008). Making sense of word senses: the comprehension of polysemy depends on sense overlap. *Journal of Experimental Psychology: Learning, Memory, and Cognition* 34(6): 1534–43.

Koenig, Jean-Pierre (1999). *Lexical Relations*. Stanford, Calif.: CSLI.

Koenig, Jean-Pierre, and Anthony Davis (2001). Sublexical modality and the structure of lexical semantic representations. *Linguistics and Philosophy* 24(1): 71–124.

Koenig, Jean-Pierre, and Anthony Davis (2003). Semantically transparent linking in HPSG. *Proceedings of the Head-Driven Phrase Structure Grammar-2003 Conference, Michigan State University, East Lansing*, 222–35.

Koontz-Garboden, Andrew (2005). On the typology of state/change of state alternations. *Yearbook of Morphology 2005*: 83–117.

Koontz-Garboden, Andrew (2009). Anticausativization. *Natural Language & Linguistic Theory* 27(1): 77–138.

Kratzer, Angelika (1996). Severing the external argument from its verb. In Johan Rooryck and Laurie Zaring (eds), *Phrase Structure and the Lexicon*, 109–37. Dordrecht: Kluwer.

Krifka, Manfred (1987). *Nominal Reference and Temporal Constitution: Towards a Semantics of Quantity*. Universität Tübingen: Forschungsstelle für Natürlich-sprachliche Systeme.

Krifka, Manfred (1992). Thematic relations as links between nominal reference and temporal constitution. In Ivan Sag and Anna Szabolsci (eds), *Lexical Matters*, 29–53. Stanford, Calif.: CSLI.

Krifka, Manfred (1995). Common nouns: a contrastive analysis of Chinese and English. In Greg N. Carlson and Francis Jeffry Pelletier (eds), *The Generic Book*, 398–411. Chicago: University of Chicago Press.

Krifka, Manfred (1998). The origins of telicity. In Susan Rothstein (ed.), *Events and Grammar*, 197–236. Dordrecht: Kluwer.

Krifka, Manfred (1999). Manner in dative alternation. *Proceedings of the West Coast Conference on Formal Linguistics 18*: 260–71.

Krifka, Manfred (2004). Semantic and pragmatic conditions for the dative alternation. *Korean Journal of English Language and Linguistics 4*: 1–32.

Kroch, Anthony S., and Aravind K. Joshi (1985). The linguistic relevance of tree adjoining grammar. MS, University of Pennsylvania. ftp://babel.ling. upenn.edu/papers/faculty/tony_kroch/papers/relevance3.pdf.

Kroeger, Paul (2005). *Analyzing Grammar: An Introduction*. New York: Cambridge University Press.

Kubota, Yusuke, and Robert Levine (2013). Against ellipsis: arguments for the direct licensing of 'non-canonical' coordinations. Presented at 'Colloque de syntaxe et sémantique', Paris.

Kunze, Jürgen (1991). *Kasusrelationen und semantische Emphase*. Berlin: Akademie.

Kunze, Jürgen (1993). *Sememstrukturen und Feldstrukturen*. Berlin: Akademie.

Labov, William (1969). Contraction, deletion, and inherent variability of the English Copula. *Language* 45(4): 715–62.

Labov, William (1973). The boundaries of words and their meanings. In Charles-James N. Bailey and Roger W. Shuy (eds), *New Ways of Analyzing Variation in English*, 340–73. Washington, DC: Georgetown University Press.

Lakoff, George (1965). On the nature of syntactic irregularity. PhD dissertation, Harvard University.

Lakoff, George (1969). *On Generative Semantics*. Bloomington: Indiana University Linguistics Club.

Lakoff, George (1987). *Women, Fire, and Dangerous Things: What Categories Reveal about the Mind*. Chicago: University of Chicago Press.

Langacker, Ronald W. (1987). *Foundations of Cognitive Grammar*, vol. 1. Stanford, Calif.: Stanford University Press.

Lapata, Maria, and Alex Lascarides (2003). A probabilistic account of logical metonymy. *Computational Linguistics* 29(2): 261–315.

Larson, Richard (1988). On the double object construction. *Linguistic Inquiry* 19(3): 335–91.

Larson, Richard (2014). *On Shell Structure*. London: Routledge.

Lees, Robert (1960). *The Grammar of English Nominalizations*. The Hague: Mouton.

Legate, Julie A. (2002). Warlpiri: theoretical implications. PhD dissertation, MIT.

Levin, Beth (1993). *English Verb Classes: A Preliminary Investigation*. Chicago: University of Chicago Press.

Levin, Beth, and Malka Rappaport Hovav (1995). *Unaccusativity: At the Syntax–Lexical Semantics Interface*. Cambridge, Mass.: MIT Press.

Levin, Beth, and Malka Rappaport Hovav (2005). *Argument Realization*. Cambridge: Cambridge University Press.

Lewis, Charlton T., and Charles Short (1879). *A Latin Dictionary. Founded on Andrews' Edition of Freund's Latin Dictionary*. Oxford: Clarendon Press.

Lewis, David (1973). *Counterfactuals*. Cambridge, Mass.: Harvard University Press.

Lichte, Timm (2013). Syntax und Valenz: zur Modellierung kohärenter und elliptischer Strukturen mit Baumadjunktionsgrammatiken. PhD dissertation, University of Tübingen.

Link, Godehard (1983). The logical analysis of plurals and mass terms: a lattice-theoretical approach. In Rainer Bäerle, Christoph Schwarze, and Arnim von Stechow (eds), *Meaning, Use and Interpretation of Language*, 302–23. Berlin: de Gruyter.

Löbner, Sebastian (2000). Polarity in natural language: predication, quantification and negation in particular and characterizing sentences. *Linguistics and Philosophy* 23(3): 213–308.

Lohndal, Terje (2012). Toward the end of argument structure. In María Cristina Cuervo and Yves Roberge (eds), *The End of Argument Structure?*, 155–84. Bingley, UK: Emerald.

Loos, Cornelia (2012). *Wenn man's bedenkt*: taking another look at applicative *be*-verbs in German. MS, University of Texas at Austin.

Malouf, Robert (1996). Mixed categories in HPSG. Presented at the Third International Conference on HPSG, Marseille.

Malouf, Robert (1998). Coherent nominalizations. Presented at the Annual Meeting of the Linguistic Society of America.

Malouf, Robert (2000). *Mixed Categories in the Hierarchical Lexicon*. Stanford, Calif.: CSLI.

Manning, Christopher D. (1994). *Ergativity: Argument Structure and Grammatical Relations*. Stanford, Calif.: CSLI.

Manning, Christopher D. (2003). Probabilistic syntax. In R. Bod, J. Hay, and S. Jannedy (eds), *Probabilistic Linguistics*, 289–342. Cambridge, Mass.: MIT Press.

Manning, Christopher D., and Ivan Sag (1995). Dissociations between argument structure and grammatical relations. In Gert Webelhuth, Jean-Pierre Koenig, and Andreas Kathol (eds), *Lexical and Constructional Aspects of Linguistic Explanation*, 63–78. Stanford, Calif.: CSLI.

Manning, Christopher D., Ivan Sag, and Masayo Iida (1999). The lexical integrity of Japanese causatives. In Robert Levine and Georgia Green (eds), *Studies in Contemporary Phrase Structure Grammar*, 39–79. Cambridge: Cambridge University Press.

Marantz, Alec (1984). *On the Nature of Grammatical Relations*. Cambridge, Mass: MIT Press.

Marantz, Alec (1997). No escape from syntax: don't try morphological analysis in the privacy of your own lexicon. *University of Pennsylvania Working Papers in Linguistics* 4(2): 201–25.

McCarthy, Diana (2009). Word sense disambiguation: an overview. *Language and Linguistics Compass* 3(2): 537–58.

McCawley, James (1968). Concerning the base component of a transformational grammar. *Foundations of Language* 4(3): 243–69.

McCawley, James (1971). Prelexical syntax. In Richard J. O'Brien (ed.), *Linguistic Developments of the Sixties: Viewpoints for the Seventies*, 19–33. Washington, DC: Georgetown University Press.

McCawley, James (1974). On identifying the remains of deceased clauses. *Language Research* 9: 73–85.

McElree, Brian, Gregory L. Murphy, and Tamara Ochoa (2006). Time course of retrieving conceptual information: a speed–accuracy trade-off study. *Psychonomic Bulletin and Review* 13(5): 848–53.

McKoon, Gail, and Talke Macfarland (2000). Externally and internally caused change of state verbs. *Language* 76(4): 833–58.

Merlan, Francesca (1985). Split intransitivity: functional oppositions in intransitive inflection. In Johanna Nichols and Anthony C. Woodbury (eds), *Grammar Inside and Outside the Clause: Some Approaches to Theory from the Field*, 324–62. Cambridge: Cambridge University Press.

Metzing, Charles, and Susan E. Brennan (2003). When conceptual pacts are broken: partner-specific effects on the comprehension of referring expressions. *Journal of Memory and Language* 49(2): 201–13.

Meurers, Walt Detmar (2000). Lexical generalizations in the syntax of German non-finite constructions. Tübingen: Universität Tübingen.

Meurers, Walt Detmar (2001). On expressing lexical generalizations in HPSG. *Nordic Journal of Linguistics* 24(2): 161–217.

Meurers, Walt Detmar, and Kordula De Kuthy (2001). Case assignment in partially fronted constituents. In Christian Rohrer, Antje Rossdeutscher, and Hans Kamp (eds), *Linguistic Form and Its Computation*, 29–63. Stanford, Calif.: CSLI.

Michaelis, Laura A., and Josef Ruppenhofer (2001). *Beyond Alternations: A Constructional Model of the German Applicative Pattern*. Stanford, Calif.: CSLI.

Minsky, Marvin (1975). A framework for representing knowledge. In Patrick Winston (ed.), *The Psychology of Computer Vision*, 211–77. New York: McGraw-Hill.

Mithun, Marianne (1984). The evolution of noun incorporation. *Language* 60(4): 847–94.

Mithun, Marianne (1991). Active/agentive case marking and its motivations. *Language* 67(3): 510–46.

Montague, Richard (1974). The proper treatment of quantification in ordinary English. In *Formal Philosophy: Selected Papers of Richard Montague*, ed. R. H. Thomason, 188–221. New Haven, Conn.: Yale University Press.

Morzycki, Marcin (2005). Mediated modification. PhD dissertation, University of Massachusetts, Amherst.

Muansuwan, Nuttanart (2001). Directional serial verb constructions in Thai. *Proceedings of the 7th International Conference on Head-Driven Phrase Structure Grammar (HPSG-2000)*: 229–46.

Muansuwan, Nuttanart (2002). Verb complexes in Thai. PhD dissertation, State University of New York at Buffalo.

Müller, Gereon (1998). *Incomplete Category Fronting: A Derivational Approach to Remnant Movement in German*. Dordrecht: Kluwer.

Müller, Stefan (1996). Yet another paper about partial verb phrase fronting in German. In Jun-ichi Tsuji (ed.), *Proceedings of COLING-96*, 800–805.

Müller, Stefan (2001). Case in German: towards an HPSG analysis. In Walt Detmar Meurers and Tibor Kiss (eds), *Constraint-Based Approaches to Germanic Syntax*, 217–55. Stanford, Calif.: CSLI.

Müller, Stefan (2002). *Complex Predicates: Verbal Complexes, Resultative Constructions, and Particle Verbs in German*. Stanford, Calif.: CSLI.

Müller, Stefan (2006). Phrasal or lexical constructions? *Language* 82(4): 850–83.

Müller, Stefan (2007a). Phrasal or lexical constructions: some comments on underspecification of constituent order, compositionality, and control. In Stefan Müller (ed.), *Proceedings of the 14th International Conference on Head-Driven Phrase Structure Grammar*, 373–93. Stanford, Calif.: CSLI.

Müller, Stefan (2007b). *Head-Driven Phrase Structure Grammar: Eine Einführung*. Tübingen: Stauffenburg.

Müller, Stefan (2010). *Grammatiktheorie*. Tübingen: Stauffenburg.

Müller, Stefan (2013a). Unifying everything. *Language* 89(4): 920–50.

Müller, Stefan (2013b). *Grammatiktheorie*, 2nd edn. Tübingen: Stauffenburg.

Müller, Stefan, and Bjarne Ørsnes (2013). Towards an HPSG analysis of object shift in Danish. In Glyn Morrill and Mark-Jan Nederhof (eds), *Proceedings of Formal Grammar 2012 and 2013*, 69–89. Berlin: Springer.

Murphy, Gregory L. (2002). *The Big Book of Concepts*. Cambridge, Mass.: MIT Press.

Nedjalkov, Vladimir P. (1969). Nekotorye Verojatnostnye Universalii v Glagol'nom Slovoobrazovanii'. In I. F. Vardul' (ed.), *Jazykovye Universalii i Lingvisticeskaja Tipologija*, 106–14. Moscow: Nauka.

Nerbonne, John (1986). 'Phantoms' and German fronting: poltergeist constituents? *Linguistics* 24(5): 857–70.

Nerbonne, John (1994). Partial verb phrases and spurious ambiguities. In John Nerbonne, Klaus Netter, and Carl J. Pollard (eds), *German in Head-Driven Phrase Structure Grammar*, 109–50. Stanford, Calif.: CSLI.

Newmeyer, Frederick (1976). The precyclic nature of predicate raising. In Masayoshi Shibatani (ed.), *The Grammar of Causative Constructions*, 131–64. New York: Academic Press.

Nunberg, Geoffrey (1979). The non-uniqueness of semantic solutions: polysemy. *Linguistics and Philosophy* 3(2): 143–84.

Nunberg, Geoffrey (1995). Transfers of meaning. *Journal of Semantics* 12(2): 109–32.

Nunberg, Geoffrey, Ivan Sag, and Thomas Wasow (1994). Idioms. *Language* 70(3): 491–538.

Nunberg, Geoffrey, and Annie Zaenen (1992). Systematic polysemy in lexicology and lexicography. In H. Tommola, K. Varantola, and J. Schopp (eds), *Proceedings of Euralex92*, pt 2, 387–98. Tampere: University of Tampere.

Nunes, Mary (1993). Argument linking in English derived nominals. In Robert D. Van Valin (ed.), *Advances in Role and Reference Grammar*, 375–432. Amsterdam: Benjamins.

Oehrle, Richard Thomas (1976). The grammatical status of the English dative alternation. PhD dissertation, MIT.

Osherson, Daniel, and Edward E. Smith (1997). On typicality and vagueness. *Cognition* 64(2): 189–206.

Parsons, Terence (1990). *Events in the Semantics of English*. Cambridge, Mass.: MIT Press.

Partee, Barbara H. (2008). Weak NPs in *have*-sentences. In Barbara Partee (ed.) *Compositionality in Formal Semantics*, 282–91. Malden, Mass.: Blackwell.

Pelletier, Francis, and Lenhart Schubert (1989). Mass expressions. In D. Gabbay and F. Guenther (eds), *Handbook of Philosophical Logic*, vol. 4, 327–407. Dordrecht: Reidel.

Perlmutter, David M. (1978). Impersonal passives and the unaccusative hypothesis. In *Proceedings of the 4th Annual Meeting of the Berkeley Linguistics Society*, 157–90. University of California at Berkeley.

Perlmutter, David M. (ed.) (1983). *Studies in Relational Grammar*. Chicago: University of Chicago Press.

Perlmutter, David M. (1989). Multiattachment and the Unaccusative Hypothesis: the perfect auxiliary in Italian. *Probus* 1(1): 63–120.

Perlmutter, David M., and Paul M. Postal (1983). Toward a universal characterization of passivization. In David M. Perlmutter (ed.), *Studies in Relational Grammar*, vol. 1, 3–29. Chicago: University of Chicago Press.

Perlmutter, David M., and Carol G. Rosen (eds) (1984). *Studies in Relational Grammar*, vol. 2. Chicago: University of Chicago Press.

Pesetsky, David (1995). *Zero Syntax: Experiencers and Cascades*. Cambridge, Mass.: MIT Press.

Pickering, Martin J., and Steven Frisson (2001). Processing ambiguous verbs: evidence from eye movements. *Journal of Experimental Psychology: Learning, Memory, and Cognition* 27(2): 556–73.

Pinkal, Manfred, and Michael Kohlhase (2000). Feature Logic for dotted types: a formalism for complex word meanings. In *Proceedings of the 38th Annual Meeting of the Association of Computational Linguistics (ACL)*, 521–8. San Francisco, Calif.: Morgan Kaufmann.

Pinker, Steven (1989). *Learnability and Cognition*. Cambridge, Mass.: MIT Press.

Pinker, Steven (1991). Rules of language. *Science* 253: 530–35.

Pinker, Steven (1999). *Words and Rules: The Ingredients of Language*. New York: Morrow.

Pollard, Carl (1996). On Head Non-Movement. In Harry Bunt and Arthur van Horck (eds), *Discontinuous Constituency*, 279–305. Berlin: Mouton de Gruyter.

Pollard, Carl, and Ivan Sag (1987). *Information-Based Syntax and Semantics*. Stanford, Calif.: CSLI.

Pollard, Carl, and Ivan Sag (1992). Anaphors in English and the scope of Binding Theory. *Linguistic Inquiry* 23(2): 261–303.

Pollard, Carl, and Ivan Sag (1994). *Head Driven Phrase Structure Grammar*. Stanford, Calif./Chicago: CSLI/University of Chicago Press.

Pustejovsky, James (1993). Type coercion and lexical selection. In *Semantics and the Lexicon*, 73–94. Dordrecht: Kluwer.

Pustejovsky, James (1995). *The Generative Lexicon*. Cambridge, Mass.: MIT Press.

Pustejovsky, James, and Pierrette Bouillon (1995). Aspectual coercion and logical polysemy. *Journal of Semantics* 12(2): 133–62.

Putnam, Hilary (1975). The meaning of 'meaning'. In *Mind, Language, and Reality: Philosophical Papers II*, 215–71. Cambridge: Cambridge University Press.

Quine, W. V. (1951). Main trends in recent philosophy: two dogmas of empiricism. *Philosophical Review* 60(1): 20–43.

Quirk, Randolph, Sidney Greenbaum, Geoffrey Leech, and Jan Svartvik (1985). *A Comprehensive Grammar of the English Language*. London: Longman.

Raffman, Diana (1994). Vagueness without paradox. *Philosophical Review* 103(1): 41–74.

Raffman, Diana (1996). Vagueness and context-relativity. *Philosophical Studies* 81(2): 175–92.

Ramchand, Gillian (2008). *Verb Meaning and the Lexicon: A First Phase Syntax*. Cambridge: Cambridge University Press.

Rappaport, Malka (1983). On the nature of derived nominals. In Beth Levin, Malka Rappaport, and Annie Zaenen (eds), *Papers in Lexical-Functional Grammar*, 113–42. Bloomington: Indiana University Linguistics Club.

Rappaport, Malka, and Beth Levin (1988). What to do with theta-roles. In Wendy K. Wilkins (ed.), *Thematic Relations*, 7–36. New York: Academic Press.

Rappaport Hovav, Malka, and Beth Levin (1998). Building verb meanings. In Miriam Butt and Wilhelm Geuder (eds), *The Projection of Arguments: Lexical and Compositional Factors*, 97–134. Cambridge: Cambridge University Press.

Rappaport Hovav, Malka, and Beth Levin (2001). An event structure account of English resultatives. *Language* 77(4): 766–97.

Rappaport Hovav, Malka, and Beth Levin (2008). The English dative alternation: the case for verb sensitivity. *Journal of Linguistics* 44: 129–67.

Rappaport Hovav, Malka, and Beth Levin (2010). Reflections on manner/result complementarity. In Edit Doron and Ivy Sichel (eds), *Lexical Semantics, Syntax, and Event Structure*, 21–38. Oxford: Oxford University Press.

Reape, Mike (1994). Domain union and word order variation in German. In John Nerbonne, Klaus Netter, and Carl J. Pollard (eds), *German in Head-Driven Phrase Structure Grammar*, 151–98. Stanford, Calif.: CSLI.

Richards, Norvin (2001). An idiomatic argument for lexical decomposition. *Linguistic Inquiry* 32(1): 183–92.

Riehemann, Susanne (1993). Word formation in lexical type hierarchies: a case study of bar-adjectives in German. Master's thesis, University of Tübingen.

Riehemann, Susanne (1998). Type-based derivational morphology. *Journal of Comparative Germanic Linguistics* 2: 49–77.

Robins, R. H. (1979). *A Short History of Linguistics*, 2nd edn. London: Longman.

Rosch, Eleanor (1975). Cognitive representations of semantic categories. *Journal of Experimental Psychology* 104(3): 192.

Rosch, Eleanor (1978). Principles of categorization. In Eleanor Rosch and Barbara B. Lloyd (eds), *Cognition and Categorization*, 27–48. Hillsdale, NJ: Erlbaum.

Rosch, Eleanor, and Carolyn B. Mervis (1975). Family resemblances: studies in the internal structure of categories. *Cognitive Psychology* 7(4): 573–605.

Rosch, Eleanor, Carolyn B. Mervis, Wayne D. Gray, David M. Johnson, and Penny Boyes-Braem (1976). Basic objects in natural categories. *Cognitive Psychology* 8(3): 382–439.

Rosen, Carol (1984). The interface between semantic roles and initial grammatical relations. In David M. Perlmutter and Carol Rosen (eds), *Studies in Relational Grammar* 2, 38–77. Chicago: University of Chicago Press.

Ross, John R. (1973). Act. In Donald Davidson and Gilbert Harman (eds), *Semantics of Natural Language*, 70–126. Dordrecht: Reidel.

Ross, John R. (1976). To have 'have' and to not have 'have'. In M. Ali Jazayery, Edgar Polomé, and Werner Winter (eds), *Linguistic and Literary Studies in Honor of Archibald A. Hill*, 263–70. Lisse: de Ridder.

Rotstein, Carmen, and Yoad Winter (2004). Total adjectives vs. partial adjectives: scale structure and higher-order modifiers. *Natural Language Semantics* 12(3): 259–88.

Rumelhart, David E. (1980). Schemata: the building blocks of cognition. In R. J. Spiro, B. C. Bruce, and W. F. Brewer (eds), *Theoretical Issues in Reading Comprehension*, 33–58. Hillsdale, NJ: Erlbaum.

Ruwet, Nicholas (1972). *Théorie syntaxique et syntaxe du français*. Paris: Éditions du Seuil.

Sag, Ivan (1981). Formal semantics and extralinguistic context. In Peter Cole (ed.), *Radical Pragmatics*, 273–94. New York: Academic Press.

Sag, Ivan (1997). English relative clause constructions. *Journal of Linguistics* 33(2): 431–83.

Sag, Ivan (2008). Feature geometry and predictions of locality. In Greville Corbett and Anna Kibort (eds), *Proceedings of the Workshop on Features*, 236–71. Oxford: Oxford University Press.

Sag, Ivan (2012). Sign-Based Construction Grammar: an informal synopsis. In Hans Boas and Ivan Sag (eds), *Sign-Based Construction Grammar*, 69–202. Stanford, Calif.: CSLI.

Sag, Ivan, Thomas Wasow, and Emily Bender (2003). *Syntactic Theory: A Formal Introduction*, 2nd edn. Stanford, Calif.: CSLI.

Sainsbury, R. M. (1996). Concepts without boundaries. In Rosanna Keefe and Peter Smith (eds), *Vagueness: A Reader*, 251–64. Cambridge, Mass.: MIT Press.

Sapir, Edward (1944). Grading: a study in semantics. *Philosophy of Science* 11: 93–116.

Saussure, Ferdinand de (1916). *Cours de linguistique générale*. Paris: Payot.

Schein, Barry (1993). *Plurals and Events*. Cambridge, Mass.: MIT Press.

Schwarze, Christoph (2001). Representation and variation: on the development of Romance auxiliary syntax. In M. Butt and T. H. King (eds), *Time Over Matter: Diachronic Perspectives on Morphosyntax*, 143–72. Stanford, Calif.: CSLI.

Shank, Roger C., and Robert P. Abelson (1977). *Scripts, Goals, Plans, and Understanding: An Inquiry into Human Knowledge Structures*. Hillsdale, NJ: Erlbaum.

Simpson, Jane (1983). Resultatives. In Lori Levin, Malka Rappaport, and Annie Zaenen (eds), *Papers in Lexical-Functional Grammar*, 143–58. Bloomington: Indiana University Linguistics Club.

Simpson, Jane (1991). *Warlpiri Morpho-Syntax: A Lexicalist Approach*. Dordrecht: Kluwer Academic.

Slobin, Dan I. (2004). The many ways to search for a frog. In Sven Strömqvist and Ludo Verhoeven (eds), *Relating Events in Narrative*, vol. 2: *Typological and Contextual Perspectives*, 219–57. Mahwah, NJ: Erlbaum.

Smith, Carlota S. (1970). Jespersen's 'move and change' class and causative verbs in English. In M. Ali Jazayery, Edgar Polomé, and Werner Winte (eds), *Linguistic and Literary Studies in Honor of Archibald A. Hill*, vol. 2, 101–9. The Hague: Mouton.

Smith, Carlota S. (1972). On causative verbs and derived nominals in English. *Linguistic Inquiry* 3: 136–8.

Smith, Carlota S. (1997). *The Parameter of Aspect*. Dordrecht: Kluwer.

Smith, Edward E., and Douglas L. Medin (1981). *Categories and Concepts*. Cambridge, Mass.: Harvard University Press.

Song, Grace, and Beth Levin (1998). A compositional approach to cross-linguistic differences in motion expressions. Presented at 72nd Annual Meeting of the Linguistic Society of America, New York.

Sorace, Antonella (2000). Gradients in auxiliary selection with intransitive verbs. *Language* 76(4): 859–90.

Sorace, Antonella, and Frank Keller (2005). Gradience in linguistic data. *Lingua* 115(11): 1497–1524.

Sorensen, Roy (2012). Vagueness. In Edward Zalta (ed.), *The Stanford Encyclopedia of Philosophy*. Stanford, Calif.: Stanford University Press. http://plato.stanford.edu/archives/sum2012/entries/vagueness/.

Spencer, Andrew (2005). Towards a typology of 'mixed categories'. In Cemil Orhan Orgun and Peter Sells (eds), *Morphology and the Web of Grammar: Essays in Memory of Steven G. Lapointe*, 95–138. Stanford, Calif.: CSLI.

Steedman, Mark J. (1991). Structure and intonation. *Language* 67(2): 260–96.

Steedman, Mark J. (2000). *The Syntactic Process*. Cambridge, Mass.: MIT Press.

Steedman, Mark J., and Jason Baldridge (2006). Combinatory Categorial Grammar. In Keith Brown (ed.), *Encyclopedia of Language and Linguistics*, 2nd edn, 610–21. Oxford: Elsevier.

Stiebels, Barbara (1991). Präpositionsinkorporierung und das Problem der Partickelverben im Deutschen. Dissertation, Heinrich Heine Universität.

Sudmuk, Cholthica (2005). The syntax and semantics of serial verb constructions in Thai. PhD dissertation, University of Texas.

Suñer, Margarita (1988). The role of agreement in clitic-doubled constructions. *Natural Language and Linguistic Theory* 6(3): 391–434.

Talmy, Leonard (1985). Lexicalization patterns: semantic structure in lexical forms. *Language Typology and Syntactic Description* 3: 57–149.

Talmy, Leonard (2000). *Toward a Cognitive Semantics*, vol. 2: *Typology and Process in Concept Structuring*. Cambridge, Mass.: MIT Press.

Taylor, John R. (1989). *Linguistic Categorization*. Oxford: Oxford University Press.

Tenny, Carol (1987). Grammaticalizing aspect and affectedness. PhD dissertation, Dept of Linguistics and Philosophy, MIT.

Tenny, Carol (1994). *Aspectual Roles and the Syntax–Semantics Interface*. Dordrecht: Kluwer Academic.

Tham, Shiao Wei (2005). Representing possessive predication: semantic dimensions and pragmatic bases. PhD dissertation, Stanford University.

Tham, Shiao Wei (2006). The definiteness effect in English *have* sentences. In Pascal Denis, Eric McCready, Alexis Palmer, and Brian Reese (eds), *Proceedings of Texas Linguistic Society 8*, 137–49. Somerville, Mass.: Cascadilla.

Tomasello, Michael (2003). *Constructing a Language: A Usage-Based Theory of Language Acquisition*. Cambridge, Mass.: Harvard University Press.

Tomasello, Michael (2008). *Origins of Human Communication*. Cambridge, Mass.: MIT Press.

Tomasello, Michael, Nameera Akhtar, Kelly Dodsen, and Laura Rekau (1997). Differential productivity in young children's use of nouns and verbs. *Journal of Child Language* 24(2): 373–87.

Van der Leek, F. (1996). The English conative construction: a compositional account. *Regional Meeting of the Chicago Linguistic Society* 32: 363–78.

Van Hout, A. (2004). Unaccusativity as telicity checking. In A. Alexiadou, E. Anagnostopoulou, and M. Everaert (eds), *The Unaccusativity Puzzle: Explorations of the Syntax–Lexicon Interface*, 60–83. Oxford: Oxford University Press.

Van Valin, Robert D. (1987). The Unaccusative Hypothesis vs. lexical semantics: syntactic vs. semantic approaches to verb classification. *Proceedings of the North East Linguistic Society 17*: 641–61.

Van Valin, Robert D. (1990). Semantic parameters of split intransitivity. *Language* 66(2): 221–60.

Van Valin, Robert D. (ed.) (1993). *Advances in Role and Reference Grammar*. Amsterdam: Benjamins.

Van Valin, Robert D. (1999). Generalized semantic roles and the syntax–semantics Interface. http://linguistics.buffalo.edu/people/faculty/vanvalin/rrg.html.

Van Valin, Robert D. (2005). *Exploring the Syntax–Semantics Interface*. Cambridge: Cambridge University Press.

Van Valin, Robert D. (2007). Review of Adele E. Goldberg, *Constructions at Work: The Nature of Generalization in Language. Journal of Linguistics* 43(1): 234–40.

Van Valin, Robert D. (2013). Lexical representation, co-composition, and linking syntax and semantics. In James Pustejovsky, Pierette Bouillon, Hitoshi Isahara, and Kyoko Kanzaki (eds), *Advances in Generative Lexicon Theory*, 67–107. Dordrecht: Springer.

Van Valin, Robert D., and Randy J. LaPolla (1997). *Syntax: Structure, Meaning and Function*. Cambridge: Cambridge University Press.

Van Valin, Robert D., and David Wilkins (1996). The case for 'effector': case roles, agents, and agency revisited. In Masayoshi Shibatani and Sandra A. Thompson (eds), *Grammatical Constructions: Their Form and Meaning*, 289–322. Oxford: Oxford University Press.

Vendler, Zeno (1957). Verbs and times. *Philosophical Review* 66(2): 143–60.

Vendler, Zeno (1967). *Linguistics in Philosophy*. Ithaca, NY: Cornell University Press.

Verspoor, Cornelia Maria (1997). Contextually-dependent lexical semantics. PhD dissertation, University of Edinburgh.

Wald, Benji (1979). The development of the Swahili object marker: a study of the interaction of syntax and discourse. In Talmy Givón (ed.), *Discourse and Syntax*, 505–24. New York: Academic Press.

Wasow, Thomas, and Jennifer Arnold (2005). Intuitions in linguistic argumentation. *Lingua* 115: 1481–96.

Wechsler, Stephen (1989). Accomplishments and the prefix *re-*. *Proceedings of the North Eastern Linguistics Society* 19: 419–34.

Wechsler, Stephen (1991). Argument structure and linking. PhD dissertation, Stanford University.

Wechsler, Stephen (1995). *The Semantic Basis of Argument Structure.* Stanford, Calif.: CSLI.

Wechsler, Stephen (1997a). Prepositional phrases from the Twilight Zone. *Nordic Journal of Linguistics* 20(2): 127–54.

Wechsler, Stephen (1997b). Resultative predicates and control. In Ralph Blight and Michelle Moosally (eds), *The Syntax and Semantics of Predication*, 307–21. Austin: University of Texas, Department of Linguistics.

Wechsler, Stephen (1999). HPSG, GB, and the Balinese Bind. In A. Kathol, J.-P. Koenig, and G. Webelhuth (eds), *Lexical and Constructional Aspects of Linguistic Explanation.* Stanford, Calif.: CSLI.

Wechsler, Stephen (2001). An analysis of English resultatives under the event–argument homomorphism model of telicity. In *Proceedings of the 3rd Workshop on Text Structure*, 1–15. Austin: Department of Linguistics, University of Texas.

Wechsler, Stephen (2003). Serial verbs and serial motion. In Dorothee Beermann and Lars Hellan (eds), *Proceedings of the Workshop on Multi-Verb Constructions.* Trondheim: Norwegian University of Science and Technology.

Wechsler, Stephen (2005a). What is right and wrong about Little v. In Mila Vulchanova and Tor A. Åfarli (eds), *Grammar and Beyond: Essays in Honour of Lars Hellan*, 179–95. Oslo: Novus Press.

Wechsler, Stephen (2005b). Thematic structure. In *The Encyclopedia of Language and Linguistics*, 2nd edn. Amsterdam: Elsevier.

Wechsler, Stephen (2005c). Resultatives under the event–argument homomorphism model of telicity. In Nomi Erteschik-Shir and Tova Rapoport (eds), *The Syntax of Aspect: Deriving Thematic and Aspectual Interpretation*, 255–73. Oxford: Oxford University Press.

Wechsler, Stephen (2008a). Dualist syntax. In *Proceedings of the 15th International Conference on Head-Driven Phrase Structure Grammar*, 294–304. Stanford, Calif.: CSLI.

Wechsler, Stephen (2008b). Punctual paths in three languages. In Susumu Kuno et al. (eds), *Harvard Studies in Korean Linguistics XII*, 3–19. Cambridge, Mass.: Harvard University Dept of Linguistics.

Wechsler, Stephen (2008c). A diachronic account of English deverbal nominals. In Charles B. Chang and Hannah J. Haynie (eds), *Proceedings of the 26th West Coast Conference on Formal Linguistics*, 498–506. Somerville, Mass.: Cascadilla.

Wechsler, Stephen (2011). Polysemy, generality, and mapping to syntax. Presented at the Workshop on Syntax–Semantics Interface, Academia Sinica International, Taipei. Taipei, Taiwan, June 17, 2011.

Wechsler, Stephen (2012). Resultatives and the problem of exceptions. In Ik-Hwan Lee (ed.), *Issues in English Linguistics*, 119–31. Seoul: Hankookmunhwasa.

Wechsler, Stephen, and I Wayan Arka (1998). Syntactic ergativity in Balinese: an argument structure based theory. *Natural Language and Linguistic Theory* 16: 387–441.

Wechsler, Stephen, and Yae-Sheik Lee (1996). The domain of direct case assignment. *Natural Language and Linguistic Theory* 14: 629–64.

Wechsler, Stephen, and Bokyung Noh (2001). On resultative predicates and clauses: parallels between Korean and English. *Language Sciences* 23(4): 391–423.

Weinreich, Uriel (1964). Webster's Third: a critique of its semantics. *International Journal of American Linguistics* 30: 405–9.

Wienold, Götz (1995). Lexical and conceptual structures in expressions for movement and space: with reference to Japanese, Korean, Thai, and Indonesian as compared to English and German. In Urs Egli et al. (eds), *Lexical Knowledge in the Organization of Language*, 301–40. Amsterdam: Benjamins.

Williams, Edwin (1980). Predication. *Linguistic Inquiry* 11: 203–38.

Williams, Edwin (1981). Argument structure and morphology. *Linguistic Review* 1(1): 81–114.

Williamson, Timothy (1994). *Vagueness*. New York: Routledge.

Williamson, Timothy, and Peter Simons (1992). Vagueness and ignorance. *Proceedings of the Aristotelian Society*, Supplementary Vol. 66, 145–77.

Wittgenstein, Ludwig (1934). *The Blue and Brown Books*. Oxford: Blackwell.

Wunderlich, Dieter (1997a). Cause and the structure of verbs. *Linguistic Inquiry* 28(1): 27–68.

Wunderlich, Dieter (1997b). Argument extension by lexical adjunction. *Journal of Semantics* 14(2): 95–142.

Yoon, Youngeun (1996). Total and partial predicates and the weak and strong interpretations. *Natural Language Semantics* 4(3): 217–36.

Zaenen, Annie (1988). Unaccusative verbs in Dutch and the syntax–semantics interface. Stanford, Calif.: CSLI.

Zaenen, Annie (1993). Unaccusativity in Dutch: integrating syntax and lexical semantics. In James Pustejovsky (ed.), *Semantics and the Lexicon*, 129–61. Dordrecht: Kluwer.

Zaenen, Annie, Joan Maling, and Höskuldur Thráinsson (1985). Case and grammatical functions: the Icelandic passive. *Natural Language and Linguistic Theory* 3: 441–83.

Zlatev, Jordan, and Peerapat Yangklang (2004). A third way to travel: the place of Thai in motion event typology. In S. Strömqvist and L. Verhoeven (eds), *Relating Events in Narrative*, vol. 2: *Typological and Contextual Perspectives*, 159–90. Mahwah, NJ: Erlbaum.

Zribi-Hertz, Anne (1982). The 'middle-*se*' construction in French and its status in the triad middle voice–passive–reflexive. *Linguisticae Investigationes* 6: 345–401.

Zucchi, Alessandro (1993). *The Language of Propositions and Events: Issues in the Syntax and the Semantics of Nominalization*. Berlin: Springer.

Zwicky, Arnold, and Jerrold Sadock (1975). Ambiguity tests and how to fail them. In J. P. Kimball (ed.), *Syntax and Semantics 4*, 1–36. New York: Academic Press.

Index of authors

Index of subjects